ASSESSMENT

— IN —

COUNSELING

A GUIDE TO THE USE OF

Psychological Assessment Procedures

SECOND EDITION

Albert B. Hood, EdD
Richard W. Johnson, PhD

AMERICAN COUNSELING ASSOCIATION

5999 Stevenson Avenue
Alexandria, VA 22304-3300

ASSESSMENT IN COUNSELING
Second Edition

10 9 8 7 6 5

American Counseling Association
5999 Stevenson Avenue
Alexandria, VA 22304

Acquisitions and Development Editor
Carolyn Baker

Managing Editor
Michael Comlish

Copyeditor
Wendy Lieberman

Cover design by Brian Gallagher

Library of Congress Cataloging-in-Publication Data
Hood, Albert B. (Albert Bullard), 1929–
    Assessment in counseling: a guide to the use of psychological
assessment procedures / Albert B. Hood, Richard W. Johnson. — 2nd
ed.
        p.   cm.
    Includes bibliographical references and index.
    ISBN 1-55620-155-9 (alk. paper)
    1. Psychological tests.   2. Counseling.   I. Johnson, Richard W.,
1934–   . II. Title.
BF176.H66   1997   96-33894
150'.28'7—dc20   CIP

CONTENTS

FOREWORD *by C. Gilbert Wrenn* .... *ix*

PREFACE .... *xi*

ACKNOWLEDGMENTS .... *xv*

ABOUT THE AUTHORS .... *xvii*

I

SECTION
Basic Concepts of Psychological Assessment

1 Use of Assessment Procedures in Counseling 3
Purpose of Psychological Assessment 4
Definition of Psychological Assessment 7
Attitudes Toward Psychological Tests 10
Surveys of Test Usage 12

2 Nature of Psychological Assessment in Counseling .. 17
Distinctions Among Psychological Assessment Procedures 18
Types of Psychological Assessment Methods 20
Standards for Evaluating Tests and Test Usage 24
Sources of Information About Assessment Procedures 28

3 Measurement Concepts and Test Interpretation 33
Norms 34
Correlation 42
Reliability 43
Validity 49
Test Development 55

4 Initial Assessment in Counseling 57

Client Orientation Toward Problem Solving 58

Defining the Problem 62

Test Selection, Administration, and Scoring 72

II

SECTION
Cognitive Assessment

5 Assessment of Intelligence 81

Popular Individual Intelligence Tests 83

Group Intelligence Tests 89

Interpreting Intelligence Test Results 92

6 Academic Aptitude and Achievement 95

Tests for Higher Education 96

Graduate and Professional School Admissions Tests 104

Administering and Interpreting Academic Aptitude Tests 108

Academic Achievement Tests 110

Study Habits Inventories 115

Cognitive Developmental Theories 116

III

SECTION
Career and Life Planning Assessment

7 Measures of Career Choice and Development 121

Attitudes Toward Career Planning 122

Career Planning Competencies 129

Measures of Career Maturity 130

Use of Career Development Measures in Counseling 135

8 Measures of Work and Personal Values *139*
Values Inventories *140*
Values Clarification Exercises *147*

9 Assessment of Interests *151*
Types of Interest Inventories *151*
Selection of Interest Inventories for Counseling *153*
Popular Interest Inventories *155*
Interpretation of Interest Inventories in Counseling *182*

10 Comprehensive Assessment Programs for Career
and Life Planning *185*
Self-Rating Career and Life Planning Programs *185*
Standardized Career and Life Planning Programs *193*
Use of Comprehensive Assessment Programs in Counseling *202*

IV

SECTION
Personality Assessment

11 Personality Inventories 207
Inventory Development 208
Self-Report Personality Inventories 209

12 Other Personality Measures 229
Projective Techniques 229
Person-Environment Interaction 232
Psychosocial Theories 235

13 Assessment of Interpersonal Relationships 239
Inventories for Marriage, Couples, and Family Counseling 240
Interpersonal Assessment Inventories 244
Genograms 246

14 Mental Health Assessment: Interview Procedures *249*

Diagnostic and Statistical Manual of Mental Disorders *250*

Suicide Risk Assessment *254*

Assessment of Alcohol Use *261*

15 Mental Health Assessment: Standardized Inventories
.... *269*

General-Purpose Measures *269*

Specific-Purpose Measures *280*

V

SECTION
Professional Practices and Considerations

16 Assessment of Minority and Special Populations *297*

Cultural Bias in Testing *297*

Aptitude and Cognitive Assessment *300*

Career Assessment *306*

Personality Assessment *308*

Assessment of Clients With Disabilities *310*

17 Communication of Test Results *315*

General Guidelines for Communicating Test Results *317*

Guidelines for the Test Interpretation Interview *319*

Report Writing *321*

18 Ethical and Social Issues in Testing *327*

Ethical Standards *327*

Client Welfare Issues *330*

Issues of Gender Bias in Testing *333*

Counseling Process Issues *337*

Final Statement *339*

CONTENTS

VI
SECTION
Appendices

A   Excerpts From American Counseling Association
Code of Ethics and Standards of Practice 1995 ...... *343*

B   Excerpts From the Responsibilities of Users of
Standardized Tests *349*

C   Excerpts From Standards for Educational and
Psychological Testing *359*

D   Names and Acronyms of Tests Commonly Used by
Counselors and the Names and Addresses of
Publishers of Those Tests *365*

PERMISSIONS *373*

REFERENCES *375*

INDEX *409*

FOREWORD

PSYCHOLOGICAL TESTS first became available in this country during the early part of the century. Lewis Terman's Stanford Binet Intelligence Test, a carefully standardized and individually administered intelligence test that initiated the famous $MA/CA = IQ$, became public in 1916. This remained a basic test for the next 7 decades and beyond. In 1921 Arthur Otis, a former student of Terman's, published the first Group Intelligence Test, a paper-and-pencil test using the extensive research performed on the Army Alpha and the Army Beta tests of World War I. E.K. Strong, Jr., opened another area when the Vocational Interest Blank was published in 1927. This test, with major revisions and additions, has become one of the most widely used tests of the century. Robert Woodworth's Rating Scale appeared early in the 1920s. Around 1930 *personality tests* began to make their appearance, with pioneering productions by Robert Bernreuter and Hugh Bell. All but one of these early productions originated at Stanford University. They became part of my life because I did my graduate work at Stanford at about that time (1928–1932) with Terman and Strong as my MA and PhD advisors. I did my bit in these early ventures by bringing out the first edition of the Study Habits Inventory in 1935.

Let me add to the personal note of these years by recalling that during my first year at Stanford I was given an appointment as what we would now call a student personnel assistant—Stanford's first. This involved counseling in the registrar's office and giving admissions tests for the university. Stanford had pioneered in those early days by giving what we would now call scholastic aptitude tests as part of the admissions process. I made trips each spring throughout the state giving the Thorndike Intelligence Test to prospective students at Stanford testing centers. Kathleen, my wife, accompanied me and scored the tests as we moved along—at 25¢ an hour!

After 8 years at Stanford, I accepted an appointment at the University of Minnesota (1936–1964) and again moved into another center of intense test activity. Over these past 75 years I have seen an accelerating development of psychological tests and other types of assessment, tests for many purposes. During World War II, tests were used in *selecting* millions of war workers, in *assigning* other millions in the Armed Forces, and in *diagnosing* the mental and social health problems of men and women under stress. Today also tests are used to make decisions *for* or *against* a client. This is not a counselor's use of tests; a counselor uses tests or other assessment measures to help clients understand themselves. The authors of this book state this very clearly in words that should appear in large black type: *"In the counseling setting. . . psychological tests are used to help the clients understand themselves. . . . [They are] used primarily to assist individuals in developing their potential to the fullest and to their own satisfaction"* (italics mine) from "Final Statement," Chapter 18, p. 339.

This a significant book in my experience, a book written by two professionals whose scholarship, depth of experience with assessment in counseling, and sheer desire to be helpful to the reader are apparent on every page. It is a pragmatic book, focusing on what has been useful to others and using a simple problem-solving model. The authors clearly indicate how tests are used differently in different counseling settings: schools, university counseling centers, hospitals and mental health centers, banks, business, government, and private practice.

The first four chapters introduce the reader to basic concepts in psychological assessment and to the statistical understandings necessary in the selection and interpretation of tests, not in their construction. The last four chapters deal with special populations, communications, and ethics in the use of tests.

Chapters 5–15 treat with care and skill the use of more than 100 tests, inventories, and other assessment measures in each of 11 categories. Numerous tables, figures, appendices, and reference citations provide a great deal of information in compact bundles. The treatment of the literature is admirable—no long quotations in varying styles of writing, but interpretations and applications all in the same simple, consistent wording of the two authors.

By this time the reader may begin to suspect that I like this book. I do indeed! I commend it to counselors and psychologists without reservation. I wish that it had been available to me during my lifetime of service. I would have been a better counselor.

—*C. Gilbert Wrenn*

PREFACE

A S WITH THE FIRST EDITION, the purpose of this book is to provide information about the various psychological assessment procedures that are specifically relevant for practicing counselors. The book deals with the use of those tests most often employed by counselors in the counseling process and includes illustrative case studies. It emphasizes the selection, interpretation, and communication of psychological test results. It also emphasizes the importance of integrating test results with other information about the client.

The book is not designed to be a textbook or desk manual on the various tests themselves. There are a number of excellent books that describe psychological tests and other assessment procedures (e.g., Anastasi, 1988; Walsh & Betz, 1994). It is expected that counselors will make use of such texts, along with other sources (such as the *Mental Measurements Yearbooks* and Kapes, Mastie, & Whitfield, 1994) and the test manuals themselves, which deal with the construction, reliability, and validity of the various assessment instruments.

Since the first edition, a number of prominent assessment instruments often used in counseling have been revised. Most notably, the Strong Interest Inventory has undergone a major revision, an adolescent version of the Minnesota Multiphasic Personality Inventory (MMPI-A) has been published for the first time, the fourth edition of the *Diagnostic and Statistical Manual of Mental Disorders* (DSM-IV) has been released, and a revised version of the NEO Personality Inventory based on the "big five" personality factors has been made available. Most of the scholastic aptitude and achievement tests discussed in the first edition have been revised; in particular, the Scholastic Aptitude Test has been revised as the Scholastic Assessment Test I and II and "recentered."

Other tests that have been subjected to significant revisions include the Wechsler Intelligence Scale for Children, Self-Directed Search, Millon Clinical Multiaxial Inventory–III, Eating Disorders Inventory–II,

California Psychological Inventory, Jackson Vocational Interest Inventory, Armed Services Vocational Aptitude Battery, Differential Aptitude Tests, Children's Depression Inventory, Career Decision-Making System—Revised, ACT Career Planning Program, COPSystem, Jackson Personality Inventory—Revised, and the 16 Personality Factor Questionnaire.

In addition to the revision of the established tests, a number of promising new instruments have been published in the past 5 years. New tests that have special interest for counselors include the Campbell Interest and Skill Survey by David Campbell, the Career Attitudes and Strategies Inventory by John Holland and Gary Gottfredson, the Career Beliefs Inventory by John Krumboltz, and Leslie Morey's Personality Assessment Inventory. Other new assessment instruments that merit attention include the Millon Adolescent Clinical Inventory, Millon Index of Personality Styles, Position Classification Inventory, My Career Thoughts Inventory, and Career Mastery Inventory. All of these recent developments in psychological assessment are described in this edition.

Also in this edition, increased emphasis has been placed on the use of assessment procedures with clients from minority populations, including clients with physical disabilities, to reflect the additional attention to this topic in the professional literature. Changes in professional codes of ethics, test reference materials, surveys of test usage, and test standards are noted. Other topics that receive increased discussion include qualitative assessment procedures, computer-based test administration and interpretation, automated social history forms, the use of the circumplex in understanding interpersonal relationships, and additional important measurement concepts.

This edition is also organized into five sections. Section I presents basic concepts of psychological assessment. It includes an introduction to the nature and use of psychological assessment procedures in counseling, briefly describes certain important measurement concepts, and discusses initial assessment procedures. It is expected that any counselor using psychological tests will have had a basic course in relevant statistical procedures and this section may provide a brief refresher of the commonly used descriptive statistical concepts but is not intended as a substitute for at least a basic knowledge of psychological statistics. The second section covers cognitive assessment and the various tests that assess intelligence, academic aptitude, and academic achievement.

The third section deals with procedures used by counselors to assist clients in making decisions regarding their careers and life plans. In Section IV, personality assessment is considered, including several personality inventories and other personality measures. This section also includes instruments used for assessment of interpersonal relationships, various aspects of mental health, and certain mental disorders. The final section deals with professional practices and considerations. It includes assessment of ethnic and special populations; guidelines for the communication of test results, both in interviews and in case reports; and a discussion of the significant ethical and social issues that arise when psychological assessment procedures are used in counseling.

Excerpts from documents outlining ethical and test standards particularly appropriate to counselors and human development professionals are reproduced in the appendices. Appendix D lists the names and addresses of publishers of tests commonly used by counselors, along with the instruments that may be ordered from those publishers.

In graduate courses that cover the use of tests and other appraisal procedures in counseling, information about the various instruments is typically covered, but actual use in the counseling process and the interpretation of results in counseling interviews must be learned by the beginning counselor primarily through trial and error. This volume should remedy that situation by providing information to assist the counselor in choosing, administering, and interpreting psychological test results.

ACKNOWLEDGMENTS

Albert B. Hood wishes to acknowledge the contributions of many colleagues at various institutions who, at formal presentations as well as informal conversations at lunches and social gatherings, have helped him stay abreast of developments in the psychological testing field. He also expresses his thanks to Ginny Travis and Reta Litton for the word processing of numerous manuscript drafts as rough notes were transformed into finished chapters both for this edition and for the original. He is also grateful for the assistance of Bob Jordan in the Paul Blommers Measurement Resources Laboratory for his help in tracking down test information.

Richard W. Johnson would like to acknowledge the influence of his mentors at the University of Minnesota who first taught him to appreciate the importance of assessment in counseling. In addition to those people acknowledged in the first edition of this book, he is thankful to his colleagues, graduate students, and clients at the University of Wisconsin–Madison who have contributed to his knowledge and understanding of the use of psychological assessment in counseling.

Both authors continue to be grateful to their wives—Jean and Adelle—for their patience with curtailed social activities and deferred home maintenance schedules during the time that this volume was being written and revised.

—Albert B. Hood
Iowa City, Iowa
—Richard W. Johnson
Madison, Wisconsin
January 1996

ABOUT THE AUTHORS

Albert B. Hood is professor of education and former chair of the Division of Counselor Education at the University of Iowa. He received his BA degree (1951) from the University of New Hampshire in psychology and his EdD degree (1957) from Cornell University in counseling and student personnel administration.

He has been the assistant director of the Student Counseling Service at Princeton University and a counseling psychologist in the Student Counseling Bureau at the University of Minnesota. In addition to using psychological tests regularly in his counseling practice, he worked with several colleagues at the Educational Testing Service in Princeton and with test authors as he conducted research studies on academic aptitude (Ralph Berdie, MSAT, MCI), interest inventories (David Campbell, SVIB), and personality measures (Starke Hathaway, MMPI). Now at the University of Iowa, he has coauthored several student development inventories and has consulted with staff members of the American College Testing Program. He held a research fellowship in Kyoto, Japan, a Fulbright lectureship in the Soviet Union, and has been a visiting faculty member at the University of Utah and at San Francisco State University.

Author of more than 100 books, monographs, and professional articles, Dr. Hood received the Contribution to Knowledge Award of the American College Personnel Association (ACPA) in 1985 and the American Counseling Association's Extended Research Award in 1994. He was the editor of ACPA's *Journal of College Student Personnel* from 1970 to 1976 and is a fellow in the American Psychological Association's Division 17 (Counseling) and in the American Psychological Society. Hood's scholarly work has dealt primarily with research on the psychological, educational, and vocational development of college students, and a large proportion of the over 60 PhD dissertations he has directed have dealt with psychological assessment.

Richard W. Johnson is director of training for Counseling and Consultation Services, a unit of University Health Services, at the University of Wisconsin–Madison, where he also serves as adjunct professor of counseling psychology. He obtained his PhD degree in counseling psychology at the University of Minnesota in 1961, after graduating with honors in psychology from Princeton University in 1956. Prior to joining the staff at the University of Wisconsin–Madison in 1968, he taught and counseled at the University of Massachusetts–Amherst and at the University of North Dakota.

Dr. Johnson has served on the editorial boards for three journals of the American Counseling Association: *Journal of College Student Development, Measurement and Evaluation in Counseling and Development,* and *The Career Development Quarterly.* He has also been a frequent contributor to *Journal of Counseling Psychology, Journal of Vocational Behavior, Journal of Applied Psychology,* and *Mental Measurements Yearbooks.* His professional interests include psychological assessment, career development, cognitive-behavioral counseling, and individual differences.

I

Basic Concepts of Psychological Assessment

1

USE OF ASSESSMENT PROCEDURES IN COUNSELING

ASSESSMENT HAS ALWAYS PLAYED an important role in counseling. During the early days, counseling and testing were virtually synonymous. Many of the counseling centers established during the 1930s and 1940s were called Counseling and Testing Centers. At that time, counseling typically involved helping students to make educational or vocational plans on the basis of test results.

In recent years, the role of counseling has broadened to include many issues beyond academic and career planning. Counselors help clients address a variety of concerns, such as self-esteem, shyness, personal growth, family and couple relationships, sexual identity, sexual abuse, cross-cultural communication, substance abuse, eating disorders, depression, anxiety, and suicidal ideation. Many counselors now work in community mental health settings, private practices, hospitals, and businesses, as well as in educational institutions. During the same time, the nature of psychological assessment has expanded to assist counselors and clients in all of these areas.

Assessment aids counseling by providing information for both counselors and clients. Counselors need the information gained in assessment to understand and respond to their clients' concerns. They also rely on assessment for program planning and evaluation. Clients use the information obtained by assessment to understand themselves better and to make plans for the future.

The assessment process can be therapeutic in itself by helping clients to clarify goals and to gain a sense of perspective (Paritzky & Magoon, 1982; Smith, 1976). Recent research indicates that clients benefit significantly from personality assessment (Finn & Tonsager, 1992), vocational interest assessment (Randahl, Hansen, & Haverkamp, 1993), and relationship assessment (Worthington et al., 1995) when the assessment is accompanied by a feedback session.

For most purposes, counseling can be conceptualized in terms of problem solving (Maloney & Ward, 1976; Walsh & Betz, 1994). This chapter begins with a discussion of the purpose of psychological assessment within the framework of a problem-solving model. The definition of psychological assessment is then considered, followed by a discussion of counselor and client attitudes toward assessment. Finally, results of surveys of psychological test usage by counselors are presented.

PURPOSE OF PSYCHOLOGICAL ASSESSMENT

The problem-solving model provides a convenient means for summarizing the purposes of psychological assessment procedures in counseling. These purposes can be described by the five basic steps in the problem-solving model presented by D'Zurilla & Goldfried (1971). Each step in the problem-solving model entails the need for information that can be gained through psychological assessment.

Problem Orientation

The first step requires that the client recognize and accept the problem. If the client denies the problem, it cannot be dealt with adequately.

Almost any assessment procedure can be used to increase sensitivity to potential problems. Instruments that promote self-awareness and self-exploration can stimulate clients to cope with developmental issues before they become actual problems.

Surveys of groups or classes can help counselors to identify common problems or concerns that can be taken into account in planning programs for clients. A number of needs assessment instruments (e.g., alcohol screening inventories and sexual behavior questionnaires) have been developed for this purpose.

Both client and counselor need to recognize the problem. As soon as a problematic situation is recognized, they can begin to approach it in a systematic fashion as indicated by the problem-solving model. The model helps to "normalize" a client's concerns. It implies an acceptance of problems as a normal part of life. The counselor provides support and perspective for the client as he or she begins to address the problem. Recognition of the problem, together with a means of addressing it, helps the counselor to establish rapport with the client.

Problem Identification

In this step, the counselor and the client attempt to identify the problem in as much detail as possible. Assessment procedures can help clarify the nature of the client's problem. For example, problem or symptom checklists can be used to assess the type and the extent of a client's concerns. Personal diaries or logs can also be used to identify situations in which the problem occurs. Personality inventories can help counselors and clients to understand personality dynamics underlying certain situations. Information gained during the course of identifying client problems can be used to specify counseling goals.

Problem identification improves communication. A client is more likely to continue in counseling if the counselor and client agree on the nature of the problem (Epperson, Bushway, & Warman, 1983; Pekarik, 1988). Identification of the problem also aids in communication with others, such as referral sources, family, and friends.

Generation of Alternatives

In the third step, the counselor and client generate alternatives to help resolve the problem. Assessment procedures enable counselors and clients to identify alternative solutions for client problems. For example, an interest inventory can suggest alternative career choices for a client. An assessment interview can be used to determine what techniques have worked for the client in the past when faced with a similar problem. Checklists (such as a study skills inventory) or free association tests (such as an incomplete sentences blank) yield data that can be used to generate alternatives.

Test results can help clients to view problems from different angles. For example, the use of instruments that measure personality styles provide clients with alternative ways of looking at their behavior or the behavior of others. Assessment exercises can identify positive self-statements of clients, which can open up alternatives for clients (Parks & Hollon, 1988). Counselors use assessment procedures to assist clients in discovering strengths upon which they can build to overcome difficulties or enhance development (Duckworth, 1990).

Decision Making

In deciding upon a solution to a problem, clients need to anticipate the consequences of the various alternatives. According to classical decision theory, choice is a function of the probability of success and the desirability of the outcome (Horan, 1979). This equation emphasizes the importance of assessing both the likelihood of success of various alternatives and the attractiveness of those alternatives for the client. Clients will usually want to consider those alternatives that maximize the likelihood of a favorable outcome.

Counselors use assessment materials to help clients weigh the attractiveness of each alternative and the likelihood of achieving each alternative. For example, the attractiveness of various alternatives can be assessed by values clarification exercises. The likelihood of achieving alternatives can be evaluated by expectancy (or experience) tables that show the success rate for people with different types of test scores or characteristics. (Anastasi, 1988). Balance sheets or decision-making grids enable clients to compare the desirability and feasibility of various alternatives (Cochran, 1983).

Counselors can use assessment data to help determine the appropriate treatment for clients. For example, scores on the Minnesota Multiphasic Personality Inventory (MMPI) can be used to help decide which type of treatment program to employ for a client (Butcher,

6

1990), and achievement test scores can be used to guide a student's course selections.

Verification

Counselors need to evaluate the effectiveness of their counseling endeavors. They need to verify that the client's problem has been resolved or reduced. The counselor should discuss with the client how the client will know when the problem has been solved. This step requires that goals be clearly specified, that they be translated into specific behavioral objectives, and that the possibility for progress in accomplishing these goals be realistically viewed by both counselor and client. Assessment procedures for this purpose include goal attainment scaling (Kiresuk & Sherman, 1968; Paritzky & Magoon, 1982), self-monitoring techniques, and the readministration of tests that the client completed earlier in counseling.

Besides serving as a guide for the counseling process, verification efforts also provide a means of accountability for the counseling agency. Positive feedback from clients can be used to gain support for the agency. Negative feedback can be used to help revise programs to make them more attractive to clients.

DEFINITION OF PSYCHOLOGICAL ASSESSMENT

According to the *Standards for Educational and Psychological Tests* (Wagner, 1987), an authoritative source for all test users, the term *assessment procedure* refers to "any method used to measure characteristics of people, programs, or objects" (American Educational Research Association, American Psychological Association, & National Council on Measurement in Education, 1985, p. 89). This is a broad definition that can be analyzed in three parts, as indicated in the following paragraphs.

For the sake of simplicity, the terms *assessment* and *testing* are sometimes used interchangeably in this book. Strictly speaking, a test refers to a task upon which people are asked to try their best, such as an aptitude or achievement test (AERA, APA, & NCME, 1985). Tests measure *maximum* performance, in contrast with questionnaires and inventories, which evaluate *typical* performance (Cronbach, 1990). Questionnaires and inventories, such as personality and interest inven-

7

tories, elicit self-reports of opinions, preferences, and typical reactions to everyday situations.

Standardized Versus Unstandardized Assessment

In the first part of the definition for assessment procedure, "any method" includes both standardized and nonstandardized assessment procedures. Standardized procedures must meet certain criteria of test construction, administration, and interpretation (Anastasi, 1988). These criteria include uniform procedures for test administration, objective scoring methods, representative norm groups for test interpretation, reliable test scores, and studies that show that the test is valid for the purposes for which it was designed. Many assessment procedures used in counseling fail to meet these criteria. Nonstandardized assessment procedures include rating scales, projective techniques, behavioral observations, and biographical measures. Because counselors frequently rely upon such nonstandardized procedures, they need to be familiar with their use.

Nonstandardized techniques produce results that are less dependable (that is, less reliable and valid) than do standardized techniques; however, they allow counselors to consider aspects of behavior or the environment not covered by traditional psychological tests. Counselors must be concerned not only about the *dependability* of test results, but also the *exhaustiveness* of the results (Cronbach & Gleser, 1965). Tests that provide highly dependable information often describe only a small part of the information a counselor needs. Assessment procedures such as interviews, projective techniques, or essays, which provide less dependable information, can nonetheless aid counselors in obtaining information on topics that would be missed by formal testing procedures. Exhaustive procedures should be used when counselors need to obtain a large amount of information pertaining to a variety of decisions (e.g., which problems to address or which treatments to consider). Information obtained in this manner can be verified in subsequent assessments with more dependable measures.

Nomothetic Versus Idiographic Assessment

The phrase "any method" in the definition of psychological assessment procedure also encompasses both nomothetic and idiographic assessment techniques (Allport, 1937). *Nomos* is the Greek word for "law"; the Greek term *idios* means "personal." In nomothetic assessment, emphasis in placed on variables that show lawful or meaningful distinctions among people. The group provides a frame of reference for determining which variables to assess and how to interpret the results. In idiographic assessment, on the other hand, emphasis is placed on those variables that can be most helpful in describing the individual. The individual serves as the reference point both to identify relevant variables and to interpret data.

Most psychological tests, such as interest and personality inventories, use the nomothetic approach. These tests use the same scales to describe all clients. Scores are interpreted in regard to a set of norms. In contrast, many informal assessment procedures, such as the interview, case study, or card sorts, employ an idiographic approach. A different set of variables is likely to be used to describe each client. Nomothetic techniques can be more readily interpreted, but they may not be as relevant or as penetrating as idiographic methods, which have been designed to measure variations in individuality (Neimeyer, 1989).

Quantitative Versus Qualitative Assessment

The second part of the definition of psychological assessment procedure, "to measure characteristics," pertains to both quantitative and qualitative assessment. It includes both refined scaling procedures (e.g., scores on individual intelligence tests) and simple classifications (e.g., "outgoing" versus "reserved" personality type).

Quantitative procedures, which include most psychological tests, yield a specific score on a continuous scale. Qualitative procedures, such as an interview or autobiography, produce a verbal description of a person's behavior or of a situation that can be placed into one of several categories. Although more research has been conducted on techniques that produce some type of continuous score, procedures that employ descriptive categories are often used in counseling. Such categories (e.g., developmental stages or personality types) can provide a means for conceptualizing a case or considering treatment strategies.

By their very nature, quantitative assessment methods have been more thoroughly studied in terms of reliability and validity. Qualitative assessment methods, on the other hand, also possess a number of advantages. Compared with quantitative methods, they provide a more holistic and integrated view of clients, they encourage greater activity on the part of clients, they more often form part of the treatment in addition to assessment, and they can more easily be adapted for clients from different backgrounds (Goldman, 1990).

Individual Versus Environmental Assessment

The last part of the definition of psychological assessment indicates that psychological assessment refers to people, programs, and objects. Counselors have usually devoted more attention to assessment of people, but assessment of the environment (that is, programs and objects) is also necessary. In recent years, counselors have paid greater attention to the influence of the environment in determining one's behavior (Chartrand, 1991; Walsh & Betz, 1994). The client's behavior depends both on individual and situational characteristics (Barrios, 1988), so counseling can be most effective when psychological assessment includes both the individual and the environment.

Counselors need to be familiar with all of the different aspects of psychological assessment included in its definition. All of those aspects are reviewed in this book.

ATTITUDES TOWARD PSYCHOLOGICAL TESTS

Psychological testing, which was very popular during and after World Wars I and II, lost some of its appeal during the time of social upheaval in the 1960s and 1970s (Haney, 1981). People became concerned about the lack of predictive validity of tests, the use of test scores to label or judge others, and test bias in regard to minority groups. In an influential article, Goldman (1972) lamented the shortcomings of standardized tests, particularly ability tests, and counselors' lack of preparation and skill in the use of such tests.

Most of the criticisms of tests have their basis in unrealistic expectations or misuse. Tests do not provide a magic answer; instead, they should be looked upon as one additional source of information that may be helpful in problem solving. The tests need to be soundly constructed and responsibly applied (Dahlstrom, 1993). Tests can be especially helpful in counseling if they are designed to stimulate self-exploration and self-development, if they are accompanied by extensive interpretive materials, and if counselors are well schooled in their use (Prediger, 1972).

Goldman (1994) has recently reiterated his reservations regarding standardized testing. He argued that most counselors should rely primarily upon qualitative assessment and that quantitative assessment should probably become a specialized field for about 10% of the counselors who are well qualified in its use.

In response, Zytowski (1994b) has pointed out that counselors should be more qualified now than they were 20 years ago because of higher standards imposed by recent licensing and certification requirements. He also noted that new tests such as the Self-Directed Search have been developed, and that old tests such as the MMPI-2 and the Strong Interest Inventory have been improved. Finally, he stressed that tests have been much more helpful in counseling when they have been used with clients as measures of similarity to different criterion groups (e.g., occupational groups or diagnostic classifications) rather than as measures of potential success in various endeavors. Similarly, Prediger (1994b) observed that tests are most effective when they are used together with other information to help a client develop "informed self-estimates," which can then be used to identify appropriate environments or treatments for that individual.

Although surveys indicate that most counselors understand and employ desirable testing practices, some areas of concern have been detected (Elmore, Ekstrom, & Diamond, 1993; Elmore, Ekstrom, Diamond, & Whittaker, 1993). These areas of concern include inadequate knowledge of test norms, too much reliance on test scores without additional information, and insufficient knowledge of possible test bias and how to use tests fairly.

To offset criticisms, counselors need to become aware of both the strengths and limitations of the various tests used in counseling. They need to understand both the psychometric properties of tests and the psychological findings regarding the behavior being assessed (Anastasi, 1992). They need to learn effective and appropriate procedures for selecting, administering, and interpreting tests with clients from diverse backgrounds. They need to be able to integrate the use of psychological assessment procedures with other aspects of counseling to help clients with self-understanding and self-determination. Principles and procedures to aid counselors in these endeavors are presented throughout this book.

SURVEYS OF TEST USAGE

Despite criticism, psychological tests continue to play an important part in counseling. Recent surveys of test usage in different counseling settings are described below. Although preferences for particular tests have changed somewhat over the years, counselors continue to make extensive use of tests for a variety of purposes.

Community Mental Health Counseling

The popularity of standardized assessment instruments among counselors in community-based work settings is shown in Table 1-1 (Bubenzer, Zimpfer, & Mahrle, 1990). The majority of the respondents indicated that they employed standardized testing in their counseling practice.

As indicated in Table 1-1, the Minnesota Multiphasic Personality Inventory (MMPI) stands out as the most frequently chosen instru-

TABLE 1-1. Usage of Psychological Assessment Instruments by Community Mental Health Counselors

Rank	Instrument	Total Mentions[a]
1	Minnesota Multiphasic Personality Inventory	227
2	Strong-Campbell Interest Inventory	92
3	Wechsler Adult Intelligence Scale–Revised	84
4	Myers-Briggs Type Indicator	77
5	Wechsler Intelligence Scale for Children–Revised	50
6.5	Sixteen Personality Factor Questionnaire	34
6.5	Thematic Apperception Test	34
8	Bender-Gestalt Visual Motor Test	33
9	Wide Range Achievement Test	27
10.5	Million Clinical Multiaxial Inventory	25
10.5	Rorschach Inkblot Test	25
12	Taylor-Johnson Temperament Analysis	24
13	Career Assessment Inventory	20
14.5	General Aptitude Test Battery	16
14.5	California Psychological Inventory	16
16	Self-Directed Search	14
17.5	Fundamental Interpersonal Relations Orientation–Behavior	13
17.5	House-Tree-Person Test	13

Note. From Bubenzer, Zimpfer, & Mahrle (1990, p. 57). © 1990 AACD. Reprinted with permission. No further reproduction authorized without written permission of the American Counseling Association.

[a]Based on the responses of 743 members of the American Counseling Association employed as counselors in community-based settings.

ment, followed by the Strong-Campbell Interest Inventory (now known as the Strong Interest Inventory), and the Wechsler Adult Intelligence Scale–Revised. The top 10 instruments include personality inventories, interest inventories, intelligence tests, projective tests, and achievement tests. The complexity and diversity of these instruments underlines the importance of adequate training in the use of psychological assessment for the counselors (most of whom are trained at the master's degree level) who work in these settings.

Career Counseling

The instruments most frequently used for vocational assessment by counseling psychologists are listed in Table 1-2 (Watkins, Campbell, & Nieberding, 1994). According to the survey respondents, these instruments are used (a) to increase client self-knowledge, (b) to help clients make career choices, and (c) to encourage client participation in career counseling.

As found in previous surveys (Zytowski & Warman, 1982), the Strong Interest Inventory continues to be the most frequently used instrument by counselors for career counseling. In general, the counselors in this study placed greater emphasis on interest measurement than they did upon aptitude measurement. The results were fairly consistent across different work settings.

School Counseling

Table 1-3 shows the results of a national survey of school counselors regarding test usage (Elmore, Ekstrom, Diamond, & Whittaker 1993). In contrast with community-based counselors and career counselors, school counselors are much more likely to use tests of maximum performance (intelligence, aptitude, and achievement tests) than tests of typical performance (personality and interest inventories). A similar test usage pattern has been noted among school counselors in earlier surveys (Engen, Lamb, & Prediger, 1982).

Approximately two thirds of the respondents indicated that testing was an "important" or "very important" part of their work. Nearly all of the respondents said that they were responsible for interpreting test results to students.

Most of the tests identified by means of the test usage surveys will be discussed in this book. Counselors need to become familiar with

TABLE 1-2. Usage of Vocational Assessment Instruments by Counseling Psychologists

Rank	Instrument	Total Mentions[a]
1	Strong Interest Inventory	461
2	Self-Directed Search	363
3	Kuder Occupational Interest Survey	279
4	Differential Aptitude Test	191
5	General Aptitude Test Battery	158
6	Career Assessment Inventory	148
7	Vocational Preference Inventory	131
8	Work Values Inventory	121
9	Vocational Sort Cards	117
10	Temperament and Values Inventory	91
11	Career Maturity Inventory	89
12	Wide Range Interest-Opinion Test	70
13.5	Career Decision Scale	69
13.5	Career Development Inventory	69
15.5	California Occupational Preference System	61
15.5	Harrington-O'Shea	61
17	My Vocational Situation	60
18	Jackson Vocational Interest Inventory	59
19	Minnesota Importance Questionnaire	51
20	Occupational Stress Inventory	47
21	Armed Services Vocational Aptitude Battery	40
22	Hall Occupational Orientation Inventory	30
23	Minnesota Satisfaction Questionnaire	28
24	Ohio Vocational Interest Survey	27
25	SES Interest Inventory	26
26	Adult Career Concerns Inventory	25
27	Cognitive Vocational Maturity Test	19
28	Salience Inventory	15

Note. From Watkins, Campbell, & Nieberding (1994, pp. 121–122). © 1994 by the Division of Counseling Psychology. Modified and reproduced by special permission of the publisher, SAGE Publications, Inc., Thousand Oaks, CA. All rights reserved.

[a]Based on the responses of 637 members of the American Psychological Association who identified counseling as their specialty.

the most popular tests so that they can use them effectively in their own practices and so that they can interpret scores from tests for clients referred to them by other counselors.

SUMMARY

1. Psychological assessment is an integral part of counseling. Assessment provides information that can be used in each step of the

TABLE 1-3. Usage of Psychological Assessment Instruments by School Counselors

Rank	Instrument	Total Mentions[a]
1	Wechsler Intelligence Scale for Children—Revised	78
2	Preliminary Scholastic Aptitude Test	77
3	California Achievement Test	67
4	Differential Aptitude Tests	64
5	Strong-Campbell Interest Inventory	62
6	Scholastic Aptitude Test	60
7	American College Testing Program	55
8	Iowa Tests of Basic Skills	53
9	Armed Services Vocational Aptitude Battery	50

Note: From Elmore, Ekstrom, & Diamond (1993, p. 75). © 1993 ACA. Reprinted with permission. No further reproduction authorized without written permission of the American Counseling Association.

[a]Based on the responses of 423 members of the American School Counselor Association.

problem-solving model. The assessment process can be therapeutic in and of itself.

2. Assessment serves the following functions: (a) to stimulate counselors and clients to consider various issues, (b) to clarify the nature of a problem or issue, (c) to suggest alternative solutions for problems, (d) to provide a method of comparing various alternatives so that a decision can be made or confirmed, and (e) to enable counselors and clients to evaluate the effectiveness of a particular solution.

3. Psychological assessment refers to all methods used to measure the characteristics of people, programs, or objects. This is a broad definition that encompasses measures that are nonstandardized, idiographic, and qualitative, as well as those that are standardized, nomothetic, and quantitative. It pertains to environmental as well as individual assessment.

4. Negative attitudes toward psychological tests can be traced to unrealistic expectations regarding tests and to the misuse of tests. Psychological assessment needs to be seen in perspective, and counselors must be trained in the proper use of tests.

5. Surveys of test usage show that counselors use a wide variety of assessment procedures. School counselors more often use aptitude and achievement tests (measures of maximum performance), whereas community-based and career counselors more often employ personality and interest inventories (measures of typical performance).

2

NATURE OF PSYCHOLOGICAL ASSESSMENT IN COUNSELING

C OUNSELORS NEED TO BE INFORMED about the basic characteristics of psychological assessment procedures. They must be able to compare and evaluate different assessment procedures. Information presented in this chapter should aid counselors in these endeavors.

In this chapter, the different criteria that have been used to distinguish among psychological assessment procedures are reviewed and then used to describe six common assessment procedures. These procedures include standardized tests, rating scales, projective techniques, behavioral observations, biographical measures, and physiological measures. The standards that have been established for evaluating tests and test usage are identified, and the chapter concludes with a list of information sources about assessment procedures.

DISTINCTIONS AMONG PSYCHOLOGICAL ASSESSMENT PROCEDURES

Psychological assessment procedures differ from each other in a variety of ways. As indicated below, these differences can be categorized by six basic questions regarding the nature of the assessment procedure itself.

Who Is Making the Assessment?

Is the person making a self-assessment or is another person making the assessment? Block (1961) differentiated between "S-data" based on self-reports and "O-data" based on the reports of others. Both types of data are needed to obtain a full appraisal of the individual. O-data can be used to validate self-reports; S-data can provide valuable insights regarding self-perception not available in the reports of others.

What Is Being Assessed?

What here refers to the subject of the assessment procedure. Is the *individual* or the *environment* the subject of the assessment? As noted in Chapter 1, counselors have usually been interested in individual assessment; however, instruments that evaluate the environment (e.g., classroom atmosphere or residence hall settings) can also provide important information for understanding or treating a problem.

If the individual is being appraised, does the content of the assessment deal primarily with *affective* (feeling), *cognitive* (thinking), or *behavioral* (doing) aspects of the individual? These three aspects of the individual may be further subdivided as discussed below.

Affective characteristics may be subdivided into *temperamental* and *motivational* factors (Guilford, 1959). Temperamental factors include the characteristics assessed by most personality inventories, for example, self-sufficiency, stability, and impulsiveness. Motivational factors, on the other hand, refer to interests or values. According to Guilford, temperament governs the *manner* in which an individual performs, whereas motivation determines *what activity* the individual will choose to pursue.

Cognitive variables may be based on learning that takes place in a specific course (*course-related*) or learning that is relatively independent of specific coursework (*noncourse-related*; Anastasi, 1988). This distinction describes a basic difference between achievement and aptitude tests. Achievement tests evaluate past or present performance; aptitude tests predict future performance. Achievement tests measure learning that has taken place in a particular course or series of courses. Aptitude tests assess capacity to learn, based on items that are relatively independent of the classroom or any formal educational experience.

Behavioral measures include responses that are *voluntary* or *involuntary* in nature. Voluntary responses may be assessed either by self-monitoring or by other-monitoring techniques. A systematic record is kept of measurable items such as calories consumed or hours spent watching television. In the case of involuntary responses (e.g., blood pressure or heart rate), various types of physiological measures are used to assess individual reactivity. Biofeedback devices, often used to teach relaxation methods, are a good example of the latter type of assessment measure.

Where Is the Assessment Taking Place?

The location in which the assessment takes place is important in the sense that it helps to differentiate between test results obtained in *laboratory* settings from those obtained in *natural* settings. Many psychological tests must be administered under standardized conditions so that the test results can be interpreted properly. For these tests, a testing room or laboratory is usually used. If the circumstances of test administration differ from person to person, differences in the testing conditions can influence test results. Some measures, such as employee ratings, are obtained in natural settings under conditions that may vary considerably for different individuals. Variations in job circumstances can greatly affect the ratings. Interpretations of the results must take into account the setting in which they were obtained.

When Is the Assessment Occurring?

The question of when an assessment takes place is of value in distinguishing between assessments planned in advance (*prospective*) as opposed to those based on recall (*retrospective*). Self-monitoring techniques are usually planned in advance. For example, students may be asked to keep track of the number of hours that they studied or the number of pages that they read during a study period. In contrast, biographical measures such as life history forms are recorded to the best of the individual's recollection after the event has occurred.

Why Is the Assessment Being Undertaken?

The question of why pertains to the reason for administering the test rather than to the nature of the test itself. The same test can be used for a variety of purposes, such as counseling, selection, placement, description, and evaluation. When tests are used in counseling, all data obtained must be regarded as confidential. Such *private data* may be contrasted with *public data*—data originally obtained for another purpose such as selection or placement. Examples of public data include academic grades, educational level, or occupational status. Counselors use public as well as private data in helping clients to address certain issues, because the public data can provide a great deal of information about the client's past performance under various circumstances.

How Is the Assessment Conducted?

How here refers both to the manner in which the test material is presented and to how the score for the assessment procedure is obtained. Is the type of behavior which is being assessed *disguised* or *undisguised*? Projective techniques (described in Chapter 12) are designed so that the respondent is typically unaware of the true nature of the test or of any "preferred" answer. Because the intent of the test is disguised, it is more difficult for respondents to fake their answers to produce a particular type of impression.

Are the scores arrived at *objectively*, that is, independently of individual judgment, or *subjectively*, depending on the scorer's best judgment? Tests that can be scored by means of a scoring stencil are objective. That is, different persons using the same scoring stencil with an answer sheet should obtain the same score if they are careful in counting the number of correct answers. In contrast, rating scales are subjective—the score assigned will often vary depending upon the individual rater.

TYPES OF PSYCHOLOGICAL ASSESSMENT METHODS

The various assessment methods used in counseling may be conveniently classified by using different combinations of the criteria discussed in the previous section. Six popular types of psychological assessment methods are described below.

Standardized Tests

Standardized tests are discussed at length throughout the book; they therefore will be mentioned only briefly here. The term *standardized tests* refers to tests that must be administered and scored according to specified procedures. The testing conditions must be uniform for all clients. All scoring must be objective. Standardized test scores are usually interpreted by means of normative data obtained from a representative sample of people. Most standardized tests have been studied in terms of their reliability and validity.

Standardized tests include the following types of tests, each of which are discussed in this book: achievement tests, aptitude (or ability) tests, personality inventories, interest inventories, value inventories, and environmental inventories. Some standardized tests designed for specialized purposes such as neuropsychological assessment (e.g., Halstead-Reitan Neuropsychological Test Battery) and the evaluation of learning disabilities (e.g., Woodcock-Johnson Psycho-Educational Battery) are not reviewed in this book.

Rating Scales

Rating scales, which provide estimates of various behaviors or characteristics based on the rater's observations, are a common method of assessment. In contrast with standardized tests, rating scales are derived from subjective rather than objective data. Rating scales include self-ratings, ratings of others, and ratings of the environment. Interview data are often summarized by means of rating scales.

Because of their subjectivity, rating scales suffer from a number of disadvantages. Three common errors associated with rating scales include (a) halo effect, (b) error of central tendency, and (c) leniency error. In the case of the halo effect, raters show a tendency to generalize from one aspect of the client to all other aspects. For example, if a person is friendly, that person may also be rated highly in unrelated areas such as intelligence, creativity, leadership, and motivation. The error of central tendency describes the tendency to rate all people as "average," or near the middle of the rating scale. The leniency error refers to the tendency to rate the characteristics of people more favorably than they should be rated.

To control for such errors, raters are sometimes asked to rank people on each rating scale. As an alternative, raters may be forced to distribute their ratings across the entire rating scale according to the normal curve or a similar system. When these techniques are applied to a large number of people, they prevent ratings from bunching up in the middle of the distribution or at the top end of the distribution. Kenrick & Funder (1988) offered the following suggestions for improving the validity of ratings: (a) use raters who are thoroughly familiar with the person being rated, (b) require multiple behavioral observations, (c) obtain ratings from more than one observer, (d) employ dimensions that are publicly observable, and (e) identify behaviors for observation that are relevant to the dimension in question. These suggestions can help counteract limitations posed by the various sources of invalidity.

Examples of rating techniques include the semantic differential and situational tests. The semantic differential technique requires raters to rate concepts (e.g., "my job") by means of a series of 7-step, bipolar scales (e.g., competitive versus cooperative). This technique can be readily adapted to a variety of situations. A list of bipolar scales that can be used to represent different dimensions appears in Osgood, Suci, and Tannenbaum (1957).

Situational tests require the person to perform a task in a situation similar to that for which the person is being evaluated. For example, the "in-basket technique" requires candidates for an administrative position to respond to the daily tasks of an administrator by means of an in-basket (work assignment basket) that simulates the actual work assignments of administrators. Situational tests can often meet the conditions suggested by Kenrick and Funder (1988) noted above. For this reason, they often prove to be beneficial in predicting performance in a situation similar to that of the test. Situational tests are frequently used to assess leadership or management skills.

Projective Techniques

Projective tests employ vague or ambiguous stimuli to which people must respond. Because the stimuli (e.g., inkblots, ambiguous pictures, incomplete sentences) are vague, people tend to make interpretations of the stimuli that reveal more about themselves than they do about the stimuli. They "project" their own personality onto the stimuli.

Responses are usually scored subjectively. Common projective techniques include the Rorschach Inkblot Test, Thematic Apperception Test, and Rotter Incomplete Sentences Blank. For many years projective tests dominated the field of personality testing, but during the past few decades objective (standardized) tests have become more popular. The use of projective techniques in counseling is discussed further in Chapter 12.

Behavioral Observations

Behavioral observations refer to behaviors that can be observed and counted. The observations are planned in advance or based on recent events. The behaviors, which usually occur in a natural setting, are monitored by the client, by an observer, such as a spouse or parent, or both. The observer usually records the frequency of a discrete behavior, for example, the number of "I" statements made in an interview or the number of conversations initiated. Frequently the duration of the response and the intensity of the behavior (as rated by the observer) are also recorded.

Behavioral observations have the advantage of pertaining directly to a behavior that a client is concerned about. The behavior can usually be included as part of a goal. The measure is directly related to the client's treatment.

Biographical Measures

Biographical measures refer to one's accomplishments or experiences as reported by the client or as reflected in historical records. For example, an employment resume or college application form usually provides an extensive amount of biographical information. Biographical measures differ from behavioral measures in that the observations are not planned in advance. They differ from rating scales in that the information is usually a matter of fact rather than a matter of judgment. Biographical data (biodata) include information maintained in cumulative records by schools or in personnel records by businesses, such as academic grades, extracurricular achievements, job promotions, hobbies, and volunteer work experiences.

The value of biographical measures in assessment is expressed in the well-established psychological maxim: "The best predictor of future performance is past performance." As a rule, the best single pre-

23

dictor of college grades for an individual is usually that person's high school grades. A person who has functioned well in a particular job in the past will probably perform well in related types of activities in the future.

Biographical data are usually collected by means of a written form or during the course of an initial interview with a client. Although this information is most often used in a qualitative manner, it can also be quantified for assessment purposes (Owens, 1983).

Biographical measures are both economical and efficient. They can provide information for areas such as leadership experiences or creative accomplishments that may be difficult to assess by other means. On the other hand, they may be inappropriate or difficult to interpret if the person's experiences have been unusual or severely limited. Biographical measures yield a broad range of information, but the meaning of the information requires additional interaction with the client or others familiar with the situation.

The Quick Job-Hunting Map (QJHM) by Richard Bolles (1990, 1991) represents an example of a biographical measure. The QJHM asks clients to review their accomplishments in terms of the transferable skills that are involved. It provides a systematic means of analyzing one's history in regard to career opportunities. Other examples of biographical measures include career assessment portfolios (McDivitt, 1994) and psychosocial inventories such as the Quickview Social History (Giannetti, 1992).

Physiological Measures

Physiological measures promise to become increasingly important in understanding and monitoring client behavior (Sturgis & Gramling, 1988). Such measures refer to bodily states or bodily functions that are primarily involuntary in nature, including skin temperature, muscle contractions, and blood pressure. Recent advances in instrumentation (e.g., biofeedback devices) make it relatively easy to include such variables in the assessment process.

STANDARDS FOR EVALUATING TESTS AND TEST USAGE

Several sets of standards have been published by professional organizations concerning the development and use of psychological assess-

24

ment procedures. Counselors should be familiar with each set of standards or guidelines for test usage presented in this section.

ACA Code of Ethics and Standards of Practice

The *American Counseling Association Code of Ethics and Standards of Practice* specifies principles of ethical conduct and standards of professional behavior for counselors (ACA, 1995). Sections of this document devoted to psychological assessment are reproduced in Appendix A. Other professional organizations have also published ethical codes that address the use of psychological assessment procedures in a similar fashion (American Psychological Association, 1993; American Rehabilitation Counseling Association, Commission on Rehabilitation Counselor Certification, & National Rehabilitation Counseling Association, 1995; American School Counselor Association, 1992). The ACA Code of Ethics is discussed further in Chapter 18 and in other sections of this book.

Responsibilities of Users of Standardized Tests (RUST Statement–Revised)

ACA (formerly known as the American Association for Counseling and Development) and the Association for Assessment in Counseling (formerly known as the Association for Measurement and Evaluation in Counseling and Development), one of the subdivisions of ACA, have published a policy statement that lists responsibilities of test users in seven categories: test decisions, qualifications of test users, test selection, test administration, test scoring, test interpretation, and communicating test results (ACA/AMECD, 1989). Counselors should be familiar with the recommendations made in this policy statement, frequently referred to as "the RUST statement." The most significant recommendations for counselors are reproduced in Appendix B.

Standards for Educational and Psychological Testing (Standards)

The *Standards* provide criteria for evaluating both the tests themselves and use of the tests. The criteria were prepared by a joint committee of the American Educational Research Association, the American Psychological Association, and the National Council on Measurement in

Education (AERA, APA, & NCME, 1985). The current version of the *Standards* represents the fifth in a series of documents on this issue beginning in 1954. Whereas previous editions of the *Standards* emphasized the responsibilities of the test developer, the present edition devotes more attention to the responsibilities of the test user. Increased emphasis on the appropriate use of tests should help to reduce criticism caused by the misuse of tests (Wagner, 1987). Excerpts from the *Standards* that pertain to the use of tests in counseling are presented in Appendix C.

The *Standards* also address, at least in part, the problem of potential bias in tests by stating a series of guidelines to be followed in testing linguistic minorities or people with disabilities. These issues will be discussed further in Chapter 16.

Test User Qualifications

The Joint Committee on Testing Practices (JCTP), which presently includes members from the American Counseling Association, American Psychological Association, American Speech-Language-Hearing Association, National Association of School Psychologists, and National Council on Measurement in Education, represents an interdisciplinary effort to identify and improve the qualifications of test users. Members of this committee have identified a total of 86 competencies required for the proper use of different instruments (Eyde, Moreland, Robertson, Primoff, & Most, 1988; Moreland, Eyde, Robertson, Primoff, & Most, 1995). Of the 86 competencies, 12 embody minimum proficencies for all test users (see Table 2-1).

Factor analytic research indicates that the 86 competencies can be reduced to seven broad factors. These include comprehensive assessment, proper test use, psychometric knowledge, integrity of test results, scoring accuracy, appropriate use of norms, and interpretive feedback. Based on research regarding test misuse, the relative significance of the seven factors varies with the particular type of test. For example, competencies in comprehensive assessment are more important in using clinical tests, whereas skills in the appropriate use of norms are more important in vocational tests (Moreland et al., 1995).

The JCTP statement stresses educational efforts, not restriction of access, as a means of ensuring qualified test users. Examples of appro-

TABLE 2-1. Twelve Minimum Competencies for Proper Use of Tests

Item No.	Competency
1.	Avoiding errors in scoring and recording
2.	Refraining from labeling people with personally derogatory terms like *dishonest* on the basis of a test score that lacks perfect validity
3.	Keeping scoring keys and test materials secure
4.	Seeing that every examinee follows directions so that test scores are accurate
5.	Using settings for testing that allow for optimum performance by test takers (e.g., adequate room)
6.	Refraining from coaching or training individuals or groups on test items, which results in misrepresentation of the person's abilities and competencies
7.	Being willing to give interpretation and guidance to test takers in counseling situations
8.	Not making photocopies of copyrighted materials
9.	Refraining from using homemade answer sheets that do not align properly with scoring keys
10.	Establishing rapport with examinees to obtain accurate scores
11.	Refraining from answering questions from test takers in greater detail than the test manual permits
12.	Not assuming that a norm for one job applies to a different job (and not assuming that norms for one group automatically apply to other groups)

Note. From Moreland, Eyde, Robertson, Primoff, & Most (1995, p. 16). © 1995 by the American Psychological Association. Adapted by permission.

priate and inappropriate test usage based on the 86 competencies and seven broad factors are provided in the casebook, *Responsible Test Use: Case Studies for Assessing Human Behavior*, published under the auspices of the JCTP (Eyde et al., 1993).

Code of Fair Test Practices in Education

The *Code of Fair Testing Practices in Education* (1988), which was prepared by JCTP, focuses on the use of educational tests. The code addresses a public as well as a professional audience. It lists standards for educational test users and developers in four areas: developing and selecting tests, interpreting scores, striving for fairness, and informing test takers. The code lists 22 standards that specify the responsibilities of counselors and other test users in each of these areas. Most of the responsibilities described by the code are discussed in appropriate sections of this book.

Test Publisher Requirements

Requirements for test usage vary depending upon the complexity of the test. In the past, test publishers often distinguished between level *a* tests (no restrictions), level *b* tests (purchasers must have completed a college course in tests and measurements), and level *c* tests (purchaser must have completed an advanced degree in an appropriate profession, belong to an appropriate professional organization, or be licensed or certified in an appropriate profession). Recently, test publishers have begun to give greater emphasis to the competencies required for the use of different types of tests rather than relying strictly on one's professional credentials.

The JCTP has worked with test publishers to prepare qualification forms for potential customers. These forms ask test purchasers to indicate the purpose for which they will use the test, their level of training, their professional credentials, their educational background, the specific training they have received in the use of tests, and their testing competencies (Moreland et al., 1995).

Counselors need to be aware of the qualifications for the specific tests they wish to use. *Counselors should not attempt to use tests for which they lack adequate preparation.*

Multicultural Assessment Standards

The *Multicultural Assessment Standards*, a publication of the Association for Assessment in Counseling (AAC), a division of ACA, lists 34 standards of test practices that are relevant for clients from multicultural populations (Prediger, 1993). The booklet lists standards compiled from different sources that should be followed in selecting, administering, scoring, and interpreting instruments for clients from minority cultures. Further information on this topic can be found in Chapter 16 and throughout this book.

SOURCES OF INFORMATION ABOUT ASSESSMENT PROCEDURES

Although there are vast numbers of tests available in the United States, and there is a constant stream of new tests and revisions of old tests on the market, most of the tests are published by a few large publishers such as the Consulting Psychologists Press, the Psychological Corporation, and Psychological Assessment Resources. These publishers distribute test catalogs from which manuals, scoring keys, and the tests themselves may be ordered. A list of the largest test publishers and some of the tests they publish appears in Appendix D.

The best general source of information about tests is the *Mental Measurement Yearbooks* series (Plake, Conoley, Kramer, & Murphy, 1991). First published in 1938 by Oscar K. Buros at Rutgers University, the series is now published at the Buros Institute of Mental Measurements at the University of Nebraska–Lincoln. The *Yearbooks* provide descriptive information about the tests, including publishers, prices, and persons for whom the tests are appropriate, along with critical reviews by one or more test experts. A complete list of published references pertaining to each test is included and updated with each new edition. The *Twelfth Mental Measurements Yearbook* contains reviews for more than 400 newly released or revised instruments (Conoley & Impara, 1995).

Critical reviews are not published for each test in each yearbook, as each new volume is designed to add to, rather than replace, information found in prior volumes. A listing of all tests currently available for purchase in English-speaking countries is provided in another publication, also initiated by Buros, titled *Tests in Print*. The most recent edition of this publication is *Tests in Print IV*, a two-volume set that contains over 3,000 test entries (Murphy, Conoley, & Impara, 1994). The tests listed in each edition of *Tests in Print* are cross-referenced to the test reviews found in all previous editions of the *Yearbooks*. Recent test entries and test reviews for these publications can be obtained by means of an online computer service at the Buros Institute at the University of Nebraska.

In addition to the publications of the Buros Institute, counselors can consult similar reference books by the Test Corporation of America. This organization began publishing *Tests* and *Test Critiques* in the mid-1980s. *Tests*, now in its third edition, provides updated information on over 3,200 assessment instruments (Sweetland & Keyser, 1991). The information includes a description of each test, its cost, scoring procedures, and publisher information. The 10 volumes of *Test Critiques* offer in-depth reviews of psychological assessment instruments (Keyser & Sweetland, 1984–1994). The reviews, which average eight pages in length, provide a discussion of the practical applications of each test as well as its technical aspects. Each volume of *Test Critiques* provides an updated cumulative index of test reviews included in all previous volumes. The Test Corporation of America also publishes a sourcebook of computer-based assessment packages for use in a variety of situations (Krug, 1993).

Educational Testing Service (ETS) acquires and disseminates information on a wide range of commercial and research measures. The ETS Test Collection contains copies of approximately 18,000 tests and measurement devices. ETS has published information on these measures in a series of *Test Collection Catalogs* (Bradley, 1995; ETS, 1993).

Most of the information required for administering and scoring any particular test is found in its test manual. Although many manuals do not provide complete information, they should contain information regarding the construction of the test together with directions for administering, scoring, and interpreting the test. Norms should be reported, including a description of the norm group and the sampling techniques used to obtain the norms. Information regarding the reliability and validity of the test scores should also be presented in the manual, which should contain enough information so that prospective test users can evaluate the instrument before determining when and how they will use it. Most test publishers offer a specimen set of a test that includes the test itself, answer sheets, scoring keys, and a test manual, at a nominal cost.

Professional books and journals also provide extensive information about tests. *A Counselor's Guide to Career Assessment Instruments* (3rd ed.) offers reviews of popular assessment procedures used in career counseling together with a list of sources of information about assessment procedures in general (Jepsen & Kapes, 1994; Kapes, Mastie, & Whitfield, 1994). Copies of selected tests together with brief test reviews can be found in recently published sourcebooks (Fischer & Corcoran, 1994; Robinson, Shaver, & Wrightsman, 1991; Schutte & Malouff, 1995). Counselors are most likely to find test information pertinent to their work in the following journals: *Measurement and Evaluation in Counseling and Development, Journal of Counseling and Development*, and *Journal of Counseling Psychology*. Recently, a wide range of test information has also become available by means of electronic mail services (Denzine, 1995).

Information may be difficult to obtain for some proprietary tests that are exclusively owned and used within an organization such as a psychological consulting firm. Counselors should be cautious in relying upon the results of a test that has not been submitted for professional review.

SUMMARY

1. Psychological assessment procedures can be distinguished from each other in terms of *who* is making the assessment, *what* is being assessed, *where* the assessment takes place, *when* the assessment occurs, *why* the assessment is undertaken, and *how* the assessment is conducted. These distinctions can be used to classify tests into six broad categories: standardized tests, rating scales, projective tests, behavioral observations, biographical measures, and physiological measures.

2. Standardized tests have been the most thoroughly studied of all psychological assessment procedures in terms of reliability and validity; however, they cover a limited domain of behavior or situations. Counselors need to employ a broad range of assessment procedures to obtain information on relevant matters not included in standardized tests.

3. Counselors should be familiar with professional recommendations for evaluating tests and test usage. Important sets of guidelines include the *ACA Code of Ethics and Standards of Practice, Responsibilities of Users of Standardized Tests* (the RUST Statement—Revised), and *Standards for Educational and Psychological Testing*.

4. The most important sources of information about psychological tests are the *Mental Measurements Yearbook, Test Critiques*, test manuals, and professional journals.

3

MEASUREMENT CONCEPTS AND TEST INTERPRETATION

T O MAKE EFFECTIVE USE OF TESTS, counselors must understand certain elementary statistical concepts that are used in conjunction with the development and interpretation of tests and test scores. In this chapter only a few descriptive statistical concepts involved in understanding and interpreting tests are presented. Neither the underlying concepts of statistics nor their calculation, elements commonly found in a basic statistics course, is included. This chapter describes (a) some of the measures used to organize and describe test information, (b) the concepts of test reliability and test validity, and (c) the interpretation of reliability and validity information.

A simple raw score on a psychological test, without any type of comparative information, is a meaningless number. If a graduate student obtains a raw score of 58 on a midsemester examination in a course called "Theories of Counseling," the student's next question will be about the meaning of that score. A student whose score falls in the top 5% of the class will obviously react very differently from one whose score falls in the bottom 5%.

Some type of interpretive or comparative information is necessary before any information is conveyed by a score. To say that a client obtained a raw score of 37 out of 60 on an anxiety measure conveys no useful information, nor does the fact that this score of 37 meant that the client answered 62% of the anxiety items. To know that the same client obtained a raw score of 48 on a 60-item measure of tolerance does not indicate that he or she is more tolerant than anxious, nor does it yield any other useful information. Some frame of reference is necessary to give a test result meaning (Anastasi, 1988).

Scores on tests can be interpreted from three points of view: (a) comparison with scores obtained by other individuals, (b) comparison with an absolute score established by an authority, and (c) comparison with other scores obtained by the same individual. The first type of comparison is usually called *norm-referenced*. This type is used most often in interpreting scores on standardized tests. The second type is often described as a *criterion-referenced* interpretation. For example, a program administrator may require students to understand 90% of the material in a course before they receive credit for that course. Scores for tests based on this course would then be compared with this 90% passing score, not with the scores of other students.

Both of the first two types of comparisons use an external frame of reference. The third type of comparison, which uses an internal frame of reference, can be best thought of as a *self-referenced* (or ipsative) measure. An article in the local newspaper carried the following headline: "Smith's is Best for Breakfast." This headline could imply that Smith's restaurant was the best restaurant in the city for breakfast. In the article, however, it was pointed out that Smith's was not a particularly good place to eat, but if one had to choose, it was better for breakfast than it was for lunch or dinner. The reporter was using a self-referenced, not a norm-referenced, type of comparison.

NORMS

Standardized tests by nature are norm-referenced. Norms are established by administering the instrument to a standardization group and then referencing an individual's score to the distribution of scores obtained in the standardization sample. The individual's raw score is converted into some type of derived score, which indicates the individual's relative standing to the normative sample. This then provides a comparative measure of the individual's performance on whatever characteristic that instrument is assumed to measure.

Rank

A person's rank or standing within a group is the simplest norm-referenced statistic, with its interpretation based upon the size and composition of the group. It is used extensively for grades—for example, a high school student who ranks 12th in grade point average in a graduating class of 140—but it is seldom used in describing psychological test results.

Percentile Rank

Percentile rank is much more often used because it is not dependent on the size of the comparison group. Percentile scores are expressed in terms of the percentage of persons in the comparison group who fall below them when the scores are placed in rank order. A percentile rank of 65 indicates a score or rank that is as high or higher than those made by 65% of those in the comparison group. A percentile can be interpreted as a rank out of 100 persons in the comparison group (see Figure 3-1). Higher scores yield higher percentile ranks and the lower the percentile, the lower the person's standing. The 50th percentile corresponds to the middle-most score or the median. The 25th percentile is the first quartile point, marking the bottom quarter of the distribution, and the 75th percentile is the third quartile point, above which is found the top one quarter of the scores. The advantage of using percentiles is that they are easily calculated and easily understood by most people (provided it is made clear that a percentile indicates ranking in the comparison group rather than the percentage of correct responses).

The principal disadvantage of percentile ranking is that the distribution of most scores resembles the familiar bell-shaped curve, whereas the distribution of percentiles is always rectangular in shape. Ten percent of the cases fall between the 40th and 50th percentiles, in the same way that 10% fall between the 80th and 90th percentiles. Because of the pile-up of scores near the center of a distribution, a

FIGURE 3-1. Relationship Among Different Types of Standard Scores and Percentiles in a Normal Population

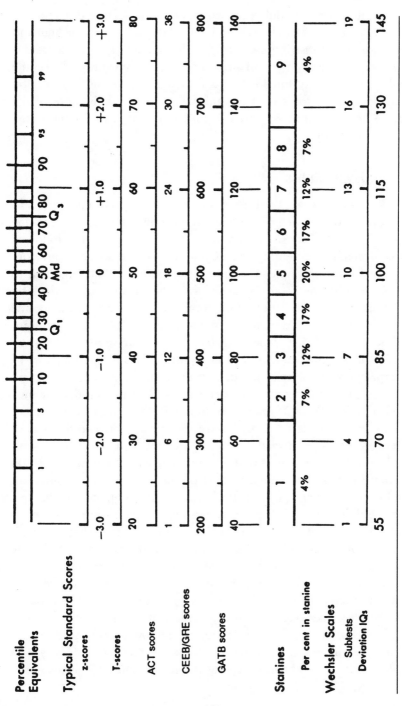

small difference in middle raw scores can yield a large difference in percentile ranks, as can be seen in Figure 3-1. At the extreme high and low ends of the distribution, on the other hand, large raw score differences may yield only small differences in percentile ranks. Percentile ranks are generally intended as a means of conveying information concerning a person's relative rank in a group, but because of the nature of percentiles, they are generally not used in additional statistical computations.

Grade Equivalents

Grade equivalents are often used on educational achievement tests to interpret how a student is progressing in terms of grade level. Grade equivalent scores consist of a number representing a grade followed by a decimal representing the 10 months of the school year from September through June. The grades range from K (kindergarten) to 12. Grades above 12 are occasionally used but are not particularly meaningful. The mean raw score obtained by students in each grade is computed, with fractions of a grade determined either by interpolation or by testing students at different times during the school year.

The principal advantage of grade equivalents is the seeming ease of interpretation to those without any understanding of measurement concepts. Actually, grade equivalents are subject to considerable misinterpretation. A sixth grader obtaining a grade equivalent score of 9.3 in arithmetic could easily be assumed by parents and teachers to have a knowledge of mathematics equivalent to the average student in the ninth grade at that time. A more correct interpretation would be that the student obtained a score on the arithmetic test equivalent to the score the average ninth grader would have obtained on that test in the unlikely event that ninth graders might have a sixth-grade arithmetic test administered to them. It would not mean that the sixth grader would have obtained a score equal to the average ninth-grade student on the ninth-grade test, which would undoubtedly have included algebraic and other mathematical concepts unfamiliar to sixth graders. Such a score would certainly indicate superior performance by a sixth grader but could not be regarded as equivalent to ninth-grade performance (Anastasi, 1988). In addition, because grade equivalents are computed from mean raw scores, students will vary in a bell-shaped curve above or below the mean. Thus a teacher might attempt to bring each student up to grade level—all students scoring above the mean. If national grade equivalents are used, this could perhaps be accomplished in a particular classroom, but if local norms are used such a feat would obviously be impossible.

Standard Deviation

If a frequency distribution is constructed of a sufficiently large number of measurements of many naturally occurring phenomena, a bell-shaped curve is likely to be produced. Results of most measurements occur close to the average and relatively few are found at either extreme. For this type of distribution the most dependable measure of variability is the standard deviation. It is the most widely accepted measure of variability for test users because (a) it is the basis for standard scores, (b) it yields a method of presenting the reliability of an individual test score as described in a later section, and (c) it is used in research studies for statistical tests of significance.

In a normal curve, the numerical value of the standard deviation divides the raw score range into six parts, with three above the mean and three below. Scores occurring above or below the distance of three standard deviations occur only very rarely. In a normal distribution, shown in Figure 3-1, approximately 34% of the sample lies between the median and one standard deviation above it and another 34% within the standard deviation below it. Thus the distance of one standard deviation in each direction encompasses approximately 68% of the sample. An additional 14% or so of the sample is found within the second standard deviation above the mean and 14% below the mean, and approximately 2% is found in each of the measurements occurring in the third standard deviation above the mean and below the mean.

A person scoring two standard deviations below the mean, therefore, falls at the second percentile, and at one standard deviation below, at the 16th percentile. A person scoring at the median or mean is at the 50th percentile; a person scoring one standard deviation above the mean is at the 84th percentile, and a person scoring two standard deviations above the mean is at the 98th percentile. These percentages and points along the normal curve are shown in Figure 3-1. Because the standard deviation is the basis of standard scores, which are used in reporting the results of most psychological tests used by counselors and human development professionals, these percentages and points along the normal curve should be thoroughly understood and memorized by anyone who makes substantial use of psychological test results.

Standard Scores

Because there are several problems related to using percentiles and other measures of variability, many tests make use of standard scores as the most satisfactory method of reporting test results. Standard scores are based on standard deviations and means. A standard score is defined as a score expressed as a distance, in standard deviation units, between a raw score and the mean. The basic standard score is the *z-score*. A z-score of -1.5 on this scale indicates that the raw score falls one and a half standard deviations below the mean of the reference group. A z-score of 0 means the raw score falls exactly at the mean, and a raw score falling two standard deviations above the mean would yield a z-score of $+2.0$. Because z-scores produce both decimals and negative values, they cause difficulties in computations and interpretation, so other types of standard scores have been developed based on a linear transformation of the z-score.

The most common standard score is the *T-score*, which is used on a number of the most widely used personality tests and interest inventories. By definition, the T-score has an arbitrary mean of 50 and an arbitrary standard deviation of 10. The T-score is rounded to the nearest whole number, and because most raw scores do not exceed plus or minus three standard deviations from the mean, T-score distributions usually range from 20 to 80.

Other test publishers have selected different scales using different means and standard deviations, which can be interpreted the same way as z-scores or T-scores. The College Entrance Examination Board and the Graduate Record Examination scores are reported in standard scores that use a mean of 500 and a standard deviation of 100. Thus a raw score falling one standard deviation above the mean, which would yield a z-score of $+1$, produces a standard score of 600. All scores are reported in increments of 10. This produces a scale that is recognizable for these instruments, although the scores may be thought of simply as T-scores with an additional zero added. This type of scale can cause a minor problem in that small differences in raw scores may seem to be much larger, because of the large scaled score differences that range through 600 points (200 to 800).

Until recently there was considerable confusion concerning the Scholastic Aptitude Test portions of the College Entrance Examination Board (which is discussed further in Chapter 6). A mean of 500 was established many years ago when a smaller proportion of college-bound students took those tests. The typical college-bound student in recent years scored less than 500. In 1995, the scores were "recentered" and 500 again became the college-bound student mean (College Board, 1994).

The American College Testing Program (ACT) uses standard scores similar to those developed for the Iowa Tests of Educational Development (ITED). The ACT and the revised Enhanced ACT have been standardized to have a mean of 18 and a standard deviation of 6, yielding a range of standard scores from 1 to 36. Standard scores developed for the General Aptitude Test Battery (GATB) used by the U.S. Employment Service yield a mean of 100 and a standard deviation of 20.

When the first intelligence tests were developed, a ratio of mental age to chronological age was developed and this ratio multiplied by 100. This ratio was later called the Intelligence Quotient or IQ. The ratio IQ had a number of problems including the fact that the ratio became invalid beginning in the adolescent years. Deviation IQ standard scores have since been developed to replace ratio IQs. Current results still report the mean at 100, as was the case with ratio IQs, but they report a standard score based on standard deviation units. Therefore, tests such as the Wechsler scales and the Stanford-Binet established a mean of 100 and a standard deviation of 15 or 16 depending upon the test. The positions at which these standard scores fall along the normal curve are shown in Figure 3-1. Again it is important in interpreting test results using any of these types of standard scores to have firmly in mind the points along the normal curve where these scores fall and the proportions of the population on which the standard scores are based that fall at various points on the normal curve.

Another type of standard score is the *stanine,* based on the term *standard nine.* Stanines have a range of 1 to 9 and a mean of 5. The stanine of 1 and 9 at the ends of the distribution contain 4% of the cases, and these increase as in the normal curve so that the center stanine of 5 includes 20% of the cases. Test scores can be converted to stanines by referring to the normal curve percentages in Figure 3-1. Stanines are infrequently used because of the difficulty in explaining their meaning. Their chief advantage lies in the single digit numbers, which do not imply greater accuracy than most tests can deliver. On the other hand, single digits can sometimes suggest a significant difference between two individuals where none exists.

CORRELATION

The correlation statistic assesses the degree to which two sets of measures are related—for example, how a tested trait or ability is related to a behavior. If a counselor had a score on a mathematics achievement test and the grades in arithmetic achieved by each student in a class, the counselor might wonder to what extent those students who scored well on the mathematics test also get good grades in arithmetic. To the extent that the rank orders of the students on each of these indices were similar—that is those who scored high on the test obtained good grades and those with lower scores obtained poorer grades—the counselor would conclude that a relationship existed between the two indices. Such a relationship is expressed through a statistic known as a correlation coefficient. Each correlation coefficient contains two bits of information: the sign of the correlation tells whether the two variables tend to rank individuals in the same order, or in their reverse order, and the magnitude of the correlation indicates the strength of this relationship. Among the several different types of correlation coefficients that can be computed, the Pearson product-moment coefficient (r) is the most common and can range in value from +1.00, a perfect positive relationship, through 0.00, no relationship or a chance relationship, to −1.00, indicating a perfect negative or inverse relationship. For example, the correlation between scores on a college entrance test and the freshman year grade point average of college students might yield a correlation coefficient of .40. Distance of students' homes from the college might yield a random or complete lack of a relationship, .00, with grades, and number of hours that students spend watching television might yield a low negative relationship with grades of −.20. It must be remembered that a substantial correlation between two variables does not imply that either variable causes the other. They can both be under the influence of a third variable. Heights of children could show a significant correlation with their scores on a vocabulary test, but both of these variables could be related to the children's ages and maturational growth.

RELIABILITY

Reliability and validity are two technical subjects that may not be of great interest to most people-oriented counselors, but they are extremely important for those who use psychological tests. They are concepts that need to be well understood when administering and interpreting psychological tests.

Inherent in the concept of reliability of psychological tests is the recognition that none of these instruments measures perfectly. Educators and behavioral scientists are interested in measuring much more complicated human characteristics than people's physical aspects. Anxiety, intelligence, depression, or potential to become a substance abuser are complex qualities that are difficult both to define precisely and to measure.

Reliability refers to how consistently a test measures, and the extent to which it eliminates chance and other extraneous factors in its results. Synonyms for reliability include *dependability, reproducibility, stability,* and *consistency.* A score that a person receives on a test is made up of two elements: the person's true score and an error score that may add to or subtract from the true score. A test with perfect reliability would be one on which everyone's scores remained in the same relative position on each administration (although they would not necessarily receive the exact same scores each time). In computing a correlation coefficient for a group of people on two sets of scores, the perfect relationship would yield a correlation of 1.00. If the test scores were completely unreliable, the relationship between the two would be a chance relationship and the correlation would be approximately 0.

Reliability is concerned both with the natural variation in human performance and with the technical aspects of psychological measurement. The stability of the trait or variable being measured obviously influences the amount of variation expected or considered normal when measured at different times. It would be expected that ability variables would have less variation than psychological states, but changes in ability measures can still occur as a result of growth and development. On the other hand, measures of personality variables, such as a state of depression, a state of anxiety, or a state of stress, could be expected to vary considerably at different times and under different circumstances.

Factors that are irrelevant to the purpose for which the test is designed represent error variance. Attempts to maintain uniform test conditions by controlling the instructions, time limits, and the testing environment are undertaken to reduce error variance and make test scores more reliable. No test is perfectly reliable, and because psychological measurement is often imprecise, it is important to check the accuracy and consistency of the instrument constantly to ensure that the unreliability is kept within reasonable limits.

Reliability coefficients usually run within the range of .80 to .95, but what is considered to be acceptable reliability varies substantially depending both on the testing circumstances and the type of reliability. For national testing programs such as the Graduate Record Examination or the Iowa Tests of Educational Development, reliability coefficients are expected to be above .90. For certain other types of psychological tests, this type of reliability is substantially lower. A score on the Depression scale of the MMPI, for example, is an indication of the person's mood at the time the inventory was administered. Because peoples' moods change, a very high test-retest reliability would be neither expected nor desired. Thus, for personality measures, interest measures, and attitudinal measures, test-retest reliability coefficients often fall below .90, although if they fall below .70, the consistency of the instrument becomes suspect (Cicchetti, 1994).

Types of Reliability

Reliability can be measured in several different ways, so there is not a single reliability for a test but different coefficients depending on how they are determined. Test scores can vary in their consistency in terms of time, test forms, or test items. There are four basic methods of estimating the reliability of an instrument based on these variables.

Test-Retest Reliability. Test-retest reliability, which is a common method of estimating traits, measures consistency over time. The correlation coefficient in this case indicates the relationship between scores obtained by the same person on two administrations of the test. Test-retest correlations tend to decrease as the interval between the test administrations lengthens. If the interval is brief, there are potential problems of practice and memory, which tend to make the reliability estimation spuriously high. If the time interval is too long, variation can be influenced by events that occur to subjects between the two test administrations, and spuriously low estimates of reliability may be obtained.

For tests that yield a profile of scores on a number of different scales, the concept of profile reliability may be more appropriate than a mean reliability coefficient from a number of different scales of varying reliability. Profile reliability is obtained by computing the overall similarity of two profiles obtained for the same person at two different times. If the profile reliability is greater than .75, there is little difference in the interpretation given to the profile by counselors (Hoyt, 1960).

Alternate-Form Reliability. Alternate-form or parallel-form reliability is computed by comparing the consistency of scores of the same individual on two alternate but equivalent forms of the same test. Because the test items are different, the effect of memory and other carryover effects are eliminated. The crucial question remains of whether in fact the two alternate forms of the test are actually equivalent.

Two tests that measure the same content or variables, and that are equivalent in difficulty level, can be administered on the same day or very close to each other without concern about the practice effect. They can be alternated so that test A is given to one group first and test B to the other group first, and the practice effect can thus be controlled.

The problem with this type of test reliability is that it is often difficult enough to come up with one good form of a test, much less two good forms. Therefore, unless there is a national testing program with a staff working on developing test forms, as is the case with some of the national testing programs such as the Medical College Admissions Test or the ACT tests, hope for this form of reliability is unrealistic.

In national testing programs, the problem of developing equivalent forms is met by administering experimental items with each test administration. The persons taking the test respond both to items that count and to those that are being tried out. The latter do not count in scoring for that administration but provide data for the construction of future forms of the test. The experimental items do not have to be the same for all those taking the test on a particular date, as item information can be collected from random subsamples. This is how national testing programs are able to produce equivalent forms year after year.

Split-Half. Split-half reliability is a popular form of establishing reliability because it can be obtained from a single administration by dividing the tests into two comparable halves and comparing the resulting scores for each individual. It is administered all at once, so no time-to-time fluctuation occurs. It can be thought of as a special case of alternate-form reliability.

In most tests, the first half and the second half would not be comparable because of differences in the difficulty of the items, as well as effects of practice and fatigue that are likely to vary from the beginning to the end of the test. Therefore, most tests are split into odd and even items, except where several items deal with a specific problem, in which case the entire group is assigned to one or the other half. An important weakness in the split-half approach lies in the general principle of sampling—that is, usually the greater the number of items, the more stable the concept being measured. All things being equal, the longer the test, the more reliable it will be. The split-half procedure cuts the test length in half, thus decreasing the reliability estimate. To correct the computed reliability, an estimate is made using the Spearman-Brown Prophecy Formula to correct for the shorter length and to yield an estimate of what the reliability would be if it were obtained on the test's full length.

Interitem Consistency. As the name implies, measures of interitem consistency indicate the consistency of responses to all of the items in the test. This estimate of test reliability is obtained from the average intercorrelations among all of the items on a test. Depending upon the type of response called for on the instrument, formulas known as the Kuder-Richardson Formula 20 for two-response answers (e.g., *true* or *false*, *yes* or *no*), or Cronbach's alpha reliability coefficient for more than two alternatives are computed. These reliability coefficients indicate the consistency with which the items sample the trait being measured.

This is a measure of internal consistency that assesses the extent to which the items on the test are related to the total score on the test and consequently are related to other items on the test. Because the individual items for each person are taken into consideration in this method, it is useful to place all of the test items for the entire sample in a computer file. A computer can analyze these indices very easily and is particularly useful when the answers can be read into the computer using mark sensing or optically scannable answer sheets. This measure of reliability is not typically used when results must be computed by hand.

Considerations in Reliability

There is no easy answer to the question of which method of reliability testing is the best. The appropriateness of a particular method depends on the nature of the trait being measured, particularly in terms of the stability of the trait. If one is interested in a measure of internal consistency and accuracy of a test, then the split-half or interitem consistency technique would be recommended; if the concern is with dependability for predictive purposes, then the test-retest or parallel forms with an increased time interval would be more appropriate.

Again, the most important consideration is the nature of the trait being measured. A paper-and-pencil IQ test with a reliability coefficient of .75 would not be acceptable, whereas the same coefficient for a measure of anxiety would be fairly acceptable for use. Reliabilities of tests can be compared with those of other similar instruments, remembering that the lower the reliability, the less confidence is possible in using and interpreting the resulting test data.

Reliability estimates are also influenced by the nature of the group on which the reliability measure was computed. In a group that is heterogeneous on the characteristic being measured, there will be a greater range and greater variability and hence a higher reliability coefficient. An introductory course at the undergraduate level is likely to have a relatively heterogeneous group of students, with the result that a relatively poorly constructed final examination may yield a considerably higher reliability coefficient than a carefully constructed final examination in a graduate level course, which will likely contain a much more homogeneous group of students. Thus, in examining the reliability of a particular instrument, it is necessary to look at the type of sample on which the reliability coefficient was obtained as well as the type of reliability that was obtained. Information on reliability in a test manual should include the means and standard deviations, as well as the demographic characteristics of the sample on which the reliability coefficients were computed.

An important point to remember regarding reliability is that longer tests are usually more reliable than shorter tests. It is also true that speed-measured tests can yield correlations that show high reliability, but the reliability is really based on how many items the person completed and not how well the test is measuring what it is supposed to measure. On speed-measured tests such as those assessing clerical aptitude or manual dexterity, individuals are likely to complete approximately the same number of odd and even items and do not receive credit for items at the end of the test because they did not get that far. This results in a similarity of performance between the two halves and therefore yields a spuriously high split-half reliability coefficient.

Reliabilities of scored essay tests have always been quite poor, a problem when national testing organizations have attempted to use writing samples as criteria for college admissions. Even well-trained raters often vary substantially in the ratings they give to writing samples required by some institutions.

Standard Error of Measurement

The standard error of measurement (SEM) yields the same type of information as does the reliability coefficient, but is specifically applicable to the interpretation of individual scores. Its most common use is to construct bands of confidence around an individual's obtained score. It represents the theoretical distribution that would be obtained if an individual were repeatedly tested with a large number of exactly equivalent forms of the same test. Such a cluster of repeated scores would form a curve, with a mean and standard deviation of the distribution, and that standard deviation is called the standard error of measurement. An individual's single score on a test is assumed to be the mean of repeated scores, and the standard error of measurement can be interpreted in terms of normal curve frequencies. Thus if a student's true raw score was 40 on a particular test and the standard error of measurement was 3, then if we repeated the test many times, 68% of the individual's scores would fall between 37 and 43 and we could be 95% confident that the individual's true score would be between 34 and 46—two standard error of measurement units above or below the obtained score.

The SEM is easily computed when the standard deviation and the reliability coefficient of the test are known by using the following formula: The SEM equals the standard deviation of the test (SD) times the square root of 1 minus the reliability of the test.

$$SEM = SD \times \sqrt{1 - reliability}$$

As an example, the SAT scores of the College Entrance Examination Board have a standard score mean of 500, a standard deviation of 100, and a reliability of approximately .90. The standard error of measurement is approximately 30, which allows one to compute the odds of a person's true score falling within 30 points above or below the obtained score. Similar estimates can be made of the true scores for individuals on the ACT test which, with a mean of 18, a standard deviation of approximately 6, and reliability coefficients of about .90, have a standard error of measurement in the vicinity of 2. In the case of the Wechsler Intelligence Scales with full scale score standard deviations of 15 (mean of 100) and reliability coefficients in the vicinity of .96, the SEM equals 3.

VALIDITY

Whereas reliability is concerned with whether or not the instrument is a consistent measure, validity asks the question of whether it measures what it is supposed to measure. Does a test that is supposed to measure arithmetic skills really measure arithmetic skills, or is it composed of word problems of such reading difficulty that it is actually measuring reading ability instead? It is possible for a test to have high reliability without validity (but in order to have good validity, high reliability is necessary).

The question must always be asked, "validity for what?" Scores on the Strong Interest Inventory, for example, have considerable test-retest reliability even when the second test is taken many years later. When it comes to validity, however, the problem becomes much more complicated. Because of the large number of scales and the different types of scales, specific definitions must be developed before they can be applied to a criterion to obtain validity. As will be seen later, when it comes to predicting the occupation that a person is likely to enter in the future, the Strong does have some validity. On the other hand, it is not particularly valid for predicting success in an occupation. Persons who enter an occupation for which they get a low score on the Strong may very well not stay in that occupation. People who score high are much more likely to stay in the occupation, but the low scorers who stay in that field are just as likely to be successful as those who score high. Therefore, a score on a Strong scale may have some validity for predicting whether people will enter an occupation, and if so, how long they will stay in it, but it will have little validity when it comes to predicting success in that occupation.

The range of validity coefficients runs much lower than that of reliability. Whereas coefficients of .80 to .90 are common for reliability, validity coefficients seldom run above .60 and are more typically in the range of .30 to .50. Validity coefficients as low as .10 and .20 can still be useful in predicting future behavior (Rosenthal, 1990; Rosnow & Rosenthal, 1988). In predicting grades in college from test scores, coefficients are almost never obtained above .60. Even when other measures of high school achievement, personality, and some type of achievement motivation are all combined, validity coefficients for college grades above .60 are seldom achieved.

Content Validity

There are several types of validity, one of which is content validity. This is the type of validity in which the items on a test are examined carefully to determine whether the items measure what the test is supposed to be measuring. If the test is designed to measure achievement in high school physics, a number of high school physics teachers, and perhaps some college physics teachers, examine the items on the test to determine whether these items are in fact measuring knowledge of what is typically taught in high school physics. Content validity involves judgment by persons competent in that field.

Content validity is not face validity, which is not really validity at all, but merely deals with the question of whether the items seem to be relevant to the person taking the test.

Criterion-Related Validity

One type of criterion-related validity is *concurrent validity*. This is a type of *empirical* validity, in which the validity of the instrument is measured against a criterion. In most cases a correlation coefficient is calculated between a test score and the scores on the criterion variable. For example, in developing a test of mechanical aptitude, it might be given to a group of working machinists, and then the ratings that they receive by their supervisors might be examined to determine whether the mechanical aptitude scores are related to their current work. Usually measures of concurrent validity are obtained because the test is going to be used in the future to estimate some type of behavior—such as the ability to do the work of a machinist.

A second type of criterion-related validity is *predictive validity.* For a scholastic aptitude test designed to predict college grades, the grades that the students earn in college are examined to determine whether the scholastic aptitude test given in high school has predictive validity. Does it predict what it is supposed to be predicting—in this case college grades?

One of the problems in measuring either concurrent or predictive validity is that the size of the correlation coefficients will be reduced if the range of scores on either the test or criterion variable is restricted in any way. Because scholastic aptitude test scores are often used to select students for a particular institution, and many students with low scores are eliminated, the group being studied to measure the test's predictive validity will have a narrower range, with a resulting lower validity coefficient. One way of avoiding this is to administer the instrument before any selection has taken place and to have the selection take place without regard to the criterion being assessed. For example, in one of the validation studies for the General Aptitude Test Battery (GATB) of the U.S. Employment Service, the entire battery was given to all applicants for jobs in an industrial plant that was being built in a particular town. Workers were then selected without regard to their GATB results. Performance ratings for the workers were obtained at a later date and these were then related to the previously obtained GATB results showing substantial concurrent validity.

Spuriously high validity coefficients can also be obtained from a form of criterion contamination if, for example, the persons doing the rating know the test results. They may be influenced by this knowledge, which could result in a higher relationship between test results and later ratings or assessments.

An important concept related to the validity of a test concerns the base rates of the characteristic that is being measured in the population. Base rates refer to the proportion of persons in a population who represent the particular characteristic or behavior that is being predicted. Base rates are important because they have a marked influence on how useful tests are in making predictions. If the base rates are either very low or very high, the predictions made from the tests are not as useful. If almost every student admitted to medical school graduates, then scores on the Medical College Admission Test (MCAT) are unlikely to determine who will graduate and who will not. The best prediction to be obtained would be not to use the test scores but merely to predict that every student admitted will graduate. Suicide rates are examples of low base rates. Although persons who obtain high scores on a scale that measures depression are more likely to commit suicide than those with lower scores, most people who obtain high scores on a measure of depression do not commit suicide. Because suicide is relatively rare, the base rate is so low that even with a high score on a depression scale, the best prediction to be made, would still be that any individual is not likely to commit suicide.

The purpose of tests is, of course, to provide more information than could be obtained by chance or other unreliable means. Validity of tests is evaluated in terms of how much they contribute beyond what could be predicted without them. *Incremental validity* refers to the extent to which a particular assessment instrument adds to the accuracy of predictions obtained from other tests or less extensive methods of assessment. It should be considered when deciding whether to use an additional assessment instrument.

When a test is used to make a dichotomous, either/or decision (acceptable or unacceptable, successful or unsuccessful, positive diagnosis or negative diagnosis) cut-off scores are usually used. Many times the rate of predicting success is high without the test (the base rate)—for example, most of the students attending medical school eventually graduate. The overall proportion graduating is called the base rate, and the real value of the MCAT comes if the correct prediction rate can be increased beyond that available without the use of the test. On the other hand, if the base rate is very low, the correct prediction rate can be low but still above that of the base rate, so that the test results could still be valuable.

Questions concerning base rates and hit rates (proportion of successful predictions) often deal with relative cost. In some cases a miss can be very costly, for example, concluding that someone is not suicidal because he or she is below a cut-off score on a suicide potential scale when in fact the person is suicidal. The cost of this type of miss could be that a suicide takes place that might have been preventable. This type of case is called a "false negative." The person fell below the cutting score and was therefore predicted not to be suicidal when in fact he or she was suicidal. A "false positive" occurs when a person obtains a score above the cutting score and, for example, is predicted to be successful on the job but in fact fails and is dismissed. Again, the time and money invested in training the person are likely to influence where the cutting score is placed and therefore to influence the proportion of false positives.

The validity of an instrument in classifying individuals into different diagnostic categories or related groups can be expressed in terms of sensitivity and specificity. *Sensitivity* of an instrument refers to the accuracy of the instrument in detecting those people who belong in a given category (e.g., clinically depressed); whereas *specificity* indicates the accuracy of the instrument in excluding those without that condition. Sensitivity and specificity will vary depending on the particular cutoff score used to select individuals considered to be meeting the condition.

Most clients who commit suicide or have seriously considered suicide obtain elevations on the Depression scale of the Minnesota Multiphasic Personality Inventory (MMPI), particularly if this elevation is combined with an elevation on the Psychasthenia scale. Thus the MMPI possesses sensitivity in regard to suicidal ideation. But the problem is that large numbers of other individuals also obtain elevations on these two scales who are not suicidal. The MMPI therefore lacks specificity in this regard (Cicchetti, 1994).

The amount of variability in a criterion that a correlation coefficient is considered to account for is determined by the square of the correlation. Thus a correlation coefficient of .30 means that the predictor accounts for 9% of the variance. In using a correlation coefficient for prediction, however, Rosnow and Rosenthal (1988) showed that the correlation coefficient can be taken to indicate the improvement in success of prediction over chance or over the base rate by the percentage indicated by that correlation. Thus a correlation of .30 means that using that variable in prediction improves the prediction by approximately 30%. When considered in this way, a moderate correlation can be seen to have considerable usefulness in counseling over

53

that which would have been obtained had that test not been taken into consideration.

Construct Validity

A third type of validity is called construct validity and is a more complex concept. This type of validity asks the question—Do the test results make psychological sense? Are the test results related to things that they ought to be related to and not related to things that they ought not be? For example, do results on the test change according to what we know about developmental changes? Do older students do better on the test than younger students, for example sixth graders doing better on arithmetic tests than third graders? Is the test picking up the kinds of changes known to occur as people develop? Two aspects of construct validity are those of *convergent validity* and *discriminant validity*. Tests should be expected to show a substantial correlation with other tests and assessments that measure similar characteristics. Measures of mathematical aptitude ought to be related to grades in mathematics. Most validation studies report convergent validity. Another aspect of construct validity is that tests should not show a substantial correlation with other tests from which they are supposed to differ—discriminant validity. A test of mathematical ability probably should not show a strong correlation with a test of clerical speed and accuracy. A measure of sociability should be negatively related to the score on a schizophrenic scale and positively related to the score on a scale of extroversion.

If an instrument is related to a particular psychological theory, then the results should fit that theory. Factor analysis is used to determine whether the test items fall together in different factors the way that the theory suggests they should. If a test is constructed along the lines of Jungian theory, such as the Myers-Briggs Type Indicator (MBTI), the resulting factors from a factor analysis should be related to such Jungian concepts as introversion versus extroversion, sensing versus intuition, and thinking versus feeling.

An additional component of construct validity is *internal consistency*. Measures of internal consistency, which are used primarily to indicate reliability, show the extent to which the items in the test are related to each other and to the total score. High internal consistency is therefore one indication of construct validity. When test scales are internally consistent, they are easier for the counselor to interpret because a single construct is being measured.

Treatment Validity

There is yet another type of validity that may be considered by counselors and clinicians. It has been termed *treatment validity*: "Do the results obtained from the test make a difference in the treatment?" (Barrios, 1988; Holland, 1985). If the test results are useful and if they make a difference in the counseling process, then the test could be said to have treatment validity. For example, a recent research study indicated that clients who had their MMPI scores interpreted to them showed significant improvement on several treatment variables (Finn & Tonsager, 1992). In a similar fashion, Randahl, Hansen, and Haverkamp (1993) found that clients who had their Strong Interest Inventory profiles interpreted to them made significant progress in their career planning.

The question, then, is not simply "Is the test valid?" but "What types of validity does the test possess and are they relevant to the purpose for which the test is being used?" Criterion-related validity is important, for example, if the test is to be used for selection, whereas content validity is important if it is to be used as a measure of achievement. In the overall construction and development of a test, various validation procedures are applied throughout the developmental stages. All the types of validity can also be conceived as contributing to the construct validity. Measures of internal consistency are built into the early stages of development, and criterion-related validation, typically, in some of the latter stages. Validation continues long after the test has been published and distributed for use.

TEST DEVELOPMENT

To produce a well designed standardized psychological test or inventory, the test developer generates a large amount of data. After the items have been written they are tried out on adequate samples and results analyzed to determine those items which are of appropriate difficulty as well as differentiating between persons who represent more and less of the behaviors or the domain that the items represent. After the resulting items have been assembled into a test and scored, the scores must be converted into a continuous scale, norms must be developed that are applicable to the groups for which the test is designed, reliability estimates must be calculated and correlations of the test with other similar variables, with background variables, and with predicted criteria must be determined. All of these analyses are facilitated by computers and some, for example internal consistency reliability, are feasible only with the ability of a high speed computer.

Test scoring services have been operating for so long that few can even remember when all scoring had to be done by hand. Almost all test publishers provide computer scoring not only for large-scale cognitive and achievement testing but also for almost all complex interest and personality inventories. With the proliferation of microcomputers, computers can be used for the actual administration of tests as well as the scoring and interpretation.

SUMMARY

In this chapter some of the basic statistical concepts necessary to understand and interpret tests were presented. These concepts include:

1. Norms and certain descriptive statistics necessary to relate an individual's score to that of the norm group, including percentiles, grade equivalents, and standard scores
2. Correlation coefficients that indicate the degree and direction of a relationship between two measures or variables
3. Reliability, including its definition, expected ranges, and its four different types: test-retest, alternate form, split-half, and interitem consistency
4. The interpretation of reliability coefficients, standard errors of measurement, and error bands
5. Validity, including its definition and four types: content, concurrent, predictive, and construct
6. The understanding and interpretation of validity data.

4

INITIAL
ASSESSMENT IN
COUNSELING

W HAT ASSESSMENT PROCEDURES should counselors pursue at the beginning of counseling? What steps can ensure that assessment procedures are appropriately selected and administered? This chapter addresses these questions.

First, the counselor needs to determine the client's orientation toward problem solving. Next, the counselor needs to assess the nature and severity of the client's problems. Assessment procedures that can aid in these endeavors are described in the first parts of this chapter, and the chapter concludes with a consideration of the principles of test selection, administration, and scoring.

CLIENT ORIENTATION TOWARD PROBLEM SOLVING

Clients differ in their readiness for counseling, their expectations of counseling, and their problem-solving styles. Counselors can be more effective with clients if they take these differences into account.

Readiness for Counseling

In their work with individuals with addictive behaviors, Prochaska, DiClemente, and Norcross (1992) noted five stages of change experienced by their clients: precontemplation, contemplation, preparation, action, and maintenance. These same stages of change pertain to clients with a wide variety of problems.

In the *precontemplation* stage, individuals are not especially aware of their problem and have no plans to change their behavior in the foreseeable future. Individuals who seek counseling while in the pre-contemplative stage usually do so at the insistence of someone else who is concerned about their problem.

Clients in the *contemplation* stage are aware of their problem, but have not yet made a serious commitment to do anything about it. Individuals in this state are considering making changes in their behavior sometime within the next 6 months; however, it may be much longer than this amount of time before they actually do make changes.

In the *preparation* stage, clients have begun to make small changes in their problematic behaviors with the intention of making more complete changes within 1 month. The *action* stage is reached when clients successfully change their behavior for short periods of time. If the changes persist for longer than 6 months, the client enters the *maintenance* stage, where the goal is to maintain the behavioral and attitudinal changes that have occurred.

Assessment of the client's stage of change is crucial for determining the most effective treatment technique. As noted by Prochaska et al. (1992), different approaches should be used for clients in different stages. For example, individuals in the precontemplation or contemplation stages can be helped most by early intervention techniques such as consciousness raising and dramatic relief, whereas individuals in the action and maintenance stages can benefit most from later intervention techniques such as reinforcement management and support groups.

It is important to note that most clients recycle through some or all of the stages several times before successfully achieving long-term changes. Although recycling is the norm, most clients learn from their previous attempts so that they make faster progress through the cycle in subsequent attempts to resolve their problems.

Models of Helping and Coping

Client expectations for counseling will vary depending on their view of the problematic situation. Clients differ in the extent to which they accept responsibility for the problem or its solution. This distinction is important because it makes it possible to separate *blame* for the problem from *control* of its solution. Brickman et al. (1982) identified four different orientations toward counseling based on the client's views. As indicated below, clients may subscribe to any one of these four models:

Moral model.   People are responsible for their problems and solutions. Clients who fit this model look upon counselors as consultants who can help direct them to resources, such as self-help books and personal growth groups, that they can implement on their own. They perceive themselves as lazy people who must work harder. Clients seek stimulation from counselors to do what they know they must do.

Compensatory model.   People are not responsible for their problems, but are responsible for solutions. Clients with this point of view perceive counselors as advocates who can help them to overcome a problem that they did not cause (e.g., poor education, which can be helped by tutorial programs). They think of themselves as deprived individuals who must assert themselves. Clients look to counselors for empowerment to help them correct problem-causing situations.

Enlightenment model.   People are responsible for their problems, but not for solutions to the problems. Clients who endorse this model look upon counselors as saviors who can provide long-term care for them by means of ongoing support groups or other methods. They see themselves as guilty persons who must submit to a higher authority.

Clients expect counselors to help provide them with discipline they lack themselves.

Medical model. People are not responsible for problems or solutions. Clients who fit this model view counselors as experts who will be able to remedy their problems by external means (e.g., by prescribing a treatment program). They regard themselves as ill people who must accept advice or treatment from the proper authority. Clients expect counselors to prescribe the solution, which they will then follow.

The problem-solving process can be aided by taking into account the orientation of the client and that of the counselor. If the counselor assumes a different viewpoint from the client in terms of responsibility for the problem or the solution, the two might be working at cross purposes. For example, clients with active coping styles (moral or compensatory models) make more progress in treatments that stress self-control rather than counselor control (Dance & Neufeld, 1988).

Counselors can usually determine their client's orientation by means of an interview. They can ask clients who (or what) is to blame for their problem, and who (or what) is in control of solving the problem. They can use the distinctions among the models indicated in the preceding paragraphs to help frame questions for clients. Internal versus external locus of control scales may also be helpful in this regard (Fisher & Corcoran, 1994). Clients who believe that they are in control of their destiny (internal locus of control) fit the moral or compensatory models; clients who believe that they are the victims of chance or their environment (external locus of control) conform to the enlightenment or medical models.

The compensatory model produces the best results for counselors in many situations (Brickman et al., 1982). It has the advantage of absolving clients of blame for the problem, thus justifying their request for assistance, at the same time that it places them in control of removing or reducing the problem. As indicated in a number of studies reviewed by Brickman et al., changes that occur as a result of counseling are most likely to persist when clients feel that they were responsible for the change. If change is attributed to the counselor's efforts, the change in client behavior is less likely to endure. Counselors can help clients to reattribute solutions for their problems to factors that they can control (Dorn, 1988).

Problem-Solving Style

Individuals differ in how they define the problem, how they solve the problem, and which part of the problem-solving process they tend to emphasize (defining the problem or solving the problem). The MBTI provides a convenient means of describing one's problem-solving style. As indicated in Chapter 11, the MBTI includes four bipolar dimensions. Each of these dimensions can be used to describe an important aspect of the client's problem-solving style.

First, the Extroverted versus Introverted dimension indicates the extent to which the person chooses to solve problems as part of a group or individually. Second, the Sensing versus Intuition dimension offers insight into the manner in which the client defines a problem. Does the client give predominant consideration to facts (Sensing type) or possibilities (Intuitive type)? Third, the Thinking versus Feeling dimension indicates the extent to which the person solves the problem by logic (Thinking type) or values (Feeling type). Finally, the Judging versus Perceiving dimension shows which function (problem definition or problem solving) the client will emphasize. Judging types place greater importance on solving the problem, whereas Perceiving types give primary consideration to defining the problem.

These same personality variables are also included as part of the new Millon Index of Personality Styles (MIPS; Millon, 1995). Counselors can use the MBTI or the MIPS to help clients to identify their problem-solving style. They can help clients to recognize strengths and weaknesses in their preferred styles. Counselors can teach clients to "stretch" their styles when necessary to include some of the advantages of the other personality styles.

Problem-solving style can also be assessed by means of several instruments specifically designed to measure the manner in which individuals cope with difficult situations. A recently developed instrument of this type, the Problem-Focused Style of Coping (PF-SOC), measures reflective, suppressive, and reactive styles of coping (Heppner, Cook, Wright, & Johnson, 1995). Individuals who score high on the Reflective factor emphasize rational techniques in solving problems, those who score high on the Suppressive factor are likely to deny or avoid the problem, and those who score high on the Reactive factor will most likely exhibit strong emotional responses and impulsivity when faced with a major life event. Other instruments of this sort include the Ways of Coping Questionnaire (Folkman & Lazarus, 1988), the Problem-Solving Inventory (Heppner, 1988), and the Coping Inventory for Stressful Situations (Endler & Parke, 1994).

DEFINING THE PROBLEM

What is the nature of the client's problem? How severe is it? How does it affect the client's life? Answers to these questions can help counselors to plan and to evaluate treatment for their clients. In this section, a number of systematic procedures for addressing these questions will be considered.

Counselors can gather significant information from clients in a short period of time by means of an intake (initial contact) questionnaire, a problem checklist, and an interview. The intake counselor uses this information in arranging counseling for the client or in making a referral.

Intake Form

An intake form contains questions about client status and presenting issues that can help guide the first counseling session. Common questions include name, address, sex, age, ethnicity, educational and work history, presenting problem(s), previous counseling, and urgency of request for counseling. Intake forms vary somewhat from agency to agency depending upon the particular type of services offered by the agency.

It is helpful to ask clients to briefly summarize their reasons for seeking counseling on the intake form. This statement can help focus the counseling and can serve as a reference point for judging progress in subsequent counseling sessions.

The intake form should be kept relatively short so that it does not become an imposition in counseling. If needed, the form can be supplemented with additional questionnaires designed for particular issues, such as career planning, study skills, or relationships, as counseling progresses.

Information obtained from the intake form orients the counselor toward the client's problem, serves as a checklist to make sure that important points are covered, and provides a record for future counseling contacts. This information can also be compiled and used to describe the nature of the clientele served by a counseling center during a given time period. These data can be helpful in budget and program planning.

The agency's intake questionnaire can be supplemented with a biographical form to provide more complete information regarding the client's background. As an example, the Quickview Social History contains 130 questions pertaining to the client's developmental history, family of origin, educational history, marital history, occupational history/financial status, and legal history, together with 105 additional questions that address psychological and medical issues (Giannetti, 1992). The client's answers are processed by computer to provide a 4- to 5-page narrative report plus a follow-up section that highlights client problems and areas that the counselor may wish to explore further with the client.

Problem Checklists

Problem checklists or screening instruments are used by many counselors in conjunction with an intake form to obtain a quick, comprehensive, and systematic evaluation of a client's concerns. These instruments usually ask clients to check which ones of a variety of problems or symptoms may have been troubling them during the past week or two. Several checklists that have been widely used or that seem to be particularly valuable for use in counseling are described below. In addition to the instruments discussed here, other popular or promising checklists or screening inventories include the College Adjustment Scale (Baker & Siryk, 1984), the Psychological Distress Inventory (Lustman, Sowa, & O'Hara, 1984), the Porteus Problem Checklist (Porteus, 1985), the Personal Problems Checklists–Adult (Schinka, 1984), the Personal Problems Checklist-Adolescent (Schinka, 1985), and the Psychological Screening Inventory (Lanyon, 1978).

Inventory of Common Problems (ICP). The ICP was developed by Jeffrey Hoffman & Bahr Weiss (1986) for use as a screening instrument in college counseling centers. It lists 24 specific problems that college students may confront (see Figure 4-1). These items represent six major types of problems as follows:

- Depression—Items 1–4
- Anxiety—Items 5–8

FIGURE 4-1. Inventory of Common Problems

Instructions: The following items represent common problems of college students. How much has each problem distressed, worried, or bothered you in the past few weeks? Please circle the answer that is most nearly correct for you.

Not at all	A little bit	Moderately	Quite a bit	Very much
1	2	3	4	5

	Not at all	A little bit	Moderately	Quite a bit	Very much
1. Feeling depressed, sad, dejected?	1	2	3	4	5
2. Blaming, criticizing, or condemning myself?	1	2	3	4	5
3. Feeling discouraged or like a failure?	1	2	3	4	5
4. Suicidal thoughts or concerns?	1	2	3	4	5
5. Feeling irritable, tense, or nervous?	1	2	3	4	5
6. Feeling fearful?	1	2	3	4	5
7. Spells of terror or panic?	1	2	3	4	5
8. Feel like I'm "going to pieces?"	1	2	3	4	5
9. Academic problems?	1	2	3	4	5
10. Difficulty caring about or concentrating on studies?	1	2	3	4	5
11. Indecision or concern about choice of career or major?	1	2	3	4	5
12. Feeling like I'm not doing as well in school as I should?	1	2	3	4	5
13. Problems with romantic or sexual relationships?	1	2	3	4	5
14. Family problems?	1	2	3	4	5
15. Difficulty getting along with others?	1	2	3	4	5
16. Feeling lonely or isolated?	1	2	3	4	5
17. Physical health problems?	1	2	3	4	5
18. Headaches, faintness, or dizziness?	1	2	3	4	5
19. Trouble sleeping?	1	2	3	4	5
20. Eating, appetite, or weight problems?	1	2	3	4	5
21. My use of alcohol?	1	2	3	4	5
22. My use of marijuana?	1	2	3	4	5
23. How many psychoactive drugs I use?	1	2	3	4	5
24. How many prescribed drugs I use?	1	2	3	4	5

If so, what? _____

Note. From "A New System for Conceptualizing College Students' Problems; Types of Crises and the Inventory of Common Problems" by Hoffman & Weiss, (1986, p. 262). Reprinted with permission of the Helen Dwight Reid Educational Foundation. Published by Heldref Publications, 4000 Albermarle St., N.W., Washington, DC 20016. © 1986.

- Academic Problems—Items 9–12
- Interpersonal Problems—Items 13–16
- Physical Health Problems—Items 17–20
- Substance-use Problems—Items 21–24.

Clients must indicate to what extent each of the 24 problems has distressed, worried, or bothered them in the past few weeks. Answers range from "1" (*not at all*) through "5" (*very much*). Scores for each scale can vary from 4 to 20; total scores can vary from 24 to 120.

Normative data for a sample of college students collected by the authors showed no significant sex differences, thus the same set of norms may be used with both male and female clients. The highest mean score (11 points) was obtained on the Academic Problems scale whereas the lowest mean score (5 points) was recorded for the Substance Use scale. The mean total score for college students was approximately 45 points with a standard deviation of about 10 (Hoffman & Weiss, 1986).

The ICP possesses sufficient reliability and validity for its use as a screening instrument, but it should not be looked upon as a diagnostic instrument (Hoffman & Weiss, 1986). The results should be used primarily to suggest topics for further exploration in counseling. It can also be readministered to clients to obtain a rough measure of progress during the course of counseling.

From a practical point of view, the ICP offers several advantages for the counselor. It can be completed by most clients within 5 to 10 minutes, it represents most of the problems that clients are likely to encounter, and it can be reproduced for little cost if the original source of the instrument is acknowledged (J. A. Hoffman, personal communication, April 18, 1988).

CASE EXAMPLE

Linda came to the university counseling center as a senior because of dissatisfaction with her major. She felt particularly uneasy because most of her peers were participating in job interviews for the next year. She was majoring in banking, but not happy with it. She did not like the competitiveness of the students in her field. According to the initial contact form that she completed at the same time as the ICP, she wanted help in "choosing a major" and "career planning." She marked all of the items except one in the first three categories (Depression, Anxiety, and Academic Problems) of the ICP as 4 or 5. She was feeling very distressed by her career indecision.

The initial contact counselor attributed Linda's problems to developmental issues, not preexisting psychopathology. Based on the counselor's judgment, short-term counseling was arranged. Linda needed help in dealing with developmental tasks, especially in resolving her career choice, not in making fundamental changes in her personality.

Linda met with a counselor for six sessions for help in acquiring decision-making and assertiveness skills and for assistance in working through conflicted feelings about her career choice. She decided to add

65

personnel management as a second major to that of banking. This combination was supported by the tests (including the Strong Interest Inventory) that she had taken and by the information that she had gained in her career exploration.

The ICP was readministered at the conclusion of counseling. Linda marked no 4 or 5 responses the second time she completed the inventory. Her total score, which dropped from 66 to 34, and all of her subscores were well within the normal range compared with other college students. The ICP was helpful with Linda both in determining the nature and the severity of her initial complaints and in evaluating the progress that she showed in counseling. Linda's rapid progress in counseling supported the perception of the initial contact counselor that her problems were developmental, not psychopathological, in nature.

Symptom Check List–90–Revised (SCL-90-R). The SCL-90-R and its forerunners have been widely used for research and clinical purposes in a variety of medical and mental health settings (Derogatis, 1983; Tennen, Affleck, & Herzberger, 1985). As indicated by its name, the SCL-90-R contains a list of 90 symptoms such as "headaches," "feeling critical of others," and "feeling tense or keyed up." Clients respond to items in terms of how much they were distressed by that symptom during the past week. Each item is answered on a 5-step scale ranging from 0 (*not at all*) through 4 (*extremely*). Most clients complete the SCL-90-R in 15 minutes. With practice it can be easily hand-scored.

The SCL-90-R provides scores for the following nine scales: Somatization, Obsessive-Compulsive, Interpersonal Sensitivity, Depression, Anxiety, Hostility, Phobic Anxiety, Paranoid Ideation, and Psychoticism. Scores for each scale show the mean response for the items in that scale. It also yields three total scores—Global Severity Index (GSI), Positive Symptom Total (PST), and Positive Symptom Distress Index (PSDI). The GSI, the best single index of psychological disturbance, shows the mean response to all 90 items. The PST indicates the number of symptoms reported (all items marked 1 or higher). The PSDI, which shows the mean response to all items included in the PST, reflects the severity of the client's symptoms.

Scores on the SCL-90-R vary depending upon age and sex. Adolescent nonpatients report more symptomatology than do adult nonpatients. Women acknowledge more symptoms than do men. The SCL-90-R manual provides separate-sex norms for adolescent nonpatients, adult nonpatients, adult psychiatric inpatients, and adult psychiatric outpatients.

The SCL-90-R scales possess adequate internal consistency and test-retest reliability over short time periods. It appears to be most valid as a broad measure of psychological disturbance. Factor analytic research indicates that the SCL-90-R primarily measures one factor, which can best be thought of as depression or general psychological distress (Cyr, McKenna-Foley, & Peacock, 1985).

The SCL-90-R is particularly valuable as a screening instrument to detect cases that need additional assessment. As a general rule, Derogatis (1983, p. 28) suggested that counselors should refer clients for psychiatric evaluation if their scores on the GSI or any two of the individual scales equal or exceed the 90th percentile compared with adult nonpatients.

At least two abbreviated versions of the SCL-90-R have been developed. The Brief Symptom Inventory (BSI) contains 53 of the 90 items on the SCL-90-R (Derogatis & Melisaratos, 1983). Administration time for the BSI is approximately 10 minutes, compared with 15 minutes for the SCL-90-R. Intercorrelations between the two sets of scales range from .92 to .99. According to its authors, the BSI has become a more popular instrument for research and clinical use than the SCL-90-R.

The Symptom Check List–10 (SCL-10) contains 10 items that have contributed most to the primary factors in the SCL-90-R based on factor analysis (Nguyen, Attkisson, & Stegner, 1983). It includes 6 items from the Depression scale, 2 from the Phobic Anxiety scale, and 2 from the Somatization scale. The SCL-10 total score correlates highly with scores on other measures of psychological distress (Nguyen et al., 1983; Sabourin, Laferriere, Sicuro, Coallier, Cournoyer, & Gendreau, 1989).

Suggestions for Using Problem Checklists in Counseling

1. Identify critical items on problem checklist (e.g., items that refer to thoughts of suicide or violent behavior) that can be used to help determine if the client is in state of crisis. Be sure to make a suicide risk assessment (see Chapter 14) if client shows signs of suicidal thinking.

2. Examine general level of responses. If a client marks a large number of extreme responses, consider the need for immediate counseling and possible psychiatric referral. Ask clients to discuss each of these responses, especially ones that they perceive to be most crucial.

3. Note the client's responses for substance abuse and health items. These problems may be overlooked in the counseling interview if the counselor does not bring them up with the client.

4. Readminister the problem checklist at conclusion of counseling or after a significant time period has elapsed to evaluate changes that have taken place during the course of counseling. Clients who have shown little improvement may need to be referred.

5. Use problem checklist scores to consult with supervisors or colleagues regarding treatment. Problem checklist scores can be used to communicate the nature and severity of client's issues within a few minutes.

6. Add items to standard problem checklists to assess matters of importance to your agency. For example, one agency added the following items to the Inventory of Common Problems to identify potentially dangerous situations: "urge to harm myself," "plan to harm myself," "urge to harm someone else," "plan to harm someone else," and "concern that someone else may harm me."

7. Administer problem checklists or screening inventories for specific topics (e.g., Michigan Alcohol Screening Test, My Vocational Situation, or Eating Attitudes Tests) when these seem to be appropriate. Ask clients to identify any issues that they might be experiencing that are not represented on the problem checklist.

8. Consider the possibility that clients could be minimizing or exaggerating their problems. Use both number and intensity of symptoms to help gauge possible distortion. If clients mark most items at a low level of intensity, they could be minimizing their problems. Similarly, if they mark a large number of problems at a high level of intensity, they could be exaggerating their concerns.

9. Keep in mind that problem checklists primarily measure general psychological disturbance. Do not place too much emphasis on individual scales or items. Use individual scales and items primarily as a means of identifying significant subject matter for discussion.

10. Use problem checklists to monitor the caseload in your agency. What types of clients are receiving treatment at the agency? How many of the clients express suicidal ideation? How many of the clients in-

dicate problems with substance abuse? Use these data to develop local norms to help interpret problem checklist responses.

Intake Interview

The purpose of the intake (or assessment) interview is to assess the nature and severity of the client's problems and to determine possible treatment programs. Initial interviews usually progress on a continuum from minimal structure to more structure. As the interview proceeds, the client may need help or direction in continuing to respond. Questions that probe or clarify can be used to obtain a clearer understanding of what the client feels or means. Statements like "Can you tell me more about . . ." or "Tell me more about how you felt when . . ." or "I don't think I understand what you mean by . . ." provide relevant information from the client's point of view and help to maintain rapport. Rephrasing of questions can sometimes help to clarify client responses if other techniques have not been effective.

Most intake interviews cover the following topics: (a) general appearance and behavior; (b) presenting problem; (c) history of current problem and related problems; (d) present level of functioning in work, relationships, and leisure activities; (e) use of alcohol or other drugs including medications; (f) family history of mental illness; (g) history of physical, sexual, or emotional abuse; (h) previous counseling; and (i) attitude of client toward counselor. At the conclusion of the interview, the counselor must help the client to decide what steps to take next. These steps include additional counseling within the agency, referral to a counselor or helping professional outside the agency, or termination of counseling at the end of the initial interview.

As part of the intake interview, it is important to ask why the client is seeking help at this particular time. Has the problem recently become worse? Have other people become concerned about the person? Has the problem begun to interfere with the client's functioning at work or home? Answers to such questions can help clarify the nature of the client's problem and assess the client's motivation for participating in counseling.

In the intake interview, counselors can help clients begin to identify themes or life stories that shape their actions (Adams, 1993). During the course of therapy, counselors can then help clients to reformulate dysfunctional stories that impede their development. Themes that pro-

69

mote healthy adjustment include searching for meaning, gaining a sense of mastery, and working toward self-enhancement (Taylor, 1989). In the same manner, counselors can help clients to identify and address "cognitive distortions," such as all-or-nothing thinking, over-generalizing, and catastrophizing, that produce psychological disturbance (Burns, 1989).

In addition to assessing problems, counselors can begin to evaluate possible solutions for clients during the intake interview. The following five questions have been found to be helpful for this purpose (Miller & Berg, 1995; Skidmore & Berg, 1994):

1. The exception question—What are the exceptions to the problem you are describing?

2. The coping question—how have you been able to cope with the problem thus far? What has kept it from getting worse?

3. The scaling question—on a 10-point scale (where 1 = *problem at its worst* and 10 = *problem resolved*), how would you rate the severity of the problem at this time? What needs to happen to help you move up one step on the scale?

4. The miracle question—if a miracle were to happen tonight while you slept, how would things be different for you in the morning when you awoke? (This question helps to clarify goals.)

5. The presession (or intersession) therapy question—what factors have helped to reduce the problem for you since making the intake appointment (or since your last appointment)?

The counselor should evaluate the client's orientation toward reality if his or her thinking seems to be confused. Does the client experience any auditory or visual hallucinations? Is the client delusional, agitated, or euphoric? For such clients, the counselor may wish to administer a mental status exam (Waldinger, 1986).

The intake counselor should also be aware of the possibility that the client's psychological symptoms may be caused by physical illness, particularly if the client has not responded well to counseling or psychotherapy, if the symptoms have not occurred previously, if the client reports physical as well as psychological symptoms, or if the client is disoriented (Diamond, 1989). If the client is on medications, possible side-effects of these medications should be checked in the current edition of the *Physicians' Desk Reference* (published annually by Medical Economics Data, Montvale, NJ 07645).

Common errors of judgment based on interview assessments include the following: (a) anchoring—placing too much emphasis on information obtained early in the interview, (b) availability—relying too much on one's favorite theory or on popular diagnoses such as borderline personality disorder or adult child of dysfunctional family, (c) diagnostic overshadowing—ignoring or minimizing problems because they are less noticeable or are of less interest to the counselor, and (d) attribution—attributing the problem primarily to the client without giving sufficient consideration to the environment. Each of these errors represents a type of *confirmatory bias*, that is, a tendency to seek and to pay attention only to those factors that support one's initial judgment (Spengler, Strohmer, Dixon, & Shivy, 1995).

Confirmatory bias can be combated by keeping an open mind and by using a multifactor, multimethod approach to assessment (Carter & Barlow, 1995). In keeping an open mind, counselors should seek not only data that may support hypotheses about a client but also data that may refute these hypotheses. Multifactor assessments, which provide data concerning a range of personality and environmental factors, enable counselors to consider alternative explanations of client problems. Multimethod assessments allow counselors to consider issues from different viewpoints including the use of interview schedules, objective instruments, and observations by the client and others.

The accuracy of judgments can be improved further by soliciting feedback from clients, by using statistical prediction formulas when they exist, and by learning as much as possible about the issue that is being evaluated (Groth-Marnat, 1990). Knowledge of base rates for particular diagnoses or behaviors in the population from which the client is drawn can be particular helpful. For example, almost one half of college students in a national survey were identified as binge drinkers (Wechsler, Davenport, Dowdall, Moeykens, & Castillo, 1994); therefore, the presence of problem drinking among college clients should be carefully assessed during the intake process.

The reliability and validity of information obtained by means of interviews can also be improved by the use of structured or semistructured interview schedules (see Hasin, 1991; Kessler et al., 1994). Interview schedules provide a series of questions that can be helpful in diagnosing a particular condition or ailment. Examples include the Structured Clinical Interview for DSM-IV (SCID), Diagnostic Interview Schedule (DIS), the Schedule for Affective Disorders and Schizophrenia (SADS), the Diagnostic Interview for Children and Adolescents (DICA), the Present State Examination (PSE), and the Composite International Diagnostic Interview (CIDI). These interview schedules are typically used for diagnostic or survey purposes.

TEST SELECTION, ADMINISTRATION, AND SCORING

Test Selection

Testing should be seen as a part of the counseling process and not as an interruption of it. People often approach tests with some anxiety. This is particularly true of aptitude and achievement tests because of fear of failure. Anxiety regarding testing can influence the entire counseling process. Even interest and personality tests can reveal aspects of a person's character that may indicate weaknesses or undesirable features. To reduce the threatening aspects of tests, the counselor should make clear that the purpose of testing is to provide self-understanding, not evaluation of the client by the counselor. The counselor needs to convey to clients the feeling that they will be accepted whatever the test results happen to be.

If at all possible, clients should actively participate in the selection of tests that will be used in counseling (Duckworth, 1990; Healy, 1990). By learning about the purpose and nature of particular tests, clients can profit more from the test results. If convinced of the usefulness of the tests, clients will be more motivated to do their best on ability tests and to be accurate and truthful in responding to items on interest and personality inventories. By having participated in the decisions to use the tests, clients are also more likely to accept the results and their interpretations with less defensiveness. They can be more objective in their perception of the results of the tests.

In the case of academic or career counseling, clients often feel dependent on tests. They perceive the counselor as an expert who will select tests that will tell them what to do. Active participation by clients in test selection helps to counteract this overreliance on the counselor.

Generally the client does not select specific tests. That is a technical matter that counselors must decide based on their knowledge of tests. Instead, the client helps to decide the types of tests that can provide the information most useful for whatever actions or decisions are going to be made. Clients are not nearly as interested in specific characteristics of tests as they are in the implications the results will have for them. The types of tests are therefore described in a general fashion. For example, a counselor should describe the Strong Interest Inventory to a client simply as "an interest inventory that enables you to compare your likes and dislikes with those of people in different occupations." The counselor should not overwhelm the client with a lengthy technical presentation of the instrument itself.

A client's statement of need for tests should not necessarily be taken at face value. An initial request for a personality test should result in an effort to explore the meaning of the request, not simply acceptance of it. The client may be experiencing a significant problem such as anxiety or depression that should be explored before tests are assigned. The client may be asking for help regarding a particular problem but having difficulty revealing the problem or asking for help directly. The request for tests serves as an avenue to get at the major problem.

Tests should not be used unnecessarily. Other sources of data should also be explored. In a college counseling center little is gained by selecting aptitude tests when a record of college entrance tests, high school grades, and college grades are readily available. Other counseling agencies, of course, often start with no previous information. Nevertheless, counselors can first attempt to explore with the client previous experiences that may provide relevant information and self-descriptions. Recall of previous experiences can provide a great deal of information either to supplement test results or to eliminate the need for particular tests.

The time it takes to administer a test is sometimes a factor in determining whether or not the test will be used. Sometimes a short test can give an approximation adequate for a decision, whereas in other cases a longer and more reliable test may be needed for important decisions. The cost of testing is also important for many institutions and agencies with limited budgets. Whether test booklets are reusable, how tests must be scored, the time needed to score and interpret tests, and the cost of computer scoring, if available, are all factors that need to be taken into consideration.

Test Administration

A test provides a sample of behavior from which behavior in other situations can be inferred or predicted. In the case of standardized

73

tests, the sample of behavior must be obtained in a specified manner under standardized conditions with standardized instructions. The person who administers the test must be familiar with the instructions and other aspects of the administration. The knowledge necessary for administering the test differs greatly depending upon the test. Standardized scholastic aptitude tests can be administered with relatively little training. On the other hand, the knowledge and skill needed to administer individual intelligence tests requires extensive coursework and practicum experience.

Inexperienced test administrators often do not fully appreciate the importance of the test administrator's role. Irregularities identified in test administrations in school settings include inaccurate timing, altering answer sheets, coaching, teaching the test, scoring errors, recording errors, and student cheating (Gay, 1990). Most test manuals provide detailed instructions for the administration of a particular test, which should be followed exactly. It is the standardization of instructions that makes it possible to compare one person's scores with those of another or with different groups.

In administering tests, it is important that the examiner elicit the interest and cooperation of the test taker. In obtaining rapport, the examiner should attempt to convince test takers that the results will be useful and that they are not wasting their time in a task that will be of little consequence or value to them. Usually clients are cooperative if they have voluntarily sought counseling. If they are being tested against their will, perhaps because of a court order or because they feel that the test information is not important, good rapport may be difficult to establish.

On performance or aptitude tests, the test administrator must encourage examinees to follow instructions carefully and to perform as well as they can. With small children, tests may be presented as a game. For interest or personality inventories, examinees should be encouraged to answer honestly and frankly to preclude invalid results.

The administrator should be familiar with the test being administered so that subjects do not doubt the administrator's competence. Self-confidence should be exhibited together with a warm and friendly manner.

The testing environment should be suitable for test administration with adequate seating, lighting, ventilation, and temperature. It should be free from noise, interruptions, and other distractions. Time limits should be followed exactly and measures taken to prevent cheating. Factors, even minor ones, that can alter test performance should be recognized and minimized. These factors contribute to the error variance in test scores. Any problems in administering the test should be noted and taken into account when interpreting the test results.

Individual versus group tests. Some tests are designed to be administered to one individual at a time by a trained examiner; others can be administered to a group of people. Group tests allow information to be obtained from many people within a short period of time at relatively little cost. Individual tests, on the other hand, allow the examiner to adapt the test administration to the needs of the client. Individual tests must be used with certain populations such as very small children and those with particular handicaps. Individual tests permit observational data to be obtained in addition to the test scores.

Speed versus power tests. Some ability tests place a heavy emphasis on speed of response. These tests often consist of a large number of easy items that a person must complete quickly. Examples of speed tests with relatively short time limits include finger and manual dexterity tests and clerical speed and accuracy tests.

In contrast, power tests contain items of varying difficulty, most of which the person is expected to complete within the time limits. If 90% of the people for whom the test is designed can complete the test within the time limits, the test can be described as a power test. Although speed can still be a factor for some students on power tests, speed would not have much influence on the total score for most students. Most intelligence tests, scholastic aptitude tests, and achievements tests are basically power tests.

Computer-based test administration. Test administration by means of computers has become widespread in recent years with the availability of low-cost microcomputers. Computer-based testing offers a number of advantages compared with traditional paper-and-pencil methods. These advantages include (a) reduced amount of time required for test administration, (b) immediate feedback concerning client performance, (c) improved standardization of test administration procedures, (d) use of new types of items that employ movement or sequential presentations, and (e) use of adaptive (or tailored) testing procedures that take into account the client's previous responses (Wise & Plake, 1990).

Examples of computer-based tests include the Test of Variables of Attention (TOVA), a game-like computer test for attention deficit disorder that employs continuous movement in the form of a target stimulus. TOVA provides scores for several variables, such as reaction time, errors of omission (inattention), errors of commission (impulsivity), and anticipatory and multiple responses, that would be difficult to obtain with paper-and-pencil testing (Greenberg, 1994). The adaptive versions of the Graduate Record Exam and the Differential Aptitude Tests represent examples of the use of the computer to administer individualized tests based upon the examinee's pattern of test responses.

Counselors are more likely to employ assessment instruments as part of the counseling process when they can be administered by the computer (Flowers, Booream, & Schwartz, 1993). Tests administered by means of a computer have been shown to yield results that are more reliable than paper-and-pencil tests (Kapes & Vansickle, 1992).

In the use of computer-based tests, counselors should make certain that clients are familiar and comfortable with the computer equipment. The computer equipment should be checked routinely to make sure that it is functioning properly.

Test Scoring

Tests can be scored by hand or by computer. Tests that are scored by hand usually involve the use of a scoring template that can be placed over the answer sheet to identify incorrect responses. In some cases, clients score their own tests by the use of "self-scorable" answer sheets that reveal the correct answers behind a seal on the reverse side of the answer sheet. Examples of measures that use self-scorable answer sheets include the Myers-Briggs Type Indicator and the Kuder General Interest Survey. If more than a few tests or scales are involved, hand scoring can become time consuming, tedious, and subject to error. If at all possible, tests that are scored by hand should also be scored by another person to ensure accuracy of results.

Compared with hand scoring, computer scoring is more rapid, more accurate, and more thorough (Wise & Plake, 1990). The computer makes it possible to undertake elaborate test scoring programs such as those required for the Strong Interest Inventory or Kuder Occupational Interest Survey that would be virtually impossible to do by hand. In addition to specific scores, computers can also generate test interpretations by means of scoring rules, or algorithms, stored in the computer's memory.

Computer-based test interpretations (CBTIs), such as those that have been developed for the Minnesota Multiphasic Personality Inventory (MMPI), provide a "second opinion" that counselors can use both to create and to test hypotheses about clients (Sampson, 1990). They should not be relied upon as the sole source of information regarding a client. Despite their popularity, the validities of CBTIs have not been well studied (Moreland, 1985). The scoring rules upon which the interpretations are based are often a "trade secret" so that it is difficult to evaluate how adequately they have been developed. In fact, the publishers of the *Mental Measurements Yearbooks* abandoned an effort to provide a separate volume of reviews of CBTIs because of the difficulty they encountered in obtaining information from the test publishers regarding the computer programs and their algorithms (Kramer & Conoley, 1992).

Counselors should examine CBTIs in light of other information that they have been able to collect about the client. They should use their best professional judgment to take into account any individual or situational factors that could alter the CBTI for a particular client. As with any test data, the results should be viewed as hypotheses that need to be confirmed or revised based upon other information that is collected regarding the particular client.

SUMMARY

1. A client's readiness for counseling can be assessed in terms of the five stages of change (precontemplation, contemplation, preparation, action, and maintenance).
2. Counselors can use the "models of helping and coping" by Brickman et al. (1982) and the MBTI to help clients identify their orientation toward problem solving. Clients should be helped to recognize the advantages and disadvantages of their particular problem-solving style.
3. The nature and severity of a client's problems can best be determined by means of an intake form, a problem checklist or screening inventory, and an intake interview used in combination. The ICP

77

and the SCL-90-R both contain comprehensive lists of client problems or symptoms that can be used systematically to clarify a client's concerns.

4. The accuracy of judgments made in interviews can be improved by keeping an open mind, by using multiple sources of data, by understanding the behavior being assessed including knowledge of base rates, by obtaining feedback from those being assessed, and by using structured or semistructured interviews.

5. The client should be integrally involved in all aspects of test selection. A variety of assessment procedures should be considered for this purpose.

6. The counselor should be careful to establish rapport with the client and to follow the prescribed procedures for test administration.

7. Computer-based test interpretations, which have become increasingly popular, require thorough knowledge and understanding of the test itself, the testing circumstances, and characteristics of the client to ensure proper use. Computer-based test interpretations do not replace the need for counselor training and experience in psychological assessment.

II

Cognitive Assessment

II

Chemical Assessment

5

ASSESSMENT OF INTELLIGENCE

C OUNSELORS WHO WORK in certain settings, such as schools, or who are involved in employment or vocational counseling, make considerable use of the results of intelligence tests. Others, working in colleges and secondary schools, constantly make use of a particular type of intelligence measure—the Scholastic Aptitude Test—whereas marriage counselors and those working with substance abusers, for example, seldom use these instruments. Some general knowledge of intelligence assessment is important, and test results influence many decisions clients make. All counselors are expected to have some knowledge of intelligence assessment and the ability to make use of test results in assisting clients to make decisions. In this chapter some of the most often used instruments are described along with considerations regarding their use. Scholastic aptitude measures are discussed in the next chapter. Assessment instruments designed for special populations are described in Chapter 16.

Intelligence has been one of the most thoroughly studied fields in the history of psychology. It was Alfred Binet in France who, in the early 1900s, conceptualized intelligence as a general ability to judge, to comprehend, and to reason well. With this definition he then went about developing a series of measures by which he could identify children for whom it was necessary to provide special educational programs. The measures he used showed that mental processes increase as a child grows older. Three-year-olds could be expected to be able to point to their nose, eyes, and mouth and repeat two digits. The typical 7-year-old could distinguish right from left and name various colors, and the 12-year-old could define various abstract words and make sense of a disarranged sentence.

In 1916, Lewis Terman, at Stanford University, revised and standardized Binet's test for use in the United States. It became known as the Stanford-Binet Intelligence Scale. Making use of the concept of mental age developed by Binet, the concept of the now-outdated intelligence quotient (IQ) was devised. This IQ score is a ratio calculated with the mental age and the chronological age. A child's mental age is divided by the child's chronological age and multiplied by 100. A child exactly 10 years of age with a mental age of 12 will obtain an IQ score of 120. This type of an IQ score has a number of problems connected with it. In the first place, answering all of the items correctly on the original Stanford-Binet yielded a maximum mental age of less than 20. Thus anyone 20 or older automatically received an IQ score of less than 100. The usefulness of the ratio score therefore disappears during the teen years. In addition, the concept of a person's IQ has been erroneously viewed by the public as a fixed measure similar to the color of a person's eyes, rather than as a particular score on a particular test at a particular time. The ratio IQ has therefore been replaced by the derived IQ standard score in order to circumvent some of these problems.

The question of what it is that actually makes up intelligence and what it is that intelligence tests actually measure has long been the subject of much controversy. One conceptualization divides intelligence into two types—*crystallized* and *fluid*. Crystallized intelligence deals with an individual's ability to solve problems and make decisions based on acquired knowledge, experiences, and verbal conceptualizations. Fluid intelligence is an individual's ability to be adaptable and flexible in solving new problems (Carroll, 1993). Most of the tests in the content areas of verbal reasoning and quantitative reasoning would be considered crystallized intelligence and those in the abstract/visual reasoning area fluid intelligence.

POPULAR INDIVIDUAL INTELLIGENCE TESTS

The Stanford-Binet

The Stanford-Binet became the best known intelligence test in the world and was used as a standard against which all other intelligence tests being developed were validated. The 1916 Stanford-Binet Intelligence Test had a number of weaknesses and was therefore revised to produce the 1937 scale, in two parallel forms (L and M). The ratio IQ score was eliminated and standard scores were calculated to provide each age with a mean of 100 and a standard deviation of 16. A 1960 revision was developed and was restandardized in 1972 to provide more adequate norms intended to be representative of the entire U.S. population.

The 1986 revision (Thorndike, Hagen, & Sattler, 1986a, 1986b) is the fourth edition of the Stanford-Binet Intelligence Scale. The authors attempted to provide a continuity with the previous editions by retaining the advantages of the early editions as an individually administered intelligence test and still take advantage of the more recent theoretical developments and new research in cognitive psychology. A wider variety of tests, particularly those of a nonverbal nature, are included.

The fourth edition includes 15 separate tests that cover four different content areas: (a) verbal reasoning, (b) abstract/visual reasoning, (c) quantitative reasoning, and (d) short-term memory. Whereas certain of the 15 subtests are administered to subjects of all ages, others have more restricted age ranges.

In the administration of the 1986 revision, as in the case of the previous editions, individuals are administered a range of tasks suited to their abilities. A level is established at which it is expected that they would have answered all of the previous, lower level items correctly and testing continues to a ceiling level. Answers on the vocabulary test along with the individual's chronological age provide a method by which the entry level is determined to begin testing on the remaining tests. Testing then proceeds on each test until at least three out of four items are missed, which determines a ceiling level on that test at which further items can be expected to be answered incorrectly.

On most of the tests each item has only one correct answer and the raw score on each test is converted into a standard age score with a mean of 50 and standard deviation of 8. Standard scores are also provided for each of the four cognitive areas along with a total composite score that reflects general mental ability. Each has a mean of 100 and a standard deviation of 16. The total testing time for the fourth edition takes approximately 1 hour and 15 minutes. No individual is administered all 15 tests—a complete battery includes 8 to 13 tests depending on the individual's entry level.

The fourth edition was standardized on more than 5,000 individuals from throughout the United States and included representative samples based on sex, age, ethnic group, and community size. Internal consistency reliabilities tend to be very high for the composite (above .95) and for each of the cognitive areas (above .93). In general, test-retest reliabilities on both the individual tests and the composites are higher for older than for younger age levels. The authors have provided validity data on the fourth edition by using (a) constructs based on current research in the field of cognitive intelligence, (b) internal consistency and factor analytic methods, and (c) correlations with other intelligence tests.

The Wechsler Scales

The Stanford-Binet was originally developed for children, with some more difficult items added for adults. David Wechsler, working at Bellevue Hospital in New York, believed that there was a need for an intelligence test more suitable for adults, and therefore developed the Wechsler Bellevue Intelligence Scale in 1939. In addition, believing that the Stanford-Binet placed too much emphasis on language and verbal skills, he developed a totally different performance scale measuring nonverbal intelligence.

The Wechsler Adult Intelligence Scale (WAIS-R). The 1939 scale was revised in 1955 to correct a number of deficiencies that had been found in the earlier form and became the Wechsler Adult Intelligence Scale

(Wechsler, 1981). The WAIS was revised in 1981 to produce the WAIS-R. It was standardized on a sample selected to match the proportions of the U.S. population in regard to race, occupational level, education, and residence as of the 1970 census and distributed over age levels from 16 to 74.

The Wechsler tests yield a profile of scores (such as that of the case example displayed in Figure 5-1 for the WAIS-R) showing the raw score and scale score for each of the 11 subtests along with verbal IQ, performance IQ, and the full-scale IQ scores. The mean and standard deviation for each of the 11 subtests are 10 and 3, respectively. For the performance, verbal, and full-scale IQ scores, the mean is 100 with a standard deviation of 15 (as compared with 16 for the Stanford-Binet). Standard error of measurement for the three IQ scores is reported to be approximately 2.5 for the full-scale IQ, 2.7 for the verbal IQ, and 4.1 for the performance IQ. A client's true full-scale score could thus be assumed at a 95% level of confidence to fall within five points in one direction or the other from the client's obtained full-scale IQ score.

CASE EXAMPLE

Peter, 24 years old and single, had the WAIS-R administered to him while undergoing treatment for alcoholism in a residential alcohol detox-ification center. He had been treated twice before for alcoholism, but, being single, without family or other support systems, found it easy to drift back into alcoholism upon discharge. He suffered from mild depression and antisocial tendencies and had been in trouble with the law in addition to his problems with alcohol. In the center, however, he was a model client and fully cooperated with the treatment and testing he received. His verbal score on the WAIS-R fell in the normal range although he scored substantially lower on the performance subtest, giving him a total score that would place him in the dull-normal range. The large difference between the verbal and performance portions of the WAIS-R may very likely have been caused by the effects of continued alcohol abuse.

Wechsler Intelligence Scale for Children (WISC-III). The Wechsler Intelligence Scale for Children (WISC) was originally developed as a downward extension of the Wechsler Bellevue Intelligence Scale for children aged 6 to 16 years. It was revised in 1974 (WISC-R) to contain more child-oriented items, to include more Black and female figures,

FIGURE 5-1. WAIS-R Summary Test Scores for Peter

WAIS-R RECORD FORM

WECHSLER ADULT INTELLIGENCE SCALE— REVISED

NAME **Peter**

ADDRESS

SEX **M** AGE **24** RACE **Anglo** MARITAL STATUS **S**

OCCUPATION **Unemployed** EDUCATION **10th grade**

PLACE OF TESTING _____ TESTED BY _____

		Year	Month	Day
Date Tested				
Date of Birth				
Age				

TABLE OF SCALED SCORE EQUIVALENTS*

Scaled Score	VERBAL TESTS						PERFORMANCE TESTS					Scaled Score
	Information	Digit Span	Vocabulary	Arithmetic	Comprehension	Similarities	Picture Completion	Picture Arrangement	Block Design	Object Assembly	Digit Symbol	
19	—	28	70	—	32	—	—	—	51	—	93	19
18	29	27	69	—	31	28	—	—	—	41	91-92	18
17	—	26	68	19	--	—	20	20	50	--	89-90	17
16	28	25	66-67	—	30	27	—	—	49	40	84-88	16
15	27	24	65	18	29	26	—	19	47-48	39	79-83	15
14	26	22-23	63-64	17	27-28	25	19	—	44-46	38	75-78	14
13	25	20-21	60-62	16	26	24	—	18	42-43	37	70-74	13
12	23-24	18-19	55-59	(15)	25	23	18	17	38-41	35-36	66-69	12
11	22	17	52-54	13-14	23-24	22	17	15-16	35-37	34	62-65	11
10	19-21	(15)16	47-51	12	21(22)	(20)21	16	14	31-34	32-33	57-61	10
9	17-18	14	43-46	11	19-20	18-19	15	13	27-30	30-31	53-56	9
8	15-16	12-13	37-42	10	17-18	16-17	(14)	11-12	23-26	28-29	48-52	8
7	13-14	11	29(36)	8-9	14-16	14-15	13	(9-10)	20(22)	24-27	44-47	7
6	9(12)	9-10	20-28	6-7	11-13	11-13	11-12	5-7	14-19	21-23	37-43	6
5	6-8	8	14-19	5	8-10	7-10	8-10	3-4	8-13	16-20	30-36	5
4	5	7	11-13	4	6-7	5-6	5-7	2	3-7	13-15	23-29	4
3	4	6	9-10	3	4-5	2-4	3-4	—	2	9-12	16-22	3
2	3	3-5	6-8	1-2	2-3	1	2	1	1	6-8	8-15	2
1	0-2	0-2	0-5	0	0-1	0	0-1	0	0	0-5	0-7	1

*Clinicians who wish to draw a profile may do so by locating the subject's raw scores on the table above and drawing a line to connect them. See Chapter 4 in the Manual for a discussion of the significance of differences between scores on the tests

SUMMARY

	Raw Score	Scaled Score	
VERBAL TESTS			
Information	**12**	**6**	__
Digit Span	**15**	**10**	__
Vocabulary	**34**	**7**	__
Arithmetic	**15**	**12**	__
Comprehension	**22**	**10**	__
Similarities	**22**	**10**	__
Verbal Score		**55**	
PERFORMANCE TESTS			
Picture Completion	**14**	**8**	__
Picture Arrangement	**9**	**7**	__
Block Design	**22**	**7**	__
Object Assembly	**25**	**7**	__
Digit Symbol	**35**	**5**	__
Performance Score		**33**	

	Sum of Scaled Scores	IQ
VERBAL	**55**	**95**
PERFORMANCE	**33**	**76**
FULL SCALE	**88**	**85**

and to provide a normative sample more representative of children in the U.S. population (Wechsler, 1974). A third revised and updated edition was published in 1991 as the WISC-III (Wechsler, 1991).

The WISC-III contains 12 subtests, 2 of which are supplementary, to be used if needed. The subtests generally parallel those in the WAIS-R and provide verbal, performance, and full-scale IQ scores similar to the WAIS-R. The two supplementary tests provided are the digit span test, which may be substituted for a verbal test, and a maze subtest, which may be substituted for the coding test in the performance battery, if the examiner meets with difficulty in administering one of the regular subtests to a particular child. As with the WAIS-R, the subtests are administered by alternating the verbal and performance subtests.

The subtests, the two partial IQ scores, and the full-scale IQ scores have means and standard deviations similar to those of the WAIS-R. Scores are provided for each 4-month age group between 6 and 16 years.

Both split-half and test-retest reliabilities for all three IQ scores fall within the range of .90 to .96. The standard error of measurement for the full-scale IQ test is approximately three points. Thus a child's true WISC-III IQ score would be estimated to be no more than six points above or below the obtained score at a 95% level of confidence.

The Wechsler Preschool and Primary Scale of Intelligence (WPPSI-R). In 1967, a downward extension of the WISC was developed for use with children 4 to 6½ years of age called the Wechsler Preschool and Primary Scale of Intelligence (WPPSI) and revised in 1989 to become the WPPSI-R (Wechsler, 1989). It includes 11 subtests, of which 10 are used in obtaining the IQ scores. Eight of the subtests represent downward extensions of those from the WISC, and 3 unique subtests were added. Normalized standard scores for subtests and IQs are similar to those on the other Wechsler tests.

The Kaufman Batteries

The Kaufmans have developed several intelligence test batteries including the Kaufman Assessment Battery for Children (K-ABC) and the Kaufman Adolescent and Adult Intelligence Test (KAIT). The K-ABC (Cohen, Swerdlik, & Smith, 1992; Kaufman & Kaufman, 1983) is composed of 16 subtests, of which 13 are administered to any one

87

child. It is designed for children 2½ to 12½ years old and contains sets of both mental processing and achievement subscores.

The KAIT (Kaufman & Kaufman, 1993) consists of six core subtests and four additional subtests in an expanded battery and is normed for ages 11 to 85 years. It yields scores on both crystallized and fluid intelligence and a composite IQ score, each with reliability coefficients above .90. A short form, the Kaufman Brief Intelligence Test (K-BIT; Kaufman & Kaufman, 1990) is administered in 15–30 minutes, consists of a vocabulary (through pictures) portion and a matrices portion using pictures and abstract designs. It is useful when time constraints preclude the use of a longer measure (Naugle, Chelume & Tucker, 1993).

Advantages of Individual Intelligence Tests

Each of these four intelligence tests is individually administered and requires a highly trained examiner. Considerable training and practice in administering each test are necessary for a competent administration that produces reliable results. An experienced examiner has the opportunity to observe and judge a variety of behaviors and aspects of the individual's personality. Thus for the competent examiner these tests provide aspects of a clinical interview as well as a standardized test.

Because these individual intelligence tests provide several different types of IQ scores, the counselor has the opportunity to pay particular attention to those clients in whom the difference between the scores is substantial. In such cases, an exploration is warranted to attempt to discern factors that might account for the differences. The different subtest scores also provide an opportunity to examine the pattern of scores that appear as a profile on the report form, such as that shown for the WAIS-R of the case example of Peter in Figure 5-1.

There have been a number of hypotheses advanced regarding emotional, neurological, and pathological problems that yield differential subtest scores. Considerable research has shown differential diagnoses resulting from patterns on such profiles to be questionable. Because the different subtests vary in reliability, difference scores obtained among the subtests can be particularly unreliable. Nevertheless, most sophisticated users of the Stanford-Binet and the Wechsler tests regard differential patterns as suggesting certain types of dysfunction. For example, higher scores on various verbal scales and lower ones on certain of the performance scales are suggestive of such problems as brain damage, drug abuse (as in the case example), or in an older person, Alzheimer's dementia. Verbal subtest scores falling well below performance scores may suggest poor reading ability or lack of motivation for academic achievement.

Many counselors do not obtain the coursework and practice to administer these instruments in their graduate training. Instead they refer clients to competent examiners and receive the results from them. Counselors should encourage such examiners to report their observations and any other information that can assist counselors in interpreting the results, particularly in regard to information that can help to explain any discrepancies.

GROUP INTELLIGENCE TESTS

Group intelligence tests are considerably more cost-efficient than individual tests in the time required for administration and scoring. They require simpler materials; typically only a printed booklet, a multiple-choice answer sheet, a pencil, and a scoring key are needed. They also usually offer more normative information as this type of data is easier to collect for group tests.

The development of group tests was stimulated by the need to classify almost 2 million U.S. Army recruits during World War I. The Army Alpha and the nonreading companion test, the Army Beta, were developed for military use. Group intelligence tests designed for educational and personnel uses were developed shortly thereafter, with these two tests as models. Such group-administered tests are now used at every educational level from kindergarten through graduate school. They are also used extensively by industry, by the military, and in research studies. In order to avoid the term *intelligence test,* because the term *intelligence* is so often misunderstood and misinterpreted, these tests, particularly those designed for school use, tend to be described as mental maturity, cognitive ability, school ability, or mental ability tests.

Group Intelligence Tests for School Use

Because these tests are administered across a number of grades throughout entire school systems, they are administered by the hundreds of thousands each year. The market for these tests is therefore a profitable one, and a large number are available for use. A half dozen of the most popular and most psychometrically sound instruments are briefly described here.

Henmon-Nelson Tests. The Henmon-Nelson Tests of Mental Ability contain four levels of tests designed to cover the grades kindergarten through the 12th grade, with each level covering three or four grades (Lambe, Nelson, & French, 1973). The tests contain verbal and numerical items, and the resulting raw scores are converted into both deviation IQs and percentiles.

Cognitive Abilities Test. The Cognitive Abilities Test is the modern version of the Lorge-Thorndike Intelligence Tests (Riverside Publishing, 1994). The test contains three different batteries, one for kindergarten and first grade, one for second and third grades, and a multilevel battery for use in grades 3 through 12. The Cognitive Abilities Test contains three separate sections providing three separate scores: verbal, quantitative, and nonverbal. The nonverbal section uses neither language nor numbers but geometric figures for tasks that require classification, analogies, or figure synthesis. In this portion, the effects of formal schooling, poor reading ability, or non-native-English speaking are minimized. Raw scores on each section can be converted into stanine and percentile scores for both age and grade levels so that the three scores can be compared both to norm groups and within each individual. In addition, the scores can be converted to standard scores that have a mean of 100 and a standard deviation of 16 to produce a deviation IQ score. The Cognitive Abilities Tests were standardized along with the Iowa Tests of Basic Skills for grades kindergarten through 9 and the Iowa Tests of Educational Development for grades 9 through 12.

Kuhlmann-Anderson Test. The Kuhlmann-Anderson Test is made up of eight separate levels for all grades—kindergarten through 12th grade—with each level containing several tests (Scholastic Testing Service, 1982). It is the contemporary version of one of the earliest and most popular intelligence tests used in the schools. It is less dependent on language than most similar tests and yields verbal, nonverbal, and total scores. Scores are presented as age- and grade-related percentile bands (confidence intervals) as well as deviation IQ (Cognitive Skills Quotient) scores.

Test of Cognitive Skills. The Test of Cognitive Skills is the contemporary version of the long-used California Test of Mental Maturity– Short Form (CTB/MacMillan/McGraw-Hill, 1993). In its original form the instrument was designed to be the group test equivalent of the Stanford-Binet, and to yield scores similar to those that would be obtained by individually administering the Stanford-Binet. In addition to verbal and nonverbal ability subtests, it also contains a section designed to assess short-term memory. There are six levels, each designed for two grade levels ranging from grade 2 through grade 12. Age and grade stanines, percentiles, and standard score norms are available for each subtest and a Combined Cognitive Skills Index provides a deviation IQ score.

Otis-Lennon School Ability Test. The Otis-Lennon School Ability Test, sixth edition (OLSAT6) has seven levels ranging from kindergarten to grade 12 (Otis & Lennon, 1989). The test is published in two forms and yields verbal and nonverbal scores based on 36-item subtests and a total IQ score. The test represents a contemporary version of a series of former Otis tests as will the seventh edition available in 1996. The OLSAT6 was jointly normed with the Metropolitan Achievement Tests 7 and the Stanford Achievement Tests 8, and the seventh edition with the Stanford 9.

Other Group Intelligence Tests

Shipley Institute of Living Scale. The Shipley Institute of Living Scale– Revised (SILS) is a 60-item (40 vocabulary, 20 abstract reasoning) intelligence test that takes approximately 20 minutes to administer. IQ and standard scores are obtained based on age-adjusted norms (Zachary, 1986). Correlations in the vicinity of .8 with Wechsler tests are reported in the manual along with reliabilities of .8 to .9 for internal consistency and .6 to .7 for test-retest. Originally constructed to assess cognitive impairment, this test is now used as a brief screening device for overall intellectual ability.

Wonderlic Personnel Test. The Wonderlic Personnel Test is a brief 12-minute, 50-item test of mental ability for adults (Wonderlic, 1983).

Sixteen forms of this paper-and-pencil intelligence test are available, along with extensive norms. It is widely used in business and industry for the selection and placement of employees. Validity data in regard to job success are undoubtedly available locally in many companies but typically are not found in the research literature. The test's validity has been questioned in regard to selection for certain positions when minorities obtaining lower scores on the instrument are screened out of various entry-level positions. This has resulted in the Wonderlic Personnel Test becoming the subject of various court cases in which its use was declared not legitimate where testing procedures resulted in denying fair opportunities to prospective minority employees but acceptable when test results were shown to be substantially related to the performance of specific jobs.

Multidimensional Aptitude Battery. The Multidimensional Aptitude Battery was developed by Douglas Jackson as a group-administered paper-and-pencil test to yield the same types of results and scores as the WAIS (Jackson, 1984a). This test battery contains five tests on the verbal scale and five tests on the performance scale that involve very similar tasks to the subtests on the WAIS but in a paper-and-pencil format. Scores on the various subtests have a mean of 50 and standard deviation of 10, and total scores on the verbal, performance, and full-scale scores have a mean of 100 and a standard deviation of 15.

In the design of the Multidimensional Aptitude Battery, Jackson made use of the capabilities of modern computers in the development of items and scales through item analysis and factor analysis techniques. The advantage of the battery is in its ease of administration and scoring; the highly trained examiner necessary to administer the WAIS or the Stanford-Binet is not required. As a group-administered battery, however, it does not provide the examiner with the observational data obtained in using individual instruments.

INTERPRETING INTELLIGENCE TEST RESULTS

The typical intelligence test administered in the United States assumes a relatively common cultural background found in contemporary society and English as the native language. For tests above the lower elementary levels, reading ability in English is also necessary to obtain valid results on most of the group-administered tests. To provide valid assessment devices useful in other cultures or for use with subcultures or minority cultures in this country, attempts have been made to develop culture-fair tests that function independently of a specific culture, primarily by eliminating, or at least greatly reducing, language and cultural content. These will be discussed in Chapter 16.

Robert Sternberg has refocused attention on some of the fundamental questions regarding intelligence (Sternberg, 1985; Sternberg, Wagner, Williams & Horvath, 1995). He has proposed a triarchic theory of intelligence with each of the three factors made up of several different elements that interact with one another. The componential (cognitive) factor deals with information processing and is made up of crystallized abilities measured by such subtests as vocabulary and reading comprehension and fluid abilities measured by subtests such as abstract analogies and series completions. His experiential (creative) factor embodies the ability to deal with novel activities and situations and the ability to automatize high levels of information processing. His conceptual (practical) factor contains the components of practical intelligence and social intelligence. Although no tests exist to measure all or even most of these components, believing that a single index of IQ does more to obscure than describe a person's abilities, Sternberg is attempting to construct certain measures that vary widely from the tasks typically involved in the more traditional attempts to assess intelligence (Sternberg, 1988).

Perhaps the most important point to remember in the interpretation of intelligence test results is that the IQ score obtained does not represent a fixed characteristic of the individual. Instead, it should be interpreted as a particular score obtained on a particular test at a particular time. As has been mentioned, this is especially important for younger clients, for whom test-retest reliabilities are lower, indicating that considerable change and development take place over time. In interpreting the result to a client, rather than say that he or she has an IQ of 112, a better interpretation would be to say that the client scored in the top quarter of his or her peers on a test that measures an ability useful in learning academic subjects.

SUMMARY

This chapter dealt with the assessment of intelligence using both individual and group assessment instruments.

1. The concept of intelligence is widely studied in psychology, but IQ scores are widely misunderstood by the general public.
2. Binet designed the first intelligence test in France in the early 1900s; it was revised in 1916 at Stanford for use in the United States. The 1986 revision of the Stanford-Binet intelligence tests contains 15 subtests, only parts of which are administered to any individual, depending on the chronological age and answers on certain of the subtests.
3. Three different Wechsler scales represent individually administered intelligence tests designed specifically for three different age ranges.
4. Large numbers of group intelligence tests are administered each year in the schools in this country, and six of these tests were briefly described in this chapter.

6

ACADEMIC APTITUDE AND ACHIEVEMENT

T HE ASSESSMENT of various aptitudes has played an important role in the field of psychological testing. An aptitude is generally thought of as an ability to acquire a specific type of skill or knowledge. In the field of aptitude testing, the assessment of scholastic aptitude is particularly important, because it is significantly related to achievement in various educational programs in high schools, colleges, and professional schools. Because of the importance of higher education as a prerequisite for entering the majority of higher status occupations and professions in today's society, achieving acceptable scores on scholastic aptitude measures is becoming increasingly crucial for those aspiring to such occupations.

Even counselors in elementary schools or mental health agencies, who seldom see scholastic aptitude test scores in their work, are expected to be knowledgeable about these tests. They will probably at least be consulted by their relatives, friends, and colleagues whose children are beginning to apply to undergraduate or professional colleges and universities. In this chapter information about the two major national college testing programs is presented, along with considerations and data useful in the interpretation of test scores. Academic aptitude tests used for admission to several of the different types of professional colleges are briefly described, followed by a few points regarding the administration and interpretation of academic aptitude tests. Examples of academic achievement test batteries commonly used in the schools are briefly described along with a discussion of the use and misuse of such test batteries. Finally, the relatively new cognitive development theories and assessment instruments are mentioned because of the expectation that they will be of increasing interest to counselors and human development professionals.

TESTS FOR HIGHER EDUCATION

Scholastic aptitude tests are used as sources of information for the selection and admission of students to institutions of higher education at the undergraduate and graduate or professional levels. They are also used in awarding financial aid and placing students in courses, as well as for academic and vocational counseling and advising. The two most commonly required college-level aptitude tests are the College Entrance Examination Board's Scholastic Aptitude Test (SAT) and that administered by the American College Testing Program (ACT).

The Scholastic Assessment Test (SAT)

The SAT has been administered since 1926 and is now taken by over a million college-bound high school students each year. Its design, administration, and reporting are carried out by the Educational Testing Service (ETS) in Princeton, New Jersey. It was revised in 1994 and renamed the Scholastic Assessment Test-I (SAT-I). It is a 3-hour primarily multiple-choice test with two major sections: (a) Verbal (V) containing multiple-choice items dealing with critical reading, sentence completion, and analogies; and (b) Mathematical (M) with multiple-choice items dealing with regular mathematics and quantitative comparisons of which 10 items require student-produced responses (College Board, 1991). It no longer includes a writing sample, which was moved to the optional SAT-II tests. The SAT-I attempts to measure developed abilities or intellectual skills and is not meant to be an achievement test tied to particular high school courses or curriculum. Reliabilities of the SAT-I Verbal and Mathematical portions have generally been found to be in the vicinity of .90.

In 1941, the mean on each section for students taking the test was set at 500 with a standard deviation of 100, and scores therefore ranging on a scale from 200 to 800. Since 1941, the college-bound cohort completing the test each year had changed drastically, and 500 no longer approximated the college-bound mean. In the spring of 1995, scores on the SAT-I were "recentered" with the mean on each of the two portions reset at 500. Students taking the SAT-I after this date will, if they score near the mean, obtain scores about 75 points higher on the Verbal portion and 25 points higher on the Mathematical portion (College Board, 1994b).

The mathematical portion of the SAT-I is more dependent on curriculum-based learning than is the Verbal portion, and the further the student progresses in mathematics courses in high school, the better the student will be prepared for the SAT-I Mathematics. Students who have not taken mathematics courses for several years should be encouraged to review some of their basic algebra and geometry before sitting for the SAT-I.

The College Entrance Examination Board also administers subject tests in 18 specific subjects known as the SAT-II in addition to the SAT-II writing test.

The Preliminary Scholastic Aptitude Test/National Merit Scholarship Qualifying Test (PSAT/NMSQT)

The PSAT/NMSQT is typically taken in the 11th grade (College Entrance Examination Board, 1988). It is considered by some students to be a practice or trial run for the SAT to be taken in the following year. It is also used to help students choose which colleges to consider in their college decision-making plans. It also plays an important role as the initial step in qualifying for National Merit Scholarships.

Scores on the PSAT/NMSQT, which range from 20 to 80, are designed to be comparable—with an additional 0 added—to the SAT scores that students would be expected to obtain when they take that test in their senior year. Like the SAT, it yields both Verbal and Math scores (from two 50-minute sections). The PSAT/NMSQT was also recentered in the fall of 1994 so that those juniors could predict the scores they would receive when they took the recentered SAT-I in 1995 (College Board, 1992a). Thus a student who receives a 50 on the PSAT Verbal and a 55 on the PSAT Math would be expected to receive scores somewhere in the vicinity of 500 on the SAT-I Verbal and 550 on the SAT-I Math. Such a student who had been planning to enter a very highly selective institution at which the majority of those students admitted score above 650 on both portions of the SAT-I might wish to reconsider his or her chances of admission to that institution. An additional score, known as the "selection index" is computed for scholarship consideration by doubling the Verbal score on the PSAT/NMSQT and adding the sum to the Math score. To become a National Merit Scholarship semifinalist, the selection index must total in the vicinity of 210, with actual cut-off scores varying among the different states to obtain the top 1% of the scholarship qualifiers from each state.

American College Testing (ACT)

The other national college testing admissions program is that of the American College Testing (ACT) Program, established in 1959 and based in Iowa City, Iowa. The ACT tests tend to be used more often by colleges in the Midwest and less often by those on the East Coast. The current revision, termed the Enhanced ACT Assessment, consists of four academic tests, an interest inventory, and a questionnaire regarding student backgrounds and plans (American College Testing Program, 1989a). The academic tests take 2 hours and 55 minutes to complete and are designed to assess academic ability in four areas: English, mathematics, reading, and science reasoning. Scores are obtained on each of the four academic tests and their seven subscales, along with a total composite score. The mean for college-bound students who take the Enhanced ACT is approximately 21 on each of the four academic tests and the composite score. Standard deviations vary from 4.5 to 6.0, and standard scores range from 1 to 36. The standard error of measurement is approximately 2 for the academic tests and 1 for the composite score.

The Preliminary ACT battery, the P-ACT+ (now PLAN), has been developed for 10th grade students (American College Testing Program, 1989b). It consists of (a) four academic tests of 20 to 45 minutes each, yielding ACT standard scores of 1 to 32; (b) a brief interest inventory; (c) a study skills assessment inventory; and (d) a student information section.

Validity of Scholastic Aptitude Tests

The ACT and the SAT are approximately equal in their ability to predict college grades. Thousands of studies have been conducted assessing the ability of these tests to predict grades, with the typical correlation ranging in the vicinity of .30 to .50 for freshmen grade point averages (GPAs). Correlations tend to be higher at institutions with more heterogeneous freshmen classes and lower among homogeneous student bodies, particularly at the very highly selective institutions with restricted ranges of student scores.

Most studies have found that high school grades are the best predictors of college GPAs but that scholastic aptitude tests are able to improve the prediction over high school GPAs or high school ranks alone. That scholastic aptitude test scores would add to the prediction of college success is not surprising. The particular high school GPA that a student obtains is dependent upon a number of factors—the general competitiveness of the high school attended, the grading curve used in that high school, the types of courses taken, and other personal factors. Thus a 3.2 high school GPA achieved by a particular student who has taken all college preparatory subjects in a school with a low grading curve and where the majority of classmates are college-bound represents a very different level of achievement than that obtained by a student from a less competitive high school who has taken a number of vocational or commercial courses. A national college admissions test represents a common task for all students and therefore can operate as a correction factor for the high school GPA. In addition, for the student with low grades but with substantially higher scholastic aptitude test scores than what would be expected from those grades, the scores may suggest hitherto unrecognized academic potential. These scores may represent a "second chance" for such a student.

Test scores tend to be greatly overemphasized by many parents and college-bound students. It is only at the most highly selective institutions that very high scores are generally required for admission. Students with good high school grades can obtain admission to most colleges unless their test scores are extremely low.

When scholastic aptitude test scores are interpreted to students and their parents, the standard error should be taken into account. On the SAT-V and SAT-M, the standard error is in the vicinity of 30 or 35, suggesting that two thirds of the time the student's true score will fall within 30 to 35 points in one direction or the other from the obtained score. For the ACT, with a standard error of approximately 2 points, two thirds of the time students' true scores could be expected to fall within 2 points on either side of their obtained ACT standard scores.

Although the number of colleges and universities in this country that require very high ACT or SAT scores is not large, with the exception of certain public colleges and universities located in a few states, almost all 4-year institutions claim to maintain some type of selective admissions policy. This selectivity varies greatly. Some public institutions will take any student in the top half of his or her high school class or one who obtains a test score at least equivalent to that level. Others take only those in the top quarter, or in the top three quarters, or have other means of selection using formulae with high school rank or high school grades and SAT scores. A few private institutions admit perhaps only one in five applicants from an already very selective applicant pool. There are many other private colleges that, although maintaining that they are selective in their admissions, in fact will admit almost every high school graduate who applies. The result is a great variation in the abilities of the average or typical student on various campuses.

It is definitely not true in this country that a particular GPA earned at one institution is equivalent to that of another and that college degrees are equivalent from wherever they are obtained (Hood, 1968). Although some differences in levels of competition among colleges are recognized to some extent by the general public, and perhaps to a greater degree by those in higher education, the actual differences are far greater than all but the most sophisticated observers of American higher education imagine. Levels of competition vary so greatly among institutions that a student obtaining an honors grade point average of 3.4 at one institution could easily fail out of a much more competitive institution.

These differences can be understood by examining the scholastic aptitude scores in various institutions. Scholastic aptitude test scores of entering freshmen at particular institutions of several different types are shown in Table 6-1. This table includes ACT-English and SAT-I Verbal scores as rough equivalents. It should be recognized that the equivalence between these two tests shown in this table were based on a large and relatively heterogeneous population, but at a single institution. Populations at particular institutions of varying ability levels and with differing proportions of the two sexes may result in concordance tables that differ substantially from this one. The equivalent scores given in this table should be read as only rough equivalents and not as exact mathematical equivalents. The scores given for the different types of institutions represent a specific institution and are provided here as general examples; they do not represent the typical or median institution of that type.

By comparing scores in this table it can be seen that, for example, the median student at the Ivy League institution falls above the 90th percentile for students at the midwestern state university. At the same time, the median student at the midwestern university falls in the lower 5% for students at the Ivy League institution. Students at the midwestern university actually tend to score well above college-bound students nationally—the median student at the midwestern university falls at about the 75th percentile of the national college-bound population. The median student at the private liberal arts college included in Table 6-1 is practically never found in an Ivy League school and falls in the bottom quarter among students at the midwestern state university. The median student at the southern state college (an accredited institution) is found only in the lower 1–2% of students at the midwestern state university, and very few students at this private liberal arts college score that low. The highest scoring student at the southern state college does not reach the mean at the midwestern state university, and only a handful of students at the Ivy League university obtain scores as low as the highest student at the southern state college. Thus, between the southern state college and the Ivy League institution, there is virtually no overlap among the scores of their students.

In assisting college-bound students in their decision making about institutions, these types of differences should be considered. Information regarding the levels of academic competition at particular insti-

TABLE 6-1. Percentiles of Students with Certain Academic Aptitude Test Scores (Verbal) in Different Types of Institutions

Enhanced ACT English Standard Score	SAT-1 Verbal Standard Score	ACT National Norms English 1993–1994 Percentile	Ivy League University (SAT-I-V) Percentile	A Midwest State University (ACT-E) Percentile	A Small Liberal Arts College (ACT-E) Percentile	A Southern State College (SAT-I-V) Percentile
33	730	—	95	—	—	—
32	700	99	80	99	—	—
30	660	98	60	94	98	—
29	640	96	45	90	95	—
27	600	90	23	74	89	—
24	540	74	3	44	71	99
20	460	47	1	14	34	91
18	420	32	—	8	19	76
12	290	4	—	1	2	44
6	270	1	—	—	—	11
1	230	—	—	—	—	2

Note. Institutions shown were selected to show the great variation among them and are not meant to be representative of those types.

tutions can be found in certain college guides such as *The Comparative Guide to American Colleges* (Cass & Birnbaum, 1995), *Profiles of American Colleges* (Barrons Educational Series, 1995), and *The College Handbook* (College Entrance Examination Board, 1995). Anyone involved in college counseling should obtain a guide that contains information regarding high school ranks and test scores of students at different institutions. Armed with the knowledge that the standard deviation on an academic aptitude test at a given institution is likely to be in the vicinity of two thirds or three quarters that of the normative standard deviation of the instrument (4 or 5 points on the ACT or 60 to 75 points on the SAT), and with the mean score or the range of the middle 50% given in one of the college guides, a counselor can easily calculate a rough estimate of the point at which the student is likely to fall in regard to academic aptitude at that institution.

Combining this with a knowledge of the student's achievement level in high school, the general level of competition that a student will find at a given institution can be estimated. Combined with other information about the student, his or her chances of obtaining admission at that institution can also be estimated. A student might therefore be encouraged to apply to several different institutions, including one or two where chances for admission and satisfactory performance are very favorable.

The level of competition a student is likely to meet if admitted should also be discussed. Although there are many, including parents, who feel that a student should attend the highest status institution to which he or she can be admitted, some evidence suggests that for many students this is not the wisest move. A study conducted a number of years ago (Werts & Watley, 1969) indicated that, holding ability constant, those students who attended an institution at which they fell in the bottom portion of the students at that institution were less likely to go on and attend graduate or professional school than those students who had attended an institution at which they were closer to or above the middle of the distribution.

When students transfer from college to college, much of the difference in the GPAs obtained at the new institutions can be accounted for by differing levels of competition. Students transferring from community colleges to more competitive 4-year institutions often experience a drop in grades known as "transfer shock." Students transferring from more competitive institutions to less competitive ones will, on the average, see their GPAs increase.

CASE EXAMPLE

Jason is just beginning his senior year in high school, and he and his parents are having a conference with his guidance counselor. He has a 2.9 grade point average in the academic program in his high school and received scores ranging from 18 to 22 for a composite score of 20 on the ACT battery that he took the previous spring. His parents want to talk about colleges and universities that he should investigate and his chances of being admitted to them. Included in their consideration is an Ivy League institution that their nephew attends.

The counselor reports to them that his score on the ACT is about an average score for college-bound students in this country. When he takes the SAT a few weeks hence, if he obtains comparable scores, they are likely to be in the 400s. She suggests that unless he were class valedictorian or a star athlete (which he is not) he has little chance of being admitted to a highly competitive institution. She tells them that because the state university admits any high school graduate who is in the top two fifths of his or her graduating class, and because he is at the 65th percentile, he would be admitted to the state university. He would, however, rank toward the bottom at that institution, both in terms of high school record and test scores, and could find it difficult to achieve more than barely passing grades.

Because he is undecided as to a career or a major, he is planning to enter a general liberal arts program and therefore has a wide range of institutions to choose from. At some 4-year institutions, he would fall well above the mean and at others, well below the mean. At the particular small college he is considering, he would be below the middle but still above the bottom third. His chances of success there would be better than at a number of other institutions that he and his parents have considered.

GRADUATE AND PROFESSIONAL SCHOOL ADMISSIONS TESTS

Graduate Record Examinations (GRE)

The GREs are administered by the Educational Testing Service of Princeton, New Jersey. They consist of two separate types. The GRE Aptitude Test consists of three portions, Verbal (GRE-V), Quantitative (GRE-Q), and Analytical (GRE-A; Educational Testing Service, 1994).

The Verbal portion of the Aptitude Test includes analogies, antonyms, sentence completion, and reading comprehension items. The Quantitative portion requires mathematical reasoning and an interpretation of graphs and diagrams, and includes items dealing with arithmetic, algebra, and geometry. The Analytical portion includes analytical reasoning questions and logical reasoning questions designed to measure the ability to apply abstract reasoning to a set of given conditions or facts. The GRE Subject Tests are available in 20 different academic areas, such as physics, psychology, and Spanish.

Scores on each of the three portions of the aptitude test are reported in standard scores, with a mean of 500 and standard deviation of 100. The scores were standardized on a group of college seniors who took the test in 1952, and scores are equated to this reference group so that scores remain constant over time. More recent means for students taking the test were in the vicinity of 480 on the verbal and 520 on the quantitative portions. The GRE Aptitude Tests show high internal consistency reliabilities (.90 or above).

An innovation in national testing programs has been the development of the computer adaptive form of the GRE Aptitude. Administrations are scheduled on an individual basis at any of a large number of testing sites across the country, eliminating the requirement that the test be taken on one of only a few national testing dates. Initially an examinee is presented with questions of average difficulty, after which the computer selects questions based on the difficulty level of the questions answered correctly and incorrectly. Scores on the three portions are based both on the number of questions correctly answered and the difficulty level of these questions and are available immediately after the test has been completed. Over a period of several years it is expected that the computer delivered test will replace the traditional paper-and-pencil version and that the national testing dates will be eliminated.

The GRE Subject (Advanced) Tests are required less often by graduate institutions or by graduate departments than is the Aptitude Test. They are each 2 hours and 50 minutes in length and have been developed by committees of faculty members in the appropriate academic departments working with the Educational Testing Service staff. The results are also reported on a standard scale resembling that of the Aptitude Test with a mean of 500; however, the actual mean, range, and standard deviation of scores are different for each of the advanced

105

tests. Certain of the advanced tests provide subscores for specific subject matter areas within the larger test, for example, a subscore on European history and one on American history within the history examination.

The GRE is used in selecting students for admission into graduate school and into specific graduate departments. Norms on the tests therefore vary greatly among institutions and among specific departments. A physics department could require substantially higher scores on the Quantitative section than on the Verbal section, whereas requirements by an English department would be the opposite. An art department might pay little attention to either. Because of these differences, use of GRE test scores to assist students in selecting institutions and departments in which they are likely to be admitted and are likely to be successful is difficult without knowledge of the norms in specific graduate institutions and departments.

Using GRE scores to predict success in graduate school is particularly difficult for a number of reasons. There is likely to be the problem of restriction in range within particular departments, because GREs and undergraduate GPAs are the major criteria on which students are selected for graduate programs, thus eliminating low scores. In addition, graduate school GPAs may be highly restricted in range because grades of A and B are often the only grades given. For a typical department, however, GRE scores plus undergraduate GPAs still provide a better prediction of academic success than any other readily available variables (Jaeger, 1985).

The Miller Analogies Test (MAT)

The Miller Analogies Test, published by the Psychological Corporation (1987a, 1994), is a second test often used for the selection of graduate students. The test consists of 100 complex analogy items drawn from the subject matter across a number of academic fields. Although the test is administered with a 50-minute time limit, it is largely a power test. It includes items of considerable difficulty so that resulting scores are purported to differentiate reliably among persons of superior intellect. It is available in a number of parallel forms, with reliabilities in the general magnitude of .90. Familiarity with the kinds of items on this type of test can significantly affect scores, with substantial improvement resulting from studying practice items or in a second attempt on an alternate form. As with the GRE, norms among graduate students in different institutions and different departments vary widely, and knowledge of normative data in relevant comparison groups is a necessity if predictive information based on the scores is to have any value. The problems of predictive validity of graduate school success discussed for the GRE are also present for the MAT.

Professional School Tests

A number of aptitude tests have been developed by different professions for selection into their professional schools. In many cases these tests are universally required for admission to such schools. Such tests include the Medical College Admissions Test (MCAT; Association of American Medical Colleges, 1994), the Dental Admission Test (DAT; Division of Educational Measurements, 1994), the Law School Admission Test (LSAT; Law School Admission Council, 1995), and the Graduate Management Admission Test (GMAT; Educational Testing Service, 1995). These aptitude tests are typically developed and administered by one of the national testing programs such as the ACT or the Educational Testing Service (ETS).

These tests usually include items similar to those found on scholastic aptitude tests, including measures of verbal and numerical ability. In addition they usually obtain subtests with items relevant to the particular profession. The LSAT includes sections that attempt to assess competence in analytical and logical reasoning. The GMAT includes a quantitative and an analytical writing section; the DAT, perceptual ability scores; and the MCAT includes scores in such areas as the physical and biological sciences as well as a writing sample. Scores on each of the tests are reported in very different types of standard scores with different means and standard deviations. For example, the MCAT yields standard scores ranging from 1 to 15 with a mean of approximately 8 and a standard deviation of approximately 2.5. The LSAT now reports scores ranging from 120 to 180 with a mean of approximately 150 and a standard deviation of approximately 10. For the DAT, scores range from 1 to 30 with a mean of 15 and standard deviation of 5. The GMAT, used by most graduate schools of business, reports subtest scores ranging from 0 to 60 with a mean of 30 and total scores similar to those of the GRE with a range of 200 to 800 and a mean of 500.

ADMINISTERING AND INTERPRETING ACADEMIC APTITUDE TESTS

Test Anxiety

In administering aptitude and achievement tests, it is generally considered a good procedure to attempt, while building rapport, to reduce test anxiety. Small but significant negative relationships have been found between test anxiety and scores on these types of tests. This relationship, of course, does not necessarily mean that high levels of anxiety cause lower test scores. Often those who have done poorly on these types of tests in the past are likely to experience more anxiety. Some studies suggest that a moderate amount of test anxiety can actually benefit test scores, whereas a high level of anxiety may be detrimental.

These results have been obtained when tests have been given under experimental conditions of high tension and relaxed situations. For example, in one study (French, 1962) students took the test under normal conditions when the scores were to be reported to the institutions to which they applied, and a second time on an equivalent form under instructions that the test results were to be used only for research purposes and not otherwise reported. The results showed essentially equal performance under both the anxious and relaxed conditions. The only difference was that certain students under the anxiety conditions attempted more of the mathematical items and therefore achieved slightly higher scores on that subtest than they did under the relaxed conditions. Apparently under the relaxed conditions they gave up a little earlier and therefore achieved slightly lower scores. In general, testing procedures that are well organized, smoothly run, and that reassure and encourage should help to reduce the anxiety felt by highly anxious test takers.

Coaching

The effect of coaching or practice on test scores is a controversial one that has received much attention and has been the subject of a number of studies. Obviously practice or coaching that provides the answers to, for example, an individual IQ test such as the Stanford-Binet or WISC would invalidate the results as an accurate assessment. On the other hand, completion of a high school course in mathematics that results in a higher score on a mathematics achievement test probably accurately reflects the student's knowledge of mathematics outside of the testing situation. The distinction therefore must be made between broad training and specific training or coaching focused on specific test items.

Coaching has been particularly controversial because of the existence of commercial coaching programs designed to raise scores on admissions tests such as the SAT, the GRE, or the MCAT. These coaching programs advertise and almost promise substantially better test performance for those who enroll in their programs. Many of the studies reported have substantial weaknesses that usually include the absence of a noncoached but equally highly motivated control group that is comparable to the coached group in all important ways, including performance on initial tests.

The College Entrance Examination Board (CEEB) has been particularly concerned for two reasons. First, if coaching could help students to improve their scores substantially, then the test results for all students would lose some validity. Second, the commercial coaching programs charge substantial fees and can represent a waste of money if coaching yields little improvement. In a number of CEEB's studies investigating different types of coaching methods among different types of students, well-controlled studies indicate that coaching is unlikely to produce substantial gains on the SAT (Messick, 1981). An ACT study showed that students' scores tend to increase on a second testing, most of which can be accounted for by the general development that has occurred as students take additional high school courses (Lanier, 1994).

A small amount of increase is perhaps due to a practice effect—familiarity with the types of problems and the problem-solving skills required. As a result, most of the testing programs—the College Board, the American College Testing Program, and the various professional school testing programs—now provide considerable information about the tests, including booklets with a number of practice test items. Thus all applicants have the opportunity to take practice tests and to become familiar with the types of items that appear. In addition to those provided by the testing programs, a number of test familiarization books have been published, with practice examinations in all of these areas. Usually entitled "How to take the. . . Examination," these books can be found in many bookstores. For certain tests such as the SAT, these materials are not limited to printed booklets but also include a variety of audiovisual and computer software materials.

It should be remembered that although specific coaching provides little improvement in test performance over that achieved by a little familiarization and practice (and this is particularly true on the verbal portions of these tests), additional training in the form of coursework is likely to result in improvement. In addition, a general review of the subject matter covered can substantially increase scores. For example, a student who has not taken any mathematics during the last 2 years in high school can improve scores on the Mathematics portion of the SAT by review of the courses in algebra and geometry that were taken earlier. A college senior who has not taken any mathematics in college since the freshman year can also improve his or her scores on the Quantitative portion of the GRE by a review of the mathematical and algebraic concepts learned in high school and as a college freshman.

Counselors often receive questions from students, parents, and those involved in the selection and interpretation of such scores regarding the efficacy of coaching programs and other review procedures. They need to be cognizant of the various studies of the effects of different types of training and other activities on test performance.

ACADEMIC ACHIEVEMENT TESTS

Hundreds of thousands of achievement tests are administered each year, primarily in educational institutions ranging from kindergarten through graduate and professional schools. Some are administered for licensing and certification in trades and professions, or in medical specialties, or for the selection and promotion of postal workers. Achievement tests differ from aptitude tests in that they attempt to assess learning that takes place under some relatively standardized conditions or as a result of a controlled set of experiences. Whereas achievement tests attempt to measure what has already been learned or knowledge or skills that have been attained, aptitude tests attempt to measure a potential ability, although such ability is usually related to that which has been developed up to the time of testing. Achievement tests are usually evaluated based on content validity criteria— that is, the extent to which the test includes content similar to that which those tested are expected to have experienced. The validity of aptitude tests is usually predictive, based on the extent to which success in whatever it is the aptitude test attempts to measure can be predicted from the test results. Aptitude tests are more typically used for prediction purposes and do not assume previous standardized learning experiences. The distinction between achievement and aptitude tests is not absolute, however. Some aptitude tests are based on some generally standardized prior experience, whereas some achievement tests are designed to measure some generalized educational experiences that are not especially uniform in nature (Anastasi, 1988). For example, the ACT serves as a scholastic aptitude test to predict success in college; however, its items represent subject matter taught in all high school curricula.

Achievement tests vary from the brief achievement test administered by a teacher to evaluate the learning that has taken place during a single lesson to the nationally available achievement test programs produced by the major commercial test publishers. These achievement test batteries are generally designed across a number of grade levels from kindergarten through the 12th grade. The test batteries provide profiles of scores in various academic skill areas. They tend to be based on the "three Rs" in the early grades and to measure information and knowledge in specific academic areas at the secondary school levels. The tests are generally carefully prepared in regard to content, with items written by teachers and consultants and examined by expert reviewers. The items are then subjected to analyses of item difficulty and item discrimination, with attempts made to eliminate gender and ethnic bias.

Representative Tests

Some of the more commonly used national achievement test batteries include (a) the Iowa Tests of Basic Skills/Iowa Tests of Educational Development, (b) the Stanford Achievement Tests, (c) the Metropolitan Achievement Tests, and (d) the California Achievement Tests. Results are usually reported in a full range of derived scores including scale scores, national and local percentile ranks, stanines, grade equivalents, and normal curve equivalents. These four are briefly described as examples of such test batteries.

Iowa Tests of Basic Skills/Iowa Tests of Educational Development. The Iowa Tests of Basic Skills (ITBS) form a battery of achievement tests covering grades kindergarten through nine (Hoover, Hieronymus, Frisbie, & Dunbar, 1993). The tests are designed to measure basic educational skills including vocabulary, reading, language, and mathematics for the early grades with the addition of social studies, science, and information use tests for the upper grades. They were jointly standardized with the Cognitive Abilities Test (IQ).

The Iowa Tests of Educational Development (ITED) are designed for use at the high school level (Feldt, Forsyth, Ansley, & Alnot, 1994). There are seven tests in the battery measuring achievement in the areas mentioned above for the ITBS at levels considered appropriate for high school. Results are reported as derived scores including standard scores (mean of 15, standard deviation of 5) and predicted ranges for both the ACT composite (within 5 points) and SAT-I College Entrance Tests (within 100 points). Results can therefore be used in counseling for making decisions about high school programs and college planning.

The Stanford Achievement Test. The Stanford Achievement Test Series, 9th edition (Stanford 9) is a series of achievement tests from kindergarten through grade 12, with separate tests for each year that do not repeat item content except for grades 11 and 12 (Harcourt Brace, 1996). Each test battery contains a number of different subtests, with the Stanford Early School Achievement Tests (SESAT) available for kindergarten and the first grade and the Tests of Academic Skills (TASK) for grades 9–12. The typical battery is composed of 10 to 12 subtests yielding total scores in six to eight subject areas.

Metropolitan Achievement Tests. The Metropolitan Achievement Tests, 7th edition (MAT7) provide overlapping batteries from kindergarten through grade 12 (Harcourt Brace, 1993). The battery consists of a varying number of subtests in basic skills areas beginning with reading, mathematics, and language to which science and social studies are added in the early primary grades and research skills and thinking skills added in the remaining grades yielding a total of seven achievement areas. Predicted scores for both the P-ACT+ and the PSAT in grades 9 and 10 and ACT and SAT scores for grades 11 and 12 are available.

California Achievement Tests. The California Achievement Tests fifth edition (CAT/5) provide another nationally standardized series of broad spectrum achievement test batteries, with 13 overlapping levels designed for grades kindergarten through 12 (CTB/Macmillan/McGraw, 1992). They exist in three formats: a basic skills battery of five subtests, a complete battery of seven subtests, or a set of brief survey tests.

Reliability and Validity

These achievement tests are highly reliable, with internal consistency reliabilities ranging from .80 to .90 or above for the various individual tests and well above .90 for composite scores based on the complete batteries. The procedures that the authors and publishers of each of the sets of tests have established for ensuring content validity are thorough and detailed. The item pools have been administered to large samples, and sophisticated item analyses to provide internal consistency and to detect gender and cultural biases are used. Although the results of these test batteries are often grossly misinterpreted by users, considerable pains have been taken to provide the results in understandable language and formats.

Most students take standardized achievement tests, which are used for a variety of purposes, at regular intervals during their first 12 years of schooling. They are used in a diagnostic way to identify the strengths and weaknesses of specific skills and achievements in individual students. As a result of such diagnoses, students can be selected for specific types of instruction, either remedial or advanced in nature. For this reason, the tests are often used as a part of the regular guidance and counseling program in an institution. Counselors become involved in interpreting the results to the students themselves, to their parents, and to teachers and other professionals.

Achievement tests are also used (and often misused) in attempts to evaluate the quality of the curricula and instruction within courses, programs, schools, or school systems. The tests can provide information regarding what has been actually taught in a course or curriculum, especially in regard to goals. They can also be used to assess change in performance over time within a school or school district or to compare the achievement of schools in a district or with national norms. Although the public is asking for accountability in education, which usually involves achievement test results, there are many important factors and complex issues, such as the academic backgrounds of the students and the goals of the educational programs, that make such comparisons difficult and often invalid. The complexity of such accountability is often not well understood.

College-Level Achievement Tests

Three testing programs by which individuals may be awarded college credit other than by enrolling in college courses are the College-Level Examination Program (CLEP; College Board, 1992b), the Advanced Placement Program (APP; College Board, 1994d) administered by the CEEB, and the Proficiency Examination Program (PEP; American College Testing Program, 1985) administered by the American College Testing Program. The CLEP contains (a) general examinations that assess college-level achievement in five basic liberal arts areas usually covered during the first 2 undergraduate years, and (b) 30 multiple-choice subject examinations each taking 90 minutes to complete covering a wide range of popular introductory college-level courses. The APP provides materials and examinations for college-level courses to be offered in secondary schools for which high school students may gain college credit or obtain advanced placement in college courses. The examinations, which are 3 hours in length, contain both multiple-choice and either essay or problem items. The APP provides 29 different examinations in 16 different academic fields. The PEP tests are designed to measure subject matter proficiency that has been attained primarily outside of the typical classroom. They cover material usually presented in one- or two-semester courses at the undergraduate level. There are 45 different examinations, many from the fields of business and nursing, with others available in a range of arts and sciences and education subjects. The exams, which range from 3 to 7 hours in length, primarily employ a multiple choice format with some also including essay portions. Most are taken for the purpose of assigning college credit, and some are used for placement at appropriate levels in the curriculum or to waive particular course requirements.

Tests of Adult Basic Education

The Tests of Adult Basic Education 7/8 (TABE 7/8; CTB MacMillan/ McGraw-Hill, 1994) are designed to assess the basic skills that adults need to live and work. They assess basic skills of adults ranging from very limited literacy to high school graduation and include college-level norms. There are five different forms representing difficulty levels ranging from less than a first-grade level to college level. A locator test of 25 vocabulary words and 25 mathematical items yields scores that indicate the appropriate level to use. Although scores are based on adult norms, grade equivalents to California Achievement Test grade levels are reported along with estimated scores on the Tests of General Education Development (GED), which are taken by candidates for high school equivalency diplomas.

STUDY HABITS INVENTORIES

Counselors in high schools and colleges often work with students who are having difficulties with their coursework or are not achieving academically up to their potential. In working with such students, a study habits inventory is often useful; first, to allow students to understand how adequate their study habits are as compared with those of other students; second, as a teaching tool, as the items on such inventories have useful instructional value; and third, to point out particular weaknesses, useful in discussing specific activities for improvement. Several of the achievement test batteries used at the high school level, such as the California or Metropolitan achievement batteries, contain subtests that assess study skills.

The Survey of Study Habits and Attitudes is a 100-item inventory with a high school form and a college-level form (Brown & Holtzman, 1984). It contains four subscales titled Delay Avoidance, Work Methods, Teacher Approval, and Educational Acceptance. The inventory yields scores on each of these scales, along with several additional scores obtained through combinations of these scales. Both internal consistency and test-retest scale reliabilities are reported in the general range of .85–.90. It also includes a counseling key that can be laid over the answer sheet to assist the counselor in focusing on various critical items.

The Study Attitudes and Methods Survey (SAMS; Michael, Michael, & Zimmerman, 1980) yields six scales from 148 items: Academic Interest, Academic Drive, Study Methods, Study Anxiety, Manipulation, and Alienation Toward Authority. The survey takes approximately 30 minutes to complete and both high school and college norms are provided.

The Learning and Study Strategies Inventory (LASSI) contains 10 seven- or eight-item scales, 5 of them assessing personal factors related to academic achievement such as attitude and time management and 5 cognitive factors such as selecting main ideas and self-testing (Weinstein, Palmer, & Schulte, 1987). The inventory is available in both secondary school and college forms, and alpha reliabilities are reported in the .7 to .8 range (Weinstein, 1987).

Through the use of such self-rating inventories counselors can assist students in improving their academic performance by examining their various study attitudes and by assisting them to design more effective study strategies. In addition to their diagnostic purposes, these inventories also act as structured exercises that can help teach good study techniques and point out ineffective attitudes and behaviors.

Knowledge that individuals prefer different types of learning styles and, in fact, often learn more effectively when the instructional technique matches their preferred learning style has lead to the development of inventories designed to assess such individual learning styles. There are four such inventories, all titled "Learning Style Inventory" (LSI; Canfield & Canfield, 1988; Dunn, Dunn, & Price, 1987; Kolb, 1985; Renzulli & Smith, 1978). They are designed to help individuals assess their preferred methods of learning and to identify differences among individual learning styles and corresponding learning environments. This information can then be used to provide more individualized instructional methods. These inventories typically yield scores on three or four dimensions of learning styles or modes, such as need for structure, active experimenting, or abstract conceptualizing. Because there are significant differences in the types of learning styles assessed by these instruments, the particular purpose for which the inventory is to be administered should be evaluated so the inventory that best meets that purpose can be selected.

COGNITIVE DEVELOPMENTAL THEORIES

In addition to the learning of substantive knowledge that takes place in school, college, work, and daily life, other types of cognitive development such as rationality, intellectual tolerance, and intellectual integrity are now beginning to be assessed as well. One of these areas is ethical development as conceptualized by Kohlberg (1969, 1971), building on the structuralist view articulated by Piaget (1965). Kohlberg's theory holds that moral values are first external, then conventional in upholding and maintaining the social order, and at the highest levels maintained through individually held principles. Rest (1974) developed a paper-and-pencil instrument using Kohlberg's hypothetical moral dilemmas called the Defining Issues Test (DIT) to assess this type of cognitive development.

Based in part on the work of both Piaget and Kohlberg, Perry (1970) developed a cognitive developmental scheme of positions of intellectual development that take place during adolescent and adult years. Perry's theory is composed of nine different positions representing a continuum of development that can be clustered into four general categories—dualism, multiplicity, relativism, and commitment in relativism. Assessing cognitive development on Perry's scheme has been difficult, although five different measures have been constructed that attempt to place individuals along these positions. Three of these (Baxter-Margolda & Porterfield, 1988; Kitchener & King, 1981; and Moore, 1988) require free responses that must be classified using trained raters—thus making for high costs in terms of money and convenience. Two inventories that make use of objective-style responses to assess cognitive development are the Scale of Intellectual Development (SID; Erwin, 1983) and the Parker Cognitive Development Inventory (PCDI; Parker & Hood, 1986). Although these inventories are in a form that could be used by counselors, more validity studies and probable revisions need to be undertaken before they will be ready for use by counselors with individual clients.

Stages of cognitive development represent important concepts for counselors to explore, as these stages influence many of the decisions that clients make and the processes by which they arrive at these decisions. These concepts can provide an understanding of why one client seeks only one "right" answer to a problem whereas another is willing to explore a number of alternatives.

SUMMARY

1. Almost all counselors can expect to be consulted about scholastic aptitude tests, even if they work in settings where they seldom make use of them.
2. Test results on the College Board, National Merit, and ACT College Admissions Tests have often been misinterpreted, even by

those with some understanding of their standard score distributions, but recent scoring modifications should make them more easily understood.

3. Scholastic aptitude tests contribute to academic selection and placement by identifying unrecognized academic potential and by acting as a correction factor for high school grades resulting from differing levels of competition.

4. There are great differences in the distribution of students in regard to academic aptitude among the different institutions of higher education in this country. These differences can greatly affect both the chances for admission and the chances for success at specific institutions.

5. Academic aptitude tests required for admission to graduate and professional programs typically have similar verbal and quantitative sections, but otherwise vary considerably in subjects that are assessed and in the types of standard scores with which they report results.

6. Although some practice and familiarity with the types of problems and skills required on academic aptitude tests may make slight improvements in scores, extensive coaching has not been shown to produce substantial gains.

7. Academic achievement tests administered widely in primary and secondary schools can provide diagnostic information regarding the strengths and weaknesses of specific skills and achievements of students. The results are often used and misused in attempts to evaluate the quality of instruction within classes, schools, and school systems.

8. Cognitive developmental theories can provide useful concepts in working with adolescent and postadolescent clients, but instruments to assess these stages need considerable additional refinement to be useful to most counselors.

Career and Life Planning Assessment

7

MEASURES OF CAREER CHOICE AND DEVELOPMENT

A CCORDING TO CAREER DEVELOPMENT THEORY, people pass through a series of stages during the course of their lives (Super, 1957, 1984). Each stage involves a number of developmental tasks that a person must master to be able to move successfully to the next stage. One of the major developmental tasks faced by individuals is choosing a career.

Measures that focus on the *process* of career choice and development are discussed in this chapter. These measures, which enable counselors to assess a clients's progress in regard to career choice and development, encompass both *attitudinal* and *cognitive* factors (Super & Thompson, 1979; Thompson, Lindeman, Super, Jordaan, & Myers, 1981, 1982). Attitudinal factors include both career beliefs and career concerns. Cognitive factors refer to decision-making skills and information about the world of work.

The measures of career choice and development discussed in this chapter are important in evaluating readiness for career planning. Factors that pertain to the *content* of career choice and development, such as work values, career interests, and special abilities, as well as environmental factors, will be considered in subsequent chapters.

ATTITUDES TOWARD CAREER PLANNING

The instruments discussed in this section assess client beliefs or concerns in regard to career planning. Career beliefs refer to the client's assumptions regarding career choice and development, for example, the belief that there is one "right" career choice for each individual or that people will not be able to change their careers as they progress through life. Career concerns include difficulties in decision making and in resolving developmental tasks such as choosing a major or career or making satisfactory progress in one's work.

Measures of Career Beliefs

Career Beliefs Inventory (CBI). The CBI identifies beliefs that may block career goals (Krumboltz, 1991). It contains 96 items answered on a Likert scale (*strongly agree* to *strongly disagree*) that provide the basis for 25 scores on scales such as Openness, Control, and Taking Risks. The beliefs are not considered to be "good" or "bad" by themselves; however, individuals frequently possess assumptions about themselves and their careers that may interfere with their career planning. Low scores indicate career beliefs that may be problematic depending on the individual's situation.

Krumboltz (1994) suggested that the CBI be used early in counseling to expose one's assumptions related to career planning that might not otherwise be addressed. The counselor can then help the client to test the accuracy of these assumptions in his or her particular situation. In a carefully planned research study, Mitchell and Krumboltz (1987) found that focusing on the career beliefs of undecided clients was more effective than teaching decision-making skills in stimulating career exploration and reducing anxiety.

The CBI scales yield modest internal consistency and test-retest reliabilities for different populations because of their brevity (2 to 10 items per scale); however, scale precision should not be considered a prerequisite given the purpose of the instrument (to serve as a stimulus for discussion). Research indicates that the CBI possesses convergent and discriminant validity. Scores on the CBI correlate significantly with measures of career satisfaction in the expected manner, but show little or no relationship with interest and aptitude measures (Krumboltz, 1991; Naylor & Krumboltz, 1994). Information from the CBI supplements the information that can be gained from interest and aptitude measures.

CASE EXAMPLE

The following case is discussed in the CBI manual (Krumboltz, 1991, p. 10): Ted, a college student, disliked his college major (pre-med), but did not believe that he had any other options. Ted obtained a low score on scale 12, Approval of Others, which indicated that approval of his career plans from someone else was very important to him. When the counselor asked him about this, he said that he wanted to please his father, who wanted him to become a physician. The counselor asked him to discuss this matter with his father, which Ted did despite fears that it was a hopeless matter. In so doing, he learned that his father's actual goal was to be supportive, not demanding, at which point Ted felt free to change his major from pre-med to art. Ted's desire to enter art had been blocked by his belief that his father would "simply die" if he did not fulfill the ambitions he had for him, a belief that was at the root of his difficulties. Use of the CBI helped to expose his thinking of this matter, which was then addressed in counseling by encouraging him to gather further evidence to test the accuracy of his thinking.

My Career Thoughts Inventory (MCTI). The MCTI measures dysfunctional thinking in career problem solving and decision making (Sampson, Peterson, Lenz, & Reardon, 1992; Sampson, Peterson, Lenz, Reardon, & Saunders, 1994). It includes 48 items designed to measure dysfunctional thinking in 8 content areas related to career choice and development, such as self-knowledge, occupational knowledge, and communication. Based on factor analysis of the 48 items, three construct scales have been developed: Decision-Making Confusion, Commitment Anxiety, and External Conflict.

Counselors are urged to discuss high scores on the content scales, construct scales, and individual items with clients. Counselors help clients to reframe negative thoughts regarding the career process into positive thoughts that are true for them. For example, clients who

mark *agree* or *strongly agree* to the item "no field of study or occupation interests me," may be encouraged to examine extracurricular
or leisure-time activities to help identify interests. They may also be
encouraged to broaden their life experiences as a means of clarifying
and developing their interests.

Measures of Career Concerns for Students

As suggested by career development theory, the career concerns of
students differ from those of adults. The inventories of career concerns
discussed below focus on the decision-making process of high school
and traditional-age college students.

All three of the measures discussed in this section contain scales
that assess the degree to which clients may be encountering difficulty
in choosing a career. Clients who score high in indecision may be in
the precontemplation or contemplation stage of change (Prochaska et
al., 1992); that is, they may not be prepared or ready to make a career
choice. They may lack the self-confidence, the independence, or the
foresight to make a decision (Savickas, 1990). Instead of administering
interest inventories or ability tests to these individuals to help them
make a decision, the counselor should explore further with them factors that underlie their indecision.

Career Decision Scale (CDS). The CDS was developed by Samuel
Osipow and his colleagues to help identify the antecedents of career
indecision (Osipow, 1987). It includes two scales: a 2-item Certainty
scale and a 16-item Indecision scale. The 16 items on the Indecision
scale represent 16 different reasons for career indecision based on the
authors' interview experiences with clients. For each item, clients indicate on a 4-point scale to what extent the item accurately describes
their situation.

The target population for the CDS includes high school and college
students in the process of deciding on a career. Because of its brevity,
the CDS can be quickly administered (about 10 minutes) and scored
(2 minutes). The manual provides normative data for high school
students, college students, and continuing education students.

For counselor purposes, the items from the CDS can be used to
explore possible causes of a client's indecision. Despite relatively low
test-retest reliabilities, results from individual items can be helpful in

suggesting hypotheses that can be explored in counseling. In general, factor analysis of the CDS indicates that it is primarily measuring (a) feelings of indecision, (b) internal and external barriers, (c) approach-approach conflict, and (d) dependency (Savickas, 1990; Shimizu, Vondracek, Schulenberg, & Hostetler, 1988).

According to Harmon (1994, p. 261) there is "probably no better measure" of career indecision than the CDS for use in counseling, evaluation, and research. Although it has some shortcomings, principally in clarifying the meaning of its scores, it has been praised for its ease of use, its applicability in counseling and research, and its extensive research support (Harmon, 1994; Vondracek, 1991).

My Vocational Situation (MVS). The MVS attempts to identify the nature of problems that may be contributing to career indecision (Holland, Daiger, & Power, 1980). Holland et al. attributed difficulties in decision making to three main factors: (a) problems of vocational identity, (b) lack of information about careers, and (c) environmental or personal obstacles. The MVS includes scales to measure client concerns in each of these areas. It also provides diagnostic information regarding career planning problems that should be helpful in selecting the most appropriate type of treatment for the client.

The first scale on the MVS, the Vocational Identity (VI) scale, contains 18 items (e.g., "I need reassurance that I have made the right choice of occupation") that must be answered *true* or *false*. True responses suggest problems with one's vocational identity. Normative data indicate that high school students mark about 7 true answers on the average while college students usually mark about 2 or 3 true responses. Individuals with a large number of true responses compared with people of their age may profit from career workshops, personal counseling, or additional work experiences.

The two remaining scales, Occupational Information (OI) and Barriers (B), each consist of one question with four parts. The OI scale provides data concerning the client's need for occupational information (e.g., how to obtain training or find a job in one's chosen career) while the B scale points out barriers (e.g., lack of needed abilities or family support) that may be impeding career development. These scales can be used as checklists to suggest specific steps that counselors can take to assist their clients in the career planning process.

When used as a checklist, the MVS can be completed by clients in the waiting room before the first counseling interview, in the same manner as other problem checklists described in Chapter 4. Counselors can quickly identify clients with vocational identity problems by counting the number of true responses to the first 18 items. They can also determine specific needs of clients by simply noting those items with yes responses on the OI or B scales. Items with such responses can be pursued in individual counseling to determine their significance for the client.

Assessment of Career Decision Making (ACDM). The ACDM is based on Vincent Harren's model of career decision making (Harren, 1979). In its current version (Form F), it contains 94 items scored on nine scales (Buck & Daniels, 1985). Three of the scales assess decision-making styles; the remaining six scales evaluate progress in resolving developmental tasks common to young people.

The Decision-Making Styles (DMS) scales measure the extent to which clients employ rational, intuitive, or dependent styles in making career decisions. People vary in their decision-making styles (Harren, 1979; Heppner & Krauskopf, 1987). Rational types emphasize logic in systematically collecting and weighing data to arrive at a decision. Intuitive types place greater importance on feelings in deciding among alternatives; they may collect data to confirm a choice they have already made. Dependent types rely primarily upon the opinions of others in arriving at their decisions. Both the rational and intuitive approaches possess merit as a means of obtaining data and resolving problems.

The Decision-Making Tasks (DMT) scales assess three developmental tasks faced by most young people: adjusting to school, choosing a major, and choosing a career. Adjusting to school is measured by one broad scale, School Adjustment, and three subscales, Satisfaction With School, Involvement With Peers, and Interaction With Instructors. The last two DMT scales, Major and Occupation, measure career development on a continuum ranging from the exploration stage of development to the commitment stage.

The ACDM can be used with either high school or college students. If it is used with high school students who do not plan to attend college, the 20 items pertaining to the Major scale should be omitted. The ACDM must be computer scored. Counselors receive an informative computer-based test interpretation; however, they do not have firsthand access to normative tables or scoring procedures.

Coefficients of internal consistency ranged from .49 (Intuitive scale) to .86 (Occupation and Major scales) with a median value of .72 for a sample of 264 high school students. Besides the Intuitive scale, the three School Adjustment subscales also had alpha reliabilities less than .70. These figures indicate that the content of these four scales is rather heterogeneous and may be somewhat difficult to interpret (Johnson, 1987).

Factor analytic studies support the arrangement of the profile in three groups of scores. Three factors (decision-making style, school adjustment, and career decision-making progress) that closely resemble the three parts of the ACDM consistently emerge from factor analytic studies.

The ACDM contributes most to the counseling process with its Decision-Making Styles scales (Prediger, 1988). These scales provide the most new information. Information obtained from the other scales can be helpful in counseling, particularly to the counselor in understanding the client; however, clients are more likely to be aware of the nature of their scores in these areas.

Measures of Career Concerns for Adults

Two measures have recently been developed to assess career issues of adults in the working world. The Adult Career Concerns Inventory measures concerns associated with the different developmental stages of adults, whereas the Career Attitudes and Strategies Inventory provides a broad measure of concerns that cuts across developmental stages.

Adult Career Concerns Inventory (ACCI). The ACCI measures the career concerns of adults at different stages in their development (Super, Thompson, & Lindeman, 1988). It contains 61 items that are scored in terms of four developmental stages (Exploration, Establishment, Maintenance, and Disengagement) and 12 substages. Clients rate each item (e.g., "settling down in a job I can stay with") on a 5-step scale ranging from *no concern* to *great concern* based on their present situation. Most clients complete the ACCI, which requires an eighth-grade reading ability, within 15 to 30 minutes. Answers can be hand scored or computer scored.

The manual reports preliminary norms for each sex and for different age groups (Super et al., 1988). Besides making normative (interindividual) comparisons, the test authors also stress the importance of ipsative (intraindividual) comparisons. Ipsative comparisons enable the counselor and the client to identify the predominant developmental tasks facing the person.

The test scores show a high degree of internal consistency. Factor analytic studies support the construct validity of the ACCI. Such studies have identified factors similar to the four developmental stages that provide the framework for the ACCI (Smart & Peterson, 1994).

The ACCI helps to clarify the nature of the developmental tasks of greatest concern to the client at the current time. It is important to note that adults who are in the process of career change can be expected to recycle through some of the early developmental stages. Instead of setting career maturity as a goal, a concept that does not fit adults who may have already successfully pursued a career or alternative activity, the authors of the ACCI use *career adaptability* as the criterion of effective career planning.

Career Attitudes and Strategies Inventory (CASI). The CASI was developed to identify and clarify career problems confronted by adults (Holland & Gottfredson, 1994a). It consists of 130 items that survey these aspects of career or work adaptation: Job Satisfaction, Work Involvement, Skill Development Dominant Style, Career Worries, Interpersonal Abuse, Family Commitment, Risk-Taking Style, and Geographical Barriers. The instrument has been designed to be self-administering and self-scoring; however, counselors are usually needed to help interpret the results.

The items for each scale are grouped together in the CASI booklet to facilitate scale interpretation. For example, clients who mark *true* or *mostly true* to items such as "family responsibilities limit my career responsibilities," "I short-change my family or partner by working too much," and "I have changed my work schedule to better meet my family responsibilities," will obtain high scores on the Family Commitment scale. As indicated by the item content, high scores on this scale indicate the realities and some of the difficulties of dual role responsibilities.

Two large samples of adults who completed the CASI obtained moderately high coefficients of internal consistency (mostly in the .80s). Scores on the scales are correlated with other measures of career concerns according to expectations (Holland & Gottfredson, 1994b).

CAREER PLANNING COMPETENCIES

Although a number of standardized inventories focus on the cognitive aspects of career development, few merit endorsement for counseling use at this time. The Career Skills Assessment Program (CSAP), which was constructed by the College Entrance Examination Board (CEEB) for use in career education classes at both the high school and college level, shows the most promise (CEEB, 1978).

The CSAP includes six units that represent the major topics taught in career education classes. The units can be used as a package or independently of each other. Each unit was designed so that it could be administered in one class hour, although the tests themselves are untimed.

Besides a total score, each unit provides scores for a number of specific skill areas as indicated below:

1. Self-Evaluation and Developmental Skills: 60 items, 5 scores
2. Career Awareness Skills: 60 items, 4 scores
3. Career Decision-Making Skills: 60 items, 7 scores
4. Employment-Seeking Skills: 70 items, 5 scores
5. Work Effectiveness Skills: 60 items, 7 scores
6. Personal Economics Skills: 60 items, 7 scores

Altogether, the CSAP contains 370 items in its six units to measure a total of 259 specific educational objectives.

Most of the units require a 9th-grade reading level. The Personal Economic Skills unit requires an 11th-grade reading level, and the Career Awareness Skills unit demands a reading ability at the college level. Reading ability of the students must be taken into account when administering the CSAP. Although the tests are untimed, approximately 10% to 20% of the students fail to finish the items for each unit. Students with low reading levels will encounter difficulties understanding some of the items.

All six exams can be easily scored by the examinees themselves. In this manner, students receive immediate feedback concerning their performance in the different units. Accompanying materials explain the reasons for the preferred answer. In essence, the students are taught the test. The CSAP serves as a combined assessment and instructional program; however, counselors or educators must assist students in their use of the materials. Students may become bored or overwhelmed with the materials if left to their own initiative.

The total scores for each unit show high levels of internal consistency. The CSAB has been validated primarily in terms of its content validity. Items were written to match specifications prepared by experts from the field of career education. All items reflect material taught in various career education courses.

Performance on the CSAP units correlates highly ($r = .65$ to $.70$) with verbal ability (CEEB, 1978). For this reason, the CSAP may be less appropriate for students who lack verbal skills. Job samples may work better for such students as a means of evaluating their career skills and motivating them to improve their knowledge in this area (Wiggins, 1985).

For most students, the CSAP should serve well as a measure of achievement in the different domains of career education. It identifies areas of weakness and provides educational materials to deal with these weaknesses.

MEASURES OF CAREER MATURITY

Measures of career maturity provide a broad assessment of career development. They include indices of both career planning attitudes and career planning competencies. In general, the construct of career maturity appears to be valid across different cultures; however, the pace of career development may vary according to the culture (Fouad & Arbona, 1994). Several career maturity instruments are discussed below.

Career Development Inventory (CDI)

Donald Super and his associates began work on the CDI more than 20 years ago (Myers et al., 1972). They designed the CDI "to assess students' readiness to make sound educational and vocational choices" (Thompson, Lindeman, Super, Jordaan, & Myers, 1981, p. 7). The present version of the CDI includes two forms. The School Form (grades 8 through 12) was published in 1979; the College and University Form was published 2 years later in 1981.

Part I of the CDI, which includes 80 items, provides two scales each for Career Development Attitudes (CDA) and Career Development Knowledge and Skills (CDK). Career Planning (CP) plus Career Exploration (CE) both indicate attitudes toward career development. Decision Making (DM) plus World-of-Work Information (WW) both reveal knowledge and skills related to career development. A Career Orientation Total (COT) score, the best single measure of career maturity from the CDI, combines the scores of all four subscales.

Part II of the CDI evaluates the client's knowledge of the occupational field to which he or she is most attracted. The Knowledge of Preferred Occupational Group (PO) scale uses the same 40 multiple-choice items for each occupational group. The correct response for each item (e.g., employment opportunities or educational requirements) varies depending upon the occupational field. Part II differs from Part I because of its emphasis on occupational knowledge that pertains to a particular occupational field instead of occupations in general. This part of the CDI should not be administered to students below the 11th grade under ordinary circumstances.

The answer sheets must be machine scored by the publisher. For each form, results are reported as standard scores with a mean of 100 and a standard deviation of 20. The manuals provide separate percentile tables by sex and year in school for both forms (Thompson et al., 1981, 1982). Although the normative samples are diverse in their makeup, the authors acknowledge that they do not represent a cross-section of high school or college students in the United States. No norms are provided for minority students. The test authors encourage test users to build local norms, which the publisher will provide when the number of students completing the CDI exceeds 100.

The reliabilities for the combined scales (CDA, CDK, and COT) are adequate; however, the reliabilities for some of the individual scales are surprisingly low (Locke, 1988). The test-retest reliability coefficients were particularly low for the PO, WW, and DM scales for high school students tested over 2- and 3-week intervals. The standard errors of measurement for these scales equal 14 to 16 points (approximately three fourths of a standard deviation).

The CDI can claim content validity by virtue of the fact that items for each scale were selected by expert judges to be representative of the different dimensions of Super's model of career development. It also possesses construct validity in that the scores for most of the scales increase for each age group in the manner suggested by Super's model (Thompson et al., 1981).

As noted by its authors, the CDI should be helpful in counseling individuals, in planning guidance programs, and in evaluating programs and research. Locke (1988, p. 179) concluded that the CDI "should yield data decidedly useful to high school and college students who desire diagnostic or survey information relating to future educational plans."

CASE EXAMPLE

The user's manual presents the case of MJ, a 10th-grade female student, to illustrate the interpretation of a CDI profile (see Figure 7-1). The test authors make the following comments about her profile (Thompson et al., 1981, p. 9): MJ's score on CP is consistent with her score on PO, but inconsistent with her scores on CE, DM, and WW. MJ reports that she has engaged in appropriate career-planning activities and feels knowledgeable about occupations. She has in fact acquired accurate information about her preferred occupational group.

However, her scores show that she does not know as much about the world of work or occupations in general as she reports, that she has engaged in only an average amount of career exploration, and that she apparently knows very little about what to consider in making vocational choices. Although MJ's profile appears at first sight to be encouraging, careful examination raises important questions, the importance of which is confirmed by her slightly below-average COT score. Her high score on PO may indicate premature specification of an occupation rather than thoughtful selection based on a genuine readiness to choose. Evaluation of her vocational choice in the light of other information (e.g., school record and test scores) may show that her vocational preference is not only premature and poorly grounded but also unrealistic and inappropriate.

In terms of next steps, the authors suggest a planned intervention that focuses on those areas where MJ showed the greatest need for improvement, including decision-making skills, information about the world of work, and perhaps career exploration. Possible interventions include individual counseling, structured learning exercises, or exploratory experiences.

FIGURE 7-1. Career Development Inventory Profile for MJ, a 10th-Grade Girl

Percentile	CP	CE	DM	WW	PO	CDA	CDK	COT

Note. Modified and reproduced by special permission of the publisher, Consulting Psychologists Press, Inc., Palo Alto, CA 94306, from *Career Development Inventory Volume 1: User's Manual* by Albert S. Thompson, Richard H. Lindeman, Donald E. Super, Jean P. Jordan, and Roger A. Myers. © 1981 by Consulting Psychologists' Press. Further reproduction is prohibited without the publisher's consent.

Career Maturity Inventory (CMI)

The CMI is based on John Crites's (1978) model of career development. According to his model, career maturity encompasses a hierarchy of factors. He hypothesized a general factor of career maturity similar to the "g" factor in intelligence testing, several group factors, and a large number of specific factors. The group factors pertain to both the process of career planning (attitudes and competencies) and to the content of career planning (consistency and realism of career choice).

The CMI resembles the CDI in its focus on the career planning process variables. It includes a set of scales for both career planning attitudes and career planning competencies in a manner similar to the CDI. It differs from the CDI in regard to the specific scales that it subsumes under each factor.

The specific scales for both parts of the CMI are as follows: Attitudes Toward Career Decision-Making (75 items)—Decisiveness, Involvement, Independence, Orientation, Compromise, and Total (Screening Form); and Competence in Career Decision Making (100 items)—Self-Appraisal, Occupational Information, Goal Selection, Planning, and Problem Solving.

In contrast with the CDI, the CMI includes only one composite score—the Attitude Total scale. The Attitude Total scale can also be administered separately as a 50-item screening inventory.

The CMI has been standardized on students in grades 6 through 12. Separate-sex norms are provided. Most people complete the CMI within 2 hours. It can be machine-scored or hand-scored.

Crites selected items for the CMI in terms of theoretical specifications and age and grade differentiations. Validity studies show that students in higher grades score higher (albeit modestly) on the scales than do students in lower grades. Scores on the Attitude Scale total correlate significantly with performance and satisfaction in both academic and work settings; however, scores on the Competence Tests lack criterion-related validity (Healy, 1994). According to Healy, the Attitude Scale is well supported for studying career development, screening for career immaturity, and evaluating career education, whereas the Competence Tests should be used only as experimental measures.

Career Mastery Inventory (CMAS)

The Career Mastery Inventory (abbreviated CMAS to differentiate it from the CMI described above) was constructed by John Crites to assess the career development of adults in the same manner that the CMI assesses the career development of adolescents (Crites, 1993). Part 1 of CMAS consists of 90 items on a 7-point Likert scale that assess work attitudes and behavior. Part 2 contains 20 multiple-choice items that measure skill in handling problems in one's work situation.

For Part 1, clients receive a Career Development total score plus scores on six career developmental tasks—Organizational Adaptability ("learning the ropes"), Position Performance, Work Habits and Attitudes, Coworker Relationships ("getting along"), Advancement ("getting ahead"), and Career Choice and Plans ("looking ahead"). For Part 2, they receive a Career Adjustment total score together with scores on three adjustment scales—Integrative (reduces anxiety and solves work problems), Adjustive (reduces anxiety only), and Non-adjustive (neither of the above).

The test booklet, which has been uniquely designed so that duplicate copies are provided by the means of carbon paper, can be both self-scored to provide immediate feedback and machine scored for aggregate data analysis and program evaluation.

The CMAS has been used primarily in business and industrial settings to help design career development programs, to identify common problems among workers within the organizational culture, and to diagnose individual career development task and job adjustment problems. High total scores on the CMAS are correlated with worker satisfaction and job success as measured by performance appraisals and standardized measures (Crites, 1993). Scores on the career development subscales are associated with one's age in the manner predicted by Crites's career development model.

USE OF CAREER DEVELOPMENT MEASURES IN COUNSELING

Several guidelines concerning the use of career development measures in counseling are listed below:

1. Use the various measures of career development to determine readiness for career planning. Estimate the client's stage of development both in terms of attitudes and competencies. Plan counseling activities that can enhance the client's level of development.

2. Use items from the career development measures themselves as a means of teaching clients about the different aspects of career maturity. "Teaching the test" can help clarify the meaning of career development and suggest topics for homework.

3. Assign career development measures to clients to stimulate their thinking about career issues. The measures can help focus the attention of clients on matters related to career planning.

4. Assess the client's decision-making style. Teach the problem-solving model to clients who wish to improve their decision-making ability. Help clients evaluate career myths or distorted beliefs about careers that may be interfering with their career development (Ellis, 1988; Mitchell & Krumboltz, 1987).

5. Distinguish between indecision and indecisiveness. Clients who are indecisive will probably need personal counseling in addition to assistance for career planning. Use individual items from career decision-making scales as a checklist to identify factors contributing to indecision. Explore these factors in counseling with the client.

6. Administer career development measures to classes or groups of students to help determine needs for different types of educational or counseling interventions. For example, information from career development measures could be used in planning activities for career orientation courses or career exploration counseling groups.

7. Ask students or clients to retake career development measures as counseling or education progresses to assess changes in dealing with developmental tasks. Use career development measures as criteria for evaluating the effectiveness of career counseling programs.

SUMMARY

1. Measures of career development process include both attitudinal and cognitive factors. These measures are important for determining the client's readiness for various counseling or educational interventions.
2. It is important for counselors to identify assumptions of clients that may be blocking their career progress. Two new inventories that counselors can use for this purpose are the Career Beliefs Inventory and My Career Thoughts Inventory.
3. Several instruments have been designed to evaluate the progress of high school and college students in making a career decision. The Career Decision Scale can help identify different types of indecision, whereas the My Vocational Situation inventory indicates factors contributing to indecision.
4. The Assessment of Career Decision Making enables counselors to distinguish among different decision-making styles (rational, intuitive, and dependent). Counselors should help clients assess the nature and the effectiveness of their preferred style.
5. The Adult Career Concerns Inventory and the Career Attitudes and Strategies Inventory focus on the career difficulties of adults. These instruments can serve as a springboard for discussing critical issues in counseling sessions.

6. Very few instruments have been developed to provide valid and reliable measures of career planning competencies. The Career Skills Assessment Program shows the most promise for this purpose.
7. The Career Development Inventory and Career Maturity Inventory both provide comprehensive measures of career maturity for high school and college students in terms of attitudes and competencies. The Career Mastery Inventory provides similar information for adults.

8

MEASURES OF WORK AND PERSONAL VALUES

COUNSELORS OFTEN NEED TO HELP CLIENTS to evaluate their motivations in regard to work or other aspects of living. Measures of both values and interests can be helpful for this purpose. Values define what a person thinks is *important*; interests refer to what an individuals *likes* to do. According to Nevill and Super (1986b, p. 3), "values are the objectives sought in behavior, whereas interests are the activities in which the values are sought." Values are more highly correlated than interests with work satisfaction (Rounds, 1990). In contrast, interests are more closely related to academic and career choices (Pryor & Taylor, 1986).

Research indicates that the structure of work values is similar across different cultures (Elizur, Borg, Hunt, & Beck, 1991). Measures of values will be considered in this chapter; measures of interests will be discussed in the next chapter.

VALUES INVENTORIES

Values can be assessed either by a values inventory or a values clarification exercise. Inventories of both work and personal values will be considered in this section.

Inventories of Work Values

The two most popular instruments for assessing work values are the Minnesota Importance Questionnaire and the Work Values Inventory.

Minnesota Importance Questionnaire (MIQ). The MIQ asks individuals to evaluate 20 different work needs or values in terms of their importance in an ideal job (Rounds, Henly, Dawis, Lofquist, & Weiss, 1981). The 20 needs derive from studies of job satisfaction based on the theory of work adjustment developed by Dawis and Lofquist (1984). In the theory of work adjustment, worker satisfaction is predicted by correspondence between worker needs and occupational rewards, assuming that the person has sufficient ability to succeed at the job. The 20 needs have been reduced to six broad factors (called values) by means of factor analysis. Table 8-1 provides a list of the 20 needs, the statement that measures the need, and the six values that summarize the 20 needs.

Two forms of the MIQ exist. One contains 190 pairs of items by which the respondent can compare every need with every other need. The other form is a simplified version, which requires the respondent to rank five different needs arranged in 21 sets. Most people prefer the simplified version, which usually takes about 20 minutes to complete. Computer scoring, available through the publisher, is recommended.

The MIQ measures intraindividual variability, that is, its scores show the range of work needs within the individual. The raw scores are converted to z-scores with a mean of 0 and a standard deviation of 1. The z-scores are adjusted for the client's tendency to make a large number of either positive or negative responses so that the scores can be compared with those of other individuals. By means of the adjustment, all negative scores indicate values that are unimportant to the individual, whereas all positive scores indicate needs that are important to the individual.

TABLE 8-1. Description of Scales and Item Content of the Minnesota Importance Questionnaire

Value (Need Factor)	Need Scale	Need Statement
Achievement	Ability Utilization	I coud do something that makes use of my abilities.
	Achievement	The job could give me a feeling of accomplishment.
Comfort	Activity	I could be busy all the time.
	Independence	I could work alone on the job.
	Variety	I could do something different every day.
	Compensation	My pay would compare well with that of other workers.
	Security	The job would provide steady employment.
	Working Conditions	The job would have good working conditions.
Status	Advancement	The job would provide an opportunity for advancement.
	Recognition	I could get recognition for the work I do.
	Authority	I could tell people what to do.
	Social Status	I could be "somebody" in the community.
Altruism	Coworkers	My coworkers would be easy to make friends with.
	Social Service	I could do things for other people.
	Moral Values	I could do the work without feeling that it is morally wrong.
Safety	Company Policies and Practices	The company would administer its policies fairly.
	Supervision—Human Relations	My boss would back up the workers (with top management).
	Supervision—Technical	My boss would train the workers well.
Autonomy	Creativity	I could try out some of my own ideas.
	Responsibility	I could make decisions on my own.

Note. From *Manual for the Minnesota Importance Questionnaire: A Measure of Vocational Needs and Values* (pp. 3–4, 7) by J. B. Rounds, Jr., G. A. Henly, R. V. Dawis, L. H. Lofquist, and D. J. Weiss. Reproduced by permission of Vocational Psychology Research, University of Minnesota, Copyright 1981.

All profiles are checked for consistency by means of the Logically Consistent Triad (LCT) score. The LCT score shows the percentage of logically consistent answers made by the client. To be logically consistent, one who has chosen item A over item B and item B over item C should rank item A over item C. If the LCT score drops to less than 33% (paired form) or 50% (ranked form), counselors should check to see if the client understood and followed the instructions.

LCT scores are used in setting error bands for each scale score to indicate how much the score might change upon retesting.

The MIQ has a fifth-grade reading level; however, it should not be used with individuals younger than age 16. Needs are not well defined for most people until that age.

Work needs as measured by the MIQ can be compared with the rewards or reinforcements provided by different occupations by means of Occupational Reinforcer Patterns (ORPs). The ORPs indicate to what extent different types of reinforcements can be obtained from a particular occupation (Stewart et al., 1986). An ORP is determined by asking a number of supervisors from an occupation to complete the Minnesota Job Description Questionnaire (MJDQ). The MJDQ lists 20 rewards offered by jobs that match the 20 needs assessed by the MIQ. For example, the work environment for vocational rehabilitation counselors provides the following reinforcements (ranked in order) according to supervisors from that occupation (Stewart et al., 1986):

- Have work in which they do things for other people
- Make use of their individual abilities
- Make decisions on their own
- Plan their work with little supervision
- Get a feeling of accomplishment
- Try out their own ideas
- Have something different to do every day
- Are busy all the time

The ORPs for 185 representative occupations are listed in the *Occupational Reinforcer Patterns Notebook* prepared by Stewart et al. (1986).

The test authors have organized the ORPs into six clusters based on the predominant factor (value) scores. For example, Cluster A includes occupations that score high on Achievement and Autonomy values and moderately high on Altruism. Sample occupations include Architect, Dentist, and School Teacher.

An individual's MIQ scores are correlated with the ORP for each occupation to determine the degree of similarity between the worker's needs and the rewards offered by different occupations. Correlation coefficients (also referred to as Correspondence or C-scores) above .50

indicate similarity of individual and job characteristics. C-scores between .10 and .50 show some similarity. C-scores less than .10 indicate no similarity. According to the test authors (Rounds et al., 1981), if the correlation is .50 or greater between an individual's MIQ score and an ORP, the individual stands at least 7 chances out of 10 of being satisfied in that occupation.

Counselors need to be more concerned about profile reliability for the MIQ than they do scale reliability because of the emphasis on rank order of scores for clients. For most people, the shape of the MIQ profiles will be very similar upon retesting after a few weeks (Hendel & Weiss, 1970).

Research indicates that when individuals work on jobs providing rewards that match their needs as measured by the MIQ, they will be happy. For example, Elizur & Tziner (1977) found that when social workers expressed needs (high social service, responsibility, and variety needs; low compensation, authority, and social status needs) that matched the reinforcements provided by their work, they were more likely to report satisfaction as defined by the Minnesota Satisfaction Questionnaire. Similar results have been reported in other validity studies (Benson, 1988). In general, the MIQ has been favorably reviewed by test critics (Lachar, 1992; Layton, 1992).

CASE EXAMPLE

Kevin, a 29-year-old college graduate in marketing, wished to consider new career possibilities. He had been employed in sales positions since graduating from college 7 years earlier. Kevin sought counseling at a continuing education counseling service at a nearby university. He completed the MIQ during the course of his counseling contacts.

He obtained his highest MIQ scores on the following scales: Ability Utilization = .5, Achievement = 2.7, Responsibility = 2.7, and Autonomy = 2.5. His sales position was not enabling him to express these values as much as he would have liked. He especially felt the need to obtain work in which he could make better use of his abilities and obtain a sense of accomplishment.

His scores on the six value factor scales were highest for Achievement (3.1) and Autonomy (2.4). These values match the reinforcements provided by occupations in Cluster A (Achievement-Autonomy-Altruism) in the MIQ scoring scheme. He expressed an interest in the following types of occupations included in this cluster: social services, health sciences, and recreation. He obtained Correspondence (C) scores of .79 for dentist

143

and .71 for lawyer, both of which he planned to explore in greater detail. The MIQ helped him to identify occupational possibilities that met his work values.

Work Values Inventory (WVI). The WVI was developed by Donald Super (1970) for career development research and counseling. Its 15 scales measure the satisfactions desired from work itself (intrinsic values) or satisfactions sought from work as a means to an end (extrinsic values). The 15 values or goals include altruism, esthetic, creativity, intellectual stimulation, achievement, independence, prestige, management, economic returns, security, surroundings, supervisory relations, associates, way of life, and variety.

Each scale contains three items with five response options ranging from 1 (*unimportant*) to 5 (*very important*). Most people can complete the WVI in 10 to 20 minutes. Hand scoring requires 5 to 10 minutes. The manual provides separate norms for boys and girls for each grade from grade 7 through grade 12, but no norms for college students or adults.

According to factor analytic research conducted by Bolton (1980), the 15 WVI scales can be reduced to six factors that account for most of the variance. Three of these factors measure intrinsic values (Stimulating Work, Interpersonal Satisfaction, and Esthetic Concerns), and two tap extrinsic values (Economic Security and Comfortable Existence). A sixth factor (Responsible Autonomy) reflects both intrinsic and extrinsic values. Five of the six WVI factors resemble the MIQ factors. In addition, the MIQ contains a status factor, which the WVI lacks, whereas the WVI includes an esthetic factor that is missing on the MIQ.

Inventories of Personal Values

The Study of Values has been used frequently for assessing personal values (Zytowski & Warman, 1982); however, it has been some time since this instrument has been revised (Allport, Vernon, & Lindzey, 1960). Two relatively new instruments, the Values Scale and the Salience Inventory, possess promise as measures of personal values.

Study of Values. The Study of Values measures the relative strength of an individual's values in six areas: theoretical, economic, aesthetic, social, political, and religious. The instrument contains 45 items that ask respondents to make choices between or among the various types of values. Emphasis should be placed on intraindividual comparisons when interpreting the test results. Because the reading level is somewhat difficult, the Study of Values is most appropriate for college students or advanced high school students. Scores on the scales significantly differentiate among people in different types of settings (e.g., seminary, medical school, business school) in expected directions; however, most of the differences are relatively small.

Values Scale (VS). Since developing the WVI, Super has collaborated with vocational psychologists from a number of different countries as part of the Work Importance Study to construct both the Values Scale and the Salience Inventory (Nevill & Super, 1986a, 1986b). The VS provides a broader measure of values than the WVI does. It possesses 21 scales which represent all 15 values measured by the WVI plus six additional values: physical activities, physical prowess, risk, advancement, personal development, and cultural identity.

Each VS scale contains five items with four response options ranging from 1 (*of little or no importance*) to 4 (*very important*). All items are prefaced by the phrase, "It is now or will in the future be important for me to. . . ." Sample items include "use all my skills and knowledge," "be physically active in my work," and "know that I can always make a living." For each scale (except Working Conditions), at least two of the five items pertain to nonwork situations, whereas at least two others pertain to work. Most people complete the inventory in 30 to 45 minutes. The VS, which is intended for people age 13 and older, requires an eighth-grade reading level. It can be easily scored by hand within a few minutes.

The norms for the VS have recently been expanded, but the instrument still suffers from low test-retest reliability and lack of validity studies (Slaney & Suddarth, 1994). At this point, the VS should just be used for intraindividual comparisons; that is, to help clients to determine the relative strength of their values when compared with each other. It should be used as an interview aid, not as an established measure of personal values.

Salience Inventory (SI). The SI measures the importance of different life roles for individuals in the context of Super's life-career rainbow

145

model (Nevill & Super, 1986a; Super, 1980). Five life roles are each assessed from three different perspectives. The importance of study, work, home and family, leisure, and community service are evaluated from the standpoint of the individual's participation, commitment, and value expectations. The SI yields 15 scores (five roles × three measures of importance for each role). The instrument, which includes 170 items rated on a 4-point scale, requires about 30 to 45 minutes to complete. It can be hand-scored easily without the use of templates.

The SI provides significant information for counseling. At the present time, the instrument can be used to help clients to assess the relative importance they place on different aspects of their lives. Counselors can use the SI to identify and explore role conflicts within clients or between clients and their environments. The SI can be particularly valuable in aiding clients to take into account cultural differences. Because the SI was developed as part of an international project, it should generate normative data for a wide range of cultures.

The SI and the VS both fall short of acceptable standards for standardized tests in a technical sense, but both instruments can provide valuable assistance to counselors who would like to have a vehicle for discussing values with clients (Hansen, 1994; Slaney & Suddarth, 1994). The structure provided by such instruments should help clients in values clarification and values implementation.

Use of Values Inventories in Counseling

The following points pertain to the use of all values inventories in counseling:

1. Use a measure of values when a client wishes to clarify work or life goals and objectives. Integrate measures of values with measures of interests in attempting to understand client motivation for work or other activities.

2. Use the scales or factors from a values inventory to provide a meaningful structure by which clients can consider their values. A structure of this sort enables the client to describe the nature of values expressed in various activities.

3. Ask clients to estimate their own profile. Ask them to separate those needs that are most important for them from those that are least important. This approach will teach clients to apply a values structure to their own situation.

4. Try to estimate the client's profile. This type of exercise helps the counselor to become more familiar with both the values inventory and the client. The counselor is forced to organize his or her thinking about the client's values in a systematic fashion.

5. Compare the client's and the counselor's estimates with the actual profile from the values inventory. If they do not match, try to determine the reasons for the discrepancies. Clarify the meaning of both estimated and measured values.

6. To what extent do the values scores agree with the client's experiences? Clients should report satisfaction with previous activities that provide rewards that agree with their needs and values.

7. Ask clients to interpret individual items in regard to their situation. What do the items mean to them, particularly those items they may be most concerned about?

8. Look at the relationship between values scores and rewards provided by different occupations or activities. Use the *Occupational Reinforcer Patterns Notebook* to obtain a list of occupations that provide rewards appropriate to clients' values. If an occupation is not listed in this notebook, ask clients to estimate the rewards offered by that occupation based on their best judgment. Clients can gather additional information about an occupation or other activities through reading and informational interviews.

9. Consider work values within a larger context of life values. Help clients to consider a range of values that may be expressed in a variety of roles and situations.

10. Use the results from values inventories to stimulate self-exploration. The results should not be used as a basis for decision making except in conjunction with other data that take into account interests, abilities, previous experiences, and opportunities.

11. Keep in mind that values can change. As values or needs are satisfied, other needs that have not been satisfied become more important. Counselors may need to help clients to review their needs as their situations change.

VALUES CLARIFICATION EXERCISES

Values clarification exercises are strategies that enable clients to identify and to make comparisons among their values. Compared with values inventories, they require clients to engage in self-assessment at a deeper level that takes into account actual behavior as well as preferences. The exercises ask clients to review their beliefs and behaviors in response to different situations. They encourage clients to assume a more active role in exploring and expressing their values. They possess all of the advantages of qualitative assessment procedures noted in Chapter 1. A value is considered to be fully developed when it meets the following seven criteria: It has been (a) chosen freely (b) from among alternatives (c) after careful consideration of the consequences, (d) prized and (e) publicly affirmed, and (f) acted upon repeatedly (Raths, Harmin, & Simon, 1978).

Simon, Howe, and Kirschenbaum (1978) provided 79 strategies to help clients to identify and clarify their values. The first strategy, for example, asks clients to list 20 things they love to do. For each activity, they are then asked to consider when the last time was that they participated in this activity, if it is something that they do with others or alone, how much the activity costs, how important that activity is compared with other activities, how much planning the activity requires, and whether or not this is a new activity for the person within the past 5 years. The exercise requires clients to analyze their activities in terms of the values expressed.

Most career planning workbooks contain several values clarification exercises (e.g., Blocher, 1989; Carney & Wells, 1995; Figler, 1993). The workbooks help clients to integrate information derived from the values clarification exercises with other information about themselves and with occupational information. Typical exercises include the values auction, values card sort, and guided fantasy. Other values clarification assessments include the use of stories in which work values are embedded (Krumboltz, Blando, Kim, & Reikowski, 1994) and the use of the Repertory Grid to help clients create their own values categories for making comparisons among occupations (Zytowski, 1994a).

The Life Values Inventory, a new inventory by Crace and Brown (1992), combines qualitative and quantitative assessment of an individual's values (Brown, 1995). It is particularly helpful for identifying and addressing both intrarole conflicts (when values held by the individual conflict with values espoused in the workplace) and interrole conflicts (when values held by an individual conflict with his or her values expressed in another role). The scales from the inventory provide a structure for analyzing the types of values demonstrated in one's life experiences or career choice. Clients repeat the quantitative section of the inventory after performing the qualitative exercises as a means of reviewing the priority of their values. This same technique can be used with other combinations of values inventories and values clarification exercises.

Kinnier (1995) noted that values clarification exercises have come under attack for the superficial and irrelevant manner in which they have been applied at times. He argued that values clarification can be most meaningful when it is applied to specific values conflicts, such as the relative importance an individual places on family versus career commitment. He described a number of strategies (both rational and intuitive) such as problem solving, cognitive restructuring, life review, incubation ("sleeping on it"), and the "two-chair technique," which can be used for this purpose. He has designed an assessment instrument, the Values Conflict Resolution Assessment (VCRA), that can be used to identify a values conflict, guide its resolution, and evaluate the desirability of the resolution (Kinnier, 1987). Preliminary research indicates that the VCRA produces reliable and valid results.

SUMMARY

1. Values refer to one's objectives or goals in work or other settings. Counselors usually assess client values by means of values inventories or values clarification exercises.
2. The Minnesota Importance Questionnaire is the most thoroughly researched measure of work values. Counselors can compare client values with work rewards by means of the Minnesota Importance Questionnaire and the *Occupational Reinforcer Patterns Notebook*.
3. Two new inventories by Donald Super and his associates extend the measurement of values to nonwork situations. These inventories enable counselors to assess personal as well as work values and to compare the relative importance of different life roles for individuals.
4. Values clarification exercises require clients to identify and to compare their values with their behaviors. As such, they can be particularly valuable in stimulating exploration and development of client values.

9

ASSESSMENT
OF INTERESTS

SINCE 1909, at least, when Frank Parsons published his classic book, *Choosing A Vocation*, counselors have tried to devise ways to assess people's career interests. Interest inventories, which ask clients to report their likes and dislikes for various activities, have proven to be particularly useful for this purpose. Several interest inventories that counselors use frequently are discussed in this chapter, together with guidelines for their selection and interpretation.

TYPES OF INTEREST INVENTORIES

Interest inventories can be classified in a variety of ways—by age level, occupational level, or type of item, for example. In many ways the most useful distinction pertains to type of scale. Two types of interest scales predominate. The first type measures the strength of one's interests in broad fields of activity, such as art, mechanical activities, or sports. These scales are frequently described as *general* or *basic* interests. They are *homogeneous* in nature because they refer to one type of activity. For this reason they are relatively easy to interpret.

In contrast, the second type of scale assesses the similarity of one's interest patterns with those of people in specific occupations. These scales, usually called *occupational* scales, are *heterogeneous* in terms of item content. The scales include a variety of items that distinguish between the interests of people in an occupation and those of people in general. Because of the mixed item content, scores on these scales are more difficult to interpret.

The first type of scale is usually constructed by a rational process. The scales are designed to include items that logically fit together. Examples include Occupational Theme scales and Basic Interest scales on the Strong Interest Inventory. Internal validation procedures such as factor analysis are usually undertaken to ensure that the item content of the scales is relatively pure. Scales of this type usually belong to a closed system of scales; that is, the system includes all the scales that are necessary to represent all the different types of interests (Clark, 1961).

Scales of the second type are based on those items that differentiate between the interests of people in an occupation and people in general. Item selection depends on an empirical process (observed differences between groups), not on theoretical or logical considerations. External validation procedures such as discriminate analysis are frequently employed to determine the effectiveness of the scales in differentiating among the interests of people employed in different occupations. Empirical scales are usually part of an open system; no one set of scales is established to represent the universe of occupational interests. New scales must be constructed as new occupations emerge or as old occupations change.

Both types of scales contribute to the career or life planning process. Because they are easy to interpret, the basic interest scales can be used in a variety of situations in which counseling contact may be limited. The basic interest scales can also be helpful in interpreting the scores on the occupational scales when both types of scores are available. The occupational scales, on the other hand, provide a means of comparing one's interest pattern as a whole with those of people in different occupations. These scales include in a single score the information that is distributed over a number of basic interest scales.

In most cases, counselors should use inventories that provide broad measures of interest with high school age or younger students. Not only are such scales easier to interpret, but they also preclude young students from focusing too early on specific occupations before they have had sufficient opportunity to explore different occupations. Inventories that show scores for specific occupations are most appropriate for college students or other adults.

SELECTION OF INTEREST INVENTORIES FOR COUNSELING

Counselors most often use interest inventories to aid clients with academic or career planning. Interest scores can be used to help clients to explore or discover new academic or career possibilities, to decide among various alternatives, or to confirm a previous choice. Interest scores can also be used for considering ways in which a job might be modified to produce greater job satisfaction or for planning leisure time activities. As indicated by Harmon, Hansen, Borgen, and Hammer (1994), interest scores can also be used as a catalyst for discussions between client and parents or other significant people in the client's life.

The following guidelines should help counselors to decide when to use an interest inventory with a client. First, counselors should keep in mind that interest inventories measure likes and dislikes, not abilities. Most studies show a negligible relationship between inventoried interests and tested abilities (Campbell, 1972). Interest inventories can identify careers or work situations that clients should find satisfying, but they do not indicate how successful the person would be in those settings.

Second, clients should be positively motivated to participate in the assessment process. Clients are more likely to benefit from taking an interest inventory if they express an interest in the results beforehand (Zytowski, 1977). They are also more likely to present an honest picture of their interests or intentions if they clearly understand and accept the purpose of testing (Gellerman, 1963). Large changes in interest scores can occur when clients change the manner in which they approach the test. Sometimes clients answer items in terms of what they think other people (especially parents) would like them to say or they may respond to the items in regard to their abilities or opportunities instead of their interests. Clients may answer the questions hastily or insincerely, especially if they take the inventory as part of a classroom administration. Test scores will be less valid and reliable under such circumstances.

Third, general interest inventories are of limited value for people who must make rather fine distinctions, such as choosing between civil and electrical engineering. Special purpose inventories such as the Purdue Interest Questionnaire for engineering and technical students (LeBold & Shell, 1986) or the Medical Specialty Preference Inventory for medical students (Savickas, Brizzi, Brisbin, & Pethtel, 1988; Zimny & Senturia, 1976) can provide some assistance in such cases. Under any circumstance, interest inventories must be supplemented with other information about the person and his or her situation, including abilities, values, previous work experiences, and job availability, before a decision is made.

Fourth, interest inventories may be inappropriate for people with emotional problems (Brandt & Hood, 1968). Disturbed people make more negative responses and endorse more passive interests than do people who are not disturbed (Drasgow & Carkhuff, 1964). Personal issues can interfere with decision making. Counselors usually must address the emotional difficulties before career planning can take place.

Fifth, scores on interest inventories can show significant changes for clients who are young or after long time periods (Johansson & Campbell, 1971). As a rule of thumb, counselors should consider readministering an interest inventory if it has been longer than 6 months since the client last completed one. Interests are most likely to change for people under age 20 who have experienced large changes in their situation (e.g., new work or school experiences).

Finally, counselors may wish to use an interest card sort instead of an interest inventory if they are interested in the underlying reasons for the client's choices (Slaney, Moran, & Wade, 1994). The card sort functions as a structured interview. As originally designed by Tyler (1961), clients sort cards with occupational titles on them into piles of "would choose," "would not choose," and "no opinion." They then subdivide the three piles into smaller piles based on their reasons for placing the cards into those piles. This technique helps counselors to understand the reasons for a client's choice. The counselor and the client together look for themes in the client's preferences that can guide the career exploration process. Examples of such card sorts include the Missouri Occupational Card Sort, Missouri Occupational Preference Inventory, Nonsexist Vocational Card Set, Occ-U-Sort, and Slaney Vocational Card Sort (Slaney et al., 1994). The Vocational Exploration and Insight Kit, which includes an 84-item card sort together with other career exploration activities, is especially appropriate for highly motivated students who wish to consider their career choices in some depth (Holland, 1992).

POPULAR INTEREST INVENTORIES

Several of the most popular interest inventories used for career or life planning are discussed in this chapter. These measures include the Strong Interest Inventory, Kuder General Interest Survey, Kuder Occupational Interest Survey, Career Assessment Inventory, and Jackson Vocational Interest Survey. Other interest inventories frequently used in counseling will be considered in Chapter 10.

Strong Interest Inventory™ *(Strong)*

The 1994 Strong is the most recent version of a series of interest inventories that began with the publication of the Strong Vocational Interest Blank (SVIB) by E. K. Strong, Jr., in 1927 (Harmon et al., 1994). The Strong replaces the Strong-Campbell Interest Inventory (SCII), a merged version of the male and female forms of the SVIB, created by David Campbell in 1974 and revised with the help of Jo-Ida Hansen in 1981 and 1985.

The new version of the Strong differs from the 1985 version in the following ways: (a) 43 items from the 1985 version were dropped, and 35 new items were added (a few other items were slightly altered); (b) the general reference samples were greatly increased in size from 300 to nearly 10,000 each for men and women; (c) the Basic scales were slightly altered and increased from 23 to 25; (d) new data were collected from 50 occupations including some tested for the first time, such as Audiologist and Technical Writer; and (e) four new Personal Style scales were added to the profile sheet (Harmon et al., 1994). In addition, the publishers plan to expand the Strong in the near future so that it will measure self-rated abilities in the six Occupational Theme areas (Consulting Psychologists Press, 1996).

As indicated in Chapter 1, the Strong has become one of the most frequently used, thoroughly researched, and highly respected psychological measures in existence. The Strong is used more frequently for vocational assessment than any other instrument by counseling psychologists working in a variety of settings (Watkins, Campbell, & Nieberding, 1994).

The Strong produces scores on five sets of scales including the Administrative indexes, General Occupational Theme scales, Basic Interest scales, Occupational scales, and Personal Style scales, each of which is discussed below. Most clients complete the Strong, which consists of 317 items in its current form, in 25 to 35 minutes. The answers must be scored by means of a computer program by Consulting Psychologists Press or one of its agents. The scores are presented on a six-page profile as seen in Figure 9-1.

A Strong profile for Juanita, an 18-year-old female freshman of Hispanic origin, is shown in Figure 9-1. While in high school, Juanita planned a career in medicine. After beginning her freshman year at a large university where she could choose from a wide variety of courses and majors, she became less certain of this choice. She sought counseling for help in exploring her career options. She took the Strong to help identify occupational fields that she might wish to consider in addition to medicine. Juanita's profile will be discussed in the course of considering the different sections of the inventory. Cross-cultural research with the 1994 Strong indicates that the results are valid for members of different minority groups, including Hispanics (Fouad, Harmon, & Hansen, 1994).

Administrative Indexes. The Administrative Indexes (see last page of profile) show the response percentages for each of the eight sections of the inventory. For each of the items in the first five sections (Occupations, School Subjects, Activities, Leisure Activities, and Types of People), clients indicate whether they *like*, are *indifferent* to, or *dislike* that particular item. The sixth section, Preference Between Two Activities, asks clients to choose which of two activities they like better. In the seventh section, Your Characteristics, clients describe aspects of their personality by marking *yes*, *?*, or *no* to various statements

156

(e.g., "Usually start activities of my group"). The last section, "Preference in the World of Work" is a new section on the Strong that asks clients to make comparisons among their preferences for working with ideas, data, people, or things.

Information concerning the distribution of a client's response percentages is helpful in interpreting a client's interest scores. Most clients divide their responses about equally among the three possible answers for those sections of the Strong that use a *like-indifferent-dislike* or *yes-?-no* response format. Juanita's subtotal responses (32% *like* or *yes*, 28% *indifferent* or *?*, and 40% *dislike* or *no*) were typical in this respect.

In addition to response percentages, the Administrative Indexes on the Strong also include Total Responses, which simply shows the number of items that the client answered, and Infrequent Responses, which is used to help determine if the client properly understood and cooperated with the inventory instructions. Juanita's score on Total Responses is 317, which indicates that she answered all 317 items. The profile becomes suspect if this score falls below 300 (Harmon et al., 1994).

A score on the Infrequent Responses scale is of concern only if it falls below zero. This scale consists of item responses infrequently selected (less than 7% of the time) by men or women in the standardization sample. The maximum possible scores on this scale are 7 and 5 for men and women, respectively (Harmon et al., 1994). Infrequent responses by clients are subtracted from the maximum score. Juanita obtained a score of 5 on the Infrequent Response scale—the highest score possible for her sex. This indicates that she made no unusual responses to any of the items and supports the validity of her responses.

General Occupational Theme (GOT) scales and Basic Interest scales. The Strong contains two sets of general or homogeneous scales: the GOT scales and the Basic Interest scales. These scales have been developed by a combination of logical and statistical means to ensure that all of the items for each scale represent a single type of interest.

The GOT scales provide a summary or overview of the Strong profile as well as a framework for interpreting the other scales. Each of the six GOT scales contains items selected to fit Holland's (1985) descriptions of the six types of occupational personalities. Holland

FIGURE 9-1. Strong Interest Inventory Profile for Juanita, a Counseling Center Client

STRONG INTEREST INVENTORY

Profile report for **JUANITA**
ID: **000000000**
Age: **18**
Gender: **Female**

Page 1 of 6

Date tested: **3/21/96**
Date scored: **3/27/96**

SNAPSHOT: A SUMMARY OF RESULTS FOR JUANITA

VH = very high interest	VS = very similar
H = high interest	S = similar
A = average interest	M-R = mid-range
L = little interest	D = dissimilar
VL = very little interest	VD = very dissimilar

GENERAL OCCUPATIONAL THEMES

The General Occupational Themes describe interests in six very broad areas, including interest in work and leisure activities, kinds of people, and work settings. Your interests in each area are shown at the right in rank order. Note that each Theme has a code, represented by the first letter of the Theme name.

You can use your Theme code, printed below your results, to identify school subjects, part-time jobs, college majors, leisure activities, or careers that you might find interesting.

THEME CODE	THEME	VL	L	A	H	VH	TYPICAL INTERESTS
A	ARTISTIC	☐	☐	☐	☐	☑	Creating or enjoying art
I	INVESTIGATIVE	☐	☐	☐	☑	☐	Researching, analyzing
S	SOCIAL	☐	☐	☑	☐	☐	Helping, instructing
E	ENTERPRISING	☐	☑	☐	☐	☐	Selling, managing
C	CONVENTIONAL	☐	☑	☐	☐	☐	Accounting, processing data
R	REALISTIC	☐	☑	☐	☐	☐	Building, repairing

Your Theme code is AIS—(see explanation at left).

You might explore occupations with codes that contain any combination of these letters.

BASIC INTEREST SCALES

The Basic Interest Scales measure your interests in 25 specific areas or activities. Only those 5 areas in which you show the *most* interest are listed at the right in rank order. Your results on all 25 Basic Interest Scales are found on page 2.

To the left of each scale is a letter that shows which of the six General Occupational Themes it is most closely related to. These codes can help you to identify other activities that you may enjoy.

THEME CODE	BASIC INTERESTS	VL	L	A	H	VH	TYPICAL ACTIVITIES
A	MUSIC/DRAMATICS	☐	☐	☐	☐	☑	Performing or enjoying music/drama
A	WRITING	☐	☐	☐	☐	☑	Reading or writing
A	ART	☐	☐	☐	☑	☐	Appreciating or creating art
A	APPLIED ARTS	☐	☐	☐	☑	☐	Producing or enjoying visual art
I	MEDICAL SCIENCE	☐	☐	☐	☑	☐	Working in medicine or biology

OCCUPATIONAL SCALES

The Occupational Scales measure how similar your interests are to the interests of people who are satisfied working in those occupations. Only the 10 scales on which your interests are *most* similar to those of these people are listed at the right in rank order. Your results on all 211 of the Occupational Scales are found on pages 3, 4, and 5.

The letters to the left of each scale identify the Theme or Themes that most closely describe the interests of people working in that occupation. You can use these letters to find additional, related occupations that you might find interesting.

THEME CODE	OCCUPATION	VD	D	M-R	S	VS
A	MUSICIAN	☐	☐	☐	☐	☑
SI	NURSE, RN	☐	☐	☐	☐	☑
AIR	TECHNICAL WRITER	☐	☐	☐	☐	☑
A	LIBRARIAN	☐	☐	☐	☐	☑
A	TRANSLATOR	☐	☐	☐	☐	☑
ARI	ARTIST, COMMERCIAL	☐	☐	☐	☐	☑
AR	ARTIST, FINE	☐	☐	☐	☐	☑
IR	AUDIOLOGIST	☐	☐	☐	☐	☑
IAR	COLLEGE PROFESSOR	☐	☐	☐	☐	☑
A	LAWYER	☐	☐	☐	☐	☑

PERSONAL STYLE SCALES measure your levels of comfort regarding Work Style, Learning Environment, Leadership Style, and Risk Taking/Adventure. This information may help you make decisions about particular work environments, educational settings, and types of activities you would find satisfying. Your results on these four scales are on page 6.

FIGURE 9-1. *Continued*

 STRONG INTEREST INVENTORY   *Profile report for* **JUANITA**
ID: **000000000**

GENERAL OCCUPATIONAL THEMES

BASIC INTEREST SCALES

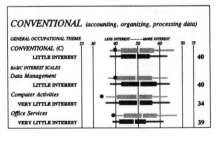

Note. Modified and reproduced by special permission of the publisher, Consulting Psychologists Press, Inc., Palo Alto, CA 94303, from Strong Interest Inventory of the Strong Interest Blanks, Form T317. © 1994 by Consulting Psychologists Press. All rights reserved. Further reproduction is prohibited without the publisher's written consent.

FIGURE 9-1. *Continued*

 STRONG INTEREST INVENTORY   *Profile report for* JUANITA
ID: 000000000

OCCUPATIONAL SCALES

REALISTIC *(building, repairing, working outdoors)*

Theme Codes Female	Male		Your Scores Female	Male
RIS	(SIR)	Athletic Trainer	6	(SIR)
R	R	Auto Mechanic	14	2
RIA	REA	Carpenter	11	3
RIS	RIC	Electrician	23	-9
RCI	RI	Emergency Medical Technician	23	20
RI	RI	Engineer	29	20
(CSE)	RC	Farmer	(CSE)	9
RI	RI	Forester	35	19
RC	RE	Gardener/Groundskeeper	21	16
RIR	RES	Horticultural Worker	4	6
(CRI)	RCR	Military Enlisted Personnel	(CRE)	8
RES	RIC	Military Officer	21	12
•	R	Plumber	•	11
RE	R	Police Officer	26	1
RIS	RI	Radiologic Technologist	35	34
(CRI)	RE	Small Business Owner	(CE)	6
RSE	RIR	Vocational Agriculture Teacher	7	1

INVESTIGATIVE *(researching, analyzing, inquiring)*

Theme Codes Female	Male		Your Scores Female	Male
IS	IA	Audiologist	53	52
IRA	IA	Biologist	43	44
IR	IR	Chemist	38	35
IR	IRA	Chiropractor	34	36
IA	IAI	College Professor	53	59
IR	IAR	Computer Progr./Systems Analyst	36	36
IRA	IR	Dentist	49	42
IRS	(SBC)	Dietitian	29	(SEC)
IRA	IA	Geographer	36	37
IRA	IRA	Geologist	25	28
IRC	ICA	Mathematician	29	20
IRC	IRR	Medical Technician	22	26
IRC	IRC	Medical Technologist	34	29
IR	IR	Optometrist	45	33
ICR	ICR	Pharmacist	43	42
IAR	IAR	Physician	48	49
IRA	IRA	Physicist	26	28
IA	IA	Psychologist	49	53
IR	IRC	Research & Development Manager	32	16
IRA	IRS	Respiratory Therapist	47	39
IRS	IRS	Science Teacher	31	26
IAR	(AI)	Sociologist	42	(AI)
IRA	IR	Veterinarian	46	37

NOTES

FIGURE 9-1. *Continued*

 STRONG INTEREST INVENTORY   *Profile report for* JUANITA
ID: **000000000**

OCCUPATIONAL SCALES (continued)

NOTES

ARTISTIC (creating or enjoying art, drama, music, writing)

THEME CODES FEMALE	MALE		YOUR SCORES FEMALE	MALE	DISSIMILAR INTERESTS 15	20	30 —MID-RANGE— 40	50	SIMILAR INTERESTS 55
AE	AE	Advertising Executive	34	51					
ARI	ARI	Architect	38	44					
ABI	A	Artist, Commercial	57	62					
AB	A	Artist, Fine	54	55					
AES	AE	Art Teacher	31	53					
AB	AB	Broadcaster	47	50					
AES	AES	Corporate Trainer	37	30					
ASE	ASE	English Teacher	42	52					
(EA)	AE	Interior Decorator	(EA)	36					
A	A	Lawyer	52	44					
A	A	Librarian	58	65					
AIR	AIR	Medical Illustrator	43	46					
A	A	Musician	63	68					
ARE	ARE	Photographer	51	41					
AER	ASB	Public Administrator	35	38					
AB	AB	Public Relations Director	34	47					
A	A	Reporter	51	51					
(AR)	AI	Sociologist	(AR)	51					
AIR	AI	Technical Writer	61	67					
A	AI	Translator	58	61					

SOCIAL (helping, instructing, caregiving)

THEME CODES FEMALE	MALE		YOUR SCORES FEMALE	MALE	DISSIMILAR INTERESTS 15	20	30 —MID-RANGE— 40	50	SIMILAR INTERESTS 55
(RIS)	SIR	Athletic Trainer	(RIS)	9					
S	•	Child Care Provider	30	•					
SE	SE	Community Serv. Organization Dir.	25	28					
SIRC	SRC	Dietitian	(RS)	18					
S	S	Elementary School Teacher	27	36					
SAR	SA	Foreign Language Teacher	32	46					
SE	SE	High School Counselor	24	20					
SE	•	Home Economics Teacher	4	•					
SAR	SA	Minister	38	41					
SCB	SCB	Nurse, LPN	26	31					
SI	SAI	Nurse, RN	62	62					
SAR	SA	Occupational Therapist	48	51					
SE	SE	Parks and Recreation Coordinator	22	24					
SRC	SR	Physical Education Teacher	8	7					
SIR	SIR	Physical Therapist	40	37					
SEA	SBC	School Administrator	30	22					
SEA	SEA	Social Science Teacher	34	29					
SA	SA	Social Worker	43	41					
SB	SEA	Special Education Teacher	22	41					
SA	SA	Speech Pathologist	39	53					

FIGURE 9-1. *Continued*

 STRONG INTEREST INVENTORY *Profile report for* JUANITA ID: ●●●●●●●● *Page 5 of 6*

OCCUPATIONAL SCALES (continued)

ENTERPRISING (selling, managing, persuading)

THEME CODES FEMALE MALE			YOUR SCORES FEMALE	MALE	DISSIMILAR INTERESTS————————SIMILAR INTERESTS
*	BCR	Agribusiness Manager	*	-6	
EC	EC	Buyer	2	3	
ERA	ER	Chef	11	16	
ES	*	Dental Hygienist	23	*	
EAS	ESA	Elected Public Official	26	24	
EAS	EAS	Flight Attendant	29	41	
EAC	EAC	Florist	13	11	
EC	EA	Hair Stylist	12	31	
ECS	ECS	Housekeeping & Maintenance Supr.	12	11	
EAS	ES	Human Resources Director	10	13	
EA	(AE)	Interior Decorator	15	(AE)	
		Investments Manager	36	15	
E	E	Life Insurance Agent	17	9	
EA	EA	Marketing Executive	35	34	
ECR	ER	Optician	19	13	
		Purchasing Agent	8	10	
E	E	Realtor	8	13	
ECR	ECR	Restaurant Manager	12	2	
ECA	ECS	Store Manager	19	12	
ECA	ECA	Travel Agent	20	17	

CONVENTIONAL (accounting, organizing, processing data)

THEME CODES FEMALE MALE			YOUR SCORES FEMALE	MALE	DISSIMILAR INTERESTS————————SIMILAR INTERESTS
CE	CE	Accountant	13	7	
CI	CI	Actuary	20	20	
CE	CE	Banker	16	6	
C	C	Bookkeeper	11	11	
CES	CES	Business Education Teacher	-1	14	
CE	CE	Credit Manager	9	16	
CSE	*	Dental Assistant	22	*	
CSE	(RC)	Farmer	10	(RC)	
CES	CES	Food Service Manager	16	16	
CE	CS	Mathematics Teacher	18	18	
C	C	Medical Records Technician	22	38	
CEB	(RCE)	Military Enlisted Personnel	18	(RCE)	
CES	CES	Nursing Home Administrator	27	36	
CE	CA	Paralegal	26	33	
CES	*	Secretary	10	*	
CE	(RE)	Small Business Owner	22	(RE)	

NOTES

162

FIGURE 9-1. *Continued*

 STRONG INTEREST INVENTORY   *Profile report for* JUANITA
                                                        ID: 000000000   *Page 6 of 6*

*PERSONAL
STYLE SCALES*

Female
Male

PERSONAL STYLE SCALES

			NOTES

WORK STYLE

PREFERS TO WORK ALONE; LIKES TO WORK WITH IDEAS, DATA, OR THINGS; ACCOMPLISHES TASKS BY INDEPENDENT ACTION OR THOUGHT.

PREFERS WORKING WITH PEOPLE, AS PART OF A GROUP OR TEAM, OR WITH ONE OTHER PERSON; ENJOYS HELPING OTHERS.

25 30 40 50 60 70 75   **44**

LEARNING ENVIRONMENT

PREFERS PRACTICAL LEARNING ENVIRONMENT; LEARNS BY DOING; PREFERS SHORT-TERM TRAINING; SEEKS TRAINING TO ACHIEVE A SPECIFIC GOAL OR SKILL.

PREFERS ACADEMIC ENVIRONMENT; LEARNS BY LECTURES AND BOOKS; WILLING TO SPEND MANY YEARS IN SCHOOL; SEEKS KNOWLEDGE FOR ITS OWN SAKE.

25 30 40 50 60 70 75   **68**

LEADERSHIP STYLE

NOT COMFORTABLE TAKING CHARGE OF OTHERS; PREFERS TO DO THE JOB RATHER THAN TO DIRECT OTHERS; MAY LEAD BY EXAMPLE RATHER THAN BY GIVING DIRECTIONS.

COMFORTABLE TAKING CHARGE AND MOTIVATING OTHERS; ENJOYS INITIATING ACTION; EXPRESSES OPINIONS EASILY.

25 30 40 50 60 70 75   **50**

RISK TAKING/ADVENTURE

DISLIKES ADVENTURE AND RISK TAKING; LIKES QUIET ACTIVITIES; PREFERS TO PLAY IT SAFE.

LIKES ADVENTURE AND RISK TAKING; APPRECIATES ORIGINAL IDEAS; ENJOYS THRILLING ACTIVITIES; TAKES CHANCES.

25 30 40 50 60 70 75   **57**

Total responses out of 317: 317
Infrequent responses: 5

SUMMARY OF ITEM RESPONSES

ADMINISTRATIVE INDEXES (response percentages)

OCCUPATIONS	24	%L	30	%I	46	%D
SCHOOL SUBJECTS	36	L	38	I	26	D
ACTIVITIES	35	L	32	I	33	D
LEISURE ACTIVITIES	38	L	14	I	48	D
TYPES OF PEOPLE	50	L	10	I	40	D
CHARACTERISTICS	48	Y	17	?	35	N
SUBTOTAL	32	%	28	%	40	%
PREFERENCES: ACTIVITIES	63	L	0	=	37	R
PREFERENCES: WORK	33	L	0	=	67	R

concluded that people could be broadly classified according to six types of interests (or abilities) as shown in Figure 9-2. This figure shows the nature of the relationship among the six categories. The closer the categories are to each other, the more highly they are inter-related.

The 25 Basic Interest scales function as subscales for the six GOT scales. They were grouped into the six GOT categories based on cor-relations between the two sets of scales. Each of the GOT scales subsumes three or more of the Basic Interest scales.

Both the GOT and Basic Interest scales have been standardized by the use of T-scores so that the general reference sample of 9,484 men and 9,467 women will obtain a mean of 50 and a standard deviation of 10. The T-scores are based on combined-sex norms; however, the test authors provide bar graphs beside the scales on the profile sheet to indicate how the scores are distributed for each sex (see Figure 9-1).

FIGURE 9-2. Holland's Classification of Personality Types

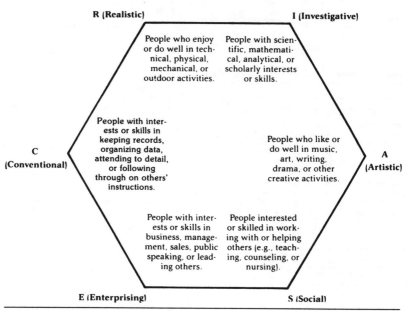

Note. From *Making Vocational Choices: A Theory of Vocational Personalities and Work Environments* (2nd ed., p. 29) by John L. Holland. © 1985. Adapted by permission of Prentice Hall, Inc., Englewood Cliffs, NJ.

Separate-sex norms are needed because of the large sex differences shown in the preferences for the Strong items. Men and women in the general reference samples differed in their *like* or *dislike* responses by at least 16 percentage points for approximately one quarter of the items on the Strong (Harmon et al., 1994). Men showed greater preference for mechanical activities, military activities, and athletics; women expressed more interest in culinary arts, art, and music/dramatics. Separate-sex norms make it is easier for people to show interest in nontraditional activities for their sex. For example, women who major in science do not express as much mechanical curiosity as do men who major in science, but they are just as successful as men in their course work (Goldman, Kaplan, & Platt, 1973). If they were held to the same standards of expressed interests as men, they would be less encouraged to enter a scientific field despite the fact that they could be just as successful.

High scores on both the GOT and Basic Interest scales are based on *like* responses, whereas low scores are based on *dislike* responses. If clients make a large number of *like* responses, they will obtain relatively high scores on these scales; if they mark a large number of *dislike* responses, their scores will be on the low side.

A large number of likes indicates broad interests; a large number of dislikes indicates fairly focused interests. In either case, the interest scores should be interpreted in relationship to one another. That is, clients should give careful consideration to their highest scores regardless of their absolute level.

The GOT and Basic Interest scales are highly reliable both in terms of internal consistency and test-retest consistency over extended time periods. Both sets of scales possess a high degree of content validity because of the manner in which they were constructed. The items for each scale were systematically selected to ensure that they would be representative of the interest domain to be measured. Empirical validity studies indicate that both sets of scales effectively discriminate among people employed in different types of occupations (Borgen, 1985; Harmon et al., 1994).

The GOT scores can be used to arrive at a Holland code to summarize a person's interest. To determine Juanita's Holland code, we must identify her three highest scores on the GOT scales. When we take sex norms into consideration, her highest scores are Artistic (A),

Investigative (I), and Social (S), in that order. Therefore, her Holland code is AIS.

The Basic Interest scales are short scales so that scores can be significantly affected by responses to a few items. The scales range in length from 5 to 21 items. The typical (median) scale possesses 12 items (Harmon et al., 1994). The Military Activities scale, for example, contains only 5 items, 3 of which pertain to marching.

As a counseling technique, it is usually helpful to ask clients to look at their four or five highest and lowest scores on the Basic Interest scales. Do they agree with this description of their interests? Can they think of ways in which they could combine the activities represented by their highest scores in a career or life plan? Juanita received her highest scores on the music/dramatics, writing, art, applied arts, medical science, and medical service scales. These scores show a pronounced interest in creative activities in addition to medical endeavors.

Occupational scales. The Strong profile provides scores for 104 Occupational scales for men and 107 Occupational scales for women. The same occupations are represented for both men and women with very few exceptions.

The Occupational scales were developed by selecting items that significantly differentiated between the interests of men or women in the occupation and men or women in general. The typical scale contains 40 to 50 items selected in this manner. Members of occupational criterion groups used to develop the Occupational scales usually possessed the following characteristics:

- Employed in occupation for 3 years or more
- Satisfied with their work
- At least 25 years of age or older
- Belong to a primary professional or business organization associated with membership in that occupation
- Perform typical duties of members of the occupation

The number of people in the occupational criterion groups ranged from 60 for female electricians to 1,187 for female librarians. All but 7 of the 211 groups exceeded 100 members. Information regarding specific characteristics of each occupational criterion group can be obtained from the Strong manual (Harmon et al., 1994, pp. 309–376).

The Occupational scales have been normed so that men or women in the occupation (depending on which sex was used for constructing the scale) obtain a mean *T*-score of 50 with a standard deviation of 10. Men and women in general obtain mean *T*-scores of approximately 20 to 35 for most scales. Scores above 40 or 45 should be looked upon as "high" scores, that is, as scores that show similarity of interests with those of people employed in the occupation.

Some clients receive few or no high scores on the Occupational scales. In such cases, it is best to interpret the scores relatively. That is, counselors should pay attention to the client's highest scores even if they are less than 40. Research indicates that clients with undifferentiated (or "flat") profiles will usually produce differentiated profiles over time. In a study conducted by Athelstan (1966) on an earlier version of the Strong, 85% of college students who had a flat profile as freshmen obtained a differentiated profile by the time they were seniors. Furthermore, the profile became differentiated in the direction indicated by the freshmen scores. Scores that had been only slightly high at that time became significantly higher by the senior year. Students with flat profiles may need additional time and experience to clarify their interests.

Scores of less than 25 on the Occupational scales indicate dissimilarity of interests compared with people in the occupation. Often profiles will contain one or two negative scores that clients sometimes find puzzling. A negative score shows that the client obtained a score more than five standard deviations below the mean compared with people in the occupation group. Negative scores are most likely to occur for those Occupational scales with uncommon interest patterns, such as medical illustrator or physicist.

Separate-sex scales have been established to take into account differences in social conditioning. The Strong printout gives the client's scores for both the male and female Occupational scales, but only plots the score on the Strong profile for the same-sex Occupational scales. Scores on the two sets of scales are highly correlated; but men tend to obtain higher scores on cross-sex scales for occupations that have traditionally appealed to men, such as military officer, whereas women tend to get higher scores on cross-sex scales for occupations that women have usually preferred such as interior decorator (Harmon et al., 1994; Johnson, 1977). Surprisingly, scores on cross-sex scales seem to be as valid as scores on same-sex scales in predicting future occupational membership (Dolliver & Worthington, 1981).

In contrast with the GOT and Basic Interest scales, high scores on the Occupational scales are based on both *like* and *dislike* responses. People can obtain high scores because they share the same dislikes as people in the occupation as well as the same likes. In essence, high scores on the Occupational scales point to occupations where individuals can pursue those activities they enjoy and avoid those they dislike.

Some Occupational scales, such as farmer, plumber, and radiologic technologist, include many items with positive weights for *dislike* responses. People in these occupations possess rather narrow or focused interests. If clients mark a large number of *dislike* responses, they will probably obtain elevated scores on these scales. On the other hand, high scores on most Occupational scales are influenced primarily by *like* responses. These include a large number of occupations in all categories, especially the Social and Enterprising categories. Such occupations appeal to individuals with broad interests.

The Occupational scores are highly reliable, particularly for older people (age 20 and beyond) and over short time periods (less than 1 year). Even over very long time periods (10 to 20 years), the Occupational scales produce similar results for most people based on research conducted with earlier versions of the Strong (Johansson & Campbell, 1971).

Concurrent validation studies show that the Occupational scales significantly differentiate between people in the occupation and people in general (Harmon et al., 1994). A number of longitudinal research studies have been conducted to examine the predictive validity of the Strong. These studies indicate that between 55% to 70% of the people who take the Strong will become employed in occupations congruent with their high scores on the Occupational scales (Brandt & Hood, 1968; Dolliver, Irvin, & Bigley, 1972; Dolliver & Will, 1977; McArthur & Stevens, 1955; Strong, 1955; Trimble, 1966).

Scores on the Occupational scales show greater validity when they are supported by scores on the Basic Interest scales that are most relevant (Johnson & Johansson, 1972). Occupational scores are also more valid when they are supported by work or volunteer experiences in those fields (Prediger & Swaney, 1985).

Research indicates that the Occupational scales predict occupational membership just as accurately for college students who are undecided as they do for those who are decided (Bartling & Hood, 1981). This finding is important inasmuch as the Strong is frequently used with students who are having difficulty in making a career decision.

When Occupational scores agree with expressed interests (career choice stated at the time that the Strong was completed), the predictive accuracy of Occupational scores significantly increases (Bartling & Hood, 1981). When Occupational scores disagree with expressed interests, the latter are more accurate. Expressed interests take into account factors that go beyond the characteristics measured by the Strong, such as values, abilities, and opportunities. McArthur and Stevens (1955) found that Harvard students from upper-class families frequently followed family traditions in choosing occupations (e.g., law, medicine, or business) instead of basing their choices on their measured interests. Counselors should recognize the limitations of an instrument such as the Strong. It provides helpful information about one's interests, but it needs to be incorporated into other relevant information.

According to several studies, people report greater job satisfaction when their occupation matches the type suggested by their Strong scores than when it does not; however, the relationship tends to be modest (Brandt & Hood, 1968; McArthur, 1954; Strong, 1955; Trimble, 1966). Presumably, factors other than interests, such as salary, opportunities for advancement, and relationships with supervisors or coworkers, account for much of one's satisfaction or dissatisfaction.

Scores on the Occupational scales can be interpreted by referring to both the GOT scales and the Basic Interest scales. For example, Juanita obtained "very similar" scores (55 or greater) on six of the Occupational scales normed on women. Five of these (Musician, Technical Writer, Librarian, Translator, and Commercial Artist) can be interpreted in terms of her high scores on the Artistic GOT scale and the Music/Dramatics, Writing, Art, and Applied Arts Basic scales. The sixth scale, Registered Nurse, reflects high scores on the Investigative GOT scale and the Medical Science and Medical Service Basic scales. The scores on the GOT and Basic scales clarify the nature of the occupational interest patterns represented by the Occupational scales.

169

Personal Style scales. Over the years, the authors of the Strong have experimented with a number of nonoccupational scales. The 1994 version of the Strong includes four Personal Style scales that measure personality factors related to educational and career planning. These four scales, each of which is bipolar in nature, are briefly described below:

- Work Style—High scorers prefer to work with people; low scorers prefer to work with ideas, data, or things.
- Learning Environment—High scorers possess academic interests associated with advanced degrees; low scorers possess practical interests associated with technical or trade school attendance.
- Leadership—High scorers prefer to direct others; low scorers prefer to lead by example.
- Risk Taking/Adventure—High scorers prefer to take chances; low scorers prefer to play it safe.

Scores on all of these scales correlate highly with scores on the GOT scales (Harmon et al, 1994, p. 164). The Work Style scale is positively correlated with scores on the Social and Enterprising GOT scales and negatively correlated with scores on the Realistic and Investigative scales. The Learning Environment scale has much in common with the Investigative and Artistic GOT scales, whereas the Leadership Style scale overlaps to a large extent with the Enterprising, Social, and Artistic scales. The Risk Taking/Adventure scale, which is very similar to the Adventure Basic Interest scale that used to appear within the Realistic GOT category, is highly correlated with scores on the Realistic GOT scale.

Campbell (1972) noted that the nonoccupational scales "are not simple to use in counseling and *their use should be restricted to professionally trained people who are aware of their pitfalls*" (p. 195). The Personal Style scales lack the established validity of the other Strong scales. Because of the high correlations with the GOT scales, and because of the danger of misinterpreting the Personal Style scales, counselors can usually best interpret these scales by referring directly to the GOT scales. Juanita's score, for example, was very high on the Learning Environment scale, which can be explained in terms of her high scores on the Artistic and Investigative GOT scales.

Interpretation of client profile. Much of Juanita's profile has been discussed in preceding paragraphs. As a means of obtaining some focus, we asked Juanita to select several occupations on the Strong profile that had the most appeal to her. We asked her to look particularly at the scales for which she received high scores, but not to exclude any occupations. She chose the following occupations, in addition to physician: technical writer, reporter, and broadcaster. She had obtained scores showing similarity between her interests and those of people employed in each of the occupations listed above. We discussed ways in which she could obtain more information about these career possibilities, which included visiting departmental representatives on campus for each of the academic majors in these fields, interviewing people employed in these fields, reading about the occupations in the *Occupational Outlook Handbook* (U.S. Department of Labor, Washington, DC) and related materials, and possibly taking a course in these areas or doing volunteer work in a related field.

She was pleased to obtain information from her Strong profile that suggested several career options other than physician for her to consider. The Strong enabled her to evaluate systematically her interests in regard to different career fields, which was the type of information that she needed at the time.

Kuder General Interest Survey (KGIS), Form E

Frederic Kuder developed a number of interest inventories, beginning in the 1930s, that have had a great impact on counseling. The various forms of the Kuder interest inventories are among the most popular assessment procedures used by counselors. The two most widely used forms at the present time are the Kuder General Interest Survey (KGIS), Form E, and the Kuder Occupational Interest Survey (KOIS), Form DD. The KOIS will be discussed in the next section.

Since 1942, all forms of the Kuder interest inventories have presented items as forced-choice triads. Clients must select which of three types of activities they prefer most and which they prefer least. For example, one forced-choice triad includes the following items: "repair a broken lock," "look for mistakes in a typewritten report," and "add columns of figures." The use of forced-choice triads controls for response styles such as acquiescence (marking *like* to most items) and deviation (making extreme responses to most items).

171

The forced-choice item format affects the interpretation of the results. The scores must be interpreted in regard to each other. A high score indicates that the person likes that type of activity more than other activities compared with members of the norm group, but it does not indicate the absolute magnitude of the interest.

The KGIS represents a revision of the Kuder Preference Record–Form C (Vocational), a broad measure of interest patterns widely used by counselors for years (Kuder, 1988). The reading level required for the inventory was reduced from the ninth grade to the sixth grade so that it could be used with middle school students and with adults who have limited reading ability.

Scales. The KGIS includes the same 10 general interest areas assessed by the Kuder Preference Record–Form C (Vocational). The 10 scales were carefully constructed to be relatively independent of each other. Few of the scale intercorrelations exceed .30. The scales are similar to the Holland scales found on many interest inventories as indicated below:

Holland scales	Comparable KGIS scales
Realistic	Outdoor and Mechanical
Investigative	Scientific
Artistic	Artistic, Literary, and Musical
Social	Social Service
Enterprising	Persuasive
Conventional	Clerical and Computational

The V-score (verification score) can be used to identify answer sheets that may been answered carelessly, insincerely, or improperly. This scale includes items that are rarely marked by students who are trying to answer honestly and who have paid careful attention to the instructions. Profiles with V-scores equal to or above 15 should be reviewed with students for possible problems.

A relatively large number of young people obtain elevated V-scores. According to the manual, 25% of middle school boys and 12% of middle school girls obtain V-scores of 15 or higher. Such scores may reflect immaturity in regard to development of interests. As a general rule, the KGIS should not be interpreted for such students. These students should be readministered the KGIS at a later point in their educational program.

Answer sheets may be self-scored or scored on a computer. One research study indicated that errors were fairly common on self-scored answer sheets (Lampe, 1985). Counselors should check to make certain that hand-scored answer sheets have been correctly scored. Most people can complete the revised instrument in 45 to 60 minutes. Additional time should be provided if students are asked to score their own answer sheets.

The publishers provide supplementary material to aid in interpretation of the results. The *Job and College Majors Charts* (available from CTB/McGraw-Hill test publishers) list a number of occupations and college majors that match the various scales, both singly and in combination.

Norms. New norms for the KGIS were assembled in 1987. Separate-sex norms are used for middle school (grades 6 through 8) and high school (grades 9 through 12) students. Unfortunately, descriptive information regarding the sample, such as ethnicity, social class, and economic class, is not available (Mehrens, 1994). Research with Native Americans indicates that separate norms may be necessary for some minority groups or subcultures (Epperson & Hammond, 1981). Kuder (1988) encouraged test users to develop local norms if they believe that their student or client population may differ from the published norms.

Reliability and validity. The KGIS scales possess adequate test-retest reliability when the results are used for academic or career exploration purposes. The median test-retest reliabilities are close to .80 for both middle school boys and girls and for high school boys and girls tested twice over a 2-week period.

In a 25-year follow-up study, Zytowski (1974) found that 53% of students tested as 14-year-olds were engaged in an occupation related to their highest scores on the Kuder Preference Record—Form B, an earlier version of the KGIS. He also found that people who were employed in occupations consistent with their interests reported greater job satisfaction than did individuals working in occupations inconsistent with their interests. Similar results have been found in other validity studies conducted with previous versions of the KGIS (Kuder, 1988).

Although the studies mentioned above support the validity of the Kuder instruments, they also show a wide range of outcomes for individuals with similar interest profiles. Zytowski (1974), for example, noted that nearly one third of the students in his sample were employed in occupations that were consistent with their lowest interest scores. Similarly, he found that the majority of the people in his study reported job satisfaction even when they were in occupations not predicted by their interest scores. The interest scores provide valuable information, but they should be looked upon as just one of a number of factors that need to be considered in academic or career planning.

Kuder Occupational Interest Survey (KOIS), Form DD

In contrast with the KGIS, which uses homogeneous scales to measure interests in broad categories, the KOIS employs heterogeneous scales to assess interests in specific occupations. The KOIS, which was established in 1966, was preceded by the Kuder Preference Record–Form D (Occupational). Kuder had constructed Form D with Occupational scales in 1956 in a manner similar to that used with the Strong Vocational Interest Blank.

Kuder used the same items for the KOIS that appeared on Form D, but radically changed the scoring procedure. Instead of selecting items that differentiated between members of an occupation and people in general, Kuder calculated correlation coefficients (called lambda coefficients) between an individual's responses to each of the 100 triads and the mean responses of occupational members to each of the 100 triads. High lambda coefficients (.45 or better) indicate that the individual's interests are similar to those of people in the occupational criterion group.

Occupational scales based on lambda correlations offer a number of advantages. Not only are they easier to construct and simpler to interpret than scales based on the use of a general reference group, but they also appear to be more effective in correctly identifying members of different occupational groups. Kuder and Zytowski (1991) found that lambda scores produced significantly fewer errors of classification than did Strong's system in a study that involved the use of both types of scales.

The KOIS has a sixth-grade reading level, but should not be used with students until they are in the 10th grade because of the specificity of the scores. Most people complete the KOIS within 30 minutes. The answer sheets must be scored by computer to calculate the lambda coefficients. The publisher provides an interpretive booklet to aid clients and counselors in understanding the test results. An audiotape is also available that can be used by students to interpret the results.

The KOIS yields four types of scores for clients—dependability measures, vocational interest estimates, college major scales, and occupational scales—each of which is discussed below. Scores on eight experimental scales are also listed for counselors; however, there is not enough research support for most of these scales to justify their use in counseling.

Dependability indices. The dependability, or validity, measures for the KOIS include the V-score (should be greater than 44), the number of unreadable responses (should be less than 15), and the magnitude of the highest lambda correlation coefficients (should be greater than .39) The V-score for the KOIS was derived in the same manner as the V-score for the KGIS, but the scoring has been reversed so that a low score instead of a high score indicates a possible validity problem. Lambda coefficients less than .40 indicate interest patterns that are not well differentiated. Profiles that have their highest lambda correlations between .30 and .40 should be interpreted with caution. If the highest lambda correlation coefficient does not exceed .30, the profile should not be interpreted at all. Such results can be attributed to chance.

Vocational Interest Estimates (VIEs). The VIEs, which were added to the KOIS in 1985, are abbreviated versions of the general interest scales found on the Kuder General Interest Survey. They are called "estimates" instead of scales because of their brevity.

The manual recommends that the VIEs be used to help interpret scores on the College Major and Occupational scales. For example, members of the criterion group for the male High School Counselor scale scored high on the Social Service, Literary, and Science scales. Inspection of the relative magnitude of an individual's scores on these scales should be helpful in interpreting that person's score on the male High School Counselor scale. For the female High School Counselor scale, the highest VIE scores were Persuasive, Social Service, and Literary. Differences between scores on the two High School Counselor

175

scales can be considered in terms of differences of scores on the relevant VIEs.

Although the VIES are relatively stable for most people, some of the individual VIES suffer from low internal consistency reliabilities. For this reason, counselors should be cautious in interpreting the meaning of scores on the VIEs.

Occupational and College Major scales. The current version of the KOIS includes a total of 109 Occupational scales (65 male scales and 44 female scales) and 40 College Major scales (22 male scales and 18 female scales; Kuder & Zytowski, 1991).

All of the Occupational and College Major scores are expressed as lambda coefficients, which, as described above, show the degree of relationship between one's interests and those of people in different college majors or occupations. The lambda coefficients are interpreted in terms of their rank order. Scales with lambda coefficients that are within .06 points of the highest score (99% confidence band) should be given primary consideration by clients. All scores within .06 points of each other can be considered to be equivalent. Differences less than .06 should be attributed to chance.

Men and women are scored on all scales, but scores for the female scales are listed separately from scores for the male scales. Most people will obtain higher scores on scales based on their own sex; however, the rank order of the scores for matching male and females scales will usually be similar (Zytowski & Laing, 1978).

Profile scores show high levels of reliability for both sexes at both the high school and college level. Median test-retest profile reliabilities over short-time periods for the Occupational scales equalled or exceeded .90 for all studies reported in the manual. Zytowski (1976b) also found relatively stable results for college students over a 12-year period.

Kuder studied the validity of the Occupational and College Major scales in differentiating among the interests of 3,000 individuals drawn from 30 "core" occupations and college majors (Kuder & Zytowski, 1991). Two thirds of the 3,000 respondents in his study obtained their highest score on their own Occupational or College Major scale. All but 10% of the total group obtained scores on their own scales that were within .06 points of their highest score (i.e., in their top group of scores). The typical scale showed very little overlap of scores with the other scales. Most overlap occurred with scales that were highly related, such as Clinical Psychologist and Social Caseworker. The scales effectively differentiated among the interests of people engaged in a variety of occupations or college majors.

The scores can also be used to predict future occupation or college major with a fair degree of success. In a 12- to 19-year longitudinal study of 882 high school and college students, Zytowski (1976a) found that 51% of the people were employed in occupations that would have been suggested to them by their KOIS scores. Approximately 55% of the high school students who went to college majored in a subject that corresponded with their high scores on the KOIS. The predictive validities for the two sets of scales compare favorably with those reported for the Occupational scales on the Strong.

Zytowski found that the predictive validities for the Occupational scales increased when any of the following conditions were met: (a) the person entered one of the occupations listed on the KOIS profile; (b) the person had a relatively large number of occupations listed within his or her top group of occupations; (c) the person went to college; or (d) the person entered a technical or scientific occupation or high-level occupation. In addition, recent research shows that both the predictive validity and the profile stability of the Occupational scales are associated with well differentiated interest patterns as indicated by a high score (greater than .50) on the client's highest Occupational scale and a low score on the Men-in-General (M) or Women-in-General (W) experimental scales (Zytowski & England, 1994).

Zytowski and Laing (1978) found that the male and female scales predicted equally well for both sexes as long as the scores were ranked separately by sex. These results suggest that counselors can use scores from opposite-sex scales for counseling purposes when same-sex scales do not exist.

A new version of the Kuder instruments is currently under development (Zytowski, 1992). This new instrument, the Kuder Career Search Schedule, will compare one's interests with those of other individuals instead of occupational groups. Clients will receive extensive descriptive information for the 20 adults in the occupational criterion samples who possess interest patterns most similar to their own. In essence, this approach will provide clients with the equivalent of 20 informational interviews with employed adults similar to themselves who have found satisfying occupations.

Career Assessment Inventory (CAI)

The CAI was first constructed in 1975 by Charles Johansson to measure career interests at the technical and skilled trades level. At that time, it complemented the Strong, which was designed to evaluate interest patterns of men and women considering business or professional occupations. Since that time, both instruments have changed. The Strong now includes a number of scales for occupations that require less than a college education. In 1986, the CAI was expanded so that it now contains a large number of scales for occupations that require a 4-year college degree or advanced training in a professional program (Johansson, 1986).

National Computer Systems (NCS), the publisher of the CAI, continues to publish the original (or "blue collar") version of the CAI as well as the new version. The original version, which has been updated several times, is now known as the CAI–Vocational Version (CAI-VV), whereas the new version is entitled CAI–Enhanced Version (CAI-EV; Johansson, 1984, 1986). The CAI-VV is shorter and has a lower reading level than CAI-EV. The former includes 305 items written at a sixth-grade reading level; the latter contains 370 items written at an eighth-grade reading level. CAI-VV should be used with secondary school students or adults who do not plan to obtain a 4-year college degree. The CAI-EV, on the other hand, should be used with individuals in the 9th grade or beyond who wish to consider a broad range of occupations, including those that require a college degree.

Both versions of the CAI consist of three types of items—Activities, School Subjects, and Occupations—each of which employs a five-step response format (L = *like very much,* l = *like somewhat,* I = *indifferent,* d = *dislike somewhat,* and D = *dislike very much*). The most recent version of the inventory provides brief definitions for each of the items that use occupational titles. For example, the term *biologist* is followed by the phrase, "Studies plants and animals."

Both versions of the CAI are patterned after the Strong. They both include the same types of scales: Administrative indices, Nonoccupational scales (called Personal Style scales on the Strong), General Theme scales (identical to the General Occupational Theme scales on the Strong), Basic Interest scales, and Occupational scales.

The Nonoccupational scales, which were added to the different forms of the CAI for the first time in 1984, include the Fine Arts–

Mechanical scale (an updated version of the Masculinity-Femininity scale that used to appear on the Strong), Extroversion-Introversion scale, Educational Orientation scale (similar to the Learning Environment scale on the Strong), and Variability of Interests scale. These scales provide some insights regarding the personality factors associated with one's career interest patterns; however, they lack the validity of the other scales on the CAI.

Scores on the General Theme scales and Basic Interest scales are highly correlated with parallel scales on the Strong for the CAI-VV and the CAI-EV (Johansson, 1984, 1986). Test-retest studies indicate that scores on these scales are highly consistent over relatively long time periods for college students and adults.

The CAI differs from the Strong by providing combined-sex scales for all of 111 Occupational scales on the CAI-EV and 32 of the 91 Occupational scales on the CAI-VV. The same scales serve both men and women. Only core items, which differentiate between the interests of both men and women in the occupation and men and women in general, are included on these scales. Items that showed significant differences for only one sex were rejected. For this reason, the scales contain fewer items than do the Occupational scales on the Strong. The reliability coefficients are slightly lower than they would be if longer scales were used; however, use of the combined-sex scales greatly simplifies interpretation of the results.

As with the Strong, the CAI Occupational scales have been coded according to Holland's classification system. The two systems produce similar results in most cases. In a manner similar to the Strong, the Occupational scales have been normed so that people in the occupation will obtain a mean score of 50 with a standard deviation of 10. Scores above 45 indicate similarity of interests with those of people employed in the occupation.

Despite the use of fewer items, the CAI Occupational scales for both versions seem to be as reliable and valid as comparable scales on the Strong. The CAI scales clearly distinguish among the interest patterns of people employed in different fields. For the typical scale, workers in the occupational criterion samples averaged about two standard deviations above the mean of those in the general reference samples. The CAI matches the success of the Strong is this regard; however, these results have not been cross-validated with independent samples.

The CAI lacks the extensive research base that has been established for both the Strong and the Kuder inventories. Test authorities have noted that both versions of the CAI have merit, but fall short in some of their technical aspects, such as limited descriptive data for the normative samples, small sizes of some of the occupational criterion samples, and insufficient predictive validity data (Rounds, 1989; Vacc & Hinkle, 1994).

CASE EXAMPLE

Tom requested counseling to help him decide upon a training program. He had already taken some coursework in his community college, but lacked a career direction. The counselor assigned the CAI-EV to Tom to assess his interests in regard to various career possibilities.

Tom obtained high scores (*T*-score greater than 57 or 75th percentile) on the Realistic General Theme scale and on each of the following Basic Interest subscales within the Realistic field: Carpentry, Athletics/Sports, Manual/Skilled Training, and Mechanical/Fixing. He also received a high score on the Performing/Entertaining scale from the Artistic field. When his likes and dislikes were compared with people in different occupations, he obtained high scores (45 or greater) on each of the following scales: Drafter, Painter, Carpenter, Firefighter, Pipefitter/Plumber, Architect, Piano Technician, Card/Gift Shop Manager, and Surveyor.

After studying his results, he expressed an interest in exploring the following occupations: drafter, photogrammetrist or cartographer (suggested by the *Occupational Outlook Handbook* as occupations similar to drafter and surveyor), painter, carpenter, and architect. He planned to read about these occupations and to visit with advisers who could provide information to him about training programs in these fields. The CAI thus helped him to focus his career exploration efforts.

Jackson Vocational Interest Survey (JVIS)

The JVIS is a relatively new interest inventory that can serve as an alternative to the interest inventories described above (Jackson, 1993). The instrument has been designed for counselors to use in educational and career planning with high school students, college students, and other adults.

Respondents must choose between 289 pairs of items that measure interests in different types of job-related activities. The items have been paired to control for response bias. Most people can complete the JVIS in 45 minutes to 1 hour. The reading level is seventh grade, although as noted by Jepsen (1994), some of the items are more conceptually difficult than the reading level would imply.

Similar to the Strong, the JVIS includes administrative indices, occupational theme scales (scales that measure the Holland categories), basic interest scales, occupational scores, and a nonoccupational scale (Academic Satisfaction). It differs from the Strong by including measures of academic interests and by its emphasis on occupational clusters instead of specific occupations. Scores are provided for a total of 17 academic major clusters, such as Performing Arts and Environmental Resource Management, and for 32 occupational clusters, such as Agriculturalists and Health Service Workers.

The JVIS differs from most other interest inventories by including items that measure interests in different types of work environments (work style items) as well as different types of work activities (work role items). Of the 34 Basic Interest scales, 8 reflect work style preferences. The work style preference Basic Interest scales, such as Independence and Job Security, are similar to the types of scales often included on values inventories.

The measures of occupational and academic major interests are unique in that these measures are derived from the scores on the Basic Interest scales. Scores for each of the 17 academic major and 32 occupational clusters are reported as correlation coefficients that show the degree of similarity between one's basic interest profile and the basic interests of people in different majors and occupations. In this manner, Jackson has been able to make use of vast amounts of archival data accumulated for the Strong Interest Inventory.

The JVIS General Theme and Basic Interest scales possess adequate test-retest reliability and internal consistency. Scores on these scales are highly correlated with similar scales on other interest inventories. Less information is known about the reliability and validity of the academic major and occupational cluster scores; however, one study indicated that the academic major scores were more successful than scores from other interest inventories in correctly identifying college students' academic majors (Jackson, 1993). Jepsen believed that clients may achieve a "greater breadth and depth in understanding the nature of their interests" (1994, p. 187) with the JVIS than with other interest inventories.

INTERPRETATION OF INTEREST INVENTORIES IN COUNSELING

Suggestions for interpreting interest inventories to clients include the following:

1. Check to make certain that the client has answered a sufficient number of items and to ensure that the client understood and followed the directions. Total response and infrequent responses indices should be helpful for this purpose.

2. Give the interest profile to the client just prior to a counseling session so that he or she will have time to read the results and formulate questions before meeting with the counselor. Allow time to study the printouts in a comfortable place. The client should come early for the appointment so that he or she still have ample time to discuss his or her results and other matters in the counseling session. After a client has studied the printout, follow the steps listed below.

3. Keep the purpose for assigning the inventory in mind. Review this purpose with the client before interpreting the results.

4. Ask the client about his or her reactions to the inventory before interpreting the results.

5. Note the percentage distribution of *like, indifferent,* and *dislike* responses for interest inventories with this type of response format. Remember that high scores on general or basic interest scales are based on *likes,* whereas low scores on these scales are based on *dislikes.* If clients mark a disproportionate percentage of any one of the responses, be sure to interpret scores relatively; that is, give greatest consideration to the highest scores, regardless of their absolute level.

6. Interpret the general (homogeneous) scales first. Help the client to determine his or her Holland code. Use these scales as a framework for interpreting the occupational scales.

7. Use separate-sex norms in interpreting scores on the interest scales. The separate-sex norms take into account the differences in the socialization process for men and women, which can affect the validity of the scales.

8. Interpret the occupational scores as measuring similarity of interest patterns compared with those of people in the occupation. Emphasize that the scores reflect interests rather than abilities. The scores can be used to help predict job satisfaction but not job success.

9. Do not overinterpret small differences in scores between scales. If *T*-scores fall within 8 to 10 points of each other, do not consider them to be significantly different from each other for most scales.

10. Refer to *dislike* as well as *like* responses in interpreting high scores on occupational scales. A client can obtain high scores for some occupational scales simply by sharing the same dislikes that people in the occupation possess.

11. Relate the scores to other information, such as work experience, academic background, career plans, and other test data concerning the client. Work together with the client in attempting to integrate the results.

12. Deemphasize scores on special scales unless these are particularly relevant. The same type of information can be obtained from the general scales in a more understandable fashion.

13. Bring into consideration occupations that are not on the profile by using Holland's occupational classification system (Gottfredson & Holland, 1989). Try to think of occupations that bridge the client's interests. Be sure to actively involve the client in the process.

14. Ask clients to identify four or five occupations suggested by the interest inventory that they would like to investigate. Suggest sources of occupational and educational information, including the *Occupational Outlook Handbook*, career pamphlets, informational interviews, and volunteer work.

SUMMARY

1. Interest inventories differ in the types of scales they use. General (homogeneous) scales, which measure interests in different types of activities, provide scores that can be easily interpreted. Occupational (heterogeneous) scales, which measure the similarity between one's interests and those of people in employed in different occupations, yield scores that summarize one's interest patterns.

2. Counselors should carefully consider the circumstances for assigning an interest inventory to a client. These circumstances include the purpose for testing, the client's motivation for taking the inventory, the client's emotional adjustment, and the availability of other interest scores, among other matters. Card sorts should be used to explore underlying reasons for career preferences.

3. The Strong Interest Inventory, which contains both general and occupational scales based on Holland's theory of career choice, represents the most thoroughly developed interest inventory for people considering business or professional occupations.
4. The Kuder General Interest Survey, which contains only general scales, is well suited for use with middle and high school students or for people whose interests are uncrystallized. The Kuder Occupational Interest Survey provides scores on both Occupational and College Major scales for senior high school students, college students, and other adults.
5. The Career Assessment Inventory–Vocational Version has been designed for use with people considering technical, clerical, or skilled trade occupations. The Career Assessment Inventory–Enhanced Version provides a broader measure of interests than the Vocational Version by also including occupations that require a college degree.
6. The Jackson Vocational Interest Survey provides a comprehensive view of one's preferences for work environments as well as work activities.
7. Counselors should use all of the scales on an interest inventory in combination to understand a client's profile. The administrative scales, especially response patterns, should be reviewed. The general scales should be used to help interpret the occupational scales.

10

COMPREHENSIVE ASSESSMENT PROGRAMS FOR CAREER AND LIFE PLANNING

C OMPREHENSIVE ASSESSMENT PROGRAMS MEASURE a combination of one's values, interests, and aptitudes. Most programs include a means of identifying academic, career, or social environments that would be compatible with a person's preferences and abilities. All of the programs use self-reports to measure interests or values; however, the programs differ in the manner in which abilities are assessed. Whereas some of the programs use self-ratings, other programs used standardized tests to determine abilities. Both types of programs are discussed in this chapter.

SELF-RATING CAREER AND LIFE PLANNING PROGRAMS

Career and life planning programs based on self-ratings include self-report inventories, computer-based programs, and career education workbooks. These programs primarily help clients organize their thinking about themselves and various opportunities. They have been validated primarily in terms of their success in encouraging people to explore various occupations and in enabling individuals to make progress in their career decision making.

Research shows that *informed* self-assessments can predict future performance as least as accurately as standardized tests in many situations (Norris & Cochran, 1977; Shrauger & Osberg, 1981). These assessments will be most accurate when clients know specifically what aspects of their behavior are being predicted, when questions are phrased as directly as possible, when the counselor helps the client to recall previous behavior in similar situations, and when clients are motivated to cooperate (Shrauger & Osberg, 1981).

Self-Report Inventories

Comprehensive self-report inventories counselors frequently use include the Self-Directed Search; the Career Decision-Making System, the Vocational Interest, Experience, and Skill Assessment; and the new Campbell Interest and Skill Survey.

Self-Directed Search (SDS). The SDS, which is based on Holland's (1985) theory of vocational choice, can be self-administered, self-scored, and self-interpreted. Although it is sometimes classified as an interest inventory, the SDS is actually an inventory of both interests and abilities. Holland referred to it as a career counseling simulation. It consists of sections that ask respondents to indicate their liking for activities (66 items) or occupations (84 items) as well as sections that inquire about competencies (66 items) and abilities (12 self-rating scales). By making comparisons between ratings for similar types of activities, counselors can learn to what extent clients perceive discrepancies between their interests and abilities.

Four versions of the SDS have been created for different populations (Holland, Powell, & Fritzsche, 1994): The Regular Form (Form R) is designed for high school students, college students, and adults; the Easy Form (Form E) is for adults or high school students who possess limited education or reading ability; the Career Planning Form (Form CP) is for people who plan to enter a profession or higher-level occupation; and the SDS Career Explorer is for middle school and junior high school students.

Each part of the SDS includes an equal number of items from each of the six Holland categories (Realistic, Investigative, Artistic, Social, Enterprising, and Conventional) described in Chapter 9. Based upon the test taker's responses, a three-letter Holland code is derived that can then be compared with the Holland code for various occupations or college majors. The *Occupations Finder*, a booklet that accompanies the SDS, lists over 1,300 occupations according to their Holland codes and the amount of education required. Holland codes for each of 12,860 different occupations defined in the *Dictionary of Occupational Titles* and its supplements are provided in a separate publication (Gottfredson & Holland, 1989). Codes for more than 750 postsecondary fields of study are given in the *Educational Opportunities Finder* (Rosen, Holmberg, & Holland, 1994). Finally, two-letter codes for over 750 leisure activities have been published for use in life planning outside of careers (Holmberg, Rosen, & Holland, 1990).

The codes that Holland and his colleagues have assigned to different occupations are based primarily on judgments of job analysts. These codes may differ from the codes assigned by authors of interest inventories based on actual test scores. For example, college or university faculty member is coded as an SEI (Social-Enterprising-Investigative) occupation by Gottfredson and Holland (1989), whereas college professor is coded as an IAS (Investigative, Artistic, Social) occupation for men and as an IAR (Investigative, Artistic, Realistic) occupation for women on the Strong (Harmon, et al., 1994). In most cases, the codes based on the two types of systems agree. When they disagree, codes derived by means of actual data should be given greater weight.

Unlike most interest inventories, the SDS uses raw scores in interpreting tests results. Holland has been criticized for this approach in that it reinforces sexual stereotypes (Hanson, Noeth, & Prediger, 1977). With the use of raw scores, men are more likely to obtain high scores on the Realistic and Enterprising scales, and women are more likely to score high on the Artistic and Social scales than they would if standardized scores based on separate-sex norms were used. Holland defended his approach because he says it reflects the real world, namely, that men and women are in fact attracted to different types of occupations.

Holland has recommended that the SDS be supplemented with another inventory that he has developed, My Vocational Situation (MVS), which measures aspects of vocational identity not measured by the SDS (see Chapter 7). Clients with a clear vocational identity probably need relatively little assistance from counselors. The SDS may be sufficient for such clients. Clients who score low on the Vocational Identity scale (indicating difficulties in self-perception) are more likely to need individual counseling or other interventions, such as career seminars or volunteer experiences, in addition to the SDS. Similarly, clients who show a need for occupational information or who face external barriers to their career development, such as lack of money, parental disapproval of career choice, or lack of ability to complete a training program, probably could profit from individual counseling. The SDS may also be supplemented with the Vocational Exploration Insight Kit (VEIK) for clients who desire a more intensified assessment (Holland, 1992).

CASE EXAMPLE

Lisa, a college sophomore, completed both the SDS and the MVS to help her in career exploration after she was dropped from her academic program for poor grades. She had been majoring in biology, with plans to become a dentist, but had lost interest in this career goal some time ago. She planned to reconsider her career plans during the next 3 to 4 months, then reapply to the university the following semester. According to the SDS, her Holland code was ESI (Enterprising-Social-Investigative). In discussing these results, she indicated that she wished to consider the possibility of pursuing a career in business with an emphasis on the environment. The MVI indicated that she lacked occupational information. She planned to take advantage of the time that she would not be in college to explore this type of career direction by talking with people in the field, reading relevant materials, and obtaining volunteer or paid employment in a related field.

Career Decision-Making System Revised (CDM-R). The CDM-R, by Harrington and O'Shea (1992), level 2 (high school students and adults) asks clients to rate themselves in terms of career fields, school subjects, school plans, job values, abilities, and interests. Greatest emphasis is placed on interests assessed by means of 120 items. Each of the six Holland interest categories are represented by 20 items.

Level 1 (grades 7 through 10), which was included as part of the CDM for the first time in the revised edition, is a simplified version of Level 2 consisting of 96 interest items. For both forms, clients score their own answer sheets by simply counting the number of responses in each category. Raw scores (instead of standardized scores) are used in the same manner as the SDS. (The authors have published a set of norms for the interest scales in the manual for those who wish to use them.)

The results are used to suggest career clusters to clients that they may wish to investigate. The CDM-R has received favorable reviews from guidance experts as a system for the delivery of comprehensive career planning services (Vansickle, 1994). It is a simple, yet relatively thorough, instrument that is well integrated with the counseling literature.

Vocational Interest, Experience, and Skill Assessment (VIESA). VIESA (pronounced "Veesa") is a self-scored, short form of the ACT Career Planning Program (described later in this chapter). Level 1 of VIESA should be used with students in grades 8 through 10; level 2 is appropriate for 11th graders through adults. VIESA has no time limits, but most students can complete all of the exercises in 45 minutes.

VIESA enables clients to assess their interests, experiences, and skills by a series of exercises based on the World-of-Work Map (see Figure 10-1; American College Testing Program, 1988b). The map shows the relationships among 23 job families grouped into 12 interest fields. The arrangement of interest fields on the map closely resembles that of the Holland hexagon (see Figure 9-2 in Chapter 9).

The job families and interest fields differ from each other in regard to two basic dimensions: *data versus ideas* and *people versus things*. Each of the exercises for VIESA are scored in terms of these two dimensions. Students use their scores for each exercise to locate on the map those occupations that match their characteristics.

For example, students who express an interest in activities related primarily to people and secondarily to data would be directed to regions 1 and 2 on the map. They would be encouraged to investigate occupations in social and government services, education and related services, and personal customer services (job families U, V, and W, respectively) as ones that might match their interests.

Because of its brevity, VIESA lacks the reliability and validity of the ACT Career Planning Program from which it was adapted. Essentially, VIESA should be looked upon as a well-designed teaching module that can serve as a catalyst for career investigation and self-exploration (Mehrens, 1988).

FIGURE 10-1. World-of-Work Map used in ACT's Career Planning Program

ABOUT THE MAP

• The World-of-Work Map arranges job families (groups of similar jobs) into 12 regions. Together, the job families cover nearly all U.S. jobs. Although the jobs in a family differ in their locations, most are located near the points shown.

• A job family's location is based on its primary work tasks. The four primary work tasks are working with—
    DATA: Facts, numbers, files, accounts, business procedures.
    IDEAS: Insights, theories, new ways of saying or doing something—for example, with words, equations, or music.
    PEOPLE: People you help, serve, inform, care for, or sell things to.
    THINGS: Machines, tools, living things, and materials such as food, wood, or metal.

• Six general areas of the work world and related Holland types are indicated around the edge of the map. Job Family Charts (available from ACT) list over 500 occupations by general area, job family, and preparation level. They cover more than 95% of the labor force.

Note. © 1996 by The American College Testing Program. All rights reserved. Reprinted with permission.

Campbell Interest and Skill Survey (CISS). After parting company with the publishers of the Strong Interest Inventory (formerly known as the Strong-Campbell Interest Inventory), David Campbell developed the CISS together with a series of other instruments known as the Campbell Development Surveys (Campbell, 1993). The CISS is similar to the Strong in that it includes both general and occupational interest scales; it differs by its inclusion of a set of self-report skill scales to match each of the interest scales.

The CISS provides interest and skill scores for 7 Orientation scales, 29 Basic scales, 60 Occupational scales (including Nurse and Engineer, which have recently been added to the profile), and 3 Special scales (Academic Focus, Extroversion, and Variety). The 7 Orientation scales are similar to the 6 Holland scales on the Strong except that they have been renamed, and the Strong Realistic scale has been subdivided into Producing and Adventuring scales. The Basic scales on the CISS bear much in common with the Basic scales on the Strong.

In contrast with the Strong, the CISS uses unisex Occupational scales instead of separate scales for men and women. These scales were formed by comparing the interests and skills of a combined sample of men and women in the occupation with a general reference sample of men and women. The proportions of men and women in the general reference sample were adjusted for each occupation to match the proportions of men and women in the occupational sample as a means of controlling for gender differences. The effectiveness of this technique in creating scales that will prove equally valid for both sexes needs further study.

Reliability studies indicate that all of the scales possess adequate test-retest reliabilities. Scores on most scales can be expected to vary by 4 to 5 points upon retesting after 3 months. The Occupational scales are valid in that they differentiate people in the occupation from people in general by approximately two standard deviations for most occupations (Campbell, Hyne, & Nilsen, 1992).

Scores on the skill and interest scales for the same occupations are interpreted in terms of the following four categories:

- Pursue—high interest, high skill
- Explore—high skill, lower interest
- Develop—high interest, lower skill
- Avoid—low interest, low skill

191

For example, individuals with a high score on the Accountant skill scale, but a relatively low score on the Accountant interest scale, are encouraged to explore this occupation more thoroughly with the thought that their interests in it might be enhanced or that they might find a niche in the occupational field that they would enjoy.

According to Fuqua and Newman (1994, p. 142), the CISS represents "a well-developed, adequately tested, and user-friendly instrument for the purposes of career exploration." In addition to the CISS, other instruments in the Campbell Development Surveys include the Campbell Organizational Survey, Campbell Leadership Index, Campbell-Hallam Team Development Survey, and Campbell Community Survey (Campbell, 1993). These instruments, which possess many characteristics in common to aid interpretation, can help counselors in their work with teams, organizations, and communities in addition to individuals.

Computer-Based Programs

A number of computer-based career and life planning programs have been developed in recent years. These programs assist clients in self-assessment, environmental assessment (i.e., educational and occupational information), and decision making. The self-assessment modules usually ask clients to evaluate their interests, values, and skills. Based on the self-evaluations, the computer generates a list of appropriate occupations.

Two popular programs are SIGI + (System of Interactive Guidance and Information), from Educational Testing Service, and DISCOVER, a creation of the American College Testing Program. (Separate versions of DISCOVER have been developed for colleges and adults, high schools, and junior high and middle schools.) Both programs are comprehensive, interactive, and simple to use, and both are updated each year. Students and counselors react positively to both programs (Kapes, Borman, & Frazier, 1989).

Research indicates that use of computer-based programs leads to increased retention of career information and to greater certainty of occupational choice (Pyle, 1984). The programs are most effective when they are used in conjunction with counseling (Kapes et al., 1989; Roselle & Hummel, 1988).

192

Career and Life Planning Workbooks

Career and life planning workbooks play an important part in comprehensive self-rating programs used by counselors. These workbooks usually include a number of exercises that can be used by clients to assess their interests, values, personality style, and skills. Additional exercises aid clients in exploring the work environment by means of informational interviews and reviews of career literature. The workbooks are well suited to career education classes or career exploration groups. They usually employ a decision-making or problem-solving model as a framework for presentation of the exercises.

Examples of effective career and life planning workbooks include *What Color is Your Parachute?* (Bolles, 1996), *Career Actualization and Life Planning* (Blocher, 1989), and *Discover the Career Within You* (Carney & Wells, 1995). All of the exercises provided in the workbooks are informal or qualitative in nature. They are meant to stimulate interest in career exploration by offering a variety of assessment procedures in a systematic fashion.

The *Quick Job-Hunting Map for Beginners*, a short self-assessment workbook, enables clients to identify transferable work skills represented in the different types of activities they have pursued in their lives (Bolles, 1990). The advanced version of this workbook provides a checklist of over 150 different types of skills clients use for evaluating their work and life experiences (Bolles, 1991). Similar types of exercises designed to aid clients in self-assessment can be found in workbooks accompanying computer-based career planning programs, such as the *Career Skills Workbook* (Center on Education and Work, 1995).

STANDARDIZED CAREER AND LIFE PLANNING PROGRAMS

As indicated by their name, standardized career and life planning programs employ a series of standardized tests to assess an individual's preferences and capabilities. Five of the most often used programs—ACT Career Planning Program, DAT Career Planning Program, Counselee Assessment/Occupational Exploration System, Armed Services Vocational Aptitude Battery, and Career Occupational Preference System—are discussed in this section. Each of these assessment batteries includes objective tests of abilities in addition to inventories of interests, values, or experiences. The measures in this section have been validated most often in terms of work or academic performance.

ACT Career Planning Program (CPP)

The CPP provides a series of measures at two levels (grades 8 through 10 and grade 11 through adult; American College Testing Program, 1994). The measures include an interest inventory, an experiences inventory, a self-rated abilities report, and timed abilities tests. It is an extended, standardized version of VIESA. The entire program requires nearly 3 hours of testing and administration time, which can be divided into three testing sessions if necessary.

The revised unisex edition of the ACT Interest Inventory (UNIACT-R), which serves as the measure of interests, consists of 90 items chosen to represent the six interest fields identified by Holland (American College Testing Program, 1995). Each of the six fields (Technical, Science, Arts, Social Service, Business Contact, and Business Operations) is assessed by means of 15 items. All items yield equivalent responses for men and women; items that showed significant sex differences were eliminated. For this reason, combined-sex norms can be used. The client's interests are compared with the activities represented in different clusters of occupations by means of the World of Work Map (see Figure 10-1).

The Work-Related Experiences Inventory contains six scales that match the six categories of the interest inventory. Sample items from level 2 of the CPP include "identified star constellations by name" and "performed in a variety show." Students answer *never, only once or twice,* or *several times* for each item. Counselors can use this information to review both the depth and the range of experience in situations related to work activities. The Experience scales add to the validity of the Interest scales. The measured interests of students possess greater predictive validity when they are supported by relevant experiences than when they are not (Prediger & Swaney, 1985).

The Self-Rated Abilities Questionnaire asks students to rate themselves in nine broad categories that are difficult to measure with existing tests of abilities. The Ability Test Battery includes six timed measures of ability: Reading Skills, Numerical Skills, Language Usage, Mechanical Reasoning, Space Relations, and Clerical Speed/Accuracy.

Each of the six tests is somewhat speeded. Counselors should take into account the speed at which the student worked in interpreting the meaning of the test scores. Norms have been established for the 8th, 10th, and 12th grades; norms are needed for community college students and adults, however.

The test-retest reliabilities were only moderately high over short time periods (2 to 5 weeks) for secondary school students. The median reliabilities ranged from .76 to .82 for the three types of measures (Interests, Experiences, and Abilities; American College Testing Program, 1988a). Scores for each scale should be interpreted as falling within one of five categories: high, moderately high, average, moderately low, or low. More precise measurement is not feasible given the level of reliability. In regard to validity, the CPP scores effectively differentiate among individuals pursuing various educational and occupational objectives.

Differential Aptitude Tests (DAT)

The DAT, a well established measure of abilities in secondary school, can be used together with the new Career Interest Inventory (CII) to generate educational and career planning reports for counselors and students. Originally published in 1947, it was most recently revised in 1990 as the fifth edition, forms C and D (Psychological Corporation, 1992). The CII replaces the Career Planning Questionnaire (CPQ) as a measure of work and school interests that can be used either together with the DAT or separately.

Both the DAT and CII include two levels of assessment: level 1 for grades 7 through 9, and level 2 for grades 10 through 12. Both levels of the DAT and level 2 of the CII may also be used with adults. When the DAT and the CII are administered together the results are integrated by means of a computerized educational and career planning report.

The DAT contains eight subtests: Verbal Reasoning, Numerical Ability, Abstract Reasoning, Perceptual Speed and Accuracy, Mechanical Reasoning, Space Relations, Spelling, and Language Usage. The eight tests require 2½ to 3 hours to complete. Although all the tests are timed, they function primarily as power tests except for the Perceptual Speed and Accuracy test. The tests can be hand-scored or computer-scored.

The CII, which is a more comprehensive measure of interests than the instrument it replaces, provides scores for 15 occupational groups for both levels 1 and 2. In addition, level 1 reports scores for 16 school subjects and 16 school activities, while level 2 yields scores for 20 school subjects.

The current version of the DAT has been normed jointly with the CII. Members of the norm groups represent students from different parts of the country, different socioeconomic classes, and different ethnic groups. The norm tables have been subdivided in terms of sex and grade. In contrast with previous editions of the DAT, extensive adult norms are also provided.

The DAT subtests possess high internal consistency and alternate-form reliability. Test scores are reported as percentile bands that take test error into consideration.

The DAT has been validated primarily in terms of educational criteria. Typically, DAT scores have been correlated with course grades from a variety of subjects. In most cases, combined scores on Verbal Reasoning plus Numerical Ability (VR + NA) produce the highest correlations with course performance. Except for Perceptual Speed and Accuracy, test scores are highly intercorrelated, so that differential prediction (the goal of the DAT) is questionable. Nonetheless, Wang (1995, p. 170) has noted that "the DAT is still the best battery of its kind."

As part of the scoring service available from the publishers, the Counselor's Report for the combined DAT and CII indicates whether or not a student's occupational plans match his or her aptitude test scores, career interest scores, educational plans, school subjects, and school activities. This report alerts counselors to students who have made inappropriate plans and who may be at risk of failing or dropping out of school.

The DAT can also be administered and scored on site by computer. This version, called the DAT Computerized Adaptive Edition (DAT Adaptive), administers only the items that are most appropriate for the student's ability level. By the use of item response theory (IRT), the computer is able to eliminate questions that would be too difficult or too easy for the student as the student progresses through each test. When the adaptive version is used, testing time is cut in half. Research indicates that scores obtained in this manner are just as reliable and valid as scores based on the complete test.

An abbreviated version of the DAT, known as the DAT for Personnel and Career Assessment, has been developed for use in organizational settings (Bennett, Seashore, & Wesman, 1989). This version, which has been derived from Form V (fourth edition) of the DAT, contains 40% fewer items. Extensive data showing the relationship between the DAT scores and job performance are provided in the technical manual.

Counselee Assessment/Occupational Exploration System

The Counselee Assessment/Occupational Exploration System of the United States Employment Service (USES) takes advantage of the extensive research conducted by this agency on career aptitudes and interests (Droege, 1987). This system uses scores from the USES Interest Inventory together with scores from the General Aptitude Test Battery (GATB) to identify career possibilities listed in the *Guide for Occupational Exploration* (Maze, 1991).

USES Interest Inventory (USES-II). The USES-II consists of 162 items arranged in 12 categories (U.S. Department of Labor, 1981). The 162 items describe various activities (e.g., "draw cartoons for newspapers," and "diagnose and treat vision problems") that are answered *like, not sure,* or *dislike.* The items represent all worker-trait groups and occupational groups in the *Dictionary of Occupational Titles* (Droege & Hawk, 1977). Factor analysis of the original item pool revealed 11 factors for both male and female samples: Artistic, Scientific, Plants & Animals, Protective, Mechanical, Industrial, Business Detail, Selling, Accommodating, Humanitarian, and Leading & Influencing. The best items were retained to form interest scales of 10 to 15 items each for the 11 factors. A 12th scale, Physical Performing, was added to represent a small group of occupations that did not fit any of the other 11 fields.

The USES-II, which may be used with high school students or adults age 16 and older, requires about 20 minutes of testing time. It possesses extensive separate-sex and combined-sex norms based on a broad sample of students and both employed and unemployed adults. Reliability studies indicate high internal consistency of scores and high test-retest reliabilities of scores over a 2-week time period. Validity studies support the predictive and factorial validity of the USES-II (Bolton, 1994).

The main advantage of the USES-II lies in the ease with which it may be related to GATB test scores and the world of work. The same subcategories are used to classify work fields both for the USES-II and the GATB. The same 12 interest fields measured by the USES-II are used in the *Guide for Occupational Exploration* (GOE; Maze, 1991) to classify all of the occupations defined by the *Dictionary of Occupational Titles* (USDOL, 1993).

For some situations, the USES Interest Check List (USDOL, 1979) serves as an alternative to the USES-II. The Interest Check List is essentially an interview aid. It consists of 210 sample tasks that have been keyed to the 66 work groups listed in the GOE. It does not require scoring or any type of specialized training to interpret. It is most appropriate for clients who are relatively certain of their career choice. For such clients, it provides an organized structure for them to convey their interests to the counselor. The information provided by the Interest Check List is not as reliable or valid as that provided by the USES-II. The counselor should use the USES-II with clients who need help in clarifying a career direction.

General Aptitude Test Battery (GATB). The GATB was first published by the U. S. Department of Labor in 1947 to be used by counselors in state employment services. It is controlled by the federal government, but its use has since been expanded to Veterans Administration offices and hospitals, vocational counseling offices, and high schools and community colleges (USDOL, 1982). Because the battery is used in some settings to select or recommend job applicants for employment, test security is important. Counselors outside of the employment service must have special training and permission to use the battery. In high schools it is sometimes administered to graduating seniors who do not plan on further education and who expect to enter the local employment market upon graduation. In community colleges it is used for counseling and guidance and occasionally for selection in the vocational programs in those institutions.

The battery yields nine aptitude scores based on 12 separate tests. The nine aptitudes comprise three cognitive (general learning ability, verbal aptitude, and numerical aptitude), three perceptual (spatial aptitude, form perception, clerical perception) and three psychomotor (motor coordination, finger dexterity, and manual dexterity) factors.

The tests are highly speeded. Ten of the 12 tests are paper-and-pencil tests; 2 tests require a special apparatus. The battery of 12 tests can be administered in approximately 2½ hours. The nine aptitude scores are expressed as standard scores with a mean of 100 and standard deviation of 20. In addition to adult norms, 9th- and 10th-grade norms are also available.

As a result of validity studies conducted by the USES, cut-off scores have been established for aptitudes that are important for success in various occupations. The cut-off scores have been used to determine occupational ability patterns (OAPs) for different work groups. All of the occupations in the *Dictionary of Occupational Titles* have been classified into 66 work groups, most of which are represented by OAPS. The OAPs have been used for counseling and job referral by employment service agencies and other agencies at which the GATB has been administered.

Median test-retest or alternate-form reliabilities generally range from .80 to .90 with the paper-and-pencil tests yielding higher reliabilities than the dexterity tests. The test reliabilities are affected by both the speed and accuracy of the respondent. Counselors should be aware that the GATB may not adequately assess the aptitudes of those who, for one reason or another, are unable to work very quickly.

Large numbers of empirical studies have been carried out, with some of them showing substantial validity coefficients for certain types of jobs. The typical validity coefficients fall in the neighborhood of .40. These validities have been obtained for individual tests or for a combination of several aptitudes. Unfortunately, the GATB suffers from the same problem noted for the DAT; that is, differential prediction is limited because of the high correlations among the subtest scores. If clients qualify for one OAP, they often qualify for many others as well.

Recently, the U. S. Employment Service has begun to use composite weighted scores instead of multiple cut-off scores to identify occupational fields that match the client's abilities (USDOL, 1992). Use of the composite weighted scores has improved the validity of the GATB for predicting job performance. Composite percentile scores are provided for a total of 179 job groups that differ in terms of field and level.

Keesling and Healy (1988) suggested that clients compare GATB scores with their own estimates of their abilities. If discrepancies occur, the client may wish to consider such matters as (a) how speed may have affected the test results, (b) what type of work or educational experience formed the basis for the self-estimate, and (c) what comparison group was used to make the self-estimate. They believed that the GATB scores help clients to make "reasoned estimates" of their abilities compared with working adults.

The GATB has been more thoroughly studied than any other occupational ability test. In general, it predicts occupational performance more effectively than other ability measures for both minority and majority group members (Bolton, 1994). The GATB and the USES-II in combination can be used to generate a list of job fields for clients to consider in which they most likely would be both successful and satisfied.

Armed Services Vocational Aptitude Battery (ASVAB) Career Exploration Program

The current versions of ASVAB (Forms 18a, 18b, 19a, and 19b), which are administered and interpreted without charge by representatives of the Armed Services, provide scores on 10 individual scales and three composite indices (U.S. Department of Defense, 1992). Test results are used by the military for recruitment and research; school counselors use the results to help high school students (grades 10 through 12) and community college students make educational and vocational plans. Testing time, including instructions, is approximately 3 hours. More than 1 million students complete the tests each year.

The 10 individual scales include Word Knowledge (WK), Paragraph Comprehension, (PC), Arithmetic Reasoning (AR), Mathematics Knowledge (MK), General Science (GS), Auto & Shop Information (AS), Mechanical Comprehension (MC), Electronics Information (EI), Numerical Operations (NO), and Coding Speed (CS). The composite scores are Verbal Ability (WK + PC), Math Ability (AR + MK), and Academic Ability (Verbal Ability + Math Ability). The ASVAB profile shows a primary and secondary ASVAB code (each with five levels) for each student based on his or her Academic Ability Composite score. In addition, a military careers score is also derived, which is based on a combination of the Academic Ability score + MC + EI for use in suggesting military careers to students. Only the composite scores are used for counseling and selection purposes.

Besides the ASVAB test scores, the ASVAB Career Exploration Program consists of the Self-Directed Search (described earlier in this chapter) and a work values checklist, both of which are included in *Exploring Careers: The ASVAB Workbook*. The student's academic ability composite code, Holland code (derived from the Self-Directed Search), work values, and educational plans are entered by the student in a booklet titled *OCCU-FIND* to identify occupations that match one's characteristics.

Internal consistency coefficients are high (.92 to .96) for the composite scores. The composite scores are significantly correlated (.30 to .60) with training and job performance in both civilian and military settings (U.S. Department of Defense, 1992). Some concerns exist regarding the use of the ASVAB with minority groups, especially African Americans and Hispanics who consistently obtain low Academic Ability composite codes (Prediger & Swaney, 1992).

In general, the ASVAB, together with its accompanying materials, has shown great improvement since its inception in 1968, especially in selecting candidates for military careers (Elmore & Bradley, 1994). From a counseling standpoint, however, it appears to place too much emphasis on general intelligence. Research indicates that informed self-estimates across a broad range of abilities (e.g., meeting people, leadership/management, and creative/artistic) can greatly enhance the effectiveness of the ASVAB in differentiating among students in various career fields (Prediger & Swaney, 1992).

Career Occupational Preference System (COPSystem)

The COPSystem includes measures of interests, values, and abilities as follows (Knapp-Lee, Knapp, & Knapp, 1990): (a) the Career Occupational Preference System (COPS) Interest Inventory assesses interests in 14 occupational clusters at different educational levels, (b) the Career Orientation Placement and Evaluation Survey (COPES) measures eight personal values related to the work one does, and (c) the Career Ability Placement Survey (CAPS) measures eight abilities that are important for different types of work.

Several versions of the COPS Interest Inventory have been developed to take into account different grade levels and reading abilities of the clients. The COPS Interest Inventory itself may be used with seventh-grade students through adults. The COPS-II (Intermediate Inventory), a highly visual, simplified version of the COPS Interest Inventory based on knowledge of school subjects and activities familiar to younger students, may be used with elementary school children or with adults who have a limited reading ability (fourth-grade level). The COPS-R (Form R) differs from the COPS Interest Inventory in that it contains sex-balanced items, combined-sex norms, and simplified language (sixth-grade reading level). The COPS-R more closely parallels the COPS Interest Inventory than does the COPS-II. The COPS-P (Professional Level) provides an advanced version for colleges students and adults who may be considering professional occupations. Finally, the COPS-PIC (Picture Inventory) use pictures only to assess the interests of nonreaders or those with reading difficulties.

Both the COPS Interest Inventory and the COPES have recently been revised (EdITS, 1995). The COPS Interest Inventory has been renormed. The COPES has been more closely integrated with other measures in the COPSystem. The COPSystem contributes significantly to the counseling process by stimulating clients to explore career fields from different viewpoints. Test experts have endorsed the COPSystem for its "versatility and usefulness" based on its continued development and refinement (Wickwire & Faldet, 1994, p. 161).

USE OF COMPREHENSIVE ASSESSMENT PROGRAMS IN COUNSELING

Several recommendations for the use of comprehensive assessment programs discussed in this chapter are listed below:

1. Use self-rating career and life planning programs such as the Self-Directed Search to promote self-examination and career exploration, especially for people who are unwilling or unable to see a counselor.

2. Use standardized career and life planning programs to obtain data to predict an individual's success and satisfaction in an educational or occupational setting.

3. Disregard small differences between test scores on multiple aptitude tests. Use percentile bands to interpret scores; if percentile bands for two scores overlap, ignore score differences.

4. Use combined verbal and numerical ability measures to predict school or job success. Not only is this measure more valid than the other test scores in most cases, but also it shows less sex difference.

5. Develop local norms for interpreting results, especially if the results are used to estimate performance in local courses.

6. Consider recommendations listed in materials that accompany comprehensive career planning programs, but proceed cautiously. Obtain supporting material from other sources before making any decisions based on these recommendations. Remember that, for the most part, aptitude tests lack differential predictive validity.

7. Help students with low scores consider how they may improve their scores through appropriate course work or related experiences.

8. Interpret aptitude scores as measures of *developed* abilities. Exposure to the subject matter represented within the test is necessary for the student to perform well on the test.

9. Use nonlanguage tests, such as the Abstract Reasoning and Spatial Relations tests from the DAT, for students with limited English language skills to determine general ability to learn new material or to perform tasks for which knowledge of English is not required.

10. Consult supplementary materials provided by publishers of comprehensive career planning programs. For example, *Using the DAT With Adults* provides suggestions for various settings. Use student workbooks to encourage active participation on the part of clients.

SUMMARY

1. Comprehensive assessment programs for career and life planning provide measures of an individual's values, interests, and abilities that can be compared with the requirements of different educational and occupational environments.

2. Comprehensive assessment programs differ in terms of their assessment procedures. Some of the programs use self-assessments of all characteristics, including abilities. Others use standardized procedures with objective measures of abilities.

3. The Self-Directed Search represents a comprehensive self-assessment career and life planning program based on Holland's model of career behavior.

4. The Campbell Interest and Skill Survey uses self-rated abilities as well as self-rated interests to assess one's similarity to people in 60 different occupations.

5. The ACT and DAT Career Planning Programs provide the most reliable and valid measures of success in educational settings.

6. The GATB and ASVAB multiple aptitude tests offer the most reliable and valid indicators of occupational performance.

7. Multiple aptitude tests have been much more effective in predicting job success in general than they have been in predicting in which job the person will be most successful.

IV

Personality Assessment

11

PERSONALITY INVENTORIES

T HE TERM *personality* is often used to cover a very broad concept. When applied to psychological assessment instruments, however, it is used more narrowly to describe those instruments designed to assess personal, emotional, and social traits and behaviors, as distinguished from instruments that measure aptitudes, achievements, and interests. The instruments discussed in this chapter are generally referred to as self-report personality inventories in which respondents check or rate items that they believe are most descriptive of themselves.

A description of the different approaches used to construct these inventories is followed by a description of 10 inventories often used by counselors.

INVENTORY DEVELOPMENT

There are four different methods by which personality tests have been constructed (Anastasi, 1988). One that uses a deductive approach is the *logical content method*. In this method, the inventory author uses a rational approach to choosing items. Statements related to the characteristic being assessed are logically deduced to be related to the content of the characteristic being assessed. The Occupational Theme scales of the Strong Interest Inventory and the new content scales of the MMPI-2 (discussed in Chapter 15) use this method. The principal limitation of this approach is that it assumes the validity of each item— that individuals are capable of evaluating their own characteristics and that their answers can be taken at face value. If a client checks an item related to "not getting along with parents," this approach assumes that that he or she is having parental difficulties.

The second approach is the *theoretical method*, in which items are developed to measure constructs represented by a particular theory of personality. After the items have been grouped into scales, a construct validity approach is taken to determine whether the inventory results are consistent with the theory. Two examples of this approach are Jackson's Personality Research Form (PRF), based on Murray's theory of needs, and the Myers-Briggs Type Indicator (MBTI), based on Jung's theory of personality types.

Two methods make use of empirical (data-based) strategies to develop personality inventories. The *criterion group method* begins with a sample with known characteristics, such as a group of diagnosed schizophrenics. An item pool is then administered to individuals in the known sample and to a control group (usually a "normal" population). The items that distinguish the known sample from the control group are then placed on a scale in a manner similar to the method used to construct the occupational scales on the Strong Interest Inventory. Typically these items are then used on another similar sample to determine whether the scale continues to distinguish between the two groups. This method can also be used with groups that present contrasts on a particular trait. For example, members of fraternities and sororities are asked to judge the five most and the five least sociable individuals in their group, and then items that distinguish between these two groups are used in the development of a sociability scale.

The MMPI and the California Psychological Inventory (CPI) are both based on the criterion group method of inventory construction.

The *factor analytic method* is the second method using empirical strategy in test development. In this method a statistical procedure is used to examine the intercorrelations among all of the items on the inventory. This technique, which can be completed effectively only on a modern computer, groups items into factors until a substantial proportion of the variability among the items has been accounted for by the dimensions that have resulted. An example of this approach is Cattell's Sixteen Personality Factor Questionnaire (16PF), which resulted from a factor analysis of 171 terms that describe human traits and that were, in turn, developed from a list of thousands of adjectives that in one way or another describe humans. The factor analytic method also includes the use of internal consistency measures to develop homogeneous scales.

Researchers using factor-analytic techniques across a number of personality inventories have synthesized personality traits into five major dimensions nicknamed the "Big Five." These five factors are (a) neuroticism—insecure versus self-confident, (b) extroversion—outgoing versus shy, (c) openness—imaginative versus concrete, (d) agreeableness—empathic versus hostile, and (e) conscientiousness—well-organized versus impulsive (Costa & McCrae, 1992; Costa & Widiger, 1994; Goldberg, 1993; McCrae & Costa, 1986). The NEO Personality Inventory–Revised (NEO-PI-R) has been developed specifically to assess these Big Five factors. The four dimensions of the MBTI are related to each of the last four of these factors, but not to neuroticism. The MMPI, on the other hand, contains numerous items related to neuroticism and fewer relating to the other four factors.

SELF-REPORT PERSONALITY INVENTORIES

The Myers-Briggs Type Indicator (MBTI)

Work on the MBTI was begun in the 1920s by Katherine Briggs when she developed a system of psychological types by conceptualizing her observations and readings (Myers & McCaulley, 1985). Upon finding much similarity between her conclusions and those of Carl Jung, who was working at the same time, she began using his theory. Together with her daughter Isabel Myers, she developed an inventory now known as the Myers-Briggs Type Indicator. The inventory, in its several forms, was slow in gaining acceptance but is now reported to be the most widely used personality inventory outside of clinical settings.

The MBTI is based on Jung's concepts of perception and judgment that are used by different types of people. Each of the several forms of the MBTI are scored on eight scales (four pairs) yielding four bipolar dimensions. Jung's theory proposes that apparently random variations in human behavior can be systematically accounted for by the manner in which individuals prefer to employ their capacities for perception and judgment. The MBTI is a self-reporting instrument designed to identify these preferences.

The first of the four dimensions involves the preference for extroversion versus introversion (E-I). Extroverts prefer to direct their energy to the outer world of people and things, whereas introverts tend to focus energy on the inner world of ideas.

The second dimension measures personal preference for mode of perceiving, and is labeled the sensing-intuition (S-N) dimension. Sensing individuals prefer to rely on one or more of the five senses as their primary mode of perceiving. Intuitive people, on the other hand, rely primarily on indirect perception by the way of the mind, incorporating ideas or associations that are related to perceptions coming from the outside.

The third MBTI dimension is designed to measure an individual's preference for judging data obtained through sensing or intuition by means of either thinking or feeling (T-F). A thinking orientation signifies a preference for drawing conclusions using an objective, impersonal, logical approach. A feeling-oriented individual is much more likely to base decisions on personal or social rationales that take into account the subjective feelings of others.

The fourth dimension measures a person's preference for either a judging or perceiving (J-P) orientation for dealing with the external world. Although individuals must use both perception and judgment in their daily lives, most find one of these orientations to be more comfortable than the other and employ it more often, in the same way that a right-handed person favors the use of that hand. Persons with a judgment orientation are anxious to employ either the thinking or feeling mode to arrive at a decision or conclusion as quickly as possible. The perceptive person is more comfortable continuing to collect information through either a sensing or intuitive process and delaying judgment as long as possible. This fourth dimension was not defined by Jung but represents an additional concept of Briggs and Myers.

Although the four dimensions of the MBTI are theoretically independent, significant correlations in the vicinity of .30 have been found between the S-N and J-P scales. This finding tends to support Jung's theory, which included only the first three dimensions. Other than the relationship between these two sets of scales, the remaining scales are statistically independent of each other.

A person's MBTI personality type is summarized in four letters, which indicate the direction of the person's preference on each of the four dimensions. All possible combinations of the four paired scales result in 16 different personality types. Thus an ENTJ is an extrovert with a preference for intuition and thinking who generally has a judging attitude in his or her orientation toward the outer world. An ISFP type indicates an introvert with a preference toward sensing and feeling who has a perceptive orientation toward the outer world. The manual provides a summary of the processes, characteristics, and traits of each of the 16 types.

When computing personality type, scores are obtained for each of the opposite preferences and then subtracted to obtain the particular type. A large difference between the two scores indicates a clear preference and yields a higher score on that type, whereas a smaller difference yields a low score, indicating a preference on that type that is considered less strong and less clear. Even though the difference is small (and the scoring formula eliminates ties), one or the other letter is included in the four-letter code type. A major criticism of the MBTI is that the variables assessed result in dichotomies, although there is little psychological evidence of such dichotomies or bimodal distributions. Instead, the variables can best be represented as continuous bipolar distributions that fall along a normal curve (Pittenger, 1993). Although an individual's type is supposed to remain relatively constant over a lifetime, norms on several MBTI dimensions change substantially between adolescence and adulthood as well as during the adult years (Cummings, 1995).

Split-half reliability studies of the MBTI have generally yielded correlation coefficients exceeding .80 and test-retest correlations ranging from .70 to .85. In terms of the four letter types, reliability data tend to be somewhat discouraging. An individual's four-letter MBTI type has only about a 50-50 chance of being identical on retesting. On the average, 75% of the persons completing the instrument will retain three of the four dichotomous type preferences on retesting.

One of the reasons the MBTI is attractive to many individuals is that there are no good or bad scores nor good or bad combinations of types. Since both polarities can be viewed as strengths, this non-judgmental quality facilitates interpreting results to clients. A score indicates a preference for certain functions or behaviors, although most individuals have the capacity to make use of the opposite preference as well. Each preference includes some strengths, joys, and positive characteristics, and each has its problems and blind spots. In the interpretive materials in the manual, as well as in a number of other publications, the strengths, weaknesses, abilities, needs, values, interests, and other characteristics are provided for scores on each of the scales as well as for the 16 types. Resources include *Gifts Differing* (Myers & Myers, 1993), *People Types and Tiger Stripes* (Lawrence, 1992), *Introduction to Type* (Myers, 1980), *Portraits of Type: An MBTI Research Compendium* (Thorne & Gough, 1991), *Type Talk* (Kroeger & Thuesen, 1988), and *Applications of the MBTI in Higher Education* (Provost & Anchors, 1987). Answer sheets can also be mailed to Consulting Psychologists Press for computer-based interpretations.

The MBTI is used in a number of counseling situations. It is often used to explore relationships between couples and among family members (see Chapter 13). It is used to develop teamwork and an understanding of relationships in work situations and in vocational counseling by examining the effects of each of the four preferences in work situations. For example, introverts like a work situation that provides quiet or concentration and may have problems communicating, whereas extroverts like variety in action and are usually able to communicate freely. People with strong thinking preferences are interested in fairness and logic and may not be sensitive to other people's feelings. Feeling types tend to be very aware of other people's feelings and find it difficult to tell people unpleasant things. Thus preferences and strengths on the MBTI can be discussed in terms of occupational functions and work environments, although solid validity data for such use still needs to be obtained.

In addition, the manual lists the types of people found in various occupations from a vast data pool of persons in different occupations who have had the MBTI administered to them. Persons with certain MBTI types are found in substantially higher proportions in certain occupations. All types may enter all types of occupations, but certain types choose particular occupations far more often than others. For example, although all types are represented among psychologists, 85% of psychologists are intuitive types and only 15% are sensing types, but they are almost exactly evenly split on the introvert-extrovert dimension. The MBTI is seldom used by itself in career counseling, but is often used along with interest inventories and other psychological test results and adds an additional dimension in vocational counseling (Tieger & Barron-Tieger, 1992).

Individuals who are intuitive, feeling, and perceptive seem to be more likely to seek counseling than individuals with other MBTI types (Mendelsohn & Kirk, 1962; Vilas, 1988). Some counselors administer the MBTI before counseling has begun so that they can use the results, along with the knowledge of their own type, in structuring the counseling process for a particular client.

Because of the wide variety of settings in which counselors use the MBTI, no specific list of guidelines for its use or interpretation is included here. Because of its popularity and seemingly simplistic interpretation of results, however, it is often administered and interpreted by those who are overly enthusiastic about its use or who have little background in psychological assessment. Counselors who make use of this personality inventory should be aware not only of its strengths and usefulness in various settings, but also its various weaknesses, including ipsative scoring and lack of criterion related validity studies in certain settings.

The MBTI should not be used to label or narrowly categorize people. Although most people have a preferred personality style that they can learn to use to their advantage, they can also learn to express the less dominant aspects of their personality when appropriate. Counselors can teach clients to become more flexible in the manner in which they respond to different situations.

The California Psychological Inventory (CPI)

The CPI (third edition) was developed for use with relatively well-adjusted persons (Gough & Bradley, 1995). Although the MMPI was used as a basis for development of this inventory (over one third of the CPI items), the CPI is designed to measure everyday characteristics that its author, Harrison Gough, calls "folk concepts," such as sociability, tolerance, and responsibility—terms that people use every day to classify and predict each other's behavior. The 1995 version of the CPI (Form 434) differs from the previous version (Form 462) in at least three ways: (a) 28 items were dropped from Form 462 because of legal proscriptions, privacy considerations, or offensive content; (b) the scales have been renormed on larger standardization samples of 3,000 men and 3,000 women; and (c) five new special purpose or research scales (e.g., Leadership, Amicability) have been added. The CPI has been restandardized in such a way that the old and new scales can be considered interchangeable.

The items deal with typical behavior patterns and attitudes with less objectionable content than that of the MMPI. The scales are designed to assess personality characteristics and to aid in the understanding of the interpersonal behavior of "normal" individuals. Thus the CPI is sometimes termed "the sane person's MMPI."

The CPI contains 20 folk scales that are organized into four separate clusters (see Figure 11-1):

1. The first cluster is designed to assess interpersonal adequacy of poise, self-assurance, and ascendency. It contains seven scales titled Dominance (Do), Capacity for Status (Cs), Sociability (Sy), Social Presence (Sp), Self-Acceptance (Sa), Independence (In), and Empathy (Em).

2. The second cluster contains measures of socialization, responsibility, and character with seven scales titled Responsibility (Re), Socialization (So), Self-Control (Sc), Good Impression (Gi), Communality (Cm), Well-Being (Wb), and Tolerance (To).

3. The third cluster contains scales measuring intellectual and academic themes useful in educational counseling. The three scales in this cluster are titled Achievement via Conformance (Ac), Achievement via Independence (Ai), and Intellectual Efficiency (Ie).

4. The fourth cluster contains a mixed group of three scales that do not fit well together nor are they highly related to scales in the other three clusters. They include Psychological-Mindedness (Py), Flexibility (Fx), and Femininity-Masculinity (F/M).

Of the 20 CPI scales, 13 were developed by the criterion-group method, four by internal consistency analysis (Sp, Sa, Sc, Fx), and

FIGURE 11-1. CPI Profile for Theresa

three by a combination of these two methods (Gi, Cm, and Wb; Gough, 1987).

Three of the scales are validity scales developed to detect faking or other test-taking attitudes. "Faking bad" is detected by T-scores of 35 or less on the Well-Being (Wb), Communality (Cm), or Good Impression (Gi) scales. Scores on the Communality scale are based on a frequency count of popular responses, with low scores suggesting that the inventory has been taken in a random or idiosyncratic fashion. When a "fake bad" profile is obtained, the counselor should ask why the individual feels a need to create an impression of serious problems. The person might in fact have very serious problems, or might be malingering for some reason, or the low score might represent a cry for help. The Good Impression scale is based on responses by normal individuals asked to "fake good" to identify persons who are overly concerned about making a good impression. "Faking good" is suggested by a Gi T-score of 65 or more with this score as the highest on the profile. Generally most other scales will also show scores in the positive direction, which makes it difficult to differentiate between an individual with an excellent level of adjustment and one who is faking good. Here an individual's history can usually help the counselor to differentiate between faking good and superior adjustment.

Standard scores (T-scores) are reported on a profile with a mean of 50 and a standard deviation of 10 (see Figure 11-1). High scores tend to indicate psychological health and lower scores psychological inadequacy or distress (except for the F/M scale). Different profiles are used to plot scores for men and women. Norms in the current version are based on 3,000 men and 3,000 women representing heterogeneous samples from high school and college students, teachers, business executives, prison executives, psychiatric patients, and prison inmates.

Reliability coefficients for some scales show substantial reliability, whereas for others coefficients are more moderate. Median alpha coefficients for the 20 folk concept scales were .72 for men and .73 for women. The large numbers of validity studies conducted with the CPI, usually exploring either predictive or concurrent validity, have yielded validity indices that have varied widely among the scales.

Based on factor analytic work, Gough developed three "vector" scales to measure broad aspects of personality structure. Because a number of the 20 scales on the CPI show considerable overlap, the three dimensions (vectors) can be used to facilitate understanding and

FIGURE 11-2. Three Vector Scores for Theresa

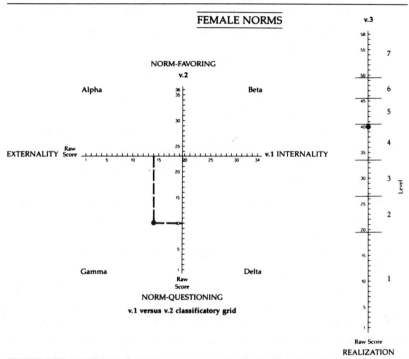

FEMALE NORMS

Note. Reproduced by special permission of the publisher, Consulting Psychologists Press, Inc., Palo Alto, CA 94306, from California Psychological Inventory/Profile Sheet by Harrison G. Gough, Ph.D. © 1987. Further reproduction is prohibited without the publisher's written consent.

interpretation of the 20-scale profile. The three vectors are described generally as (a) internality versus externality, (b) norm favoring versus norm questioning, and (c) self-realization and self-actualization. These factors have been placed in an interpretive three-dimensional model (see Figure 11-2). The first two vectors measure personality type, whereas the third vector measures levels of personality adjustment.

- Vector 1: High scorers tend to be viewed as reticent, modest, shy, reserved, moderate, and reluctant to initiate or take decisive social action. Low scorers are talkative, outgoing, confident, and poised.
- Vector 2: High scorers are viewed as well organized, conscientious, conventional, dependable, and controlled. Low scorers are seen as rebellious, restless, self-indulgent, and pleasure-seeking.

217

- Vector 3: High scorers are described as optimistic, mature, in-sightful, free of neurotic trends and conflicts, and as having a wide range of interests. Low scorers are seen as dissatisfied, un-sure of themselves, uncomfortable with uncertainty and complexity, and as having constricted interests.

The intersection of vectors 1 and 2 form four quadrants. Personality characteristics can be inferred from membership in one of these four categories: Alphas are ambitious, productive, and socially competent; Betas are responsible, reserved, and conforming; Gammas are restless, rebellious, and pleasure-seeking; Deltas are withdrawn, reflective, and detached.

The CPI has been shown to be useful in predicting success in a number of educational and vocational areas. Achievers in both high school and college have been shown to obtain relatively high scores on the Ac, Ai, Re, and So scales. Studies making use of CPI scale scores have been shown to predict school and college performance beyond that using IQ scores or Scholastic Aptitude Test scores alone. Other scores have been shown to be related to achievement in different types of vocational training programs. The CPI has not been shown to be effective for clinical assessment, as it was not designed for that purpose. An individual's general level of adjustment or maladjustment is indicated by the overall level of the profile, but the scales do not yield much information related to a specific diagnosis. Juvenile delinquents and criminals tend to have low scores on the Re and So scales. Solitary delinquents tend to obtain lower scores on the Ie and Fe scales, whereas higher Sy, Sp, and Sa scores are obtained by social delinquents.

When interpreting the CPI results, the three validity scales should be inspected first. If the CPI results are valid, the three vector scales should then be reviewed to provide a broad overview of the results. After that, the profile for the 20 individual scales should be analyzed.

In analyzing the CPI profile, the counselor should begin by paying attention to the overall height of the profile. Higher scores represent psychologically healthy responses, and these should be compared not only with the standard scores on the profile but also, where possible, with an appropriate norm group. The mean on most of the scales, for example, is higher for college students than for high school students. Next, attention should be paid to the highest score on the profile and the lowest score. The next step in examining the profile is to attend to

TABLE 11-1. Examples of Interpretive Sentences for the CPI
Self-Acceptance (Sa) Scale

Score	Interpretation
Above 64.5	Has a strong sense of personal worth, even to the point of being self-centered and egotistic; optimistic concerning personal prospects; articulate and persuasive in dealing with others; socially outgoing and responsive
59.5–64.5	Is sure of self and at ease in most situations; presents self well; is verbally fluent, versatile in interpersonal relations—can take the initiative or can defer to others
54.5–59.5	Is at ease and comfortable in most situations; is good at avoiding interpersonal friction and conflict; is usually liked and accepted by others
45.5–54.5	Is not strongly characterized either by a firm sense of personal worth or its lack; is reasonably self-confident and enterprising; adapts well to most situations; has average or better verbal skills
39.5–45.5	Is somewhat self-doubting; often behaves in an inhibited and subdued manner; prefers not to engage in direct, personal competition with others; tends to be self-denying
34.5–39.5	Is anxious when decisions must be made or when action is necessary; tries to avoid any form of interpersonal conflict; doubts own ability and worries about the future
Below 34.5	Feels inferior to others; either avoids any kind of conflict or gives in; is withdrawn and shy in behavior; sets minimal goals for self and even then often anticipates failure

Note. Reproduced by special permission of the publisher, Consulting Psychologists Press, Inc., Palo Alto, CA 94306, from California Psychological Inventory/Computer Narrative by Harrison G. Gough, Ph.D. Further reproduction is prohibited without the publisher's consent.

the height of the scores within each of the four clusters. The cluster in which the scores tend to run the highest and those in which they tend to run the lowest are examined and interpreted. Continuing to examine the profile, the highest scales within each cluster and the lowest scales within each cluster are interpreted and discussed. Finally, attention is paid to the scales that remain on the profile to be described and interpreted. Using this method, the most important aspects of the profile are discussed first and receive the most emphasis and are less likely to become lost by the client in the detailed interpretation that follows.

The manner in which the elevation of the scales can be interpreted is seen in Table 11-1 for the Self-Acceptance (Sa) scale from the CPI computer narrative (Gough, 1987). Similar information for all the CPI scales individually or in combination can be found in McAllister (1996).

Because of the care with which the CPI was originally constructed and has since been revised, along with the many hundreds of studies employing this instrument, the CPI has become one of the best and most popular personality inventories available. Because the majority of the scales were empirically constructed and scale scores can be compared with different norm groups, the counselor can make use of the instrument in assessing and comparing the strength of various personality characteristics of clients, and clients can use the interpretation to assess their own strengths and weaknesses in comparison with normative samples. Computer-based profile interpretation is also available. A limitation of the CPI is that few studies have examined the meaning of elevations on more than one scale, in contrast to the considerable research that has been conducted on two and three high point codes of the MMPI.

CASE EXAMPLE

The CPI for Theresa, a 35-year-old divorced secretary, is shown in Figures 11-1 and 11-2. She sought counseling because of a general dissatisfaction with her current situation. She is not happy with her job; she has had three serious relationships with men since her divorce, none of which have developed into marriage; and she is often in conflict with her 15-year-old daughter. After graduation from high school, she attended college sporadically for 2 years, earning less than 40 credits and a grade point average of 1.6. She attributes her poor record to a lack of goals and interest in liberal arts subjects and to "too much partying."

The validity scales from Theresa's CPI profile show a tendency to present herself in a negative fashion (Gi = 35). Her personality type, *Gamma*, suggests self-confidence and social competence together with restlessness, pleasure-seeking, and nonconforming beliefs and behaviors. At level 4 (out of 7 levels) on vector 3 (Realization), she shows average integration and realization of potential. As a Gamma at this level she may feel somewhat alienated from society. At a higher level, she might be seen as creative or progressive; at a lower level, she might be viewed as antisocial.

In general, the scores on Theresa's profile fall near the midpoint, which corresponds with a level 4 score on vector 3. Her two high scores (T-score of 60 or above) indicate that she is "self-sufficient, resourceful, detached" (In) and that she "likes change and variety," that she is "easily

220

bored by routine life and everyday experience," and that she "may be impatient, and even erratic" (Fx; Gough, 1987, pp. 6–7). Her three low scores (T-score of 40 or below) indicate that she "insists on being herself, even if this causes friction or problems" (Gi), that she is "concerned about health and personal problems; worried about the future" (Wb), and that she "has difficulty in doing best work in situations with strict rules and expectations" (Ac; Gough, 1987, pp. 6–7). Theresa used the information from the CPI together with other information to gain a better understanding of herself and her situation.

The Sixteen Personality Factor Questionnaire (16 PF)

The 16 PF (5th edition) is a personality inventory developed through the factor analytic technique by Raymond B. Cattell and others (Cattell, Cattell, & Cattell, 1993; Russel & Karol, 1993). Based on the theory that if a human trait exists, a word in the language would have been developed to describe it, Cattell began from a list of all adjectives that could be applied to humans from an unabridged dictionary and produced a list of 4,500 trait names. These were combined to reduce the list to 171 terms that seemed to cover all of the human characteristics on the longer list. He then asked college students to rate their acquaintances on these terms, and, through factor analysis, arrived at 16 different factors that were developed into the 16 scales. Additional scores are now also obtained on five global factors—extroversion, anxiety, tough-mindedness, independence, and self-control as well as for a number of additional derived scales.

The adult edition now contains 185 items. High and low scores on each of the scales represent opposite characteristics. Thus the scales are labeled by such terms as Practical Versus Imaginative, Trusting Versus Suspicious, Concrete Versus Abstract, Shy Versus Socially Bold, and Relaxed Versus Tense. Norms are available based on nine separate norm groups of adults, college students, and high school juniors and seniors, with one set for men, one set for women, and one set for combined-sex groups. Several sets of equivalent forms of the inventory have been developed. In addition, the adult level has been extended downward to develop a form for high school students age 12 to 18 (the High School Personality Questionnaire) and another one for use with children age 8 to 12 (the Children's Personality Questionnaire).

Three different validity scales have been developed, one to detect random responding, one to detect faking good responses (called the

Motivational Distortion scale), and a third to predict attempts to give a bad impression (called the Faking Bad scale). Additional adaptations of the 16 PF have been published and promoted for use in marriage counseling, career counseling, job proficiency, and for the assessment of managers.

One approach in using the 16 PF is to compare the client's overall profile with that of typical profiles of certain groups. This approach is aided by the use of computer programs available for such interpretation.

The 16 PF is based on a large amount of research both in the construction of the instrument and in examining its reliability and validity (Schuerger, 1992). Test-retest reliability coefficients over short periods tend to range from .60 to .85. The reliability coefficients are somewhat low because the scales are made up of relatively few items (10 to 13 items per scale). A wide variety of validity data are available, including the prediction of academic grades and mean profiles for many groups such as delinquents, neurotics, and workers in a variety of different occupations.

Eysenck Personality Questionnaire–Revised (EPQ-R)

The EPQ-R offers a brief, broad, and well-researched measure of personality characteristics (Eysenck & Eysenck, 1993). It yields scores for three personality scales, an addiction scale, and a validity scale. The three personality scales—Extroversion, Neuroticism, and Psychoticism—measure independent factors that account for most of the variance among different personality measures. The scales were designed to be used primarily with a nonpathological population; however, extreme scores on the Neuroticism or Psychoticism scales usually indicate psychopathology. The Lie scale measures the extent to which a client may have distorted his or her answers to give a good impression. The 96 items on the EPQ-R describe behaviors that fall primarily within the normal range, not psychiatric symptoms.

For normal clients, the Neuroticism scale can be relabeled as a measure of "emotionality" and the Psychoticism scale as a measure of "toughmindedness." The Lie scale, although it is primarily a measure of dissimulation, also may reflect social naivete.

The EPQ-R has been validated primarily in terms of factor analysis and related procedures. These analyses attest to the construct validity of the instrument. The statistical analyses show that the scales do represent independent dimensions of personality that are important in describing variations in human behavior. The scales significantly discriminate among different groups (e.g., mental patients, criminals, business leaders) in the expected manner. They possess satisfactory test-retest reliabilities for short time periods and moderately high alpha reliabilities.

Separate age and sex norms are needed. Men score higher on the Psychoticism scale; women score higher on the Neuroticism and Lie scale. Men score higher than women on the Extroversion scale when they are young (less than age 50), but lower than women as they get older. Both sexes obtain lower scores on the Psychoticism and Neuroticism scales as they get older. Scores on the Lie scale are positively correlated with age. A separate form of the EPQ-R, the EPQ Junior, should be used for younger age groups.

The NEO Personality Inventory–Revised (NEO PI-R)

The NEO PI-R was developed to assess the Big Five personality factors previously mentioned (Costa & McCrae, 1992). It consists of five 48-item scales answered on a 5-point agree-disagree continuum. Scores are obtained on each of the five domains of (a) Neuroticism, (b) Extraversion, (c) Openness, (d) Agreeableness, and (e) Conscientiousness. Each of the five global dimensions are composed of six subscales of eight items each designed to measure facets of the global dimension. The Neuroticism domain includes facet subscales such as: anxiety, hostility, and depression, whereas the Conscientiousness domain includes facets such as competence, order, and self-discipline. Reliability coefficients ranging from .8 to .9 are reported for the global dimensions with the facet scales ranging from .6 to .8. Separate profile sheets are provided with differing norms for males, females, and for college students. The inventory is easy to administer and hand score although computer scoring and interpretation are available. Considerable concurrent validity has been reported primarily with other personality measures, which have yielded moderate to strong correlations in expected directions.

The NEO-PI was originally developed on populations available from two large studies of aging adults, indicating that the inventory can be used throughout the full range of adult ages. Since it was developed primarily with adults, different norms are necessary if it is to be used with adolescents and college-age adults as they tend to achieve particularly high scores on certain of the inventory's five dimensions. In addition to the individual form, an additional form is available with the same items but designed to be completed on an individual by another rater—someone who knows the individual well, such as a spouse or peer. The scores representing an individual's self-perception and another's perception can then be compared. Correlations that range from .5 to .7, which are typically obtained between individual and spouse or peer ratings, can be interpreted as evidence of the validity of the instrument. A shortened version—the NEO Five Factor Inventory (NEO FFI), which yields scores only on the five domains, is also available. A rapidly increasing number of research studies using the NEO PI-R are being conducted. It is emerging as one of the better inventories available for the assessment of normal adult personality.

The Personality Research Form (PRF)

The PRF is one of two personality inventories authored by Douglas Jackson that represent a method of test construction using the availability of high speed computers (Jackson, 1984b). It is based on Murray's (1938) personality theory and yields scores on 20 personality traits, such as Affiliation—friendly and accepting of others, Endurance—patient and perserving, Nurturance—sympathetic and comforting, and Play—easy-going and participates in many "fun" activities. In addition to the 20 personality scales, there are two validity indices: a Social Desirability scale and an Infrequency scale. High scores on the Social Desirability scale indicate that the clients may be distorting their answers by primarily saying socially desirable things about themselves. Low scores suggest faking bad or malingering by saying undesirable things about themselves. High scores on the Infrequency scale, which is based on items with highly unlikely responses, suggest careless or random responses.

Jackson Personality Inventory–Revised (JPI-R)

The JPI-R was also developed by Jackson to assess normal personality characteristics but is designed to provide a more practical orientation than the PRF (Jackson, 1994). It consists of 300 true-false items yielding 15 scales measuring traits such as anxiety, energy level, conformity, responsibility, risk taking, and social adroitness. The norms are based on samples of college students and white- and blue-collar workers. Each of the 15 scales yields a standard score with a mean of 50 and a standard deviation of 10. The instrument is designed to be easily and quickly scored (10 minutes). High scores represent the traits mentioned by the scales. For example, a high scorer on the Cooperativeness scale is described as susceptible to group influence and pressure and tends to modify behavior consistent with standards set by others. High scorers are described as compliant, agreeing, and cooperative. Low scorers tend not to go along with the crowd and are independent in thought and action. Low scorers on this scale are described as individualistic, self-reliant, and contradicting. Alpha reliabilities, which are somewhat low, range from .65 to .90 with a median of approximately .80. Validity studies, primarily correlations with appropriate scales on other personality inventories, indicate reasonable concurrent validity.

Both of the Jackson instruments represent a contemporary method of constructing psychometrically sound personality instruments, but they are not well known and have not yet received much use in counseling and other applied settings. Jackson has accomplished the construction of psychometrically sound inventories but has been slower to produce the interpretive materials that make them useful in applied settings.

Millon Index of Personality Styles (MIPS)

The MIPS is a newly developed inventory designed to assess personality styles for adults within the normal range (Millon, 1995). It is intended to be useful in various counseling situations involving relationships, career placement, or clients experiencing problems in daily living. It contains 24 scales, which measure opposite styles on 12 personality dimensions, plus an overall adjustment index. The scales are grouped into three categories: (a) motivating aims, which assess a person's style of adapting to the environment, such as modifying/accommodating, individuating/nuturing; (b) cognitive styles, which assess a person's preferences for information processing, such as sensing/intuiting, thinking/feeling; and (c) interpersonal behaviors, which assess the ways people relate to others, such as outgoing/retiring, controlling/yielding. The inventory is expected to be useful for counseling and helping professionals including those in family and career settings.

Millon has also authored the Millon Adolescent Personality Inventory (MAPI), which can be used to assess the personality of adolescents who have at least a sixth-grade reading level (Millon & Davis, 1993).

Coopersmith Self-Esteem Inventories (SEI)

Stanley Coopersmith, who devoted a large part of his career to the study of factors related to self-esteem, defined the concept as "the evaluation a person makes and customarily maintains with regard to him- or herself" (Coopersmith, 1981, p. 5). He reasoned that people who have confidence in their abilities will be more persistent and more successful in their activities than will those who perceive themselves negatively. He looked upon self-esteem as a global construct that affects a person's evaluation of his or her abilities in many areas. Because of its importance to the individual, in terms both of school or work performance and of personal satisfaction, he believed that counselors and teachers in particular should be aware of deficits in children's self-esteem and that they should be aware of methods for helping to improve self-esteem.

He developed three forms of the Coopersmith Inventory (so named to avoid influencing responses) to measure self-esteem. The longest and most thoroughly developed form is the School Form. This form, which contains 58 items and six scales, was designed for students age 8 to 15. An abbreviated version, the School Short Form, was constructed from the first 25 items in the School Form for use when time was at a premium. (The School Form requires about 10 to 15 minutes for most students, whereas the School Short Form can usually be answered in about 5 minutes.) The Adult Form, which also contains 25 items, was adapted from the School Short Form. All items, such as "I'm a lot of fun to be with," are answered *like me* or *unlike me*.

The School Form provides six scores: A total self-esteem score, four scores derived from subscales that measure self-esteem in regard to peers, parents, school, and personal interests, and a score based on a lie scale that checks for defensiveness. The School Short From and the Adult Form yield only one score—the total self-esteem score. Measures of internal consistency show high reliabilities for both the subscores and the total scores. Studies based on the School Form show significant relationships between self-esteem and school performance (Peterson & Austin, 1985; Sewell, 1985).

As a check on the individual's self-report on the SEI, Coopersmith and Gilberts (1982) developed the Behavioral Academic Self-Esteem (BASE) rating scale for teachers to use in evaluating a student's performance in 16 situations. Sample items include "this child is willing to undertake new tasks," and "this child readily expresses opinions." Teachers rate students on a 5-point scale based on the frequency with which they perform the behavior indicated. The BASE provides outside information to check the accuracy of one's self-perception. Counselors can profit from both types of information in helping clients to enhance their self-esteem.

Tennessee Self-Concept Scale (TSCS)

This 90-item instrument, which yields a total of 14 scales for counseling purposes, assesses self-concept in terms of identity, feelings, and behavior (Roid & Fitts, 1988). Items are answered on a 5-point scale ranging from *completely false* to *completely true*. Eight different measures of self-concept have been derived for areas such as identity, physical self, moral/ethical self, self-satisfaction, and social self. In addition to the eight self-concept scales, there are summary, response defensiveness, and variability scales. The inventory can also be scored for a number of clinical scales with such labels as Neurosis, Psychosis, and General Maladjustment. The instrument is designed for individuals 12 years of age or older and is written at a fourth-grade reading level. A similar instrument designed for younger children is the Piers-Harris Children's Self-Concept Scale, an 80-item instrument designed for children in grades 3 through 12 and written at a third-grade level (Piers, 1984).

SUMMARY

1. To interpret results of a personality inventory competently, it is necessary to understand both the personality characteristics being assessed and the approach used to develop the various inventory scales.
2. The Myers-Briggs Type Indicator has gained great popularity and is used in many settings in addition to its use by counselors and clinicians.

3. The California Psychological Inventory, the 16 Personality Factor Questionnaire, and the Eysenek Personality Questionnaire-Revised are carefully developed inventories with much research backing that assess everyday personality traits.

4. The NEO Personality Inventory–Revised provides measures of the Big 5 personality factors that account for most of the variance among personality measures.

5. The Personality Research Form and the Jackson Personality Inventory are two relatively new inventories that have capitalized on the capabilities of modern computers in their construction. The Millon Index of Personality Styles is another new inventory that has potential usefulness for counselors.

6. Two inventories useful in assessing self-concept are the Self-Esteem Inventory and the Tennessee Self-Concept Scale.

12

OTHER PERSONALITY MEASURES

ECHNIQUES USED TO ASSESS personality include the interview, behavioral observations, and personality inventories, as discussed in the previous chapter. In this chapter three of the most commonly used projective personality measures are discussed briefly because they are less often used by counselors due to both practical and psychometric considerations.

Also described are instruments constructed to assess different environments in which individuals find themselves. The chapter concludes with a summary of the assessment of adolescent and post-adolescent psychosocial development.

PROJECTIVE TECHNIQUES

In using projective techniques as a method of assessment, unstructured tasks are presented to the examinee and responses to these tasks are expected to reflect needs, experiences, inner states, and thought processes. This concept is known as the projective hypothesis—that responses to ambiguous stimuli reflect a person's basic personality. Examinee responses are usually in the form of completed sentences, associations, or descriptive or storytelling responses (Anastasi, 1988).

Because there is an infinite variety of possible responses to ambiguous stimuli, no particular conclusion can be drawn from any single response. Responses may be classified, however, and from a number of responses general impressions and inferences regarding a person's personality may be derived. The administration and scoring of most projective instruments require considerable training and experience on the part of the examiner. The scoring process may be quite complex or subjective. In addition, even highly experienced examiners frequently disagree on the interpretations and inferences drawn from projective data.

The Rorschach Ink Blot Test

The most widely used projective test has been the Rorschach Ink Blot Test (Goldfried, Stricker, & Weiner, 1971), developed in 1921 by Hermann Rorschach, a Swiss psychiatrist. Placing ink on a piece of paper and folding the paper to form ink blots, he asked people to say what images the ink blots suggested to them and used the responses to assess personality. A series of 10 ink blots have become the standardized stimuli, some of them in gray and several with combinations of colors. Several different methods of administration have been developed along with various systems to score the responses. Responses are classified and scored according to set criteria as the location of the response on the ink blot, the feature that determined the response, as well as the content of the response. Exner's (1986) procedure seems to be emerging as the most popular scoring scheme and has been shown to have considerable interscorer reliability. Even though the Exner system has been shown to have considerable validity in identifying certain personality characteristics, the reliability and validity of interpretations resulting from Rorschach scoring have not been high. Although there are psychometric and theoretical reasons along with practical ones to avoid using this instrument, the Rorschach Ink Blot Test has continued to remain a popular instrument in many clinical settings.

Thematic Apperception Test (TAT)

The Thematic Apperception Test (TAT) was developed by Christina Morgan and Henry Murray based on Murray's theory of needs (*apperception* means to perceive in terms of past perceptions; Murray, 1943). It consists of 30 black-and-white picture cards, most containing one or more human figures, and one completely blank card. Twenty of the 30 cards are presented in a test administration, the selection of the 20 depending on the age and sex of the examinee. The examinee is asked to make up a story about each picture and to include what is currently happening in the picture, what led up to that situation, how the people in the story feel, and how the story ends. If examinees fail to include any of these elements, they are asked to fill in the information after the initial story has been completed.

When the entire test is administered, it is usually broken down into two sessions on two different days with 10 cards administered at each session. The cards that illustrate more threatening material are usually included in the second session. Many of those who use the TAT do not use all 20 cards but select 10 or 12 of them and administer them in a single session. The TAT is usually not scored in any objective fashion, but the frequency of various themes, the intensity and duration of the stories, and the outcomes are taken into account. It is assumed that the hero in the story is the person with whom the examinee identifies. The assumption in interpreting the results is that examinees reveal their conflicts, experiences, needs, and strivings in their storytelling responses. A number of more objective scoring systems have been developed for the TAT to assess such concepts as achievement, ego development, or gender identity, but most are complex and do not provide the overall qualitative view of the individual usually sought by those employing this instrument.

The TAT is widely used and has many supporters, but has been attacked primarily on psychometric grounds. Subjective interpretations of TAT results often result in different or opposite conclusions even by experienced users. Instead of administering the entire TAT, counselors often select a few cards for use in an early interview. The cards can be used as a method of initially gaining rapport and as a method of encouraging the client to open up and talk during the counseling session. At the same time, the storytelling responses can yield considerable insight into the needs and personality of the client.

The Rotter Incomplete Sentence Blank

In the sentence completion technique, a person is asked to complete a number of sentence fragments that are related to possible conflicts or emotions. The most popular sentence completion test is the Rotter Incomplete Sentence Blank (Rotter & Rafferty, 1950), which consists of 40 sentence fragments. Most of them are written in the first person such as "my mother. . ." or "what bothers me most is. . ." There are three forms, one for high school, one for college, and one for adults. It is expected that attitudes, traits, and emotions will be expressed in the responses. Responses are compared to sample answers in the manual and scored on a continuum of 6 to 0, from unhealthy or maladjusted through neutral to healthy or positive responses (higher scores suggest greater maladjustment). Thus a single overall adjustment score is produced that makes this particular form useful as a gross screening instrument.

Because sentence fragments are easy to construct, counselors often develop their own incomplete sentence instruments to deal with various types of conflicts and problems presented by clients. Thus one counselor-constructed incomplete sentence instrument will deal with problems and conflicts revolving around educational/vocational decision making, another might deal with family conflicts, another with interpersonal conflicts, and yet another with school difficulties.

Early Recollections

Alfred Adler's use of early recollections has been described as the first truly projective test (Aiken, 1996). Emphasizing the importance of early experiences in the formation of personality, the technique involves asking the client to "tell me your earliest memory." It is sometimes used by counselors as a brief projective device. The memories, which should be specific rather than general, are analyzed for cognitive and behavioral patterns. The themes, outlooks, and attitudes revealed by the recollected behavior are examined and interpreted rather than the behavior itself.

PERSON-ENVIRONMENT INTERACTION

Other influences on personality include both environmental and developmental factors. Several theories have been advanced regarding the effect of interaction with the environment, and several others regarding the developmental changes that occur as an individual moves through various life stages. Instruments designed to assess the effect of these influences and to substantiate the relevant theories have been constructed, but at this point they are not yet ready for use in individual counseling. Nevertheless, these two concepts are important for counselors to take into consideration in their work with individuals and groups, and several examples of theories related to these concepts are presented.

Almost all of the developments of applied psychology on which the field of counseling is based have concentrated on the individual and his or her specific traits, states, aptitudes, and attitudes. Except for the fields of academic and career planning, relatively little attention has been paid to the environments in which individuals function, although some theorists such as Williamson (1939) have emphasized environmental manipulation as a counseling tool. Certain behavioral settings have a very strong and often coercive influence on individuals, and it is necessary to pay particular attention to the perceived situations and environments that influence human behavior. The emphasis thus far has been an attempt to assess the environment and thereby help people to understand and organize their behavior in the social environments in which they find themselves, in order to behave more effectively. Several theories have been developed that emphasize the importance of the environment in the way that individuals think and behave. They emphasize the value that can often result from changes in the environment; as opposed to the more typical counseling approach of assisting the individual to adapt to the situation.

Person-environment interaction theories are usually based on the work of Kurt Lewin (1935) and his famous formula $B = f(PE)$, in which behavior (B) is a function (f) of the interaction of the person (P) and the environment (E). These theories give particular attention to the environment portion of this formula, emphasizing the important role that environments play in shaping behavior. Another theorist (Barker, 1968) maintained that individuals tend to behave in similar ways in similar environments even though, as individuals, they differ from each other in many important ways. He pointed out that human environments often have a coercive effect on behavior. Environmental or situational variables are seen as the primary influences on behavior, with individuals behaving in a variety of ways depending on the social environments in which they find themselves.

233

Holland's theory of vocational choice was discussed in a previous chapter. In his theory, human behavior is a function of the interaction between personality and environment, and the choice of a vocation is in part an expression of personality. The ways people think about occupations and vocational stereotypes influence vocational preferences. People with particular personality types create the environments within these occupations, and thus the process is a circular one. People in each of Holland's six personality and environmental types create an atmosphere that reflects that type, and people search out and choose environments in which their interests, attitudes, and personalities fit. Their behavior is thus determined by an interaction between their personality and their environment. Individuals choose environments because of their personalities and remain in these environments because of the reinforcements and satisfactions they obtain there.

Holland has also developed the Position Classification Inventory (PCI; Gottfredson & Holland, 1991), an 84-item inventory that enables an employee or a supervisor to assess and classify work environments in terms of their demands, rewards, and opportunities. Occupational positions are thus assessed on Holland's six-category classification system and can be used to examine person-job fit and for understanding satisfaction and dissatisfaction with a position or occupation.

Several researchers have developed instruments to use in the assessment of different environments. Rudolph Moos (1974; Moos & Moos, 1994a) studied social climates in such widely varying institutions as hospitals, military companies, nursing homes, school classrooms, and university student living units. He developed a series of inventories to assess the psychosocial dimensions of environment in these settings. His scales provide information about how those in a particular psychosocial environment perceive that environment. The inventories can be used to compare perceptions of different environments over time or to evaluate how individuals or groups of people differ in their perceptions of an environment.

One of Moos's findings was that the social environments in a variety of settings can be described by common sets of dimensions. These dimensions generally fall under three categories. The relationship dimension refers to the extent to which individuals are involved in the setting, the extent to which they generally support and help each other, and the extent to which they feel able to express themselves. The

234

personal growth dimension includes the extent to which personal growth and self-enhancement occur within the basic functions of the setting. The third dimension is that of system maintenance or change and includes the extent to which the environment is structured and expectations are clear, the extent to which control is maintained in the setting, and how changes can occur.

Individuals are usually more satisfied and successful in those environments where positive social climates exist. Under these circumstances workers report greater satisfaction with their jobs, psychiatric patients become less depressed, and students show more interest and become more engaged in their course materials (Moos, 1976).

Pace has developed the College Student Experiences Questionnaire (CSEQ; Pace, 1987) to assess the quality of students' college experiences. The questionnaire assesses eight dimensions of college environments in addition to 14 dimensions of college activities and 21 estimates of outcomes of undergraduate education (Brown, 1985). The College Environment scales are composed of eight 1-item rating scales, of which five reflect the purposes of the environment: scholarship, aesthetic awareness, critical analysis, vocational emphasis, and practical or personal emphasis. The other three dimensions focus on the supportiveness of interpersonal relationships at the college among students, with faculty, and with the administration.

PSYCHOSOCIAL THEORIES

Young people develop in psychosocial areas, and various psychosocial developmental theorists have presented ways to describe positions students achieve in those areas and how these developmental changes occur.

These theorists have generally built upon the work of Erik Erikson (1968) and believe that an individual develops through a sequence of stages that define the life cycle. Each stage is created by the convergence of a particular growth phase and certain developmental tasks. These include learning certain attitudes, forming particular facets of the self, and learning specific skills that must be mastered if one is to successfully manage that particular life phase. In these theories, the development follows a chronological sequence: at certain times of life a particular facet of the personality emerges as a central concern that must be addressed. The particular timing and methods by which the concerns are addressed are influenced by the individual's society and culture. Psychosocial theorists examine these particular concerns or personal preoccupations that occur at various points in the life cycle. The adolescent is likely to be preoccupied with the concerns of "Who am I?" or "What am I to believe?" The young mother wonders, "What type of parent shall I try to be?" and the older worker, "What identity will I have when I retire from my professional position?"

Analogous to the moral and cognitive theories in Chapter 6 advanced by Kohlberg and Perry, Arthur Chickering (Chickering & Reisser, 1993) developed a theory of college student development that is an elaboration of Erikson's stages of identity and intimacy. Chickering focused on the particular developmental concerns of students that are relevant to the social situation in which they find themselves during their years at the university. He attempted to construct a framework of the developmental changes occurring in young adulthood in a more detailed way than did the psychosocial theorists such as Erikson. This framework has been presented in a form that draws on and gives coherence to the wealth of empirical data on college student change reported by a variety of researchers who have studied college students.

He has postulated seven vectors or dimensions of development, rather than the developmental tasks or developmental stages used by other theorists. The seven vectors along which development occurs in young adulthood are as follows: achieving competency, managing emotions, developing autonomy, establishing identity, freeing of interpersonal relationships, developing purpose, and developing integrity.

Two sets of inventories have been developed to assess status on these developmental vectors. They include the Student Developmental Task and Lifestyle Inventory (Winston & Miller, 1987) and the Iowa Student Development Inventories (Hood, 1986). These inventories are designed to assess status on these vectors and the changes on them that occur during the college years. Recommendations regarding activities students might undertake to help them develop on those vectors on which they feel they would like to grow might be made from an individual's scores on these instruments. At this point, however, they do not represent instruments on which reliance can be placed in regard to differential diagnoses or selection.

SUMMARY

This chapter included a description of three projective instruments along with two personality theories useful to counselors and human development professionals.

1. For a number of both practical and psychometric reasons, projective instruments such as the Rorschach Ink Blot Test and the Thematic Apperception Test (TAT) are seldom used by counselors.
2. A condensed version of the TAT is sometimes used by counselors as a rapport-building technique that may also yield insight into the client's personality.
3. Person-environment theories and inventories emphasize situational variables that often have been overlooked by counselors and human development professionals who have traditionally placed more emphasis on the assessment and treatment of individuals.
4. Psychosocial developmental theories offer useful concepts when counselors and human development specialists use assessment techniques to assess individuals with particular concerns that occur at various points in the life cycle.

13

ASSESSMENT OF INTERPERSONAL RELATIONSHIPS

C OUNSELORS WHO DEAL WITH educational and vocational issues often make extensive use of interest and aptitude tests,
and those who deal with personal adjustment problems often
make use of personality tests. When working with clients on marriage
or relationship issues, psychological tests are infrequently a part of the
counseling process. When tests are used in marriage counseling, they
are often those commonly used in other types of counseling, such as
the MMPI or the MBTI. There are a number of instruments designed
specifically for marriage and relationship counseling, some of which
are routinely used by some counselors and occasionally used by others.
Several of the more commonly used instruments of this type are briefly
discussed in this chapter. There are also a large number of instruments
that have been developed but do not receive much use. Most of these
lack substantial amounts of normative and validity data. In addition,

there are a number of additional marriage, family, and relationship instruments that can be considered experimental at this point but are often the assessment instruments used in research studies in this field.

INVENTORIES FOR MARRIAGE, COUPLES, AND FAMILY COUNSELING

The Marital Satisfaction Inventory (MSI)

The MSI (Snyder, 1981) is a self-report inventory designed to assess marital interaction and the extent of marital distress. Scores are obtained on 11 different scales, such as Affective Communication, Problem-Solving Communication, Disagreement about Finances, Sexual Dissatisfaction, Conflict Over Child-Rearing, and a Global Distress Scale, which measures general unhappiness and uncertain commitment in the marriage. A Social Desirability scale (conventionalization) is included as a check on the response set of the test taker. The scales contain 15 to 43 items per scale.

The MSI is intended to be used in couples counseling, with both the husband and wife taking the scale and the results being displayed on a single profile that indicates areas of agreement and disagreement. It is typically administered during the initial contact with the counselor or agency so that results are available for the ensuing counseling sessions. The MSI provides useful information for counselors by providing a picture of the couple's overall marital distress, the general quality of their communication, and the differences between their perceptions of aspects of their relationship. Validity studies of the MSI scales generally show reasonable correlations with other measures of marital satisfaction. The MSI significantly differentiates between various criterion groups experiencing marital dissatisfaction. The manual for the MSI reports internal consistency coefficients and test-retest reliability coefficients in the .80 to .95 range.

The Derogatis Sexual Functioning Inventory (DSFI)

The DSFI (Derogatis, 1979) yields 12 scores from 10 scales with titles such as Information, Experience, Psychological Symptoms, Gender Role Definition, and Sexual Satisfaction. A total score and the subject's evaluation of current functioning are also included. The Information subscale consists of 26 true-false items measuring the amount of a subject's accurate sexual information. The Experience subscale lists 24 sexual behaviors ranging from kissing on the lips to oral-genital sex. The Sexual Drive subscale measures the frequency of various sexual behaviors, and the Attitude subscale measures the diversity of liberal and conservative attitudes.

The entire inventory can take 45 minutes to 1 hour to complete and was designed to assess individual rather than couple sexual functioning. The DSFI is designed to assess current functioning, although the Sexual Experience and the Sexual Fantasy subscales ask the subject to report lifetime experiences. Because the DSFI is one of the most thoroughly studied instruments in sexual research, several different types of norms are available for the instrument. Certain of the subscales, such as Sexual Information, Sexual Desire, and Gender Roles, have relatively low internal consistency coefficients of below .70. Others tend to be more adequate, falling in the .80 to .92 range. The instrument can provide counselors with considerable information regarding sexual functioning.

Taylor-Johnson Temperament Analysis (TJTA)

The TJTA is designed for use in individual, premarital, and marital counseling (Taylor, Morrison, & Nash, 1985). It consists of 180 items equally divided among nine scales measuring traits such as Nervous-Composed, Depressive-Lighthearted, Responsive-Inhibited, Dominant-Submissive, and Self-Disciplined-Impulsive. Norms are based on large samples, including a separate set of norms based on high school students. An additional edition is available for use with populations whose vocabulary and reading comprehension are below the eighth-grade level.

A unique feature of this instrument is the "criss-cross" procedure in which one person records his or her impressions of another person. This can be valuable in family counseling involving parent-adolescent interaction, in situations involving sibling conflict, or in premarital or marital counseling.

Stuart Couples' Precounseling Inventory (SCPI)

The SCPI is a revision of the former Marital Precounseling Inventory (Stuart & Stuart, 1975). Norms are now based on a small representative sample (60 couples) that includes nonmarried heterosexual and homosexual couples. The purpose of the instrument is for use in planning and evaluating relationship therapy based on a social learning model. Scores are obtained in 13 different areas with such titles as Communication Assessment, Conflict Management, Sexual Interaction, Child Management, Relationship Change Goals, General Happiness with the Relationship, and Goals of Counseling. In taking the instrument, couples describe current interaction patterns rather than personality characteristics. Items tend to emphasize positive characteristics, and, if taken with some seriousness by the couple, the instrument can be educational and therapeutic.

Family Environment Scale (FES)

The FES (2nd edition) is one of a number of social climate scales developed by Moos and his associates (Moos & Moos, 1986). This 90-item inventory yields 10 scores from scales such as Cohesion, Intellectual-Cultural Orientation, Active Recreational Orientation, Moral-Religious Emphasis, Expressiveness, and Control. In addition, a "family incongruence score" can be obtained by summing the differences in subscale scores for various pairs of family members.

The 10 scales are grouped into three underlying domains: the relationship domain, the personal growth domain, and the system maintenance domain. The assumption behind all of the social climate scales is that environments, and in this case families, have unique personalities that can be measured in the same way as individual personalities. Norms are based on a group of 1,125 "normal" and 500 distressed families. The items on the Family Environment Scale are statements about family environments originally obtained through structured interviews with family members. Validity evidence is based primarily on the difference in mean scores between normal and distressed families.

Triangular Love Scale (TLS)

The TLS is a 45-item scale that measures the three components of romantic relationships identified by Sternberg (1987): intimacy, passion, and commitment. According to Sternberg, all three components must be assessed in evaluating the quality of a romantic relationship.

Myers-Briggs Type Indicator (MBTI)

The MBTI (see Chapter 11) is also often used in counseling with couples and families (Myers & McCaulley, 1985). Here its use is to help couples understand their differences in the four dimensions measured by the MBTI and therefore to help them use these differences constructively rather than destructively. Data accumulated by the Center for Applications of Psychological Type (CAPT) indicate that people are only slightly more likely to marry individuals of similar than of opposite types (Myers & McCaulley, 1985). The proportion of couples alike in three or all four dimensions is only slightly higher than would be expected from a random assortment of types. The MBTI thus can be used to assist couples in understanding their differences and similarities.

When couples differ on the thinking-feeling dimension, feeling spouses may find their partner cold, unemotional, and insensitive, whereas the thinking spouse can become irritated with the seeming lack of logic of feeling types. Counselors can help thinking types to improve relationships by openly showing appreciation and by refraining from comments that sound like personal criticism. They can encourage feeling types to state wishes clearly, so the thinking partner does not have to guess their wishes.

One spouse may be an extrovert needing considerable external stimulation, whereas the other, an introvert, needs sufficient time alone. This becomes a problem when the introverted partner expends a good deal of energy in extroverted work all day and has little energy left for sociability in the evening. The extroverted partner, on the other hand, may work in a more solitary setting, and look forward to an evening of social stimulation and activity.

Problems arising from judging-perceiving differences can be found when planning, order, and organization are important to the judging partner whereas freedom and spontaneity are important to the perceptive partner, who also has a great deal more tolerance for ambiguity.

In using the MBTI with couples, couples are sometimes asked to guess the types of their partners after having the types briefly described. It is also possible to have each partner answer the MBTI twice, once for themselves and once as they believe their partner will respond. In either case the accuracy of type descriptions of partners can be discussed, and these differences can be useful to them as they see how they affect their relationship.

The MBTI can also be useful in family counseling in discussing difficulties in communication and differences in child-rearing styles and in attitudes toward other family members. For example, a counselor can help an orderly, practical, sensing-judging parent to see that it is easier for him or her to raise a sensing-judging child, who desires structure and organization, than it is for that parent to raise an independent, intuitive-perceptive child, who rebels against structure and order.

INTERPERSONAL ASSESSMENT INVENTORIES

Contemporary theories of interpersonal functioning assert that an individual's behavior can be understood only in relation to transactions with others and not for the individual in isolation. In the generally accepted model of interpersonal theory each interaction represents a combination of two basic dimensions of interpersonal behavior: control (dominance-submission) and affiliation (friendliness-hostility; VanDenberg, Schmidt, & Kiesler, 1992). In any interaction (including client and counselor) individuals continually negotiate these two relationship issues—how friendly or hostile they will be and how much in control they will be in the relationship. This approach uses a circular rather than a linear model; behavior is viewed not solely by situational factors or psychic motivation but instead within a group of two or more persons exerting mutual influence. These two dimensions are incorporated into a model called the interpersonal circle or circumplex. It is organized around the horizontal and vertical axes representing affiliation and control (Tracey & Schneider, 1995).

Among the inventories designed to assess interpersonal interactions are the Checklist of Interpersonal Transactions (CLOIT), a 96-item interpersonal behavior inventory, and the Checklist of Psychotherapy Transactions (CLOPT), a parallel version of the CLOIT for rating clients and counselors, both developed by Kiesler (1987).

The Interpersonal Adjective Scales (IAS), a recently developed self-report instrument that assesses the two primary interpersonal dimensions of dominance and nurturance, is based on experience with other previously developed interpersonal assessment inventories (Wiggins, 1993). The IAS yields scores on eight interpersonal variables, which are ordered along the two primary axes of the interpersonal circumplex. It is designed to provide information about how an individual typically behaves in different interpersonal situations. The instrument consists of 64 adjectives that are descriptive of interpersonal interactions and are responded to in an 8-point Likert format with respondents rating how accurately each word describes them as individuals. Responses yield octant scores, which are then plotted on the circumplex. The titles of the eight interpersonal octants are shown on the circumplex profile in Figure 13-1. Based on scores shown on the circumplex profile, this individual would be described as anxious, depressed, passive, introverted, and socially withdrawn.

FIGURE 13.1 IAS profile of extreme depression in a former bank manager

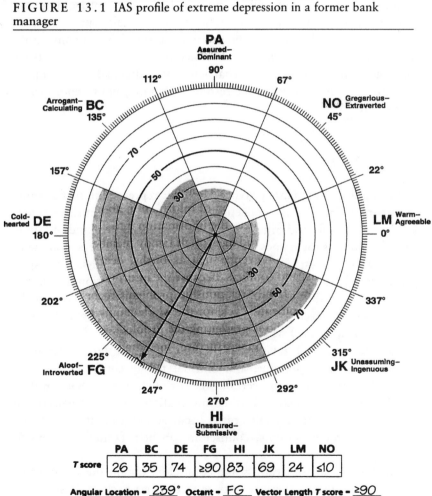

	PA	BC	DE	FG	HI	JK	LM	NO
T score	26	35	74	≥90	83	69	24	≤10

Angular Location = 239° Octant = FG Vector Length T score = ≥90

In interpreting the results of the circumplex profile, counselors should interpret it as a whole using all of the information provided on the profile and not focus solely on the highest segment score or scores. By paying attention to only one or two octants, considerable information regarding the client's interpersonal behavior is missed, and the advantage of the circumplex model is lost. Since interpersonal transactions include those between the client and counselor, the counselor's perception of client interactions should be compared with those of the client's self-report represented by the circumplex profile. Counselors can examine the components of a client's interpersonal functioning and identify topics that will be more or less anxiety provoking to a client. Many client difficulties can be viewed as maladaptive transactional patterns. Clients can be helped to understand the predominantly automatic and unaware manner in which they communicate to others through their verbal and nonverbal behavior. Individuals often employ a narrow range of interpersonal responses that may not be appropriate to the situation.

GENOGRAMS

A genogram is a map that provides a graphic representation of a family structure. It involves the collection of information about three generations of a family and organizes the information into a kind of family tree. It contains the names and ages of all family members along with information about major events such as births, deaths, marriages, divorces, adoptions, and conflicts. Because the information is collected in this way, it allows family relationship problems to be seen in the context of the developmental cycle for the whole family in addition to that of the individual who is presenting the problem.

By examining the relational structure, including family composition, sibling constellations, and unusual family configurations, the counselor can hypothesize certain roles or relationships that can then be checked out by eliciting further information. Repetitive patterns of functioning and relationships often occur across generations, and by recognizing these patterns, counselors can help family members to alter them.

In drawing a genogram, some counselors obtain the basic information to structure the genogram and then go back and ask about each individual on it and their relationships with other family members, both within and across generations. Others obtain this information as each individual is placed on the genogram. Some counselors obtain only a basic genogram illustrating the general family structure; others, through the use of figures, abbreviations, and symbols, develop a genogram that contains a great deal of organized data about the generations of a family system (McGoldrick & Gerson, 1985). A sample genogram for the couple Joseph and Paula is shown in Figure 13-2.

The construction of a genogram is a cooperative task between the counselor and the client. Clients readily become very interested and involved in the construction of a genogram; they enjoy the process and usually reveal a great deal of information about various relatives and their relationships with them. Counselors often find that genogram construction provides much insight into both the family constellation and the individual's interpersonal relationships within that system. Even from reticent clients, both the quantity and the emotional depth of the data produced are often superior to that obtained through the typical interview process, and are more easily obtained as well. The construction of genograms in marriage and relationship counseling as well as in other types of counseling has thus been enthusiastically embraced by many counselors and has become an increasingly common assessment technique.

SUMMARY

1. Personality inventories such as the Minnesota Multiphasic Personality Inventory, the California Psychological Inventory, and especially the Myers-Briggs Type Indicator, commonly used in other types of counseling, are most likely to be used by counselors with clients concerned with marriage or relationship issues.
2. There are instruments specifically developed to assess marital satisfaction, sexual functioning, communication issues, and family environments with which counselors can assist clients to understand and deal with relationship problems.
3. Through the cooperative construction of a multigeneration graphic family structure—the genogram—insight into family constellations and interpersonal relationships within the family can be revealed to both the counselor and the client.

FIGURE 13.2 Genogram of Joseph and Paula

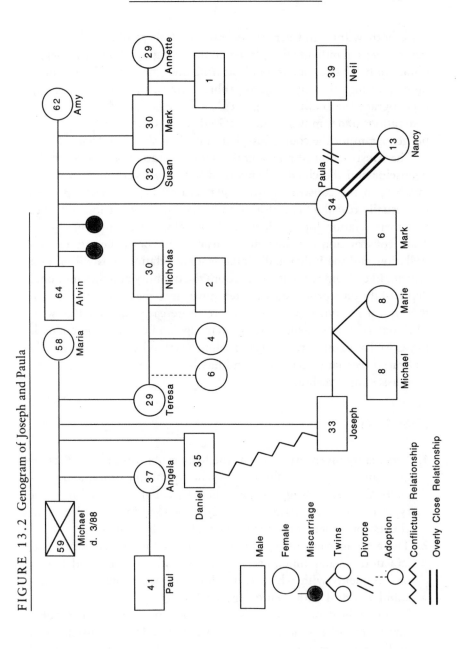

14

MENTAL HEALTH ASSESSMENT: INTERVIEW PROCEDURES

I N THE COURSE of helping people solve problems, counselors will work with a number of clients who could be diagnosed as mentally ill. In the first national survey of a representative sample of the population based on a structured psychiatric interview, Kessler et al. (1994) found that nearly 30% of the respondents suffered from a mental disorder within a 12-month period. The most common disorders occurring during this time period were anxiety disorders (17 %), substance abuse disorders (11%), and affective disorders (11%). Approximately one half of the participants in the survey met the psychiatric diagnostic criteria for a mental disorder sometime in their lifetime. These figures are higher than those of previous epidemiological studies based on less comprehensive procedures (Regier et al., 1988; Robins et al., 1984).

Other research also shows that a significant proportion of the clients at university counseling centers or mental health centers are psychopathologically disturbed. In one study, approximately 30% of the students at a university mental health clinic met the medical criteria for mental illness (Hersh, Nazario, & Backus, 1983). In another study, one fourth to one third of the clients at a university counseling service showed signs of a psychiatric disorder (Johnson, Ellison, & Heikkinen, 1989).

These studies indicate the need for counselors to be familiar with procedures for assessing mental illness. Many of their clients will exhibit symptoms of mental disorders, especially depression and anxiety. Many of the people in the population they serve will also show signs of mental illness even though they do not seek treatment. Counselors must be able to recognize the symptoms of mental illness and to provide at least a preliminary assessment of the client's mental state. They must be able to determine when services such as crisis intervention, psychiatric consultation, and long-term treatment may be necessary. Interview procedures to aid counselors in this endeavor are presented in this chapter. The use of standardized inventories for this purpose will be discussed in the next chapter.

DIAGNOSTIC & STATISTICAL MANUAL OF MENTAL DISORDERS, FOURTH EDITION (DSM-IV)

The DSM-IV provides a means of classifying psychiatric and psychological disorders for treatment and research purposes (American Psychiatric Association, 1994). The DSM-IV, which assumes an atheoretical position, classifies disorders based on descriptive, not etiological, factors. The diagnostic categories used by the DSM-IV serve as the official means for classifying mental disorders in most medical and psychological settings in the United States.

The DSM-IV employs a multiaxial classification system:

- Axis I. Clinical disorders and other conditions that may be a focus of clinical attention
- Axis II. Personality disorders and mental retardation
- Axis III. General medical conditions
- Axis IV. Psychosocial and environmental problems
- Axis V. Global assessment of functioning

The clinical disorders included on Axis I encompass all mental disorders except personality disorders and mental retardation. The Axis I disorders are classified into 15 broad categories, such as mood, anxiety, and adjustment disorders. The broad categories are further subdivided into subcategories, such as major depressive, dysthymic, bipolar I or II, or cyclothymic disorders for the mood disorder category. In addition to the clinical disorders, nonpsychiatric conditions that may be a focus of clinical attention are noted on Axis I. These conditions include the V-codes, which pertain to relational problems, bereavement, identity problems, phase of life problems, academic problems, occupational problems, and other issues often addressed in counseling.

Each disorder is defined in terms of specific criteria. For example, the diagnostic criteria for dysthymic disorder (DSM-IV code number 300.4), a chronic state of low-grade depression, are listed below (American Psychiatric Association, 1994, pp. 345–349):

- Depressed mood for most of the day during the majority of the days over a 2-year period (1-year period for children and adolescents)
- Presence of at least two of the following six symptoms while depressed: poor appetite or overeating, insomnia or hypersomnia, low energy, low self-esteem, poor concentration or difficulty making decisions, and feelings of hopelessness
- Symptoms that cause significant distress or impairment in social, occupational, or other areas of functioning

In addition, the person must never have been without these symptoms for more than 2 months during the 2-year period (1 year for children and adolescents) and must not meet the criteria for a major depressive episode during this time period. It is also important to differentiate the disorder from other disorders such as cyclothymic disorder, chronic psychotic disorder, substance abuse, or general medical conditions, such as hypothyroidism.

Note that the criteria describe the frequency, duration, and severity of the symptomatic behaviors. A person must meet all of these criteria to be classified as suffering from dysthymic disorder.

Axis II differs from Axis I by focusing on personality disorders or mental retardation conditions that may underlie the presenting problem. Developmental disorders such as learning, motor skills, and communication disorders, which used to be classified on Axis II, are now classified on Axis I.

Personality disorders refer to lifelong maladaptive behavior patterns that are often triggered by specific events in the person's life. DSM-IV defines a total of 10 personality disorders grouped in three categories as indicated below:

- Cluster A: *Emotional withdrawal and odd behavior* includes paranoid, schizoid, and schizotypal personality disorders
- Cluster B: *Exaggerated, dramatic emotionality* includes antisocial, borderline, histrionic, and narcissistic disorders
- Cluster C: *Anxious, restive submissiveness* includes avoidant, dependent, and obsessive-compulsive disorders

In addition, Personality Disorder Not Otherwise Specified (NOS) is a diagnostic category for individuals who meet the general definition, but who do not fit neatly into any of the 10 categories.

Personality disorders represent extreme forms of personality traits (i.e., enduring and pervasive patterns of behavior) that have become dysfunctional for the person. The trait is expressed in such a rigid or inappropriate manner that it interferes with that person's adjustment.

People with personality disorders usually lack insight into the source of their difficulties. Clients do not usually seek counseling because of a personality disorder itself, but because of difficulties associated with the disorder. For example, a person with a dependent personality disorder might seek counseling because of loneliness or indecisiveness, but not for dependency. The counselor needs to look beyond the symptoms to find the personality disorder.

According to Fong (1995, p. 636), any of the following signs may suggest a client with a personality disorder:

- Counseling comes to a sudden stop in progress after initial success
- The client is unaware of the effect of his or her behavior on others
- The problems are acceptable to the client
- The client is underresponsive or noncompliant with the therapeutic regime

- The client enters into intense conflictural relationships with institutional systems

She recommended the use of a semistructured interview such as the Personality Disorder Interview–IV (Widiger, 1995) to ascertain the presence of a personality disorder.

The third axis of DSM-IV lists any current physical illness or condition of the individual. In some cases, a physical illness may mask itself as a psychiatric ailment. The counselor needs to be aware of physical disorders that might be influencing a client's mental state.

The first three axes provide the official classification of psychiatric patients for most purposes; however, information provided by the last two axes allows the counselor to gain a more complete picture of the person. The fourth axis identifies psychosocial stressors faced by the client, such as problems with a primary support group or occupational problems. The fifth axis rates the client's general level of functioning on a 100-point scale at the time of evaluation. The five axes together offer an integrated view of a client's problems from the standpoint of a biopsychosocial model of human functioning.

Use of DSM-IV in Counseling

The following points should be considered when using the DSM-IV in counseling:

1. Use the DSM-IV with clients who appear to be suffering from a psychiatric disorder. Use of the DSM-IV classification system improves the reliability and validity of the assessment process.

2. Become familiar with case studies and interviewing techniques for determining DSM-IV classifications (La Bruzza & Mendez-Villarrubia, 1994; Morrison, 1995a, 1995b; Spitzer, Gibbon, et al., 1994). Appropriate use of the DSM-IV requires systematic training and experience in its use.

3. Consider using a structured interview, such as the Primary Care Evaluation of Mental Disorders (PRIME-MD; Spitzer, Williams, et al., 1994), to assist in the screening and diagnostic process. Use the decision-tree approach described in the back of the manual to help make differential diagnoses (American Psychiatric Association, 1994, Appendix A).

253

4. Keep in mind the distinction between symptom-oriented interviewing and insight-oriented interviewing. The first yields descriptions of the client's behavior, which is necessary for DSM-IV classifications. The second provides possible explanations for the client's behavior. Both types of interviewing need to be pursued in counseling.

5. Be careful to use the DSM-IV categories to classify a client's condition, not to label the client. For example, a client should be viewed as a person with schizophrenia, not as a schizophrenic. Labeling can lead to stereotyping and self-fulfilling prophecies.

6. Use the DSM-IV classification system to form diagnostic impressions of clients in communicating with mental health referral sources. Most agencies require that clients or patients be assigned a DSM-IV code for third-party payments.

7. Be cautious when using the DSM-IV to make diagnoses for people from different ethnic groups or cultural backgrounds. The DSM-IV provides guidelines that take into account cultural, age, and sex variations within most of the diagnostic categories. A glossary of culture-bound syndromes, such as *ghost sickness* (preoccupation with death and the deceased, as found among American Indian tribes), *brain fag* ("brain fatigue," from the challenges of school, a condition initially noted in West Africa), and *susto* (fright or "soul loss," a Latino folk illness), is provided in Appendix I of the DSM-IV. To some extent, all sets of psychiatric diagnoses are affected by cultural factors.

8. Keep in mind the limitations of the DSM-IV system. Because of its categorical nature, it does not adequately indicate the severity of a particular condition, nor does it sharply differentiate among individuals classified within the same categories (Clark, Watson, & Reynolds, 1995). Furthermore, the categories themselves suffer from artificial boundaries and extensive overlapping.

SUICIDE RISK ASSESSMENT

Counselors must always be ready to evaluate the risk of suicide among the clients they see. As indicated in Chapter 4, it is a good practice to routinely ask clients about any recent thoughts of suicide. Approximately 30% of the clients (474 of 1,589) seen at one university counseling service during a 1-year period indicated that they had experienced "thoughts of ending their life" during the week prior to their first counseling session (Johnson, Heikkinen, & Ellison, 1988). Counselors need to respond to this issue by undertaking a systematic assessment of suicide risk. The counselor should be careful to establish rapport with the client so that the assessment can be as complete and as accurate as possible.

Clients should be asked directly about their suicidal thoughts if there is any hint of suicidal thinking. Counselors can usually approach this with a series of questions. For example, the counselor might ask, "How have you been feeling lately?" "How bad does it get?" "Has it ever been so bad that you wished you were dead?" "Have you had thoughts of suicide?" If clients have had thoughts of suicide, counselors need to inquire about the extent of these thoughts.

Some counselors are apprehensive about bringing up the topic of suicide with a client for fear that this will encourage the client to think about suicide as an option. In reality, clients who have had suicidal thoughts need the opportunity to talk about these thoughts. In this respect, assessment is part of the treatment. Talking about suicidal thoughts helps to validate the client's experience. It provides a sense of relief and communicates hope to the client that the problem can be addressed. In contrast, clients who have not had suicidal thoughts will usually reassure the counselor that this is not a concern. In fact, it is sometimes a relief for such clients to see their problems from this perspective: Even though they are struggling with a problem, things are not so bad that they think of suicide.

In making a suicide risk assessment, counselors should be both calm and direct. Calmness indicates that it is acceptable for clients to talk about the things they find most troubling. Counselors help clients to look at problems in depth and from different points of view. They should make a point of using the words *suicide* or *kill yourself* while conducting the suicide risk assessment. The enormity of the act should be faced directly. It should not be romanticized.

Significant Factors in Suicide Risk Assessment

The assessment of suicide risk is basic to the formulation of a treatment or intervention plan. The assessment should involve a consideration of the six significant factors discussed below (Cesnik & Nixon, 1977; Stelmachers, 1995).

1. *Self-reported risk*. After a client has acknowledged suicidal ideation, they will usually tell the counselor of their perception of their risk level when asked. Questions such as "How likely do you think it

is that you will act on your thoughts of suicide?" or "How long can you continue to tolerate the situation as it is?" will often generate responses that will be helpful in the assessment process. A self-report of high risk must always be taken seriously.

2. *Suicide plan.* If the client does express thoughts of suicide, the counselor should ask if the client has considered a plan. Information about the plan is critical in helping to assess a client's suicide potential. The counselor should evaluate the plan in terms of (a) its lethality, (b) the availability of the means, and (c) the specificity of the details.

First, some plans are much more lethal, or likely to succeed, than others. Guns, jumping from great heights, and hanging are highly lethal. Holding one's breath until one dies or starving oneself to death are much less likely to succeed.

Second, does the client have access to the means of killing him- or herself? Is a gun available? Has ammunition been purchased? The counselor needs to get clear answers to these specific questions. At times, it may be necessary to interview friends or family members to obtain this information.

Finally, how detailed are the client's plans? The risk of suicide increases as plans become more detailed and specific. For example, has the client made plans to give away possessions? Has the client considered what he or she might write in a note? Where would the suicide take place? When would it take place? A client who has worked out a detailed suicide plan with a high likelihood of success demands immediate attention. Even more alarming are clients who have started to act on their plans, for example, those who have written a suicide note or given a pet animal to a friend. Provisions for further psychological or psychiatric assessment and treatment must be undertaken at once for these people.

3. *Suicide history.* Approximately 30% to 40% of the people who commit suicide have made previous attempts (Maris, 1992). About 10% of those who have attempted suicide in the past will eventually succeed in killing themselves (Murphy, 1985). If a person has attempted or seriously thought about suicide at some earlier time, the risk of suicide for that person is significantly increased.

The counselor should also check on the history of suicide in the family and among friends. Have family members or friends committed suicide or made suicide threats or attempts? If so, what was the nature of the relationship between that person and the client? Did that person represent a model for the client? What does the client feel about those situations? When did the suicide or attempt take place? Anniversary dates can sometimes provide the impetus for suicide attempts.

4. *Psychological symptoms.* Clients who are suffering from mental disorders or psychological distress are much more likely to commit suicide than those who are not (Klerman, 1987). All client symptoms should be reviewed. The SCL-90-R (discussed in Chapter 4), if used as part of the intake procedure, could be used for this purpose.

Suicidal ideation can be predicted by asking clients the following four questions regarding symptoms of depression experienced within the past year (Cooper-Patrick, Crum, & Ford, 1994, p. 1761):

- Have you ever had a period of 2 weeks or more when you had trouble falling asleep, staying asleep, waking up early, or sleeping too much?
- Have you ever had 2 weeks or more during which you felt sad, blue, depressed, or when you lost interest and pleasure in things that you usually cared about or enjoyed?
- Has there ever been a period of 2 weeks or more when you felt worthless, sinful, or guilty?
- Has there ever been a period of time when you felt that life was hopeless?

Clients who respond positively to any of these items should be asked if they have thoughts of suicide. According to experts on the topic, hopelessness stands out as "the most powerful antecedent" of suicide (Stelmachers, 1995, p. 374). Restlessness or agitation associated with any of the above symptoms increases the risk for suicide.

Sometimes signs of improvement can increase the risk of suicide. Clients may become more actively suicidal as they begin to come out of a deep depression, that is, when they acquire enough energy to act on their suicidal thoughts. In a similar fashion, clients sometimes will give an appearance of improvement when they have resolved their ambivalence by deciding to commit suicide.

Symptoms that suggest severe mental illness such as schizophrenia, bipolar disorder, or other psychotic disorders demand prompt attention. Has the client lost contact with reality? Does the client hear voice commands (auditory hallucinations) telling him or her what to do? All psychotic persons with thoughts of suicide should be hospitalized immediately to provide protection and relief from their psychosis. Many people who kill themselves are people with severe and persistent mental illness.

Alcohol or other drug abuse also increases the risk of suicide for a client. Approximately 15% to 25% of alcoholics eventually commit suicide (Klerman, 1987). Medications can also be associated with suicide. The side effects of many medications includes depression. The counselor should note if the client is taking any medications, including any recent change in medications. Medications are also frequently used as a means of suicide. As a safety precaution, antidepressant medications prescribed for highly suicidal persons should be controlled by others.

5. *Environmental stress.* Stressful situations are often the precipitating cause of suicidal ideation. What is the nature of the client's environment? Why is the client feeling suicidal at this particular time? What are the precipitating factors? How would the client benefit from suicide? Clients who wish to commit suicide to escape from stressful situations represent a greater risk than do clients who see suicide as a means of manipulating the environment.

To what degree can the client cope with the stress that he or she may be encountering? For example, can the client identify a solvable problem? Can the client distinguish between wanting to die and wanting to be rid of a problem? Can the client see more than one solution to a problem? Some clients experience "tunnel vision" so that they cannot conceive of options other than suicide for dealing with their stress. Does the client benefit from the counselor's attempts to provide assistance? Positive answers to these questions help to reduce the risk of suicide for the client.

Has the client encountered significant changes in his or her life, such as divorce, death of a family member, sickness, loss of job, academic failure, or an overwhelming work assignment? Any change, even one that is positive, such as a job promotion or the end of an unhappy relationship, can be perceived as stressful. Change involves loss. Losses that pose the greatest threat include loss of a relationship, loss of a significant role, loss of a dream, or a large financial loss. Sometimes anticipating a loss can be more stressful than the actual loss. Loss can be particularly stressful if the client accepts most of the blame. Client stress can be evaluated thoroughly by means of the Life Events Scale (Sarason, Johnson, & Siegel, 1978) or the Life Stressors and Social Resources Inventory—Adult or —Youth Form (Moos & Moos, 1994a, 1994b).

Sometimes stress can relate to events that may have happened years earlier if these events have not been addressed. Such events include sexual abuse, physical abuse, the suicide of a parent or sibling, and other traumatic events. Ask the client if there are things from his or her past that he or she finds very difficult to talk about. If so, help the client to begin to look at these issues in a supportive atmosphere. Recognize the need for long-term treatment for many of these issues.

6. *Available resources.* A counselor needs to determine what resources are available for the client. Three levels of resources should be considered: (a) internal; (b) family, close friends, neighbors, coworkers, and others who may have contact with the client; and (c) professionals.

First of all, what are the client's internal resources? In trying to assess these resources, ask what has helped the client in the past in similar situations. What is keeping the client from committing suicide? How is the client responding to your interactions? Does the client have plans for the future?

Second, find out what type of support system the client has. If nobody seems to be involved with the client at the present time, ask who used to care. Does the client have regular contact with anyone else? Does the client have any confidants? Would the client be willing to share his or her concerns with family members or close friends? In some respects, suicide can be looked upon more as a social than as a psychiatric phenomenon. Evaluation of the client's social support system is critical from this point of view. One's social support system can be systematically assessed by means of the Multidimensional Scale of Perceived Social Support (Zimet, Dahlem, Zimet, & Farley, 1988) or the Life Stressors and Social Resources Inventory—Adult or —Youth Form (Moos & Moos, 1994a, 1994b).

What community resources are available for the client? Possibilities include a 24-hour crisis phone line, emergency treatment center, or mental health specialist with whom the client has good rapport. Would the client make use of these resources in case of a crisis? Will the client sign a contract that he or she would contact the counselor or another mental health professional before attempting to commit suicide?

Not all of these points need to be covered with all clients. Move from the general to the specific. Ask for more detail in those areas in which you detect a problem. A review of each of the factors listed above should help you to evaluate the risk of suicide for your client. It also helps to give the client a sense of reassurance that you are taking his or her concern seriously. In many cases, talking about suicide can serve as a substitute for attempting suicide. Suicide can be looked upon as a desperate means of communication. Honestly confronting this level of desperation in counseling can provide a great relief for the client.

If you are having difficulty in making a suicide risk assessment, consult with another mental health professional. Clients who are at risk for suicide often need to be referred for psychiatric evaluation. Psychiatrists can evaluate the client's need for medication, hospitalization, or long-term treatment. The assessment and treatment of suicidal clients frequently requires a team approach.

SAD PERSONS Scale

The SAD PERSONS scale provides a convenient acronym for 10 basic points to keep in mind when assessing a client for suicidal risk (Patterson, Dohn, Bird, & Patterson, 1983). The 10 points are listed in Table 14-1. The demographic characteristics of sex and age are included in these points because of their relationship with suicide (Patterson et al., 1983). Even though women make more suicide attempts than do men, three times as many men as women actually kill themselves. People are also more likely to attempt suicide when they are under 25 or over 45 years old than they are in midlife. The other 8 points have been discussed above.

Guidelines for interpreting scores based on the SAD PERSONS scale are shown in Table 14-1. These guidelines are not meant to substitute for clinical judgment. The counselor will need to weigh all aspects of the situation in making a decision. Some points may deserve greater weight than other points depending upon the particular situation.

Students who have been taught how to use the SAD PERSONS scale make judgments similar to those of experienced psychiatrists (Juhnke, 1992; Patterson et al., 1983). Those who do not know how to use the scale tend to overestimate the suicide risk of the people they evaluate.

TABLE 14-1. The SAD PERSONS Scale for Assessing the Risk of Suicide

Items from the SAD PERSONS Scale	
Sex	Previous attempt
Age	Ethanol abuse
Depression	Rational thinking loss
	Social support loss
	Organized plan
	No spouse
	Sickness

One point is scored for each factor deemed present. The total score thus ranges from 0 (very low risk) to 10 (very high risk).

Guidelines for Interpreting Scores from SAD PERSONS Scale

Total points	Proposed clinical action
0–2	Send home with follow-up
3–4	Consider hospitalization
5–6	Strongly consider hospitalization, depending on confidence in follow-up arrangements
7–10	Hospitalize or commit

Note. From "Evaluation of Suicidal Patients: The SAD PERSONS Scale" by W. M. Patterson, H. H. Dohn, J. Bird, and G. A. Patterson, 1983, *Psychosomatics, 24,* pp. 343–349. © 1983 by American Psychiatric Press, Inc. Reprinted by permission.

ASSESSMENT OF ALCOHOL USE

A section on the assessment of alcohol use is included in this chapter because of the prevalence of abusive drinking and alcohol-related problems in our culture. According to a national study of psychiatric disorders, more than 25% of the people in this country will meet the diagnostic criteria for substance abuse or dependence at some time in their lifetimes (Kessler et al., 1994). Most of the substance use disorders involve the use of alcohol. Because denial is a central issue in the abuse of alcohol or other drugs, counselors may not learn of the problem if they do not systematically review this matter with clients.

A variety of assessment procedures may be used to evaluate alcohol use. In most cases, the interview will probably be used to determine the nature and the gravity of drinking problems. The interview can be supplemented by self-monitoring methods and physiological indices such as blood alcohol concentration (BAC) levels. Standardized measures (to be discussed in the next chapter) may also be used as part of the assessment process. In addition to individual assessment, the counselor will often need to assess the environment in which the drinking takes place.

Diagnostic Criteria for Alcohol Dependence or Abuse

Although this chapter focuses on assessment of alcohol use, the DSM-IV employs similar diagnostic criteria to determine dependence or abuse for all psychoactive substances. Psychoactive drugs include all drugs that alter one's mood or thought processes by their effect on the central nervous system. DSM-IV recognizes 10 classes of psychoactive drugs (alcohol, amphetamines, cannabis, nicotine, cocaine, PCP or phencyclidine, inhalants, hallucinogens, opioids, and sedatives) that can lead to dependence. The drugs show some differences in respect to tolerance and withdrawal symptoms as indicated in the DSM-IV.

The specific criteria used to determine alcohol (or other substance) *dependence* are summarized below (American Psychiatric Association, 1994):

- Tolerance, that is, markedly increased amounts of the substance are needed over time to attain intoxication or desired effect, or markedly diminished effect occurs with continued use of same amount of the substance
- Withdrawal symptoms that significantly interfere with everyday functioning when the substance is no longer available. Alcohol withdrawal symptoms include "the shakes," transient hallucinations or illusions, anxiety, depressed mood, headache, insomnia, rapid heart rate, or sweating
- Compulsive use of the substance as indicated by consuming the substance in larger amounts than intended or by any of the additional criteria listed below
- Unsuccessful efforts to cut down on use of the substance
- Expenditure of a great deal of time obtaining the substance, using it, or recovering from its effects
- Reduction or cessation of important social, occupational, or recreational activities because of substance use
- Continued use of the substance despite the physical or psychological problems that it is known to produce

Of the seven criteria listed, three or more must be manifested over a 12-month period for a person to be diagnosed as alcohol dependent. The diagnostic classification includes the specifier "with physiological dependence" if the person shows evidence of either tolerance or withdrawal (American Psychiatric Association, 1994, p. 181).

Alcohol *abuse* refers to problematic drinking that does not fulfill the criteria for dependence. People who suffer from this condition continue to drink within a 12-month period despite significant problems including failure to fulfill role obligations at work or home, repeated use in dangerous situations (e.g., driving while intoxicated), recurrent legal problems, or recurrent social and interpersonal problems.

Counselors will often see clients because of the problems produced by the drinking, such as deterioration in work performance, conflicts with others, depression, or poor health. The counselor will need to be careful to assess for drinking (or other substance) abuse that may have caused the problem. In general, counselors should assess clients' ability to control their use of alcohol and the degree to which alcohol use causes problems in their lives.

Interview Schedules

A number of interview schedules have been developed to aid in the assessment of alcohol use (Miller, 1976). The CAGE questionnaire (named for the key words in each of four questions) can be readily used to screen clients for problems related to alcohol use (Ewing, 1984; Kitchens, 1994). It consists of the four questions listed below, each of which significantly differentiates between individuals who are alcoholic and those who are not:

- Have you felt a need to *cut down* drinking?
- Have you ever felt *annoyed* by criticism of drinking?
- Have you had *guilty* feelings about drinking?
- Do you ever take a morning *eye-opener*?

If clients respond *yes* to any of these questions, additional inquiry should be undertaken.

Heck (1991) found that the effectiveness of the CAGE questionnaire in identifying problem drinkers could be significantly improved

263

by asking clients about their social drinking habits, driving habits, and the age at which they began to drink. Problem drinkers rarely or never choose nonalcoholic beverages at social events, frequently drive while under the influence of alcohol, and started drinking on a regular basis while they were still in high school.

Two extensive schedules that may be particularly valuable for counselors are the Comprehensive Drinking Profile (CDP) and the Time-Line Follow-Back (TLFB). The CDP is a structured intake interview procedure requiring 1 to 2 hours for completion (Marlatt & Miller, 1984). It provides detailed information regarding the history and current status of an individual's drinking problems and related matters. It assesses both consumption and problematic behaviors. A short form of the CDP, the Brief Drinker Profile, is also available, as well as the Follow-up Drinker Profile (a measure of client progress) and the Collateral Interview Form (an instrument for obtaining information from other people who are close to the client).

The TLFB enables the client and the counselor to reconstruct the client's drinking behavior for the past year (Sobell et al., 1980). It analyzes the patterns (e.g., daily, weekly, sporadically) and the intensity (e.g., light, heavy) of drinking behavior. Connections between drinking episodes and significant events ("anchor points") in the person's life are studied. Research indicates that the TLFB is highly reliable and relatively accurate. TLFB reports obtained from clients agree reasonably well with those obtained from the clients' spouses or partners. This procedure yields information that is highly informative to clients as well as to counselors (Vuchinich, Tucker, & Harllee, 1988).

Self-Monitoring Methods

Self-monitoring can enhance assessments made by means of interview procedures in a number of ways. Because self-monitoring is based on planned observations, data obtained in this manner should be more accurate and more complete than data based on recall. Self-monitoring has the added advantage of helping clients to see more clearly the relationship between certain events and their drinking behavior. Finally, self-monitoring provides a means of plotting the client's progress in controlling drinking behavior.

Self-monitoring charts typically include the amount of alcohol consumed in a given period of time, the situations in which the alcohol was consumed, and the presence of other people (Vuchinich et al., 1988). The thoughts or feelings of the person at the time may also be recorded. Temptations to drink, as well as actual drinking behavior, may be tracked.

Situational Factors

Besides assessing individual factors, counselors should help clients look at environmental factors that may encourage abusive drinking. Miller and Munoz (1982, p. 75) provided a checklist of 10 such situations:

- Drinking after work, especially after hard days
- Drinking after a stressful or emotional experience
- Drinking beer from barrels, kegs, or pitchers
- Drinking directly from the bottle (except beer)
- Drinking during automatic or boring activities
- Drinking during or with rewarding activities
- Drinking with heavy drinkers
- Drinking when thirsty or hungry
- Drinking with those who pressure you to drink faster or more
- Drinking "the usual" in the usual place

In a survey conducted by Ziemelis (1988), approximately 60% of college students reported that they often found themselves in situations in which they were encouraged to drink more than they wished.

A recent study of problem drinkers indicated that drinking style (that is, when, where, how, and with whom) predicted problem drinking more accurately than other variables (Yu & Williford, 1992). According to this research, problem drinkers often drink alone and early in the day.

Use of Alcohol Assessment Procedures in Counseling

Guidelines concerning the assessment of problems related to alcohol or other substance use are listed below:

1. Be sure to ask about the use of alcohol or other drugs as part of the initial contact procedure.

2. Inquire about problems related to drinking. Abusive drinking may be most evident in the problems it produces. Ask if other people

have been concerned about the client's drinking behavior. Use the CAGE questions as part of the screening process.

3. Keep the DSM-IV criteria in mind in assessing for alcohol dependence or abuse. Determine frequency, duration, and severity of pertinent symptoms. Remember that these same criteria can be used in assessing other types of psychoactive substance dependence or abuse.

4. If alcohol or other drug problems are detected, use a more thorough assessment procedure to gain a better understanding of the problem or refer the client to specialists for this purpose. Interview schedules such as the CDP or TLFB or the Alcohol Use Inventory (briefly discussed in the next chapter) could be used for a more extended assessment.

5. Engage the client in self-assessment. Self-monitoring of drinking behavior can be helpful both in defining the problem and in gauging the success of treatment efforts.

6. Help clients to become aware of those situations that may trigger drinking behavior for them. Also help them to identify problems associated with drinking. Use of checklists can be helpful for this purpose. For example, the Alcohol and Other Drugs Self-Test includes 50 items that can be used to stimulate greater self-awareness (Wisconsin Clearinghouse, 1996).

7. Teach the use of Blood Alcohol Concentration (BAC) tables to clients with drinking problems so that they can assess the influence of alcohol consumption on their judgment and reaction time (Kishline, 1994). Help them to use these tables to set limits.

8. When clients do not accept the fact that they have a problem of control of their drinking behavior (an essential feature of dependency), ask them to try to limit their drinking to a certain amount (e.g., no more than three drinks) on any one occasion for a period of 3 months. This has sometimes been referred to as the "acid test" of one's ability to control drinking behavior.

9. If denial appears to be a problem, obtain permission from the client to speak with other family members as a means of gaining information about his or her drinking behaviors. Interview these people with the client present in the room.

10. Refer clients with persistent drinking problems to specialists for assessment and treatment. Inpatient or intensive outpatient treatment in a multidisciplinary setting may be necessary.

SUMMARY

1. Mental illnesses, particularly anxiety and mood disorders, occur frequently in the United States. Counselors need to be able to detect psychopathology among clients within their caseload.
2. The DSM-IV offers a clear and comprehensive means of diagnosing possible mental disorders among clients.
3. All counselors should be able to undertake suicide risk assessments and substance abuse assessments within the counseling session.
4. If counselors are concerned about a client's suicide risk, they should ask about suicide intentions, specific suicide plans, previous suicide attempts, psychological symptoms, environmental stress, and available resources.
5. Alcohol assessment should focus on the client's ability to control his or her drinking and the problems in the client's life associated with drinking. The DSM-IV criteria can be used to diagnose alcohol dependence or abuse.

15

MENTAL HEALTH ASSESSMENT: STANDARDIZED INVENTORIES

S TANDARDIZED MEASURES of mental health are presented in this chapter. General-purpose measures contain a variety of scales that can be used to assess different aspects of psychopathology. Specific-purpose measures, on the other hand, focus upon a particular type of psychological problem, such as depression, anxiety, alcohol abuse, or eating disorders that counselors are likely to confront.

GENERAL-PURPOSE MEASURES

The Minnesota Multiphasic Personality Inventory (MMPI) has been used more than any other personality inventory to assess psychopathology for both adults and adolescents (Archer, Marvish, Imhof, & Piotrowski, 1991; Watkins, Campbell, Nieberding, & Hallmark, 1995). In the past several years, the MMPI has been updated and restandardized as two distinct versions—one for adults (MMPI-2) and one for adolescents (MMPI-A). The characteristics and use of both of these instruments are discussed below. In addition, three other broad measures of psychopathology that can serve as alternatives to the MMPI are also reviewed.

Minnesota Multiphasic Personality Inventory-2 (MMPI-2)

The MMPI-2 replaces the MMPI, which was first constructed over 50 years ago (Butcher, Dahlstrom, Graham, Tellegen, & Kaemmer, 1989). This instrument, which requires a sixth-grade reading level, may be used with clients beginning at age 18. The MMPI-A, the adolescent version of the MMPI, should be used with boys and girls age 14 to 18 (Butcher et al., 1992).

The original MMPI, as developed by Starke Hathaway and J. Charnley McKinley, contained a total of 4 validity scales and 10 clinical scales that formed the standard MMPI profile (see Table 15-1). The validity scales enable the counselor to assess the client's attitude toward the testing process. Most of the clinical scales consist of items that significantly differentiate between people in a particular psychiatric diagnostic category (e.g., depression) and people in the general reference group (often referred to as "the Minnesota normals"). For example, the Depression scale (Scale 2) contains 60 items that depressed people endorsed significantly more (or less) often than did the Minnesota normals.

Subsequent research has indicated that the MMPI scales cannot be used to classify individuals into psychiatric categories with a high degree of accuracy. Instead, the scales are most useful in providing descriptions of personality and as a source of inference regarding a person's behavior. Because of the large amount of research that has been conducted with the MMPI, the scales convey a wealth of information about an individual's personality that transcends the original purpose of the scale. For this reason, the original names for the MMPI scales have been replaced by the scale numbers for most purposes (e.g., Scale 7 instead of *Pt* or Psychasthenia).

The MMPI-2 authors have corrected problems with the original normative sample and brought the instrument up to date (Butcher, Dahlstrom, et al., 1989). The total number of items (567) remains about the same. Ineffective, offensive, and repeated items have been

TABLE 15-1. Description of Standard Scales on Minnesota
Multiphasic Personality Inventory

Scale	Original Name and Abbreviation	Behaviors Associated With Elevated Scores
Validity scales		
?	Cannot say (?)	Indecisiveness, rebelliousness, defensiveness
L	Lie (L)	Faking good, naivete, scrupulosity
F	Frequency (F)	Faking bad, unusual behavior, confusion while taking test
K	Correction (K)	Faking good, defensiveness, self-reliance
Clinical scales		
1	Hypochondriasis (Hs)	Bodily complaints, fatigue, weakness
2	Depression (D)	Dejection, dissatisfaction, tendency to give up
3	Hysteria (Hy)	Denial of problems, desire for social acceptance, psychosomatic symptoms
4	Psychopathic deviate (Pd)	Impulsivity, acting out, not bound by rules
5	Masculinity-femininity (Mf)	Men: Cultural-aesthetic interests, passivity, academic achievement Women: Outdoor-mechanical interests, dominating, competitive
6	Paranoia (Pa)	Sensitive, suspicious, preoccupied with rights and privileges
7	Psychasthenia (Pt)	Anxious, obsessive, compulsive
8	Schizophrenia (Sc)	Unusual thoughts or behavior, detached, introspective
9	Hypomania (Ma)	High energy level, restless, distractible
0	Social introversion-extroversion (Si)	Introverted, reserved, reticent

eliminated. Sexist or dated items have been reworded. New items tap areas not well represented in the original MMPI item pool, including family relationships, eating disorders, and drug abuse.

The authors of MMPI-2 have left the standard MMPI scales virtually intact. None of these scales lost more than four items. Scores obtained on MMPI-2 standard scales correlate highly (.66 to .92) with scores obtained on similar scales from the original MMPI (Ben-Porath & Butcher, 1989). The order of the items has been changed so that all of the standard scales can be scored by having a client complete the first 370 items in the MMPI-2 booklet.

In contrast with the original standardization procedures, members of the new normative sample (1,462 women and 1,138 men) were selected so that they would be representative of the adult U.S. population in terms of age, marital status, ethnicity, and geography. Some questions about the success of the revision have been raised in regard to the educational level of the normative sample (Adler, 1990). The percentage of college graduates in the new normative sample is much higher than that found in the original sample or reported by the U.S. Census Bureau. According to Butcher (1990a), the change in the educational level of the normative sample should have a minimal impact on the interpretation of the MMPI-2 scores.

With the new norms, the cut-off score used to detect psychological problems has dropped from 70 on the MMPI to 65 on the MMPI-2. Research indicates that a T-score of 65 provides optimal separation between clinical groups and the standardization sample (Butcher, Dahlstrom, et al., 1989). The scores on the MMPI-2 have also been adjusted so that the distribution of the profile scores will be the same for the eight clinical scales (all but Scales 5 and 0) used to assess psychopathology. For example, a T-score of 65 equals the 92nd percentile (based on the restandardization sample) for each of these scales.

The MMPI scales should be interpreted in conjunction with the other scales on the profile, not in isolation. Common MMPI patterns are listed in MMPI reference books (e.g., Butcher, 1990b; Butcher & Williams, 1992; Duckworth & Anderson, 1995, Graham, 1993, Greene, 1991; Lewak, Marks, & Nelson, 1990). Counselors should be acquainted with the vast literature pertaining to the MMPI if they work with mentally disturbed clients; however, they cannot expect to become proficient in its use without specialized training and extensive clinical experience.

Counselors should note critical items that the client has checked as well as scale scores. For example, if the client marked True to Item 506, "I have recently considered killing myself," or Item 524, "No one knows it but I have tried to kill myself," the counselor should review these items with the client. Clients might not bring these topics up on their own. They may assume that the counselor already knows this information from their responses to these items on the MMPI-2.

Several critical item lists have been developed. Most of these items consistently separate normal from psychiatrically disturbed samples. Lachar & Wrobel (1979) identified 111 items that suggest psychopathology in 13 different areas. All but 4 of these items have been retained in the MMPI-2. A revised version of the Koss-Butcher critical item set has been prepared for the MMPI-2 (Butcher et al., 1989). This list contains 78 items related to six crisis areas. Most computer-based MMPI scoring programs will flag critical items checked by the clients (see Butcher, 1989a, 1989b). This information can also be obtained by means of hand scoring. The critical item lists provide a simple and straightforward means for counselors to discuss MMPI results with clients and to determine which topics should be pursued in counseling.

A number of additional scales have been created for the MMPI that can be used to help interpret the clinical scales. Most of the clinical scales have been divided into subscales that can help clarify the meaning of scores (Harris & Lingoes, 1968, cited by Graham, 1993). For example, the Depression scale has been divided into the following subscales: Subjective Depression, Psychomotor Retardation, Physical Malfunctioning, Mental Dullness, and Brooding.

Besides the subscales, 15 content scales devised by Butcher, Graham, Williams, and Ben-Porath (1989) can also be used to clarify the meaning of the MMPI-2 profile scores. In contrast with the clinical scales, which were developed by empirical means, the content scales were constructed by logical analysis of the item content. The scales were refined by statistical procedures to ensure homogeneity. Scales developed in this fashion are easier to interpret than empirical scales. The content scales also assess aspects of personality not measured by the standard scales, including type-A behavior, work interference, family problems, and negative treatment indicators.

In addition to the scales discussed thus far, many other scales have been constructed from the MMPI item pool for various purposes. Popular supplementary scales include A (Anxiety), R (Repression), and Es (Ego Strength). A and R represent the two main factors derived from factor analyses of the clinical scales. As such, they offer a quick summary, or overview, of MMPI-2 results. Scale A provides a measure of anxiety or general maladjustment; Scale R shows the client's tendency to repress or deny psychological difficulties. The Es scale is based on items that differentiate between clients with psychological problems who responded to therapy and those who did not. In contrast with most of the scores on the MMPI-2, high scores on Es should be interpreted favorably.

Current research on the MMPI-2 indicates that it can be used effectively with clients from minority groups if moderator variables such as socioeconomic status, education, and acculturation are taken into account (Anderson, 1995; Greene, 1991). These variables have a greater influence than ethnic status on MMPI-2 scores. A recent study by Timbrook and Graham (1994) of the MMPI-2 found that it predicted criterion variables (based on partner ratings) as accurately for African Americans as it did for White men and women.

Although the MMPI-2 has many advantages, it is not without faults. In a comprehensive review, Helmes and Reddon (1993) criticized the MMPI-2 on the following counts: (a) lack of a consistent measurement model, (b) heterogeneous item content within clinical scales, (c) suspect diagnostic criteria, (d) overlapping item content among scales, (e) lack of cross-validation of scoring keys, (f) inadequate measures of response styles, and (g) suspect norms. They urged clinicians to consider alternative measures such as the Millon Clinical Multiaxial Inventory, Personality Assessment Inventory, and Basic Personality Inventory, because these measures are "more likely to incorporate modern developments and have fewer serious conceptual problems" (Helmes & Reddon, 1993, p. 467).

CASE EXAMPLE

Janet, a 19-year-old college sophomore, requested counseling because of low self-esteem, relationship difficulties, family conflict, and eating concerns. She marked 5 (*very much*) to the following items on the Inventory of Common Problems:

- Feeling irritable, tense, or nervous
- Feeling fearful
- Feeling lonely or isolated
- Eating, appetite, or weight problems

She also completed the Beck Depression Inventory as part of the initial contact session, for which she received a raw score of 32, indicating "severe depression." The counselor asked Janet to complete the MMPI-2 during her next visit to the counseling center to assess more thoroughly the nature and the level of her psychological problems. She obtained the profile shown in Figure 15-1.

The scores on the three validity scales—L, F, and K—indicate self-criticism and a possible plea for help. Her low L and K scores indicate that she is describing herself in a negative fashion. The elevated F score suggests self-criticism together with moderately severe psychopathology. Among the clinical scales, she obtained elevated scores on scales 2, 6, 7, and 0. Her highest two scores are Scales 7 and 2. According to Graham, individuals with this type of profile configuration "tend to be anxious, nervous, tense, high-strung, and jumpy. They worry excessively, and they are vulnerable to real and imagined threat. They tend to anticipate problems before they occur and to overreact to minor stress. Somatic symp-

FIGURE 15-1. MMPI-2 Profile for Counseling Center Client

Raw Score __0__ __9__ __9__ __12__ __29__ __25__ __23__ __39__ __15__ __31__ __24__ __18__ __43__

? Raw Score ____

K to be Added __5__ __4__ __9__ __9__ __2__

Raw Score with K __17__ __27__ __40__ __33__ __20__

From Minnesota Multiphasic Personality Inventory-2 (MMPI-2). Copyright © by the Regents of the University of Minnesota, 1942, 1943 (renewed 1970), 1989. This profile form 1989.

toms are common" (1993, p. 89). Because of their acute discomfort, they are likely to respond well to psychotherapy. They are most likely to receive a psychiatric diagnosis of anxiety disorder, depressive disorder, or obsessive-compulsive disorder.

Janet's elevated scores on Scales 6 and 0 both indicate possible difficulties in interpersonal relationships. According to the MMPI-2 Manual scores between 66 and 75 on scale 6 can possibly be interpreted as follows: Angry and resentful, displaces blame and criticisms, hostile and suspicious, rigid and stubborn, and misinterprets social situations (Butcher, Dahlstrom, et al., 1989, p. 39). Similarly, scores between 66 and 75 on Scale 0 suggest behavior that is introverted, shy and timid, lacking self-confidence, moody, submissive, and rigid (Butcher, Dahlstrom et al., 1989, p. 43).

The counselor provided counseling to Janet to help her deal with her immediate situation. At the same time, she made arrangements to refer Janet to a psychiatrist for a more complete assessment of some of the psychological problems suggested by the MMPI-2.

Minnesota Multiphasic Personality Inventory– Adolescent (MMPI-A)

Prior to the construction of the MMPI-A in 1992, adolescents were frequently administered the adult version of the MMPI despite the difficulties in adapting this version for adolescents (Archer, Marvish, Imhof, & Piotrowski, 1991; Butcher et al., 1992). The adolescent version of the MMPI is similar to the new adult version in that it retains the same basic scales as the old MMPI and also includes a new set of content scales.

The MMPI-A differs from the MMPI-2 in regard to its norms, its item content, and the nature of some of its scales. The MMPI-A provides separate-sex norms for adolescents ages 14 through 18 years. (The authors recommend that the MMPI-2 be used with 18-year-olds who have moved away from their parental home.) The MMPI-A contains 89 fewer items than the MMPI-2 to help encourage client cooperation. Most of the omitted items are items that were not scored on any of the clinical scales, items found on Scales 5 and 0 (both exceptionally long scales on the MMPI-2), or items on the Fears content scale (which has been dropped from the MMPI-A). The MMPI-A includes a number of items from the original MMPI that have been rewritten to pertain to adolescents, as well as a number of new items that deal specifically with adolescent issues (peers, teachers, parents, school).

Whereas 11 of the 15 content scales on the MMPI-A are similar to those found on the MMPI-2, 4 of the scales—School Problems, Low Aspirations, Alienation, and Conduct Disorder—have been designed specifically to address issues common to adolescents. The F validity scale, which often produced high scores for adolescents on the MMPI, has been redesigned for the MMPI-A by including only those items answered infrequently (20% of the time or less) by adolescents. The MMPI-A also includes a new supplementary scale, the Immaturity scale, not found on the MMPI-2.

Research reported in the manual indicates that the basic and content scales possess adequate test-retest reliability and internal consistency. The content scales have proven to be valid in predicting external criteria, such as record reviews and ratings by parents and treatment staff (Williams, Butcher, Ben-Porath, & Graham, 1992). Much of the validity for the MMPI-A can be inferred from validity established for the MMPI because of the comparability of the instruments. As with the MMPI-2, *T*-scores of 65 or greater suggest psychopathology. Scores between 60 and 65 should also be viewed as indicating possible psychological problems.

Millon Clinical Multiaxial Inventory-III (MCMI-III)

The MCMI-III provides an alternative to the MMPI-2 for diagnosing psychopathology (Millon, Millon, & Davis, 1994). It is considerably shorter than the MMPI-2, containing 175 items compared with 567 items on the MMPI-2. Most people can complete the MCMI-III in 20 to 30 minutes. It is also more closely tied in with the DSM-IV than is the MMPI-2, so that psychiatric classifications can be made more easily. The MCMI-III is also more closely related to psychological theory than is the MMPI (Millon, 1969, 1981, 1990).

The MCMI-III provides two broad sets of scores that correspond with Axis I (clinical syndromes) and Axis II (personality disorders) on the DSM-IV. The scales are scored in terms of base rates so that the percentage of people classified by means of the MCMI-III as suffering from a particular psychological problem correspond with the actual percentages found in society. Because of the scoring procedure, it is important that the MCMI-III be used only with people who fit the normative population, that is, people suspected to be suffering from a mental disorder. The MCMI-III will overpathologize for people who do not fit this population. Clients should be screened by other criteria such as an interview, the Beck Depression Inventory, or the Inventory of Common Problems, before they are assigned the MCMI-III.

The MCMI-III, released in 1994, differs from the MCMI-II by addition of two new personality scales (Depressive Personality and Posttraumatic Stress Disorder), revisions in the item weighting procedure (less weights are now used), and a reduction in the number of items per scale to improve scale validities. Of the 175 items, 90 have been rewritten or replaced with new items.

The MCMI-III has been validated in terms of its effectiveness in differentiating individuals with particular psychiatric diagnoses from other psychiatric patients. This is a more rigorous criterion than simply differentiating the disturbed individual from nondisturbed individuals in general. The former technique has proved to be more accurate in identifying the psychiatric diagnoses of patients in subsequent studies than has the latter technique.

MCMI-III answer sheets must be scored by means of computer-based scoring programs available from the publisher. The scoring programs provide comprehensive narrative interpretations of the scores, together with suggested psychiatric diagnoses and treatment possibilities.

Counselors should consider the use of the MCMI-III with adult clients whom they believe may be suffering from a psychiatric disorder. For adolescents, counselors should use the Millon Adolescent Clinical Inventory (MACI), the "junior version" of the MCMI-III (Millon & Davis, 1993). Considerable training and experience are required for the use of either instrument. As noted by Millon et al. (1994), the instruments provide a series of "tentative judgments" rather than a set of clinical statements. The counselor can use information gained from these instruments in the referral of clients for psychiatric assessment and treatment.

Personality Assessment Inventory (PAI)

The PAI was designed to provide information on "relevant clinical variables" for individuals 18 years of age and older (Morey, 1991). Content areas for the PAI were selected on the basis of current diagnostic schemes and treatment planning. The PAI consists of 344 items (selected from an original item pool of 2,200 items), which are scored on 22 scales. Final items for the PAI were carefully selected on the basis of expert ratings, statistical analysis, and related criteria in a 10-stage process.

The 22 full scales on the PAI include 4 validity scales (Inconsistency, Infrequency, Negative Impression, and Positive Impression), 11 clinical scales, 5 treatment scales, and 2 interpersonal scales. The 11 clinical scales, which resemble many of the MMPI clinical scales, can be subdivided into three broad categories of disorders: (a) neurotic spectrum scales—Somatic Complaints, Anxiety, Anxiety-Related Disorders, and Depression; (b) psychotic spectrum scales—Mania, Paranoia, and Schizophrenia; and (c) behavior disorder scales—Borderline Features, Antisocial Features, Alcohol Problems, and Drug Problems. The 5 treatment scales, which focus on issues important in treatment not necessarily apparent from the clinical scales, include Aggression, Suicidal Ideation, Stress, Nonsupport, and Treatment Rejection. Finally, the 2 interpersonal scales measure two critical dimensions in interpersonal relations: domination versus submission (Dominance scale) and friendliness versus hostility (Warmth scale). Information is also provided on the client's answers to 27 critical items, which were selected because of their potential seriousness and low endorsement rates.

Because of the heterogeneous nature of the clinical scales, nine have been divided into subscales. For example, the Anxiety scale includes Cognitive, Affective, and Physiological subscales, and the Anxiety-Related Disorders scale includes Obsessive-Compulsive, Phobias, and Traumatic Stress subscales. The treatment scale for aggression has also been divided into three subscales: Aggressive Attitude, Verbal Aggression, and Physical Aggression.

The PAI, which has a fourth-grade reading level, requires about 50 minutes to complete. The item response format provides four alternatives: *false—not at all true, slightly true, mainly true*, or *very true*. All of the scales can be easily handscored without the use of a template in 10 minutes or less. In contrast with the MMPI, none of the full scales contain overlapping items.

The PAI has been carefully normed on a sample of 1,000 community-dwelling adults selected to match the characteristics of the 1995 census projections in terms of sex, race, and age. In addition to the adult norms, comprehensive norms have also been established for college students and clinical populations.

The full scales exhibit adequate test-retest reliabilities over short-time periods and relatively high internal consistency coefficients. The PAI possesses substantial convergent and discriminant validity based on its correlations with scales from other psychological measures.

The PAI is a promising new instrument because of its ease of scoring and interpretation. It has been carefully constructed and appears to be psychometrically sound.

Basic Personality Inventory (BPI)

The BPI is intended for use with both adolescents and adults in clinical and nonclinical populations (Jackson, 1989). It consists of 240 true-false items scored on 11 clinical scales and 1 critical-item scale (20 items per scale). The categories for the clinical scales were derived from factor analysis of other personality inventories including the MMPI. As a result, the clinical scales on the BPI hold much in common with the clinical scales on the MMPI.

The 11 clinical scales measure neurotic tendencies (Hypochondriasis, Depression, Anxiety, Social Introversion, and Self-Depreciation), psychotic tendencies (Persecutory Ideas, Thinking Disorder), and antisocial tendencies (Denial, Interpersonal Problems, Alienation, and Impulse Expression). Items for each scale were selected to maximize item-scale correlations and minimize interscale correlations.

The BPI, which requires approximately 35 minutes to complete, can be handscored in less than 10 minutes. The manual provides separate-sex norms for both adults and adolescents. The manual reports respectable reliability and validity data. Validation procedures primarily involved correlating the scores on the BPI scales with clinical ratings and other measures of psychopathology.

In comparison to the MMPI-2, the BPI has been praised for its brevity, ease of administration and scoring, and "purity" (homogeneity) of its clinical scales (Urbina, 1995; Yelland, 1995). On the other hand, it lacks the diagnostic utility and extensive normative data, especially for ethnic populations, of the MMPI-2.

SPECIFIC-PURPOSE MEASURES

In this section, the use of standardized inventories that have been designed to assess psychological problems in specific areas will be discussed. These areas include emotional states such as depression, anxiety, and anger, as well as psychological disorders such as alcohol abuse and eating disorders. Measures of emotional states serve as "emotional vital signs" that can be used to assess the individual's psychological well being in the same sense that physical vital signs such as heart rate and blood pressure are used to evaluate one's physical health (Spielberger, Sydeman, Ritterband, Reheiser, & Unger, 1995). Measures of specific psychological disorders can be used to determine to what extent an individual may be suffering from a particular problem.

Most of the specific-purpose instruments (sometimes referred to as focus measures or rapid assessment instruments) discussed in this section are relatively brief and easy to administer and score. For this reason, they can readily be readministered to monitor a client's progress in dealing with a specific issue. Fischer and Corcoran (1994) have provided a collection of over 320 such instruments in their two-volume sourcebook.

Depression

One of the most common psychiatric disorders suffered by people in the United States is depression. In the National Comorbidity Study conducted by Kessler et al. (1994), more than 17% of the sample reported lifetime incidences of a major depressive episode and more than 10% reported such an episode within the past year.

A large number of self-rating scales have been devised to assess depression. Ponterotto, Pace, & Kavan (1989) identified 73 different self-report measures for depression used by mental health professionals for research or counseling purposes. Among these instruments, the Beck Depression Inventory was used 10 times as often as the next most popular measure.

Beck Depression Inventory (BDI). The BDI was first developed to assess the severity of depression among adults and adolescents by Aaron Beck and his associates in 1961. The original version was revised in 1971 both by rewording some of the items and by changing the instructions so that the instrument could be self-administered instead of being orally administered by a trained examiner. The BDI, which has a fifth-grade reading level, includes 21 items that describe symptoms of depression of an affective, cognitive, behavioral, or physiological nature. Each item uses a 4-point scale of severity ranging from 0 to 3. Clients mark the level of severity for each symptom that best describes how they have been feeling during "the past week, including today." The BDI instructions and sample items are shown in Figure 15-2.

Most clients complete the BDI within 5 to 10 minutes. Scoring, which involves tallying answers for 21 items, takes just a minute. For this reason, it can easily be administered, scored, and interpreted as part of a regularly scheduled counseling interview.

Ponterotto et al. (1989) rated the BDI higher in terms of its overall effectiveness than any other self-report measure of depression. They gave it the highest possible rating for utility, that is, ease of use by counselor and client. They also rated it highly (4 on a 5-point scale)

FIGURE 15-2. Instructions and Sample Items From Beck Depression Inventory

BECK DEPRESSION INVENTORY

On this questionnaire are groups of statements. Please read each group of statements carefully. Then pick out the one statement in each group that best describes the way you have been feeling the PAST WEEK, INCLUDING TODAY. Check the box beside the statement you picked. If several statements in the group seem to apply equally well, check the box for each one. *Be sure to read all the statements in each group before making your choice.*

☐ I do not feel sad.
☐ I feel sad.
☐ I am sad all the time and I can't snap out of it.
☐ I am so sad or unhappy that I can't stand it.

☐ I don't have any thoughts of killing myself.
☐ I have thoughts of killing myself, but I would not carry them out.
☐ I would like to kill myself.
☐ I would kill myself if I had the chance.

Note. © 1983, 1987 by Aaron T. Beck. Reproduced by permission of the publisher, The Psychological Corporation. All rights reserved.

for both reliability and validity. Based on their analysis, counselors should give first consideration to the BDI when attempting to assess depression in a client.

Beck and Steer (1993b) recommend that BDI scores be interpreted by means of the following classification system:

  0–9 = Minimal depression
10–16 = Mild depression
17–29 = Moderate depression
30–63 = Severe depression

The cutoff scores shown above should be looked upon as general guidelines. The counselor will need to obtain more information to judge the severity of a client's depression. The duration of the symptoms and the possible cause of the symptoms (e.g., loss of a loved one) need to be considered. If the symptoms are of short duration (less than 2 weeks) or if they can be attributed to a grief reaction, they are less likely to indicate psychopathology.

As a general rule, if the score exceeds 25, especially for two administrations of the BDI separated by at least a week, the counselor should consider referring the client for psychiatric evaluation. Beck and Steer (1993b) noted that the item content for the BDI can be divided into two broad categories: cognitive-affective (items 1 through 13) and somatic-performance (items 14 through 21). Responses to items in the first part of the test can provide valuable clues to dysfunctional thinking that can be addressed in counseling (see Burns, 1989). Scores are likely to be elevated for items appearing on the last part of the BDI for clients with physical health problems or for clients suffering from endogenous depression, that is, depression caused by physiological factors. Individuals with endogenous depression often benefit from antidepressant medication.

The item content of the BDI can be easily reviewed with clients to obtain more information about a symptom. It usually helps to ask clients which items they are most concerned about. Counselors should pay particular attention to symptoms of hopelessness (item 2) and suicidal thinking (item 9). The counselor should be sure to evaluate the risk of suicide for such clients (Beck & Steer, 1993b).

Scores on the BDI are internally consistent, but subject to change over time. The BDI was designed to be highly sensitive to changes in mood over short time periods. If people experience significant changes in their lives, or if they are responding positively to a counseling program, their BDI scores should reflect these events.

Hammen (1980) noted that BDI scores for college students often dropped upon retesting even without treatment. Depression for these students may be caused by situational factors, such as impending exams or relationship conflicts, which can change rather quickly. Such factors must be taken into account. For this reason, it is a good idea to readminister the BDI periodically during the course of counseling to help monitor changes that may occur. Information obtained from readministrations of the BDI can often be helpful in trying to decide if a client should be referred for additional assessment or treatment or if he or she can be successfully discharged from counseling.

In general, clients can be considered to be full responders to treatment if their scores on the BDI drop by 50% or more from their baseline score. Clients whose scores decrease by 25% to 50% show partial improvement, whereas clients whose scores drop by less than 25% should be thought of as nonresponders (Ambrosini, Bianchi, Metz, & Rabinovich, 1994).

Children's Depression Inventory (CDI). The CDI is a self-report measure of depression for children and adolescents ages 8 to 17 years

(Kovacs, 1992). This instrument, which is a downward extension of the Beck Depression Inventory, consists of 27 self-report items written at a third-grade reading level. For each item, the child or adolescent chooses the one statement from among three listed that most closely describes his or her thoughts, feelings, or behaviors for the past 2 weeks. The CDI yields a total score together with five factor scores: Negative Mood, Interpersonal Problems, Ineffectiveness, Anhedonia (inability to find enjoyment in any activities), and Negative Self-Esteem. The manual provides separate-sex norms for children (ages 7 through 12) and adolescents (ages 13 through 17). The author has also created a 10-item version of the CDI for group administration when time is limited.

The CDI is one of the most thoroughly researched of all instruments designed to measure depression in children. Although it was developed primarily for research purposes, it has been used increasingly for clinical purposes because of the lack of effective instruments in the field. The author recommends that a *T*-score of 65 be used to indicate possible depression in screening situations. If a client exceeds a *T*-score of 65 on two administrations, he or she should then be evaluated by means of a diagnostic interview.

In a recent study, the CDI total score and the CDI factor scores clearly differentiated between adolescent inpatients diagnosed with major depression and those diagnosed with other psychiatric disorders (Craighead, Curry, & Ilardi, 1995). Studies reported in the manual, however, indicate mixed results in using the CDI to predict psychiatric diagnoses of depression, partly because the diagnoses themselves possess limited reliability and validity (Kovacs, 1992). At this point, the CDI can best be used an adjunct to other diagnostic tools, including the clinical interview.

Hamilton Depression Inventory (HDI). The HDI is a new paper-and-pencil version of the Hamilton Depression Rating Scale (HDRS), a well-established measure of depression for adults based on a clinical interview. In contrast to the BDI, it assesses both severity and frequency of depressive symptoms. Some of its 23 questions include subquestions so that a total of 38 items are covered. In addition to the total score, the HDI also provides a relatively pure measure of melancholia, that is, endogenous depression. Scores on the HDI have proven to be highly effective in differentiating individuals diagnosed with clinical depression from nondepressed individuals (Reynolds & Kobak, 1995).

Anxiety and Fear

Approximately one fourth of the population in the United States can be expected to suffer from an anxiety disorder sometime during their lifetime (Kessler et al., 1994). Anxiety disorders, which include social phobias, panic disorder, agoraphobia, simple phobia, generalized anxiety disorder, and related ailments, also tend to be chronic. Approximately 17% of the population are likely to have experienced an anxiety disorder during any given year.

Popular measures of the symptoms of anxiety and fear are discussed below. *Anxiety* can be defined as "a pervasive feeling of dread, apprehension, and impending disaster" (Goldenson, 1984, p. 53). The cause of the anxiety is usually unknown or unclear. In contrast, fear is a response to a known danger, such as snakes or crowded places.

State-Trait Anxiety Inventory (STAI). The STAI, the most popular and well researched of all anxiety measures, was first published by Charles Spielberger and his associates in 1970; the current version (Form Y) was published in 1983 (Spielberger, Gorsuch, Lushene, Vagg, & Jacobs, 1983). The STAI consists of two scales—a State-Anxiety scale (S-Anxiety) that measures transitory anxiety and a Trait-Anxiety scale (T-Anxiety) that measures persistent anxiety. Both scales consist of 20 items marked on a 4-point scale.

Instructions for the S-Anxiety scale ask clients to indicate how they feel "at this moment"; they indicate to what degree (*not at all, somewhat, moderately so,* or *very much so*) they may be experiencing different feelings, such as tense, secure, or calm. Instructions for the T-Anxiety scale ask clients to rate how they "generally feel"; they indicate how often (*almost never, sometimes, often,* or *almost always*) they experience different feelings, such as pleasant, nervous and restless, or satisfied with self. Responses to the S-Anxiety scale show the *intensity* of one's anxious response at the time of measurement; responses to the T-Anxiety scale show the *frequency* of such responses.

The STAI is untimed, but can usually be completed within 10 minutes. The instrument can be easily hand scored; however, the scorer must take into account that approximately one half of the items measure the absence of anxiety whereas the other half measure the presence of anxiety. For those items that measure the absence of anxiety, the scoring must be reversed.

Scores on the S-Anxiety scale are internally consistent, but can change substantially over time depending on the individual's circumstances. For example, scores on this scale can be expected to rise markedly when a person is confronted with a threatening situation, such as an exam or surgery. Individuals who score high on the S-Anxiety scale are usually experiencing a number of symptoms associated with activation of the autonomic nervous system, such as rapid heart rate, perspiration, shortness of breath, shakiness, and hot or cold flashes.

Scores on the T-Anxiety scale are both internally consistent and relatively stable over time. Individuals who score high on the T-Anxiety scale will usually show a larger increase in their S-Anxiety scores in a threatening circumstance, especially in situations that involve social evaluations, than will individuals who score low on this scale. In addition to measuring anxiety proneness, the T-Anxiety scale also taps a range of other psychological problems. According to Chaplin (1985), the T-Anxiety scale can probably best be viewed as a measure of general dissatisfaction with one's life.

A children's version of the STAI, The State-Trait Anxiety Inventory for Children (STAIC), has also been established for counselor use. The STAIC provides extensive norms for fourth, fifth, and sixth graders. Because the reading level for the STAIC is relatively high (above sixth grade level), the STAIC should be used only with elementary school students who possess above average reading ability (Walker & Kaufman, 1984).

Beck Anxiety Inventory (BAI). The BAI was designed to measure symptoms of anxiety that are relatively independent of depression (Beck & Steer, 1993a). The BAI parallels the Beck Depression Inventory in its manner of construction and interpretation. Similar to the BDI, it contains 21 items, each of which is answered on a 4-point scale. Each item measures a separate symptom of anxiety. Raw scores on the BAI are interpreted in terms of four categories (minimal, mild, moderate, or severe anxiety). As with the BDI, the BAI can easily be administered during the course of the counseling interview to monitor a client's progress. The results can be analyzed in terms of four clusters of scores—neurophysiological, subjective, panic, and autonomic—that can be helpful in differentiating among different types of anxiety disorders.

Other measures of anxiety or fear. Other standardized inventories of anxiety or fear of interest to counselors include the Test Anxiety Scale (Sarason, 1980), Mathematics Anxiety Rating Scale–Revised (Plake & Parker, 1982), Achievement Anxiety Scale (Alpert & Haber, 1960), and Fear Questionnaire (Marks & Mathews, 1978). The Achievement Anxiety Inventory contains scales that distinguish between facilitating (or motivating) anxiety and debilitating (or interfering) anxiety in regard to academic achievement. The Fear Questionnaire measures the extent to which a client may be suffering from a particular type of phobia (e.g., agoraphobia, blood-injury phobia, and social phobia).

Anger

Anger is a universal emotion that underlies hostile attitudes and aggressive behaviors. Assessment of anger can aid in crisis intervention and improved understanding of factors related to one's anger.

An individual's anger can be assessed by means of the State-Trait Anger Expression Inventory (STAXI; Speilberger, 1988). The STAXI is analogous to the State-Trait Anxiety Inventory in that it provides measures of anger as a state (actual anger at any point in time) and as a trait (potential anger). Based on factor analytic work, the Trait-Anger (T-anger) scale has been divided into two subscales: Temperamental Anger and Reactive Anger. Individuals who score high on Temperamental Anger are readily angered by a broad variety of situations. Individuals who score high on Reactive Anger are upset only by particular situations; that is, certain incidents trigger their anger. People who score high on Reactive Anger are more likely to suffer from somatic ailments than those who score high on Temperamental Anger.

In addition to the Trait and State anger scales, the STAXI contains three scales that pertain to the manner in which anger is expressed. The Anger-In scale measures tendencies to internalize anger and not to express it in an outward manner. People who score high on this scale are more likely to suffer from psychosomatic illnesses. In contrast, the Anger-Out scale reveals the extent to which individuals release anger in their behavior. Finally, the Anger-Control scale indicates the extent to which people try to control their anger without necessarily holding it in. People who score high on this scale try to express their anger in more socially desirable forms than those who score high on the Anger-Out scale.

The STAXI provides a comprehensive assessment of one's anger in a relatively short period of time. It can be useful in counseling clients with issues related to anger, hostility, and aggression.

Alcohol Abuse

As indicated in Chapter 14, alcohol abuse is relatively common in this country. No single personality type represents all alcoholics. Graham and Strenger (1988) identified six different personality types for alcoholics, but none of these were unique to alcoholics. The authors emphasized the individual differences among the alcoholic patients they studied.

Michigan Alcoholism Screening Test (MAST). The MAST was designed to be administered orally by the counselor, but it can also be completed directly by the client (Selzer, 1971). It is a brief instrument that can be answered by the client within a few minutes. The items describe symptoms of excessive drinking, problems (social, family, work, legal, and health) that one may have encountered as a result of drinking, concerns expressed by others about one's drinking, and efforts that one may have made to control drinking or to obtain treatment for excessive drinking. The instrument and the scoring weights for each item are shown in Figure 15-3. Scores of 5 or more indicate alcoholism, scores of 4 suggest the possibility of alcoholism, and scores of 3 or less indicate the absence of alcoholism.

Research indicates that the MAST has been highly successful in distinguishing between alcoholics and nonalcoholics (Selzer, 1971). MAST results should be confirmed by means of other assessment procedures. It can be used with all clients in an agency to detect possible alcohol problems that otherwise might be missed. According to one study, 22% of new clients at a university counseling center scored high enough on the MAST to suggest possible alcoholism (Hay, 1988).

FIGURE 15-3. Items and Scoring Weights (Shown in Parentheses) for Michigan Alcoholism Screening Test

MICHIGAN ALCOHOLISM SCREENING TEST (MAST)

Instructions: Please answer each question "Yes" or "No" as it pertains to you.

(2) *1. Do you feel you are a normal drinker?

(2) 2. Have you ever awakened the morning after some drinking the night before and found that you could not remember a part of the evening before?

(1) 3. Does your spouse (or do your parents) ever worry or complain about your drinking?

(2) *4. Can you stop drinking without a struggle after one or two drinks?

(1) 5. Do you ever feel bad about your drinking?

(2) *6. Do friends or relatives think you are a normal drinker?

(0) 7. Do you ever try to limit your drinking to certain times of the day or to certain places?

(2) *8. Are you always able to stop drinking when you want to?

(5) 9. Have you ever attended a meeting of Alcoholics Anonymous (AA)?

(1) 10. Have you gotten into fights when drinking?

(2) 11. Has drinking ever created problems with you and your spouse?

(2) 12. Has your spouse (or other family member) ever gone to anyone for help about your drinking?

(2) 13. Have you ever lost friends or girlfriends/boyfriends because of drinking?

(2) 14. Have you ever gotten into trouble at work because of drinking?

(2) 15. Have you ever lost a job because of drinking?

(2) 16. Have you ever neglected your obligations, your family, or your work for two or more days in a row because you were drinking?

(1) 17. Do you ever drink before noon?

(2) 18. Have you ever been told you have liver trouble? Cirrhosis?

(5) 19. Have you ever had delirium tremens (DTs), severe shaking, heard voices, or seen things that weren't there after heavy drinking?

(5) 20. Have you ever gone to anyone for help about your drinking?

(5) 21. Have you ever been in a hospital because of drinking?

(2) 22. Have you ever been a patient in a psychiatric hospital or on a psychiatric ward of a general hospital where drinking was part of the problem?

(2) 23. Have you ever been seen at a psychiatric or mental health clinic, or gone to a doctor, social worker, or clergyperson for help with an emotional problem in which drinking had played a part?

(2) 24. Have you ever been arrested, even for a few hours, because of drunk behavior?

(2) 25. Have you ever been arrested for drunk driving or driving after drinking?

*Negative responses to these items indicate alcoholism; for all other items, positive responses indicate alcoholism.

Note. From "The Michigan Alcoholism Screening Test: The Quest for a New Diagnostic Instrument" by M. L. Selzer, 1971, *American Journal of Psychiatry, 127*, p. 1655. Copyright 1971 by the American Psychiatric Association. Reprinted by permission.

CASE EXAMPLE

(handwritten in left margin: Michigan Alcol Screening test)

Sally, a client at a community counseling service, received a score of 16 on the MAST. She answered Items 1, 2, 5, 6, 8, 10, 11, 12, and 23 in the scored direction. Sally had been brought to the counseling agency by friends because of problems related to her drinking. The score of 16 far surpasses the cutoff score of 5 used on MAST to signal alcoholism.

The MAST contributed to counseling by emphasizing the importance of her drinking problem. Information obtained from MAST was confirmed by other information related to Sally's drinking habits. Her alcohol consumption (13 drinks per week) surpassed more than 82% of American adults who drink (Miller & Munoz, 1982). Counseling with Sally revealed that she came from a troubled family, and she frequently fought with her mother while she lived at home. Sally suffered from low self-esteem and a perfectionistic nature. She was demanding and dependent in her relationships. Testing with the California Psychological Inventory revealed that she was highly critical of herself (low Good Impression score; $T = 34$), undercontrolled (low Self-Control score; $T = 39$), and lacking confidence (low Capacity for Status; $T = 39$). Her personality type was Gamma (externally oriented and norm-questioning) at the midpoint (level 4 of 7 levels) of self-realization.

The counselor worked with her on family issues and relationship matters. Sally became more self-sufficient during the course of counseling and more confident in her relationships with others. She began to deal with some of the personal issues represented by her drinking problem. By addressing unresolved problems, and by the use of self-monitoring techniques, Sally was able to reduce the amount of her drinking during the course of counseling.

Additional measures of alcohol or other drug problems that counselors may wish to use for screening purposes include the Personal Experience Screening Questionnaire (Winters, 1991), the Multidimensional Addictions and Personality Profile (Craig & Craig, 1995), the Adolescent Drinking Index (Harrell & Wirtz, 1989), and the AUDIT—Alcohol Use Disorders Identification Test (Saunders, Aasland, Amundsen, & Grant, 1993).

Alcohol Use Inventory (AUI). The AUI is a self-report inventory that "identifies distinct patterns of behavior, attitudes, and symptoms associated with the use and abuse of alcohol" for individuals 16 years and older (Horn, Wanberg, & Foster, 1986). Most people complete the AUI, which requires a sixth-grade reading level, within 35 to 60 minutes. It contains 24 scales based on 228 items organized at three levels: 17 primary scales, 6 second-order scales, and 1 general alcohol use scale. The scales evaluate alcohol usage in terms of benefits, styles, consequences, and concerns. It is most appropriate for individuals who enter a treatment program as a result of alcohol dependence or abuse. It can be used to establish a treatment plan for a person with alcohol-related issues.

Other comprehensive measures of substance abuse include the Personal Experience Inventory (PEI) for adolescents ages 12 to 18 years and the Personal Experiences Inventory for Adults (PEI-A). Both inventories include a problem severity section and a psychosocial section (Winters, 1991; Winters & Henley, 1989).

Eating Disorders

The number of persons, particularly women, with eating disorders or problems has increased dramatically in recent years (Garner, 1991; Mintz & Betz, 1988). The major eating disorders include anorexia nervosa (self-induced starvation), bulimia (binge-purge syndrome), and bulimarexia (a combination of the two). The DSM-IV does not list obesity as an eating disorder because it is not usually associated with a specific psychological syndrome.

According to the DSM-IV, the essential features of anorexia nervosa include refusal to maintain body weight (e.g., the person weighs less than 85% of expected body weight), intense fear of gaining weight, a disturbed body image, and loss of menstrual cycle for females. Anorexia nervosa, which means nervous loss of appetite, is a misnomer; the person resists eating, but actual loss of appetite is rare. Bulimia nervosa, on the other hand, is characterized by binge eating (rapid consumption of food in a short period of time), a feeling of lack of control of one's eating behavior while binge eating, drastic attempts to prevent weight gain (e.g., self-induced vomiting, use of laxatives or diuretics, strict dieting or fasting, or vigorous exercise), and persistent overconcern with body shape and weight (American Psychiatric Association, 1994). Some individuals, who can be classified as bulimarexics, share the symptoms of both disorders.

Individuals suspected of meeting the DSM-IV criteria for an eating disorder should be referred to an eating disorders clinic or health service with a multidisciplinary team including a physician, nurse, dietitian, and mental health professional. The person may require a complete medical examination, nutritional assessment, and psychological assessment. Treatment also entails cooperation among the different disciplines to help clients address medical complications, alter eating habits, and alleviate psychological problems by such means as improving social skills and self-image.

Individuals with eating disorders typically wait several years from the onset of the disorder before entering treatment. Early assessment of a person's eating problems can reduce the length of this time period. Counselors can help determine the need for referral of a client to an eating disorder clinic by the use of the standardized tests discussed below. The Eating Attitudes Test and the Eating Disorders Inventory are the two most widely used standardized measures available for evaluating eating problems (Rosen, Silberg, & Gross, 1988).

Eating Attitudes Test (EAT). The EAT contains 40 items that measure the symptoms and behaviors associated with anorexia nervosa and other eating problems (Garner & Garfinkel, 1979). Total scores on the EAT have clearly differentiated between patients diagnosed as anorexic and control groups of "normals" in research investigations. The scores are sensitive to treatment so that recovered anorectics obtain scores similar to normals.

The EAT can be scored in terms of three subscales—Dieting, Bulimia, and Oral Control—to help determine the nature of the eating problems. Rosen et al. (1988) found that scores on each of the three subscales correlated significantly with scores on the Restraint Scale (a measure of restrained eating) and self-reported diet behavior (skipping meals, fasting, using diet pills, vomiting, and taking laxatives).

CASE EXAMPLE

Joan's counselor asked her to take the EAT as a means of reviewing her eating habits and assessing the need for a referral to the eating disorders clinic at the local hospital. Joan had come to the community mental health service for assistance with relationship issues, family conflicts, and eating problems. She binged on bakery goods and sweets about once a week, then used laxatives to purge the extra food.

Joan obtained a score of 36 on the EAT, which placed her almost two standard deviations above the mean (98th percentile) of adult women. Scores above 30 suggest serious eating concerns. She marked *always* or *very often* to items such as "am terrified about being overweight," "am

292

preoccupied with a desire to be thinner," and "feel that food controls my life." Her score indicated that she could probably profit from a referral to an eating disorders clinic with a multidisciplinary staff for a more thorough assessment of her eating and nutritional habits as well as her physiological and psychological well-being. After discussing the matter with her, her counselor made arrangements for such a referral.

Eating Disorders Inventory–2 (EDI-2). The EDI-2 consists of 91 items (64 original items plus 27 new items) that assess the psychological and behavioral characteristics that underlie anorexia nervosa and bulimia (Garner, 1991). It differs from the EAT by the inclusion of personality items as well as behavioral and symptomatic items. The EDI-2 retains the eight scales of the EDI, five of which measure psychological traits— Ineffectiveness, Perfectionism, Interpersonal Distrust, Interoceptive Awareness, and Maturity Fears—and three that measure behavioral or attitudinal factors—Drive for Thinness, Bulimia, and Body Dissatisfaction. In addition, three new provisional scales—Asceticism ("oral self-restraint"), Impulse Regulation, and Social Insecurity—that assess constructs important in the diagnosis and treatment of eating disorders have been added to the inventory.

Clients also complete a 4-page checklist concerning symptoms they may be experiencing in regard to eating disorders. Information from the checklist on matters related to dieting, exercise, binge eating, purging, laxatives, diet pills, diuretics, and menstrual history can be helpful in forming a DSM-IV diagnosis.

The EDI-2 manual provides normative tables for patients with anorexia nervosa (restricting type), anorexia nervosa (bulimic type), and bulimia nervosa as well as for the total eating disorder sample. Separate norms are also provided for college females, college males, high school females, and high school males. The normative study for high school students found that girls scored particularly high on two of the three scales that directly pertain to eating disorder symptoms (Drive for Thinness and Body Dissatisfaction; Rosen et al., 1988). Although separate-sex norms are necessary, separate norms based on age, socioeconomic class differences, and race do not seem to be warranted.

The EDI-2 scales produce reliable (internally consistent) results for people with eating disorders. The results are somewhat less reliable for nonpatient samples, presumably because of the restricted range of scores for these samples. Validity studies indicate that the original EDI scores correlate highly with clinician ratings. Scores on the original

EDI scales also differentiate eating disorder patients from both non-patients and recovered patients (Garner, 1991). Additional research needs to be undertaken to determine the validity of the three new provisional scales.

SUMMARY

1. The MMPI-2 provides a more comprehensive assessment of a client's mental health than any other personality inventory. The MMPI-A provides comparable information for adolescents.
2. The MCMI-III represents a viable alternative to the MMPI-2 for assessment of client psychopathology. It is shorter and more closely related to theory and to the DSM-IV categories than is the MMPI-2.
3. Two promising new measures of psychopathology are the Personality Assessment Inventory and the Basic Personality Inventory. Both of these instruments can be self-scored, contain scales that are relatively easy to interpret, and circumvent some of the difficulties inherent in the MMPI-2.
4. The Beck Depression Inventory serves as a quick, yet relatively thorough, measure of a client's state of depression. It is particularly helpful for monitoring changes in depression over time.
5. The State-Trait Anxiety Inventory yields valid and reliable scores for anxiety that can be distinguished as either transitory (state anxiety) or enduring (trait anxiety). In a similar fashion, the State-Trait Anger Expression Inventory measures one's actual and potential anger, as well as providing information on how anger is likely to be expressed.
6. Problems related to alcohol use can be detected by the Michigan Alcohol Screening Test. Individuals with problems can be further evaluated by means of the Alcohol Use Inventory.
7. The Eating Attitudes Inventory and the Eating Disorder Inventory–2 can be used to screen clients for possible eating disorders.

Professional Practices and Considerations

16

ASSESSMENT OF MINORITY AND SPECIAL POPULATIONS

CONTROVERSY HAS SURROUNDED psychological tests almost from their beginnings. The development of the Army Alpha for testing World War I recruits caused much debate (Haney, 1981), particularly when differences between socioeconomic and ethnic groups became known. Since then controversy has continued, especially regarding multiple-choice aptitude tests used for selection procedures (Gross, 1962; Neisser et al., 1996).

CULTURAL BIAS IN TESTING

There are three commonly considered ways in which tests may be biased against a person or groups of persons. They may contain items that favor one group over another. For example, an item on a verbal analogies test that includes the word "toboggan" might tend to favor persons from northern states over those from southern states. Similarly, a test may be biased because it includes language or values that are typical to White middle-class people but not to Blacks, Hispanics, or other distinct cultural groups (Lonner & Sundberg, 1987). Many sociocultural factors—ethnicity, socioeconomic class, region, and situation—contribute to mismatches between the language of test takers and that of test makers.

The second source of bias comes from test-related factors such as the motivation, anxiety, or test sophistication of those taking the test—sources of bias that are external to the test itself. Extreme forms of test anxiety, self-esteem, and achievement motivation have been found to be related to test performance, but there is little evidence that there are substantial differences in these areas between races, sexes, or, in most cases, social classes. However, clients from minority groups who are not motivated to perform well on a test or not sophisticated in regard to the nature of the test items cannot be expected to perform as well as those from the dominant culture where these factors have been emphasized.

A third possible source of bias comes from the use of test results in selection for employment or college admissions—if the model used for selection and prediction varies greatly among different groups. When the use of a test or other selection procedure results in a substantially higher rejection rate for minority candidates than for nonminority candidates, the use of the tests must be justified by proving it is valid for the job in question (Anastasi, 1988).

Recognizing that increasing diversity in clients' backgrounds presents special challenges in testing, a committee of the Association for Assessment in Counseling (AAC) developed a set of multicultural counseling standards containing 34 standards grouped according to the assessment-related task (Prediger, 1994a). Of these 34, the majority addressed the selection of assessment instruments appropriate to multicultural populations since if the instrument is inappropriate, counseling based on interpretations will also probably be inappropriate (Prediger, 1993). Both the American Psychological Association (APA, 1993) and the American Counseling Association (ACA, 1995) have stated in their ethical codes that professionals should consider socioeconomic, ethnic, and cultural backgrounds, beliefs, and values when administering and interpreting psychological tests.

In discussing the problem of test bias or group differences, it is important to distinguish between test results and innate aptitude. The statement that men as a group achieve higher levels of competence in mathematics than women is a statement regarding past achievement on a given test. This does not imply that men possess a greater aptitude for mathematics than women—a statement that suggests innateness or biological or genetic determinism. Almost no one these days believes that intellectual functioning, no matter how it is measured—by tests or academic achievement—is exclusively a function of either one's heredity or one's environment; it is a complex function of both.

An understanding of the client's worldview is important, because the initial step in the counseling process is to understand the client and his or her issues and problems. Worldview includes the individual's perceptions of human nature (good or evil); focus on the past, present, or future; the emphasis given to individual or group goals; and locus of responsibility (internal or external). Based on the knowledge of the client's worldview and the client's cultural group, counselors are better able to determine the approaches, techniques, and goals needed for a specific client (Lonner & Ibrahim, 1985; Sue, 1978).

It is important in the assessment and treatment of multicultural clients for the counselor to display both the sensitivity to be aware of the cultural variables that affect assessment and the competence to translate this awareness into effective assessment. To competently assess and counsel members of multicultural groups, counselors must consider the level of the client's acculturation and determine the potential impact of this variable (Dana, 1993). *Acculturation* is defined as the degree of integration of new cultural patterns into the original cultural patterns. To assess the level of a client's acculturation, the counselor should take into account the age of the client, the number of generations in the new culture (e.g., first, second, third), the language generally preferred, and the extent of activities and relationships within and beyond the client's own cultural group (Paniagua, 1994).

In using standardized tests in counseling with a person from another culture, it is a general rule that the less the counselor knows of the client's culture, the more errors the counselor is likely to make. It is important to be knowledgeable regarding the culture of the person being assessed and develop skills for dealing with culture-related behavior patterns. On the other hand, it is important not to "overculturalize." Culture is important in understanding an individual, but it is not the only variable influencing human behavior. Attempting to remove all cultural differences from a test is likely to compromise its validity as a measure of the behavior it was designed to assess. There are many factors that all people experience that lead them to seek to counseling, and these are all important in assessing a person (Lonner & Sundberg, 1987).

Culture has an influence on psychopathological expression, and differences on personality tests across cultures should be taken into account. Psychological tests are measures of behavior, and to the extent that culture effects behavior its influence is going to be detected by tests. Resulting psychological and educational diagnoses made as a result of such testing data should be made with caution (Sue, 1990).

APTITUDE AND COGNITIVE ASSESSMENT

A basic assumption of standardized testing is that it is perfectly appropriate for the test taker to be willing to provide obvious information and to give a performance for a total stranger—the examiner. These basic social assumptions may be in conflict with the interactional rules for individuals in some cultures. For example, it might be hypothesized that Black working-class children or Native American working-class children are less oriented to public performance for unfamiliar adults than are White middle-class children. It might even be argued that child-rearing practices of many White middle-class parents, which encourage public verbal performance for strangers, program their children for eventual success on standardized tests.

The combination of constriction imposed by most American schools and the competition encouraged there can conflict with aspects of African American and Native American cultures. Such conflict may lead to the alienation of these students from both the experiences and products of education, of which assessment instruments are a part (Neisser et al., 1996).

Black Americans

Although tests could be biased against any minority, the most serious controversy exists over the fact that, as a group, Black Americans score approximately one standard deviation below White Americans on most standardized tests of cognitive ability. Even more aggravating is the fact that the magnitude of this difference persists from preschool children through college applicants. There is, however, some evidence that this differential is decreasing among children and adolescents (Neisser et al., 1996). Of course, there is a great deal of overlap between the two distributions, with almost 20% of Blacks scoring above the mean for Whites and 20% of Whites scoring below the mean for Blacks. Because counselors usually deal with individuals rather than total populations, group differences are of less importance. The counselor is concerned only with the particular ability of a particular individual, whether Black or White. The counselor is not concerned with overall mean differences among populations, but with the question of whether a particular aptitude test score has equal validity; that is, whether it predicts equally well for Black as for White Americans.

Because Blacks as a group have experienced great racial discrimination in the past and this discrimination has had an impact on their socioeconomic status, their opportunities, and their home environments, it is not surprising that this would have an effect upon test results. Much of the controversy centers on the cause of the differences. Some attribute the differences to the disadvantages that Black Americans suffer in their economic status and their educational and occupational opportunities. Others attribute much of the difference to genetic factors, although little direct evidence supports this position (Neisser et al., 1996).

A frequently offered argument is that intelligence tests and other measures of cognitive aptitude are constructed by and for White middle-class individuals and therefore are biased against lower socioeconomic individuals and others who are not members of the majority culture. Some of this cultural bias could be found in the items on which suburban children might have more familiarity than inner-city or rural children. Children, brought up using a Black dialect or nonstandard American English might be less able to comprehend the language used on such instruments. Test developers have now become extremely sensitive to this issue and have established panels of experts that include representatives from many cultural groups. Most of this content bias has therefore been eliminated from many of the current forms of these tests, although such changes have been shown to have little if any effect on the scores obtained by minority individuals (Walsh & Betz, 1994; Friedenberg, 1995).

If the validity of cognitive aptitude tests is different for majority and minority groups, and if counselors encourage or discourage clients about pursuing different levels of education or types of jobs based on these test results, then this type of bias could affect counseling outcomes. Numerous studies have been conducted predicting various criteria both for education and job performance for Black and White groups. In general, results have shown that ability tests are equally valid for both minority and majority groups. These studies have used IQ tests to predict school achievement, scholastic aptitude tests to predict college grades, and job-related aptitude tests to predict job success. Both correlations and regression lines tend to be similar for both groups, and in the cases where minor differences have occurred, there has been a tendency for the test to slightly overpredict the achievement of Black students—contrary to what might be expected if the tests were significantly racially biased (Messick, 1980; Neisser et al., 1996).

Hispanics

Although Spanish-speaking individuals often share the poor economic conditions of Black Americans, their difficulties do not lie solely in their poverty. The Spanish-speaking student meets difficulties in communication and understanding no matter what his or her social background. A Hispanic student who scores low on a standardized test in English may actually have obtained a remarkably good score if the student has been learning English for only a short period. A Hispanic client or one from another cultural background may receive a very low score on the information subtest of the WAIS, not because of a lack of intelligence but because the client lacks information about the total population of the United States, the number of senators, and other general knowledge expected from the average American. Similar problems would arise from the vocabulary section and scores on the picture completion and picture arrangement subtests, because they include materials that are not part of the client's culture (Paniagua, 1994). The counselor must consider individual differences and circumstances in interpreting the test results of clients for whom English is not the native language.

In the case of Hispanic individuals, a Spanish edition of an assessment instrument may be appropriate, and Spanish language editions have been developed for several popular tests, including the Strong Interest Inventory, the MBTI, the Wechsler intelligence scales, the Self-Directed Search, the 16 PF, and Cattell's Culture-Fair Intelligence Test.

Native Americans

In counseling Native American individuals, caution must be used in interpreting the results of various assessment procedures. There is a wide range of differences with regard to culture among various Native American tribes, and because of such large differences few generalizations are possible. In norming samples of tests, very small numbers of Native Americans are likely to have been included in the sample, and even those are likely to represent only a few of the many different cultures from which Native Americans come.

In testing situations, Native Americans may underestimate the seriousness of tests, lack test-taking skills, or lack motivation to perform on tests. For some, tribal beliefs may discourage the type of competitive behavior often present in test-taking situations. They may also have learned English as a second language, and learned their first language as a nonwritten language—factors that can easily affect English reading skills (Brescio & Fortune, 1989). In addition, because they often come from isolated, rural, or impoverished settings, they may lack the type of knowledge and experience expected on certain test instruments.

Asian Americans

Test results and the interpretations of these results vary greatly for different Asian American clients. They come from widely divergent cultural backgrounds and range all the way from fourth and fifth generation Asian Americans to the more recent Filipino and Vietnamese immigrants.

The later generations of Japanese and Chinese Americans come from backgrounds in which the mean income level equals or surpasses that of Whites, and they hold many attitudes and values similar to the majority culture. There are aspects of their cultures, however, that influence them to place increased emphasis on the results of achievement and aptitude tests and less on other types of performance. In addition, education, especially higher education, is much valued and supported, with particular value placed on attending prestigious institutions of higher education. Thus there is considerable pressure to attain high enough scores on academic aptitude tests to gain entrance to colleges and universities.

Test results for recent Southeast Asian immigrants have much less validity because these individuals are affected by all of the language problems, vast cultural differences, and economic difficulties common to newly arrived immigrants.

Culture-Fair Tests

The typical intelligence test administered in the United States assumes a relatively common cultural background found in contemporary society along with English as a native language. For tests above the lower elementary levels, literacy in English is also necessary to obtain valid results on most of the group-administered tests. To provide valid assessment devices useful in other cultures or for use with subcultures or minority cultures in this country, attempts have been made to develop culture-fair tests that function independently of a specific culture, primarily by eliminating, or at least greatly reducing, language and cultural content.

Cattell's Culture-Fair Intelligence Test. This test is a paper-and-pencil test that has no verbal content and is designed to reduce the effects of educational background and cultural influences (Cattell, 1973). The test consists of four parts in multiple choice formats: (a) series—a figure must be chosen to complete the series, (b) classification—the object is to choose the figure that is different from the series, (c) matrices—the pattern of change occurring in the figures must be completed, and (d) conditions—the alternative with similar conditions to the example figure must be chosen. The test is available in two parallel forms and for three different age or ability levels: (a) children ages 4 through 8 years and adults with mental retardation, (b) children ages 8 through 14 years and average adults, and (c) college students and adults with above-average intelligence. Within particular age levels the raw scores can be converted to normalized deviation IQ scores that have a mean of 100 and standard deviation of 16.

Raven's Progressive Matrices. Raven's Progressive Matrices is a widely used culture-fair test that requires the subject to solve problems involving abstract figures and designs by indicating which of various multiple-choice alternatives complete a given matrix (Raven, Court, & Raven, 1993). Progressive changes occur in the vertical dimension, horizontal dimension, or both dimensions in a series of matrices. For each item the examinee must determine the principle by which the matrices are progressively changing and select the correct alternative from six answers that are provided. It is available in two forms, a black and white version for grade 8 through adulthood, and the Coloured Progressive Matrices for children ages 5 to 11 years and for adults with mental retardation. Developed in England, Raven's Progressive Matrices has been used in a large number of cross-cultural studies in many countries. Results of certain of these studies suggest that although this test is one of the best available, it might better be described as culturally reduced rather than culture-fair or culture-free. Norms are based on samples of English children and adults, and one drawback for its use in this country is lack of normative data in the United States.

Raven's Progressive Matrices and other attempts to develop culture-fair tests not only represent attempts to increase the fairness of intelligence tests, but also provide interesting ways of studying this type of ability. Most studies in this country have found that children in lower socioeconomic groups score substantially lower than middle-class groups on these tests, as well as on the more common culturally loaded intelligence tests. In addition, culture-fair tests typically do less well in predicting academic achievement or job performance than do the standard culturally loaded tests. This is not surprising, because academic achievement and job performance often include much culturally important content.

Cultural Differences

Test results based on norms of White middle-class students or adults cannot be appropriately applied to ethnic minorities (Dana, 1993). In schools in which the counselor has considerable influence in determining guidance and testing procedures for these students, he or she can influence the adoption of appropriate programs and policies to prevent the misuse of test results.

The melting pot philosophy of cultural assimilation of all minorities into the Anglo-American culture has been generally rejected in favor of a multiethnic culture. Counselors who hold positive attitudes toward cultural differences are better able to accommodate the cultural predispositions of students from other ethnic backgrounds. The positive attitudes of counselors are more valuable than specific techniques or special materials. As students are accepted by counselors, they accept themselves and their abilities, as well as their limitations.

CAREER ASSESSMENT

A major question with regard to the use of vocational interest inventories is whether minority students are sufficiently familiar with the vocabulary, the examples, the occupational terms, and the problems that are used in these tests. Because many minority students differ from middle-class White students in their experiences, orientations, and values, their view of available occupations may be restricted even though the minority students' aspirations may equal or exceed those of the middle-class White student. Students from disadvantaged backgrounds are likely to be less aware of the great variety of occupations and the skills required for certain occupations. They may also view potential occupations in ways that are quite different from that which is implied in occupational literature. Minority students tend to enter narrower ranges of fields of study (Arbona, 1990; Muhs, Popp, & Patterson, 1979).

Within minority communities there is often a lack of continuity and values between school and family as well as a lack of diversity in the occupations that exist as models for children from these backgrounds. On various interest inventories minority students may achieve relatively low scores, because such students indicate liking fewer occupational titles or interests than did students in the norm group.

Studies have shown that despite these differences, interest measures have similar validities among various minority groups in this country. Interest inventories can therefore be used with minority clients with the same amount of confidence as with Whites, with the possible exception of those coming from particularly disadvantaged backgrounds. Studies have also shown that interest measures predict college majors similarly for students from various minority backgrounds. Differences have been found on interest measures among different minorities, but these differences have equal predictive value (Hansen & Fouad, 1984; Lamb, 1974). For example, Blacks who tend to score higher on social interests are more likely to enter social occupations, whereas Asian American students who obtain higher scores on biological and physical science interests and lower scores on social and sales interests, are more likely to pursue scientific occupations. Counselors should also be aware that some of the female-male differences found among Whites are similar but more extreme for Hispanic women.

There is a tendency among Asian Americans to choose vocations in business, science, mathematics, or engineering fields to the exclusion of humanities, social sciences, or law. When interpreting the results of interest inventories in educational and vocational counseling, this tendency to consider a narrow range of possible career goals should be kept in mind. Expanding the range of occupations being considered may well be one of the goals of such counseling.

For minority students, the development of appropriate attitudes and behaviors can be enhanced by using representative minority models and pointing out their accomplishments in various fields. In this way counselors can assist minority students in understanding and appreciating the contributions that have been made and continue to be made by members of their own group.

Counselors must evaluate the testing and appraisal instruments to determine whether they meet criteria for nondiscrimination. Are data provided that assist in making sound occupational choices? What is the racial and socioeconomic makeup of the population on which the test is based?

Several interest inventories have been translated into a number of other languages. A question that needs to be asked in administering such a version of the inventory is whether the person taking the test is from a culture that has similar expectations and social customs as that for the culture in which the test was devised. Unfamiliarity with the nature and purpose of tests could be a problem, as could different ways of responding. Clients from a culture in which the emphasis is on agreeing with nearly everything (because it is considered impolite to disagree) may obtain test results that lack validity.

PERSONALITY ASSESSMENT

Although racial bias has less often been a major issue in personality measurement, there is some evidence that various minority groups obtain scores on personality inventories that differ from those typically obtained in a White majority population. For example, Asian clients are more likely to express psychological problems in terms of somatic complaints. Therefore an elevation on the Hypochondriasis Scale (Scale 1) on the MMPI with Asian clients should be interpreted in light of this cultural phenomenon (Paniagua, 1994). A Pacific Islander's deviant scores on the MMPI could easily be accounted for by cultural and language differences from the original sample on which it was normed. If personality measures such as the MMPI are to be used for selection purposes, such as in selecting airline pilots or graduate students in clinical psychology, then it is possible that some minority group members could be unfairly discriminated against if the instruments were used inappropriately. Diagnoses of schizophrenia are more commonly found with Black clients than with White clients, whereas depression is reported more frequently for White than Black clients (Paniagua, 1994). Differences on personality tests among minority groups and those from other cultures are to be expected and should be taken into consideration by counselors in their interpretations of personality test results. Studies of various personality inventories, however, usually indicate that the scales predict the same types of behavioral and personality characteristics for both minority and majority group members and therefore with caution can be appropriately used in counseling and psychiatric situations (Duckworth & Anderson, 1995; Geisinger, 1994; Novy, Nelson, Goodwin & Rowzee, 1993).

In general, test results obtained from Black clients on the MMPI should be interpreted with care. Greene (1987), in reviewing a large number of studies examining differences between Black and White Americans on the MMPI, reported no consistent pattern to such differences on any of the standard validity and clinical scales. Although Blacks frequently score higher on the F scale and Scales 8 and 9 than do White Americans, differences usually disappeared if the groups were matched on education and severity of psychopathology. Black Americans may also score higher on Scales 8 and 9 because of higher levels of nonconformity, alienation, or impulsivity or because of different types of values and perceptions (Groth-Marnat, 1990). Timbrook and Graham (1994) also reported only small differences on MMPI-2 scales between Black and White Americans when matched by age, education, and income. Although there were some statistically significant differences—Black men scoring higher on Scale 8 and Black women scoring higher on Scales 4, 5, and 9, these differences were less than five *T*-score points and therefore of little clinical significance. They reported a slight underprediction of psychopathology for Black men, which is in the opposite direction of that suggested in the literature.

No consistent differences have been found in comparing Hispanics and White Americans on these scales. A number of other variables such as socioeconomic status, education, and intelligence seem to be more important determinants of MMPI performance than ethnic status.

There is some evidence that Native Americans tend to score higher on the clinical scales on the MMPI than do Whites (Greene, 1987). A Native American client with a particular score on a personality inventory might be told, "This score suggests that you are quite reserved and timid, lack interest in many activities, and that you are a shy person. My understanding is that among many American Indian tribes, these behaviors are culturally accepted so we probably need to talk more about these behaviors to ensure that they are not a part of the problem you talked to me about earlier" (Paniagua, 1994).

Asian Americans tend to underuse counseling and mental health services and less often share experiences and emotions with those outside the family. They are more likely to express concerns in an indirect manner, such as physical symptoms. Thus somatic complaints are likely to be found on an instrument such as the MMPI (Sue & Sue, 1974). There have been few studies of the scores on personality inventories of Asian students as compared with Whites, but there is some suggestion that Asian Americans may score higher on Scale 2 of the MMPI, which should be interpreted in terms of this cultural phenomenon (Greene, 1987).

Projective techniques are personality assessment instruments that undoubtedly have less value as assessment tools for minority clients. This is probably true for lower socioeconomic groups in general, as interpretations of protocols of persons from different cultures or lower socioeconomic classes tend to result in diagnoses of more severe illness (Jenkins & Ramsey, 1991).

Inaccuracies in the assessment and diagnosis of mental disorders can have three consequences: overdiagnosis, underdiagnosis, and misdiagnosis. Bias in testing can be an important factor in such inaccuracies. Attempts have been made to eliminate or control bias in the assessment and diagnosis of multicultural groups by the translation of tests into the language of the group being tested or through the development of culturally appropriate norms. In spite of these attempts the general sense among researchers and counselors is that bias in cross-cultural testing still exists. It is important for counselors to use tests and inventories in the assessment of multicultural groups; however, they need to determine how to best use these instruments with clients from different cultural backgrounds (Paniagua, 1994).

ASSESSMENT OF CLIENTS WITH DISABILITIES

According to recent estimates, nearly one fifth of the U.S. population aged 15 years and over suffer from a physical disability (Centers for Disease Control and Prevention, 1994). Assessment of clients with physical disabilities in rehabilitation settings may involve three different approaches to vocational evaluation. One approach is psychological testing, a second involves the use of work activities or work samples, and the third is evaluation of actual on-the-job activities (Berven, 1980).

For some clients with disabilities, psychological testing that provides relatively objective and reliable measures of individual abilities and interests can yield sufficient data to assist in decisions regarding vocational choice, training, and job placement while avoiding the great additional amount of time and expense involved in the other types of evaluation. For others, employability can better be explored through work samples and on-the-job evaluations. The employer becomes directly involved with the problems of the client, client characteristics can be ascertained (particularly in relation to the ultimate objective of more independent living), and a functional appraisal of job-related characteristics can be provided. Disadvantages include dependence on the good will of potential employers, plus insurance, wage laws, and regulations that make cooperation by employers difficult. Considerable evaluative information about clients must be obtained in advance if job tryouts are to be successful.

Personality measures, interest inventories, general intelligence tests, measures of specific aptitudes, and tests of achievement or current skills have potential for use with various types of special populations. In using such instruments, however, results must be viewed with caution; for example, the inclusion of items related to general health and physical symptoms on a personality test may be answered in a "deviant" direction by persons who are physically ill or disabled and therefore yield scores that are difficult to interpret or are easily misinterpreted.

Section 504 of the 1973 Rehabilitation Act requires that testing be adapted for disabled students so that it measures what it is designed to measure while allowing for the student's disability. For students with disabilities, academic standards should be maintained while appropriate accommodations in test administration are made. Considerable information regarding the assessment and testing of persons with physical disabilities is found in a monograph published by Technical Education Research Centers (1977). Included in this monograph are lists of assessment instruments appropriate for particular types of disabilities, with recommendations for modifications where necessary.

The Americans With Disabilities Act of 1990 includes a section that speaks directly to the testing (primarily employment testing) of individuals with disabilities. Any tests administered to a job applicant or employee who has a disability must accurately reflect the skills or aptitudes the test purports to measure rather than reflecting the individual's particular disability. As employers must make reasonable accommodations for otherwise qualified employees to perform a particular job, so must reasonable accommodations be provided in the testing process to ensure that the test accurately measures the abilities of the candidate rather than reflecting the disability (unless the disability relates directly to the skill the test measures). Reasonable accommodations can include administering tests in accessible locations, modifying the testing materials (timed versus untimed, written versus braille, or oral versus sign language; LoVerde, McMahon & Morris, 1992).

The national testing programs such as ACT and the College Board provide special test forms and special testing arrangements for examinees with disabilities who are unable to take the test under standard testing conditions. These options include audiocassettes, braille and large-type editions, use of a reader, use of an amanuensis to mark responses, or extended time for testing. In general, predictions of college grades obtained from the special testing situations are less accurate, and more emphasis should be placed on other data (Laing & Farmer, 1984).

A number of the widely used school achievement tests are available in braille, large type, or both. The verbal scales on the WISC-R and the WAIS-R and certain parts of the Stanford-Binet are widely used with blind and partially sighted persons. Certain of the comprehension items need rephrasing to be appropriate, and attention should be paid to the possibility that lower scores on certain subtests may result from experiential deprivation. The performance scales have less validity if visual impairment is more than minimal. Interest inventories such as the Strong or Kuder are frequently used with visually impaired persons by reading items aloud or by tape recording.

For hearing impaired clients, the performance scale on a Wechsler is one of the most accurate instruments for such assessment, whereas a number of tests that make up the verbal scale are not appropriate. Norms for hearing impaired clients are available for the WISC-R. Certain tests and inventories may be administered to this population with American Sign Language (ASL). Responses can also be communicated through an ASL interpreter. Norms for hearing impaired clients also exist for the Metropolitan and Stanford Achievement Tests. Hearing impaired children do not perform as well on such tests as do other students. This is undoubtedly due to the lack of modified curriculum methods designed to meet their needs and the obstacles to language acquisition they face that affects their reading levels (Cohen, Swerdlik, & Smith, 1992).

The Peabody Picture Vocabulary Test and the Raven Progressive Matrices are two intelligence tests that require only a pointing response and are useful for the assessment of persons with cerebral palsy and other physical handicaps. Verbal scales of the Wechsler tests can also be used for severely motor impaired clients. Certain of the performance subtests are not easily adapted because they require both adequate vision and some arm and hand use.

Adaptive devices for computers can provide clients with disabilities with options other than paper-and-pencil responses or the traditional computer keyboard. As a result, disabled individuals can complete a test with minimal staff assistance. Examples include voice input, simplified keyboards, joysticks, pneumatic controls, head pointers, and braille keyboards. Without computers, persons with disabilities have typically completed tests with the assistance of another person who read or responded to test items for the test taker. The problem with an intermediary is that that person may influence the test taker's response or the test taker may modify their responses due to the presence of another individual. The practice also has the potential of reinforcing dependence of persons with disabilities on others (Sampson, 1990).

Because cognitive disabilities cause problems adjusting to the demands of the environment, the diagnosis of mental retardation is usually made not only on the basis of individual intelligence tests but also on the basis of an assessment of adaptive behavior. Intelligence and adaptive behavior are obviously closely related, but adaptive behavior is more synonymous with such terms as *social maturity, personal competence,* and *social competence,* that is, how effectively individuals cope with and adjust to the natural and social demands of their environment. Can they function and maintain themselves independently and can they meet the culturally imposed demands of personal and social responsibility? Measures of adaptive behavior generally consist of behavioral rating scales administered in an interview or by observation (Cohen, Swerdlik, & Smith, 1992).

The Vineland Adaptive Behavior Scales (Sparrow, Balla, & Cicchetti, 1985) are available in an interview, an expanded interview, and a classroom edition. The interview, which follows a semistructured format, is conducted with the client's parents or caregivers. The classroom edition, which is designed to be completed by either the regular school teacher or the special education teacher, deals primarily with adaptive behavior in the classroom. The interview is conducted without the client being present. The Vineland Adaptive Behavior Scales were developed from the original measures designed to assess social competence by Edgar Doll of the Vineland Training School in Vineland, New Jersey. The interview edition contains 297 items and takes 20–60 minutes to complete, the expanded interview edition contains 577 items taking 60–90 minutes to complete, and the classroom edition with 244 items takes 20–30 minutes. The items tap four domains: daily living skills (self-care, dressing, washing), communication (receptive and expressive language), socialization (interpersonal interactions and play), and motor skills (gross and fine coordination). The expanded form also includes the maladaptive behavior domain assessing undesirable behaviors that interfere with adaptive behavior. The standardization sample included 3,000 individuals, 100 in each of 30 age groups stratified to represent the U.S. Census population. Test-retest reliabilities are reported from .80 to over .90, and interrater reliability from .60 to .75 (Sattler, 1989). As might be expected, the expanded form was the most reliable of the three forms and the short classroom form the least reliable. The scales are designed to assess adaptive behavior from birth to 18 years old and among low functioning adults. The instrument is not only used with mentally retarded individuals but also with those who are emotionally disturbed or who are physically, hearing, or visually impaired to develop individually educative treatment programs or vocational rehabilitation programs. Supplementary norms are available for each of these groups.

SUMMARY

1. The increasing diversity of cultural backgrounds in the United States population will present challenges both now and in the future, so that counselors who make use of psychological assessment instruments will need to become more culturally competent as the population becomes more diverse.
2. Counselors need to be aware of problems associated with the cross-cultural use of psychological tests, which include the difficulty in establishing equivalence across cultures, the difficulty of not possessing appropriate norms, differences in response sets across different cultures, the nature of the test items, and the differing attitudes toward psychological testing across cultures.
3. Cultural factors influence not only aptitude test results but scores on interest and personality inventories as well.
4. With different types of accommodations, psychological test data can provide useful information in counseling individuals with disabilities, but results obtained under atypical testing conditions must be viewed with caution.

17

COMMUNICATION OF TEST RESULTS

O NE OF THE MOST IMPORTANT ASPECTS of the assessment process is the communication of results. Counselors and human development professionals are constantly required to interpret assessment results both to clients and to others—parents, agencies, and other professionals. This chapter contains three sets of guidelines for such communications. The first lists some general guidelines regarding the communication of assessment procedures and the results. The second pertains to the actual interpretation of tests in the interview with the client. In the final section, the format and content of a typical written report on an assessment procedure are outlined.

Most of the research studies on the interpretation of test results have been related to career counseling and have been conducted with either high school or college students as subjects. These studies have usually shown that clients who receive test interpretations experience greater gains than those in control conditions who do not receive results. Thus counselors may have confidence that the interpretation of test results to clients generally has a positive effect. There is little research evidence that outcomes are differentially affected by one type of interpretation over another, although clients generally prefer individual integrative interpretations over self-interpretations or group interpretations (Goodyear, 1990).

The counselor's theoretical orientation usually determines how the test scores are interpreted to the client. Counselors whose orientation is client-centered are likely to present clients with key scores or percentiles and encourage clients to join in the process of interpretation. They pay particular attention to how clients feel about the test results and the interpretations. More directive counselors typically review the purpose of testing, present the scores, clarify what they mean, and discuss their implications. Both types should consider assisting clients to make their own interpretations. The advantage of helping clients to interpret and react to test results assists the counselor in obtaining more insight about the client. Also, clients may become accepting of the results more readily by participating in the discussion and may be more likely to make use of the information when making decisions. Client participation in the interpretations, of course, usually takes more time on the part of both the counselor and the client, and this must be weighed when determining the type of approach to be used.

It is necessary to have a thorough understanding of tests, particularly of their theoretical foundations, if a counselor is to function as a professional interpreting the test rather than as a technician using a simple cookbook approach. Tests are used to diagnose and predict; interpretations must lead to the desired understanding and results. It must be remembered that a huge number of factors are involved in producing a particular test score. These include clients' inherited abilities; their educational, cultural, family, and other experiences; their experiences with other tests, particularly psychological tests; their motivation; their test anxiety; the physical and psychological conditions under which they took the test; and the lack of consistency in the test itself.

Psychological and educational diagnoses of culturally diverse clients made as a result of testing data should be made with extreme caution. Culture has a strong influence on psychopathological expression, which can yield significant bias related to the assessment of psycho-pathology across cultures. There have also been studies indicating that ethnically and racially diverse individuals have received more negative psychological diagnoses. Thus counselors should be knowledgeable of culture-specific behaviors that may influence the traditional diagnostic process. In the report writing of psychological and educational assessments, counselors should be aware of the implications of test scores. All of the factors that have contributed to the scores should be considered when reporting predictions and recommendations. Counselors know very well that Miller Analogies or Graduate Record Exam scores account for only a small fraction of the variance in predicting which students will become skillful counselors. Therefore test results should always include a statement about the validity of the entire testing situation. Counselors should also include in their report social, ethnic, racial, and cultural variables that may effect intelligence, achievement, or personality test scores (Hinkle, 1994). Counselors should interpret cross-cultural test scores with caution and when necessary include a disclaimer for limitations in the report.

It is in the interpretation of the test that the various types of validity become extremely important. In every kind of test interpretation there is the assumption of a definite relationship between the person's score or result on a test and what it is being related to in the interpretation. It is therefore important to understand the construction and development of the test as well as its validity as determined by its relationship to that aspect or construct to which it is being related. Often this relationship is expressed in statistical terms. These include correlation coefficients, descriptive and comparative statistics, or expectancy tables. These statistics can often be presented to clients through profiles and other graphic means.

GENERAL GUIDELINES FOR COMMUNICATING TEST RESULTS

1. The first step in interpreting a test is to know and understand the test manual. In this way the validity of a test can be related to the purpose for which the test was used. The manual is also likely to contain information regarding the limits to which the test should be held and suggestions for interpreting the results.

2. In interpreting test results it is important to review the purposes for which the client took the test and the strengths and limitations of the test.

3. In interpreting results, the procedure by which the test is scored should be explained, along with an explanation of percentile ranks or standard scores if they are to be included in the interpretation.

4. Where possible, the results should be presented in terms of probabilities rather than certainties or specific predictions.

5. The emphasis should be on increasing client understanding and, where appropriate, encouraging clients to make their own interpretations.

6. The test results should be presented as they relate to other available information about the client.

7. The counselor should ensure that the interpretation of the test information is understood by the client and that he or she is encouraged to express reactions to the information.

8. Any relevant information or background characteristics, such as sex or disabilities, should be examined, along with any apparent discrepancies or inconsistencies that appear.

9. Both strengths and weaknesses revealed by the tests results should be discussed objectively.

Some of the more difficult tests to interpret are those in which a pattern or profile of scores is provided and one on which the client's pattern is a flat profile with no particularly high or low scores. In educational and vocational counseling, flat profiles on interest inventories are often encountered by the counselor because it is the client's indecision that both brings the client into counseling and yields a flat profile. In other circumstances the individual's response set when taking the test may be a factor. If the client makes little differentiation among the responses—all are high, neutral, or low—validity indices and response patterns should be examined before results are interpreted. With some inventories on which some scale scores are either slightly higher or slightly lower, there may be patterns that can be pointed out and discussed. Other relevant information such as past experiences, values, life-style goals, and previous work activities can be investigated.

On aptitude and achievement tests, flat profiles indicate a general level of performance in all areas that may be average, above average, or below average. Again, results from other types of tests and relevant past experiences may be taken into consideration in assisting with decision making.

GUIDELINES FOR THE TEST INTERPRETATION INTERVIEW

1. Show confidence in the client's ability to understand and make use of the test information. Emphasize the importance of adding the test data to other information that clients have about themselves. Emphasize the importance of clients themselves using the test information to help them in making the decisions they are facing.

2. Ask clients to tell how they feel about the particular tests they took before beginning the interpretation process. This may yield information about their attitudes toward the particular tests and provide information about the usefulness or validity of some of the results. An understanding of how clients perceive the test is often useful in the interpretation process. Stress to clients that they can ask questions, that you, as a counselor, are particularly interested in their reactions to the interpretation, and that you want to know their thoughts about the results.

3. Do not begin discussing the results of any test without reminding clients which test is being discussed. Refresh their memory about it, for example, "Remember the test where you checked whether the two sets of names and numbers were exactly the same or were different? That was a test designed to measure clerical aptitude or ability. . . ."

4. Try to make sure that clients are involved in the interpretation process. Do not merely state the results. Ask clients about their reactions before disclosing the results of a particular measure. After refreshing clients' memories about an instrument, ask, "What were your reactions to that test? How do you think you did on it?"

5. Be prepared with a brief, clear description of what the instrument measures, including what the results mean and what the results do not mean. Be sure to clarify the differences between interests and aptitudes or abilities and personality characteristics. For example, "These are some of the activities you indicated you liked and these are some that you said you did not like. Your interests seem to be more like those of people in social service fields and unlike those of most people in mechanical and technical occupations."

6. Emphasize the usefulness of the tests for clients' decision making rather than for information it provides to the counselor: "With this set of scores you can see how you compare with other college-bound students regarding your ability to learn academic subject matter," rather than "these results confirm my belief that you have the ability to do well in most colleges."

7. Discuss the test results in the context of other information, particularly relating the test results to past, present, and future behavior. Past information and current test results should be related to current decisions and to future longer range plans rather than treating each of these subjects separately.

8. Present the purpose of a test in useful and understandable terms, trying to stay away from psychological jargon. Adjust the pace of the instructions and interpretations to clients' ability and understanding. Have clients summarize often to make sure the results are being understood. If necessary, additional information or alternative methods of interpretation can be used.

9. Where possible, use a graphic representation of the results in addition to a verbal explanation. Remember to turn test profiles so that clients can read them directly. If anyone is going to have to read the profile upside-down, it should be counselors, who are familiar with profile sheets, rather than clients. It is probably better to position chairs so that you and your clients can go over the results together from similar angles. Complicated profile sheets should be grouped and summarized; this way a number of scores can be more easily assimilated. It should not be assumed that most clients have the ability to do this on their own. The results should be explained simply, without the use of elaborate statistics.

10. Avoid overidentifying with the test results. Discuss a clients' rejection of low test scores. The primary concern is what the results mean to the client, not what they mean to the counselor. Low performance scores should be expressed honestly but with perspective. They should not be ignored or attributed to inadequate measures or chance.

11. Make alternative plans sound respectable without imposing the biases of the typical middle-class counselor. Encourage clients to make their own plans rather than simply agreeing with the counselor's suggestions.

12. Be certain that you and your client relate the test information to other data available on the client. For example, scholastic aptitude scores should be related to school grades. Remember that the usual

purpose of a scholastic aptitude test is to predict academic course grades. When such grades are available, emphasis should be placed on actual grades rather than on test results that merely predict those grades.

13. Whenever possible use the types of norms that are most relevant to clients. When such norms are not directly appropriate, information about this should be presented to clients and the interpretation of the results should make certain that this is clear.

14. Use only tests that you, the counselor, have personally taken, scored, and interpreted for yourself. Know the reasons a particular test was administered, what was expected from its interpretation, and the validity of the test for the purpose for which it was used.

15. Be aware that psychological tests should not be used to provide information that can be easily gathered in other ways. Only in exceptional circumstances would a student with high academic achievement or scholastic aptitude test scores need the administration of an IQ test. Tests should not be overused.

16. Toward the end of the interview, have clients summarize the results of the entire interview rather than attempting to do this for them. Allow enough time to discuss this summary and to discuss discrepancies or misunderstandings. Attempt to end on a positive note even though some portions of the interview have not yielded information that the client has been happy to receive. If clients have received discouraging information about educational, vocational, or other types of plans, try to broaden the scope of alternatives that might be considered. Emphasis should not only be placed on narrowing the focus of future plans, but also on broadening them.

17. Remember that in counseling there is almost always an implicit future orientation. Even though the immediate goal is to help clients to make a particular decision or to understand themselves better in a specific situation, there is also the belief that it is important for people to know themselves better. Ultimately, the self-knowledge gained in counseling will enable individuals to have more effective and satisfying lives and to make wiser and more realistic plans.

REPORT WRITING

In writing a report it is important to have some conceptualization of what is necessary to include and a conceptualization of the client or person about whom you are writing the report. In writing a test report, the focus of the report and the way it is to be used are the first considerations in determining its content. The reasons for testing and the general purposes of the tests used provide the decisions about whether the report will be primarily oriented toward an objective summary of test results or an overall description of the individual being examined. Often there is a large amount of information available, and the report writer must decide what information should be included and what excluded (Drummond, 1988).

The first decision is determining the principal idea that should be communicated and what other types of information play an auxiliary role. One of the ways of emphasizing material is by the order in which it is presented, with the most important information first. Another way is through the adjectives and adverbs used in describing the person and his or her behavior. It can also be done through illustrations, using the most vivid example that points out the information you wish to emphasize. Another mode is repetition. Obviously repetition needs to be handled skillfully to avoid repeating the same material more often than necessary. Repeating information in the summary or conclusion is another way of adding emphasis.

Problems that should be avoided include (a) poor organization, in which the results are not integrated as a whole; (b) use of psychological jargon that will not be understood; (c) use of terms that do not have clearly understood definitions; or (d) lack of integration between the test results and other information and recommendations related to the individual based on observation or other data.

What Gets Included in a Case Report

The following is an outline of a typical case report:

1. *Brief description of client.* Including some of the demographic information, a description might begin by saying "This is a 32-year-old man of medium build, with wrinkled and soiled clothes, who was extremely verbal and articulate in the interview." This beginning gives a bit of an impression and may include some identifying information such as age, race, and perhaps occupation or year in school.

2. *Reason for counseling or referral.* The next piece of information is the reason that the person is seeking counseling, the problem they present, or the reason they were referred for testing. A brief description of a client along with a brief description of the nature of the problem

and the reason for undertaking the evaluation give a general focus for the report.

3. *Relevant background information.* Next to be included might be some additional demographic data and some of the information available from the referral source. The background information should be relevant to the purpose of the testing, should be related to the overall purpose of the report and should be as succinct as possible. It is likely to include the client's educational background, occupation, family background, health status, and current life situation. It should also include other aspects of personal history that are related to the reason for testing and that help to place the problem or reason for testing in its proper context.

4. *Evaluation procedures.* Evaluation procedures can be briefly described, giving the rationale for testing, the names of the tests used, and why the particular tests were selected.

5. *Behavioral observations.* Specific behaviors that were observed during the interviews and during the tests can be included in the next section. The way the client approached the test, any problems that arose, and any other factors that might bring into question the validity of any of the tests used should be mentioned. Only relevant observations should be included. This section is likely to be very brief if the behaviors were normal and much more lengthy if behaviors were unusual.

6. *Test results and their interpretation.* Next is a report of the test results, an overall interpretation, and diagnostic impressions. The description of the test results does not necessarily need to include the actual test scores, but they should be included if the report is for other professionals who are knowledgeable about testing. The most important part of this section is the interpretation of the results. Here all of the test data are integrated, along with the behavioral observations and relevant background information. A discussion of the client's strengths and weaknesses is included. A statement regarding the client's future prospects in relation to the reason for the testing often needs to be included. This statement would include both favorable and unfavorable predictions.

7. *Recommendations.* The primary reason for testing and the subsequent case report is usually to gain recommendations. Particularly if the case is a referral, recommendations can include further testing or activities that the client or others should undertake in relation to

323

the problem. Recommendations should relate to the problem and to the general purpose of the testing and report. They should be as practical and specific as possible.

8. *Brief concluding summary.* A summary paragraph should succinctly restate the most important findings and conclusions (Maloney & Ward, 1976).

Writing Style

Writing a report is often much easier if an overall case conceptualization is developed first. Reports often include the general theoretical framework that is followed by the counselor. When psychoanalytic theory was the primary theory followed by counselors, a great deal of emphasis was placed on early childhood experiences. Those who follow Rogerian theory probably pay particular attention to the person's self-concept. The Gestalt theorist looks specifically at current relationships, and the behavioral counselor will be interested in things that reinforce particular behaviors. Counselors may not feel they have a particular theory of behavior, but in the case report their general theory of personality often emerges because it influences what they perceive from the interviews and test results and therefore what they report.

In reporting test results it is a good idea to stay away from testing jargon. It is also important in writing a report to avoid the extremes of focusing either too much or too little on the test results themselves. It is possible to report extensive test results without relating them to the individual and the individual's situation and future plans, and thus not offer much in the way of conclusions or practical suggestions. It is also possible to depart too much from the test results and downplay them, particularly if the test information does not come out as expected or if it is not likely to be seen in positive terms by the client.

It should also be remembered that it is better to prepare a report immediately after counseling and testing rather than letting a considerable period of time go by. Counselors enjoy working with people much more than writing reports, so it is easy to put these aside. Timeliness becomes particularly important when a number of clients are seen each day. It is important to at least write down the information that will be needed to write a report, even if it is not possible to write the final report immediately. In writing a report it is necessary to come out and say what needs to be said, making clear statements and clear recommendations. On the other hand, where results must be considered inconclusive, this also needs to be said.

SUMMARY

The influence of the counselor's theoretical orientation and the importance of case conceptualization are related both to the interpretation of the test results and the content of a report of the results of an assessment. Nine general guidelines for communicating test results were presented in this chapter, along with 17 counselor behaviors useful in the test interpretation interview. A sample outline provided eight topics typically included in a written case report.

18

ETHICAL AND SOCIAL ISSUES IN TESTING

T HERE ARE A NUMBER of situations when psychological tests are used in counseling and placement in which ethical principles are called into question. In this chapter important ethical issues related to tests are discussed, along with the accompanying ethical principles that need to be considered. The second portion of the chapter includes several social issues related to testing that have not been included in previous chapters.

ETHICAL STANDARDS

Because of the number of cases that have arisen in the past regarding the ethical use of psychological tests, each of the professional organizations whose members make use of tests have developed, among their codes of ethics, principles that deal specifically with psychological testing. The American Counseling Association's (ACA) *Code of Ethics and Standards of Practice* (American Counseling Association, 1995) and the American Psychological Association's (APA) *Ethical Principles of Psychologists and Code of Conduct* (APA, 1993) each contain a section related to educational and psychological testing. In addition *The Responsibilities of Test Users* (The RUST Statement Revised; AACD, 1989) and the Joint Committee *Standards for Educational and Psychological Testing* (AERA, APA, & NCME, 1985), both of which were discussed in Chapter 2, also contain statements of test user responsibilities and ethical standards. Excerpts from the ACA Code, the RUST Statement, and the Joint Committee *Standards* most relevant for test use in the counseling process are presented in Appendices A, B, and C.

Ethical Standards for Test Quality

A portion of *Standards for Educational and Psychological Testing* deals with the technical quality of tests and test materials and standards to be followed by test developers and by test publishers before distributing the test. Test publishers and authors make money from the royalties of tests that are sold, and there is an obvious temptation to exaggerate the usefulness or the validity of such tests. This is an area on which the committee that developed the standards placed considerable emphasis to put pressure on publishers to maintain "truth in advertising" in test publishing. These standards include providing evidence of reliability and validity, information regarding the method of estimating reliability and the population on which it was measured, and types of validity evidence, including validity relevant to the intended purpose of the test.

Certain of the standards are designed to prevent the premature sale of tests for general use and to specify when the test is to be released for research purposes only. The standards emphasize that the test manual should not be designed to sell the test but should include adequate information about the administration, scoring, norms, and other technical data to permit the potential user to evaluate the test itself and its potential use, as well as to properly interpret its results.

Counselor Competence in Testing

An important ethical issue is the competence of the counselor to use the various available assessment instruments. The issue is whether those who use various tests have sufficient knowledge and understanding to select tests intelligently, and to interpret their results (ACA Code E.2). Because different tests demand different levels of competence for their use, users must recognize the limits of their competence and make use only of instruments for which they have adequate preparation and training. The administration and interpretation of individual intelligence tests such as the Stanford-Binet or the Wechsler tests, certain personality tests such as the MMPI, or projective personality tests such as the Rorschach or the Thematic Apperception Test, require advanced training and practice to obtain the necessary background and skill for their appropriate use.

In an attempt to deal with this problem, a number of publishers will sell tests only to those who are qualified and require a statement of qualifications from purchasers of psychological tests. In cooperation with the Test User Qualifications Working Group (see Chapter 2), publishers have produced forms that must be completed by those purchasing the tests regarding their educational background and experience. Tests are graded in regard to the amount of background and experience required and are sold only to those who meet the standards required for particular tests. These statements of qualifications are usually included in the test publishers' sales catalogs. Counselors must provide relevant information regarding their qualifications before purchasing test supplies. Typically a master's degree and a course in psychological assessment are the minimum qualifications required to purchase many of the tests commonly used by counselors. Graduate students who need to purchase particular tests for training or research purposes must have the order signed by the graduate instructor, who takes on responsibility for seeing that the tests are properly used.

The major responsibility for the proper use of tests, however, is that of the professional who makes use of them (ACA Code E.6; Standards 9.1–9.6). Is the test appropriate for the person who is being tested? How are the results going to be used? Are the test scores reliable enough? Does the test possess enough validity to be used for the purpose for which it is planned? Counselors who are well trained select tests that are appropriate both for the person to whom they are administered and for the specific purpose for which the person is being tested. They are also sensitive to the many conditions that affect test performance. They are knowledgeable enough about individual differences and human behavior not to make unwarranted interpretations of test results.

CLIENT WELFARE ISSUES

Occasionally an ethical issue arises regarding the welfare of the client in the testing process. Is the welfare of the client being taken into consideration in the choice and use of tests (Standards, 6.4–6.7)? Except in such cases as court referrals or custody determinations, this is seldom an issue in counseling because tests are usually used to help the client and not for other purposes.

Another client welfare issue deals with the questions of privacy and confidentiality (ACA Code E.4; Responsibilities, VIII). In counseling situations, clients are typically willing to reveal aspects about themselves to obtain help with their problems; thus the invasion of privacy issue, often a concern in psychological testing elsewhere, is seldom a concern in counseling. Clients obviously would not wish this information to be disclosed to others. Test data, along with other records of the counseling relationship, must be considered professional information for use in counseling and must not be revealed to others without the expressed consent of the client. Certain types of test results, such as those assessing intelligence or aptitude and those that ask for or reveal emotional or personality or attitudinal traits, often may deal with sensitive aspects of personal lives or limitations that an individual would prefer to conceal.

Problems of confidentiality often arise when the counselor is employed by an institution or organization, which results in conflicting loyalties. In these circumstances counselors should tell clients in advance how the test results will be used and make clear the limits of confidentiality. In general, ethical principles state that the test results are confidential unless the client gives his or her consent for the test results to be provided to someone else. The limits of confidentiality and the circumstances under which it can be broken (such as clear and present danger or court subpoena) must be communicated to and understood by the client.

In addition, the Family Education Rights and Privacy Act of 1974 requires that educational institutions release test result information to parents of minor students and to students who are 18 years of age or older. In reporting results to others who have a reason and need to make use of the results, counselors must ensure that the results of the assessment and their interpretations are not misused by others. Is the person receiving the information qualified to understand and interpret the results? It is incumbent on the counselor to interpret the results in a way that they can be intelligently understood by those receiving them, including teachers and parents (Responsibilities, VII, VIII). In addition, the counselor has an obligation to point out the limitations of the results and any other important information about reliability or validity, as well as a description of the norms used and their appropriateness.

Clients, of course, have the right to know the results of tests, with interpretations of the results communicated to them in a language they can clearly understand. They must be interpreted to clients in such a way that clients understand what the tests mean and also what they do not mean. It is important that clients not reach unwarranted conclusions from the interpretation they receive (Responsibilities, VII).

The manner in which tests results are communicated to others (when appropriate) should be carefully considered. Results should usually be presented descriptively rather than numerically. The use of labels that can be misinterpreted or damaging should be avoided. Labeling someone as having schizophrenia or intellectually retarded can stigmatize a person even when such terms can be justified. They not only suggest a lack of any chance to grow or change, but they may also become self-fulfilling prophecies. Instead, interpretations should be presented in terms of possibile ranges of academic achievement or formulations of interventions to assist the individual in behaving more effectively.

To help ensure confidentiality, test results should be kept in a place accessible only to authorized individuals. They should be maintained in school or agency files only so long as they serve a useful purpose. With the advent of computerized record keeping, the difficulty of keeping test results secure and inaccessible to all but authorized users has increased. Effective measures for protecting the security of individual records must be maintained.

Tests must be administered in a standardized fashion if the results are to be adequately interpreted. One problem in the area of test administration involves test security. It is obvious that test results will not be valid if people can obtain the tests in advance. For tests such as the College Boards or the Medical College Admission Test, elaborate procedures are established to ensure that there is adequate security for these tests on which important decisions will be based. In addition, tests need to be accurately scored and accurately profiled if the results are to have valid meaning.

Another ethical issue, probably a minor one for counselors, is in regard to what might be called impersonal service in using tests. It is possible for a counselor or a psychologist to use tests in which test booklets are sent to clients, returned, scored, and interpreted through the mail. A fee is charged, but the counselor does not meet the client face to face. Considerable money in fees could be generated by this service. Without knowing why the person is requesting the tests, the purposes for which test results are to be used, or the interpretation that clients could give to the results, such a practice would constitute a misuse of testing. Therefore this practice, along with other types of impersonal psychological services, is considered unethical.

The opportunity for such practices has increased with the use of computer interpretations. As noted in Chapter 4, test publishers have increasingly relied on computers to prepare narrative reports of test results. Computer interpretations of such inventories as the Strong Interest Inventory or the MMPI can produce interpretations that run 10–20 pages in length. Such interpretations provide a distillation of the information that has been accumulated in the professional literature and of the pooled experience of a number of experts. Narrative computer printouts are obviously no better than the wisdom and clinical experience on which they are based; however, they protect the client from possible bias or inexperience of an individual counselor while expediting what can be a time consuming and tedious chore of report writing. The client may either take the test itself on a computer or have the test scored and interpreted by a computer. These computer interpretations are, of course, based on norms, which are not necessarily appropriate for a particular individual. The narrative does need to be evaluated by a counselor who knows other facts about the client, the rationale for testing, and the reasons for such evaluation. The misuse of such computer-generated test interpretations has become an issue of increased concern to the counseling and psychological professions.

A final issue deals with the ethical use of psychological tests in research. When tests are given for research purposes, the first principle to be employed is that of informed consent—having had the procedures explained to them, individuals must have the opportunity to choose not to participate. Minors should also be informed, to the extent of their comprehension, and parental consent is often necessary as well. A particular problem arises in testing research when knowledge regarding the specific objectives of a test has a substantial effect on the attitude of the person taking it, therefore yielding invalid research results. In research studies there are also the ethical issues of privacy and confidentiality.

In general, counselors have had fewer ethical problems in the use of tests than have various other professionals, because counselors typically use tests in their activities on behalf of the client—to assist the client in regard to decision making or to provide additional information for treatment. They do not usually use tests for institutional purposes such as selection or placement.

ISSUES OF GENDER BIAS IN TESTING

During the past several decades, testing has been a controversial subject that has become involved with a number of social issues. In particular, testing has been attacked for its discrimination against minority groups (see Chapter 16). Tests are designed to measure differences among individuals, but when they reveal differences among ethnic or gender groups they are considered to be biased.

These issues have led to much disenchantment with psychological tests—particularly intelligence and academic aptitude tests. Much of the controversy has resulted when test scores have shown group differences. There is less controversy when the discussion is restricted to individual differences, and it is individual differences with which counselors are typically concerned.

Gender Bias in Aptitude Testing

Intelligence tests have not been shown to produce significant differences between men and women. Mean scores for both sexes are essentially the same. On specific aptitudes, however, women tend to score higher than men on tests of verbal ability, whereas men obtain higher scores on numerical and spatial aptitudes (Eagly, 1995; Maccoby & Jacklin, 1974; Neisser et al., 1996). Women tend to achieve higher grades in elementary school, high school, and in college (Han & Hoover, 1994), although the difference in college tends to diminish when controlled for types of majors and types of courses (Hood, 1968).

The question regarding lower scores on mathematical ability is a controversial one at the present time; some argue that the difference is an inherent sex-related difference, whereas others argue that it is due to stereotypical attitudes on the part of parents and teachers, which result in the two sexes being differentially encouraged to learn mathematics. Recent evidence yields at least partial support for the latter explanation; the gap has decreased among adolescents over the past 40 years and has virtually disappeared in unselected populations (Eagly, 1995; Hoover & Han, 1995). The widely reported substantial sex differences are now found only in specific populations, such as college-bound youth on the SAT or on the National Merit test. Again, this mean difference is of less consequence to counselors as they work with individual students of either sex who may obtain scores anywhere throughout the entire range.

A recent development dealing with the gender bias of tests is related to the awarding of scholarships to the top 1% or 2% of scorers on the basis of a scholastic aptitude test. In the case of awarding certain scholarships, this has resulted in a higher proportion of men receiving scholarships than women. A major cause of this problem is the difference in the variance on test scores between the sexes in a number of academic areas including mathematics (Eagly, 1995; Han & Hoover, 1994). On such measures, including quantitative reasoning, men vary over a greater range than do women (Benbow, 1988). Thus as the top 1% contains more men than women, so does the bottom 1%. There is pressure to develop tests to qualify for scholarships that eliminate this type of bias, but if the variance hypothesis holds, this will be a difficult task. In the case of the National Merit Testing Program, different cut-off scores are already used for different states, so that the top 1% of the students in each state qualify. If this practice were extended to the sexes, then qualifying scores could be established to ensure that the top 1% of both men and women would qualify.

Gender Bias in Personality Measurement

Although most of the controversy regarding bias in tests has centered around aptitude or intelligence tests, certain of the tests used in counseling, such as interest and personality measures, have not been entirely free of bias. Most personality measures are scored on norms developed for each sex, and thus a particular score on a particular personality trait achieved by a man or a woman is scored on the respective male or female norms; thus the bias that would result if men and women tended to score particularly differently on a personality characteristic is eliminated. Counselors using particular tests, such as the MMPI, should be aware that certain behavior patterns likely to be attributed to certain profile types often differ for men and women.

Gender Bias in Interest Measurement

During the decades of the 1960s and 1970s, charges of gender bias were leveled against vocational interest inventories and their use in the vocational and educational counseling of women. Several of the interest inventories used only male pronouns and male-oriented occupational names and listed primarily stereotypical occupations for each sex. Earlier versions of both the male and female forms of the Strong Interest Inventory were particularly criticized for this bias. The bias that existed has been examined by several national committees, with resulting recommendations to eliminate both the sexually stereotypical language that exists among the inventories and also to eliminate the tendency of test results to channel students on the basis of sex and limit their consideration of certain careers.

There are several methods by which publishers have attempted to eliminate, or at least reduce, gender bias on interest inventories. One is by using single-sex norms. In the case of the Strong Interest Inventory and the Kuder Occupational Interest Survey, the occupational scales are based on separate criterion groups for each sex. All clients receive scores on both the male and female scores. Thus individuals can compare their interests with those of both sexes in a wide variety of occupations. On basic interest scales, profiles now show scores for both male and female norm groups; thus gender bias is eliminated by use of the inclusion of norms for both sexes. In the case of the earlier forms of these instruments, many more occupations were shown for men than for women, which has the tendency to limit the number of careers considered by women. In recent years test authors have attempted to develop the same number and type of scales for both men and women. The only exceptions are occupations in which it is very difficult to find a norm group of one sex, such as male home economics teachers or female pilots. Virtually all inventories have eliminated sexist language, for instance, replacing *policeman* with *police officer* and *mailman* with *postal worker*.

Another method by which publishers of interest inventories have attempted to make them free of gender bias has been to include only interest items that are equally attractive to both sexes. For example, on an interest inventory containing items related to the six Holland themes, many more men than women respond to a realistic item such as "repairing an automobile," and many more women to a social item such as "taking care of very small children." Through the elimination of items that are stereotypically masculine or stereotypically feminine, such differences can be largely avoided. For example, realistic items such as "refinishing furniture" or "operating a lawn mower" or a social item such as "teaching in high school" tend to receive approximately equal responses by both men and women (Rayman, 1976). An interest inventory such as the UNIACT (American College Testing Program, 1995), published by the American College Testing Program, is a sex-balanced inventory, increasing the probability that men will obtain higher scores on the social scale and women on the realistic scale, and thus that each sex would be more likely to give consideration to occupations in a full range of fields.

Holland has resisted constructing sex-balanced scales on his Self-Directed Search, believing that the use of sex-balanced scales destroys much of the predictive validity of the instrument (Gottfredson, 1982; Holland & Gottfredson, 1976). An inventory that predicts that equal numbers of men and women will become automobile mechanics or elementary school teachers is going to have reduced predictive validity given the male and female socialization and occupational patterns found in today's society. When such inventories are used primarily for vocational exploration, however, an instrument that channels interests into stereotypical male and female fields can be criticized for containing this gender bias.

By including scores on all occupational scales for both sexes, including norms for both sexes on interest scales, by eliminating stereotypical language and, for some instruments, developing sex-balanced items, gender bias in interest testing has been greatly reduced. It must be remembered, however, that gender-based restrictions in interest preferences and career choices will continue as long as societal influences limit the experiences men and women are exposed to or are able to explore (Walsh & Betz, 1994).

COUNSELING PROCESS ISSUES

It is probably to be expected that tests used for selection into desirable programs and occupations will be criticized, particularly by those not selected. The use of tests in counseling situations, however, has been much less controversial. Counselors and human development professionals typically use tests for problem-solving purposes to assist the individual. In other settings, test results do not necessarily get shared directly with clients; in counseling, test results are almost always discussed with clients. The client is seen as the primary user of test results with the counselor acting more as a facilitator. Although counselors use the clinical interview and behavioral observation, tests provide an opportunity to obtain standardized information concerning individual differences that can be useful both to plan counseling interventions and to promote clients' understanding of themselves. Counselors help clients explore and identify their abilities, personality characteristics, patterns of interests, and values in assisting their clients in making choices and changes that can improve their sense of well-being or their life-styles.

Personality inventories can reveal information useful in the counseling process, and interest and aptitude test results can assist in educational and vocational planning. Diagnostic tests in academic areas such as reading or arithmetic skills can help to identify those who need special instruction in particular areas and to plan future educational programs. Because of criticisms leveled against psychological tests when used in selection procedures (and perhaps in part due to some counselors' own experiences with scholastic aptitude tests used for selection purposes), counselors occasionally develop a bias against psychological tests. They refuse to use them in individual counseling programs, where they can often be particularly valuable.

Much of the criticism of psychological testing and assessment and attacks on their use in educational institutions and employment situations has resulted mainly in constructive effects. Increased awareness of the utility and limitations of testing has resulted in the need for more carefully trained users of test results as the personal and social consequences of testing have become increasingly apparent. Consistent with these needs, the primary objective of this book has been to improve the knowledge and understanding of counselors who administer and interpret the results of these assessment procedures.

Counselors should not blame the tests themselves when tests have been used inappropriately. Obviously tests are often misused and occasionally misused by counselors and other human development professionals, but that does not mean the tests are at fault. When pliers are used on a bolt for which an adjustable wrench is needed, it is not the pair of pliers nor its manufacturer that is criticized.

One of the earlier criticisms of psychological tests was that they were dominating the counseling process. With the development of many new counseling theories and techniques, there are few, if any, strict practitioners of what was known as trait-and-factor counseling, for whom psychological tests totally dominated their practices.

When using tests in counseling, it is important that the counselor attempt to understand the frame of reference of the client. If the counselor is knowledgeable about tests, he or she can then better help the client understand the information that tests can provide. In interpreting test results, the counselor must help the client to understand their implications and their limitations, to help clients integrate the test information into their self-perceptions and decision-making strategies.

It has been suggested (and even mandated by legislative action) that tests should not be used because certain disadvantaged groups make poor showings on them. In these situations, the test results are often indicative of symptoms of a societal ailment, analogous to a fever thermometer that indicates an illness. When the tests reveal that the disadvantaged have not had the opportunity to learn certain concepts, there should be an attempt to provide these opportunities, not to dispose of the instruments that reveal such symptoms.

Another criticism of using tests in counseling is the point that validity coefficients are based on groups of persons, and it is not possible to discern the validity of any test score for any one individual. It is in the counseling process that the counselor attempts to help clients determine the validity of that test score for that individual. To use tests properly in counseling, the counselor must know as much about the client and the client's environment as possible. The Counselor must also be well informed about tests and have a basic familiarity with them. Although a counselor does not need to have a great deal of understanding regarding the technical aspects of test development and standardization, he or she does need to have a clear understanding of the general purposes of the particular tests, the uses to which they can be put, and the role these tests can play in the counseling process.

In the information age, test results will continue to provide important data needed for many decisions. In addition to individual personal and career decisions, there will be increased reliance on tests to determine minimum skills and competencies for educational institutions, licensing and certification, and personnel selection.

The increasing automation of psychological assessment will make the administration and scoring of tests, as well as the interpretation of their results, more efficient, more extensive, and more complex. Already many tests commonly administered by counselors are available for administration, scoring, and interpretation with a microcomputer (e.g., CPI, DAT, Millon, MMPI, MBTI, 16 PF, Strong, and Wechsler tests). Standardized interview data can also be obtained through interaction with a computer.

FINAL STATEMENT

Psychological tests are used by personnel staff to select employees, by school psychologists to track pupils, by clinical psychologists to diagnose patients, by college admissions staff to admit students, and by forensic psychologists to determine sanity. In the counseling setting, however, psychological tests are used to help clients understand themselves. With the prevalence of negative attitudes toward psychological tests, counselors may be reluctant to make adequate use of them in assisting clients, but they should remember that the use of tests in counseling differs from other test use. Counselors use tests primarily to assist individuals in developing their potential to the fullest and to their own satisfaction. Test results are designed to be used by the clients themselves, and only in the ways in which they decide to make or not to make use of them. In counseling, tests are not used by others to make decisions for or against a client.

The concept of individual differences is a basic tenet of counseling. Assessment procedures enable counselors to measure and compare the different characteristics of clients and their environments. Tests and assessment data can provide important behavior samples useful in the counseling process to assist counselors to understand their clients better and clients to understand themselves.

The purpose of this text has been to help current and future counselors and human development professionals, as well as others in the helping professions, to become better consumers and interpreters of psychological and educational tests and assessment procedures. We have attempted to cover some of the philosophical and ethical principles related to the use of tests, basic knowledge about certain tests, when tests should be used, and how to interpret and report test and assessment results.

By using tests ethically, appropriately, and intelligently, counselors can assist their clients to understand their problems, make use of their potential, function more effectively, make more effective decisions, and live more satisfying lives.

Appendices

IV

Appendices

A

Excerpts From American Counseling Association Code of Ethics and Standards of Practice 1995

CODE OF ETHICS, SECTION E: EVALUATION, ASSESSMENT, AND INTERPRETATION

E.1. General

a. *Appraisal Techniques.* The primary purpose of educational and psychological assessment is to provide measures that are objective and interpretable in either comparative or absolute terms. Counselors recognize the need to interpret the statements in this section as applying to the whole range of appraisal techniques, including test and nontest data.

b. *Client Welfare.* Counselors promote the welfare and best interests of the client in the development, publication, and utilization of educational and psychological assessment techniques. They do not misuse assessment results and interpretations and take reasonable steps to prevent others from misusing the information these techniques provide. They respect the client's right to know the results, the interpretations made, and the bases for their conclusions and recommendations.

E.2. Competence to Use and Interpret Tests

a. *Limits of Competence.* Counselors recognize the limits of their competence and perform only those testing and assessment services for which they have been trained. They are familiar with reliability, validity, related standardization, error of measurement, and proper application of any technique utilized. Counselors using computer-based test interpretations are trained in the construct being measured and the specific instrument being used prior to using this type of computer application. Counselors take reasonable measures to ensure the proper use of psychological assessment techniques by persons under their supervision.

b. *Appropriate Use.* Counselors are responsible for the appropriate application, scoring, interpretation, and use of assessment instruments, whether they score and interpret such tests themselves or use computerized or other services.

c. *Decisions Based on Results.* Counselors responsible for decisions involving individuals or policies that are based on assessment results have a thorough understanding of educational and psychological measurement, including validation criteria, test research, and guidelines for test development and use.

d. *Accurate Information.* Counselors provide accurate information and avoid false claims or misconceptions when making statements about assessment instruments or techniques. Special efforts are made to avoid unwarranted connotations of such terms as IQ and grade equivalent scores (See C.5.c).

E.3 Informed Consent

a. *Explanation to Clients.* Prior to assessment, counselors explain the nature and purposes of assessment and the specific use of results in language the client (or other legally authorized person on behalf of the client) can understand, unless an explicit exception to this right has been agreed upon in advance. Regardless of whether scoring and interpretation are completed by counselors, by assistants, or by computer or other outside services, counselors take reasonable steps to ensure that appropriate explanations are given to the client.

b. *Recipients of Results.* The examinee's welfare, explicit understanding, and prior agreement determine the recipients of test results. Counselors include accurate and appropriate interpretations with any release of individual or group test results (See B.7.a and C.5.c).

E.4. Release of Information to Competent Professionals

a. *Misuse of Results.* Counselors do not misuse assessment results including test results, and interpretations, and take reasonable steps to prevent the misuse of such by others. (See C.5.c.)
b. *Release of Raw Data.* Counselors ordinarily release data (e.g., protocols, counseling or interview notes, or questionnaires) in which the client is identified only with the consent of the client or the client's legal representative. Such data are usually released only to persons recognized by couynselors as competent to interpret the data. (See B.1.a.)

E.5. Proper Diagnosis of Mental Disorders

a. *Proper Diagnosis.* Counselors take special care to provide proper diagnosis of mental disorders. Assessment techniques (including personal interview) used to determine client care (e.g., locus of treatment, type of treatment, or recommended follow-up) are carefully selected and appropriately used (See A.3.a and C.5.c).
b. *Cultural Sensivity.* Counselors recognize that culture affects the manner in which clients' problems are defined. Clients' socioeconomic and cultural experience is considered when diagnosing mental disorders.

E.6. Test Selection

a. *Appropriateness of Instruments.* Counselors carefully consider the validity, reliability, psychometric limitations, and appropriateness of instruments when selecting tests for use in a given situation or with a particular client.
b. *Culturally Diverse Populations.* Counselors are cautious when selecting tests for culturally diverse populations to avoid inappropriateness of testing that may be outside of socialized behavioral or cognitive patterns.

E.7. Conditions of Test Administration

a. *Administration Conditions.* Counselors administer tests under the same conditions that were established in their standardization. When tests are not administered under standard conditions or when unusual behavior or irregularities occur during the testing session, those conditions are noted in interpretation, and the results may be designated as invalid or of questionable validity.
b. *Computer Administration.* Counselors are responsible for ensuring that administration programs function properly to provide clients with accurate results when a computer or other electronic methods are used for test administration (See A.12.b).
c. *Unsupervised Test-Taking.* Counselors do not permit unsupervised or inadequately supervised use of tests or assessments unless the tests or assessments are designed, intended, and validated for self-administration and/or scoring.
d. *Disclosure of Favorable Conditions.* Prior to test administration, conditions that produce most favorable test results are made known to the examinee.

E.8. Diversity in Testing

Counselors are cautious in using assessment techniques, making evaluations, and interpreting the performance of populations not represented in the norm group on which an instrument was standardized. They recognize the effects of age, color, culture, disability, ethnic group, gender, race, religion, sexual orientation, and socioeconomic status on test administration and interpretation and place test results in proper perspective with other relevant factors (See A.2.a).

E.9. Test Scoring and Interpretation

a. *Reporting Reservations.* In reporting assessment results, counselors indicate any reservations that exist regarding validity and reliability because of the circumstances of the assessment or the inappropriateness of the norms for the person tested.
b. *Research Instruments.* Counselors exercise caution when interpreting the results of research instruments possessing insufficient technical data to support respondent results. The specific purposes for the use of such instruments are stated explicitly to the examinee.

c. *Testing Services*. Counselors who provide test scoring and test interpretation services to support the assessment process confirm the validity of such interpretations. They accurtely describe the purpose, norms, validity, reliability, and applications of the procedures and any special qualifications applicable to their use. The public offering of an automated test interpretations service is considered a professional-to-professional consultation. The formal responsibility of the consultant is to the consultee, but the ultimate and overriding responsibility is to the client.

E.10. Test Security

Counselors maintain the integrity and security of tests and other assessment techniques consistent with legal and contractual obligations. Counselors do not appropriate, reproduce, or modify published tests or parts thereof without acknowledgment and permission from the publisher.

E.11. Obsolete Tests and Outdated Test Results

Counselors do not use data or test results that are obsolete or outdated for the current purpose. Counselors make every effort to prevent the misuse of obsolete measures and test data by others.

E.12. Test Construction

Counselors use established scientific procedures, relevant standards, and current professional knowledge for test design in the development, publication, and utilization of educational and psychological assessment techniques.

B

Excerpts From the Responsibilities of Users of Standardized Tests (The RUST Statement Revised)

by
The Association for Measurement and Evaluation in
Counseling and Development (AMECD) and
The American Association for Counseling and
Development (AACD)
March 1989

II.   *TEST DECISIONS:* Decisions should be based on data. In general, test data improve the quality of decisions. However, deciding whether or not to test creates the possibility of three kinds of errors. First, a decision not to test can result in misjudgments that stem from inadequate or subjective data. Second, tests may produce data which could improve accuracy in decisions affecting the client, but which are not used in counseling. Third, tests may be misused. The responsible practitioner will determine, in advance, the purpose for administering a given test, considering protections and benefits for the client, practitioner, and agency.

A. Define purposes for testing by developing specific objectives and limits for the use of test data in relation to the particular assessment purpose:
   1. Placement: If the purpose is selection or placement, the test user should understand the programs or institutions into which the client may be placed and be able to judge the consequences of inclusion or exclusion decisions for the client.
   2. Prediction: If the purpose is prediction, the test user should understand the need for predictive data as well as possible negative consequences (e.g., stereotyping).
   3. Description: If the purpose is diagnosis or description, the test user should understand the general domain being measured and be able to identify those aspects which are adequately measured and those which are not.
   4. Growth: If the purpose is to examine growth or change, the test user should understand the practical and theoretical difficulties associated with such measurement.
   5. Program Evaluation: If the purpose of assessment is the evaluation of an agency's programs, the test user should be aware of the various information needs for the evaluation and of the limitation of each instrument used to assess those needs, as well as how the evaluation will be used.
B. Determine Information Needs and Assessment Needs:
   1. Determine whether testing is intended to assess individuals, groups, or both.
   2. Identify the particular individual and/or group to be tested with regard to the agency's purposes and capabilities.
   3. Determine the limitations to testing created by an individual's age; racial, sexual, ethnic, and cultural background; or other characteristics.
   4. Avoid unnecessary testing by identifying decisions which can be made with existing information.
   5. Assess the consequences for clients of deciding either to test or not to test.
   6. Limit data gathering to the variables that are needed for the particular purpose.

7. Cross-validate test data using other available information whenever possible.

III. *QUALIFICATIONS OF TEST USERS:* While all professional counselors and personnel workers should have formal training in psychological and educational measurement and testing, this training does not necessarily make one an expert and even an expert does not have all the knowledge and skills appropriate to some particular situations or instruments. Questions of user qualifications should always be addressed when testing is being considered.

Lack of proper qualifications can lead to errors and subsequent harm to clients. Each professional is responsible for making judgments on this in each situation and cannot leave that responsibility either to client or to others in authority. It is incumbent upon the individual test user to obtain appropriate training or arrange for proper supervision and assistance when engaged in testing.

Qualifications for test users depend on four factors:
A. Purposes of Testing: Technically proper testing for ill-understood purposes may constitute misuse. Because the purposes of testing dictate how the results are used, qualifications of test users are needed beyond general testing competencies to interpret and apply data.
B. Characteristics of Tests: Understanding the nature and limitations of each instrument used is needed by test users.
C. Settings and Conditions of Test Use: Assessment of the quality and relevance of test user knowledge and skill to the situation is needed before deciding to test or to participate in a testing program.
D. Roles of Test Selectors, Administrators, Scorers and Interpretors: Test users must be engaged in only those testing activities for which their training and experience qualify them.

IV. *TEST SELECTION:* The selection of tests should be guided by information obtained from a careful analysis of the characteristics of the population to be tested; the knowledge, skills, abilities or attitudes to be assessed; the purposes for teaching; and the eventual use and interpretation of the test scores. Use of tests should also be guided by criteria for technical quality recommended by measurement professionals (i.e., the APA/AERA/NCME "Standards for Educational and Psychological Tests" and the APA/AERNNCME/AACD/ASHA "Code of Fair Testing Practices in Education").

A. Relate Validity to Usage.

B. Use Appropriate Tests.

C. Consider Technical Characteristics.

D. Employ User Participation in Test Selection: Actively involve everyone who will be using the assessments (administering, scoring, summarizing, interpreting, making decisions) as appropriate in the selection of tests so that they are congruent with local purposes, conditions, and uses.

VI. *TEST SCORING:* Accurate measurement of human performance necessitates adequate procedures for scoring the responses of examinees. These procedures must be audited as necessary to ensure consistency and accuracy of application.

A. Consider Accuracy and Interpretability: Select a test scoring process that maximizes accuracy and interpretability.

B. Rescore Samples: Routinely rescore samples of examinee responses to monitor the accuracy of the scoring process.

C. Screen Test Results: Screen reports of test results using personnel competent to recognize unreasonable or impossible scores.

D. Verify Scores and Norms: Verify the accuracy of computation of raw scores and conversion to normative scales prior to release of such information to examinees or users of test results.

E. Communicate Deviations: Report as part of the official record any deviation from normal conditions and examinee behaviors.

F. Label Results: Clearly label the date of test administration along with the scores.

VII. *TEST INTERPRETATION:* Test interpretation encompasses all the ways that meaning is assigned to the scores. Proper interpretation requires knowledge about the test which can be obtained by studying its manual and other materials along with current research literature with respect to its use; no one should undertake the interpretation of scores on any test without such study.

A. Consider Reliability: Reliability is important because it is a prerequisite to validity and because the degree to which a score may vary due to measurement error is an important factor in its interpretation.

　1. Estimate test stability using a reliability (or other appropriate) coefficient.

　2. Use the standard error of measurement to estimate the amount of variation due to random error in individual scores and to evaluate the precision of cut-scores in selection decisions.

　3. Consider, in relationship to the uses being made of the scores, variance components attributed to error in the reliability index.

　4. Evaluate reliability estimates with regard to factors that may have artificially raised or lowered them (e.g., test speededness, biases in population sampling).

　5. Distinguish indices of objectivity (i.e., scorer reliability) from test reliability.

B. Consider Validity: Proper test interpretation requires knowledge of the validity evidence available for the intended use of the test. Its validity for other uses is not relevant. Indeed, use of a measure for a purpose for which it was not designed may constitute misuse. The nature of the validity evidence required for a test depends upon its use.

　1. Use for Placement: Predictive validity is the usual basis for valid placement.

　　a. Obtain adequate information about the programs or institutions in which the client may be placed to judge the consequences of such placement.

　　b. Use all available evidence to infer the validity of an individual's score. A single test score should not be the sole basis for a placement or selection recommendation. Other items of information about an individual (e.g., teacher report, counselor opinion) frequently improve the likelihood that proper judgments and decisions will be made.

353

c. Consider validity for each alternative (i.e., each placement option) when interpreting test scores and other evidence.

d. Examine the possibility that a client's group membership (socioeconomic status, gender, subculture, etc.) may affect test performance and, consequently, validity.

e. Examine the probability of favorable outcomes for each possible placement before making recommendations.

f. Consider the possibility that outcomes favorable from an institutional point of view may differ from those that are favorable from the individual's point of view.

2. Use for Prediction: The relationship of the test scores to an independently developed criterion measure is the basis for predictive validity.

a. Consider the reliability and validity of the criterion measure(s) used.

b. Consider the validity of a measure in the context of other predictors available (i.e., does the test make a valid contribution to prediction beyond that provided by other measures).

c. Use cross-validation to judge the validity of prediction processes.

d. Consider the effect of labeling, stereotyping, and prejudging people (e.g., self-fulfilling prophecies that may result from labeling are usually undesirable).

e. If a statistically valid predictor lacks both construct and content validity, analyze the mechanism by which it operates to determine whether or not its predictive validity is spurious.

3. Use for Description: Comprehensiveness of information is fundamental to effective description, since no set of test scores completely describes an individual.

a. Clearly identify the domain assessed by any measure and the adequacy of the content sampling procedures used in developing items.

b. Clarify the dimensions being measured when multiple scores from a battery or inventory are used for description.

c. Distinguish characteristics that can be validated only empirically and those for which content specifications exist.

4. Use for Assessment of Growth: Assessment of growth or change requires valid tests as well as valid procedures for combining them.

a. Specifically evaluate the reliability of differences between scores as measures of change.

b. Establish the validities of the measures used to establish change in relation to one another as well as individually.

c. Consider comparability of intervals in scales used to assess change.

d. Assess potential for undesirable correlations of difference scores with the measures entering into their calculations (e.g., regression toward the mean).

e. Recognize the potential lack of comparability between norms or differences derived from norms and norms for differences derived from differences (i.e., mathematically derived norms for differences are not necessarily equivalent to norms based on distributions of actual differences).

5. Use for Program Evaluation: Assessments of group differences (between groups or within groups over time) are based on research designs which to varying degrees admit competing interpretations of the results.

a. Use procedures in the evaluation which ensure that no factors other than those being studied have major influence on the results (i.e., internal validity).

b. Use statistical procedures which are appropriate and have all assumptions met by the data being analyzed.

c. Evaluate the generalizability (external validity) of the results for different individuals, settings, tests, and variables.

C. Scores, Norms, and Related Technical Features: The result of scoring a test or subtest is usually a number called a raw score which by itself is not interpretable. Additional steps are needed to translate the number directly into either a verbal description (e.g., pass or fail) or a derived score (e.g., a standard score). Less than full understanding of these procedures is likely to produce errors in interpretation and ultimately in counseling or other uses.

1. Examine appropriate test materials (e.g., manuals, handbooks, users' guides, and technical reports) to identify the descriptions or derived scores produced and their unique characteristics.

    a. Know the operational procedures for translating raw scores into descriptions or derived scores.

    b. Know specific psychological or educational concepts or theories before interpreting the scores of tests based on them.

    c. Consider differential validity along with equating error when different tests, different test forms, or scores on the same test administered at different times are compared.

2. Clarify arbitrary standards used in interpretation (e.g., mastery or nonmastery for criterion-referenced tests).

    a. Recognize that when a score is interpreted based on a proportion score (e.g., percent correct), its elements are being given arbitrary weights.

    b. Recognize that the difficulty of a fixed standard (e.g., 80 percent right) varies widely and thus does not have the same meaning for different content areas and for different assessment methods.

    c. Report the number (or percentage) of items right in addition to the interpretation when it will help others understand the quality of the examinee's performance.

3. Employ derived scores based on norms which fit the needs of the current use of the test.

    a. Evaluate whether available norm groups are appropriate as part of the process of interpreting the scores of clients.

    b. Choose a score based on its intended use.

D. Administration and Scoring Variation: Stated criteria for score interpretation assume standard procedures for administering and scoring the test. Departures from standard conditions and procedures modify and often invalidate these criteria.

1. Evaluate unusual circumstances peculiar to the administration and scoring of the test.
   a. Examine reports from administrators, proctors, and scorers concerning irregularities or unusual conditions (e.g., excessive anxiety) for possible effects on test performance.
   b. Consider potential effects of examiner-examinee differences in ethnic and cultural background, attitudes, and values based on available relevant research.
   c. Consider any reports of examinee behavior indicating the responses were made on some basis other than that intended.
   d. Consider differences among clients in their reaction to instructions about guessing and scoring.
2. Evaluate scoring irregularities (e.g., machine scoring errors) and bias and judgment effects when subjective elements enter into scoring.

VIII. *COMMUNICATING TEST RESULTS:* The responsible counselor or other practitioner reports test data with a concern for the individual's need for information and the purposes of the information. There must also be protection of the right of the person tested to be informed about how the results will be used and what safeguards exist to prevent misuse (right to information) and about who will have access to the results (right to privacy).
   A. Decisions About Individuals: Where test data are used to enhance decisions about an individual, the practitioner's responsibilities include:
      1. Limitations on Communication:
         a. Inform the examinee of possible actions that may be taken by any person or agency who will be using the results.
         b. Limit access to users specifically authorized by the law or by the client.
         c. Obtain the consent of the examinee before using test results for any purpose other than those advanced prior to testing.
      2. Practitioner Communication Skills:

357

a. Develop the ability to interpret test results accurately before attempting to communicate them.

b. Develop appropriate communication skills, particularly with respect to concepts that are commonly misunderstood by the intended audience, before attempting to explain test results to clients, the public, or other recipients of the information.

3. Communication of Limitations of the Assessment:

a. Inform persons receiving test information that scores are not perfectly accurate and indicate the degree of inaccuracy in some way, such as by reporting score intervals.

b. Inform persons receiving test information of any circumstances that could have affected the validity or reliability of the results.

c. Inform persons receiving test information of any factors necessary to understand potential sources of bias for a given test result.

d. Communicate clearly that test data represent just one source of information and should rarely, if ever, be used alone for decision making.

4. Communication of Client Rights:

a. Provide test takers or their parents or guardians with information about any rights they may have to obtain test copies and/or their completed answer sheets, to retake tests, to have test rescored, or to cancel test scores.

b. Inform test takers or their parents or guardians about how long the test scores will remain on file along with the persons to whom, and circumstances under which, they may be released.

c. Describe the procedures test takers or their parents or guardians may use to register complaints or have problems resolved.

C

Excerpts From Standards for Educational and Psychological Testing

by
Committee to Develop Standards for Educational and
Psychological Testing
American Educational Research Association (AERA)
American Psychological Association (APA)
National Council on Measurement in Education (NCME)
1985

6. GENERAL PRINCIPLES OF TEST USE

Standard

6.1   Test users should evaluate the available written documentation on the validity and reliability of tests for the specific use intended.

6.2   When a test user makes a substantial change in test format, mode of administration, instructions, language, or content, the user should revalidate the use of the test for the changed conditions or have a ra-

tionale supporting the claim that additional validation is not necessary or possible.

6.3	When a test is to be used for a purpose for which it has not been previously validated, or for which there is not supported claim for validity, the user is responsible for providing evidence of validity.
6.4	Test users should accurately portray the relevance of a test to the assessment and decision-making process and should not use a test score to justify an evaluation, recommendation, or decision that has been largely on some other basis.
6.5	Test users should be alert to probable unintended consequences of test use and should attempt to avoid actions that have unintended negative consequences.
6.6	Responsibility for test use should be assumed by or delegated only to those individuals who have the training and experience necessary to handle this responsibility in a professional and technically adequate manner. Any special qualifications for test administration or interpretation noted in the manual should be met.
6.7	Test users should verify periodically that changes in populations of test takers, objectives of the testing process, or changes in available techniques have not made their current procedures inappropriate.
6.8	When test results are released to the news media, those responsible for releasing the results should provide information to help minimize the possibility of misinterpretation of the test results.
6.9	When a specific cut score is used to select, classify, or certify test takers, the method and rationale for setting that cut score, including any technical analyses, should be presented in a manual or report. When cut scores are based primarily on professional judgment, the qualifications of the judges also should be documented.

6.10   In educational, clinical, and counseling applications, test administrators and users should not attempt to evaluate test takers whose special characteristics—ages, handicapping conditions, or linguistic, generational, or cultural backgrounds—are outside the range of their academic training or supervised experience. A test user faced with a request to evaluate a test taker whose special characteristics are not within his or her range of professional experience should seek consultation regarding test selection, necessary modifications of testing procedures, and score interpretation from a professional who has had relevant experience.

9. TEST USE IN COUNSELING

Background   Uses of tests in counseling differ from most other test uses in that the test taker is viewed as the primary user of test results. Accumulated experience and research evidence have shown that standardized tests can be a valuable part of the counseling process. If used appropriately, tests can provide useful information to clients. However, because test takers do not typically have professional testing knowledge and skill, they need assistance and guidance from counselors and developers of interpretive materials, who have a unique role in facilitating the appropriate and effective use of tests.

Counselors are concerned with a range of assessment and guidance activities related to the life-span development and decision-making activities of individuals. Typical counseling concerns include the individual's personal and social skills, educational achievement, developed abilities, educational and vocational interests, occupational knowledge and preferences, occupational values, career development, study skills, coping and problem solving skills, and plans and values for other important roles in adult life, such as relationships with others, work, and parenting. These characteristics of the individual are assessed in counseling by a variety of formal and informal procedures—paper-and-pencil inventories, tests, work samples, interviews, card sorts, checklists, and so on. All such measures that yield classifications and raw or converted scores that result in suggestions for exploration or recommendations for action are considered tests and require evidence of reliability and validity.

Standard	
9.1	Testing for counseling should have as its primary goals the acquisition of relevant information and the reporting of that information with appropriate interpretations so that clients from diverse backgrounds can be assisted in making important educational, personal, and career decisions.
9.2	Counselors should review the interpretive materials provided to clients to evaluate accuracy, clarity, and usefulness of the materials. Manuals for tests or computer-based interpretations should be evaluated for evidence of the validity of specific interpretations made.
9.3	Counselors should review technical data and develop a rationale for the decision to use combined or separate norms for females and males in reports to test takers.
9.4	If a publisher packages tests that are to be used in combination for counseling, the counselor should review the manual for the rationale for the specific combination of tests used and the justification of the interpretive relationships among the scores.
9.5	Counselors should examine test manuals for any available information about how suggested or implied career options (i.e., the vocational program or occupation suggested by the highest scores on the test) are distributed for samples of the typical respon-

362

dents of each gender and relevant racial or ethnic groups.

9.6	Counselors should review the test materials that are provided to the test takers to be sure that such materials properly caution the test taker not to rely on the test scores solely when making life-planning decisions. The counselor should encourage the test taker to consider other relevant information on personal and social skills, values, interests, accomplishments, experiences, and on other test scores and observations.
9.7	Counselors should encourage multiple valid assessments of an individual's abilities, social skills, and interests.
9.8	Counselors should review the interpretire materials for ability or interest measures and for other tests that are used with people who are reentering employment or education or changing work settings for their appropriateness for these clients. A counselor should consider the age, experience, and background of the client as they are compared with the characteristics of the norm groups on which the scores are based.
9.9	Counselors should review interpretive materials for tests to ensure that case studies and examples are not limited to illustrations of people in traditional roles.

D

Names and Acronyms of Tests Commonly Used by Counselors and the Names and Addresses of Publishers of Those Tests

TESTS AND TEST PUBLISHERS

American College Testing Program, P.O. Box 168, Iowa City, IA 52243-0168. 319-337-1000.
Career Planning Program (CPP)
DISCOVER
PLAN (formerly P-ACT+)
Proficiency Examination Program (PEP)
Vocational Interest, Experience and Skill Assessment (VIESA)

American Guidance Service, P.O. Box 99, Circle Pines, MN 55014-1796. 800-328-2560.
Harrington-O'Shea Career Decision-Making System–Revised (CDM-R)
Kaufman Adolescent and Adult Intelligenct Test (KAIT)

Kaufman Assessment Battery for Children (K-ABC)
Kaufman Brief Intelligence Test (K-BIT)
Kaufman Functional Academic Skills Test (K-FAST)
Peabody Picture Vocabulary Test—Revised (PPVT-R)
Vineland Adaptive Behavior Scales

Chronicle Guidance Publications, Inc., Aurora Street, P.O. Box 1190, Moravia, NY 13118-1190. 800-622-7284; fax: 315-497-3359.
Career Maturity Inventory
Chronicle Career Quest

Consulting Psychologists Press, 3803 East Bayshore Road, P.O. Box 10096, Palo Alto, CA 94303-0979. 800-624-1765; fax: 415-969-8608.
Adjective Check List (ACL)
Adult Career Concerns Inventory (ACCI)
California Psychological Inventory (CPI)
Career Beliefs Inventory (CBI)
Career Development Inventory (CDI)
College Major Interest Inventory (CMII)
Coping Resources Inventory (CRI)
Coopersmith Self-Esteem Inventories
FIRO Awareness Scales (FIRO)
Guilford-Zimmerman Temperament Survey (GZTS)
Myers-Briggs Type Indicator (MBTI)
Salience Inventory (SI)
Strong Interest Inventory (SII)
Values Scale (VS)

CTB/McGraw-Hill, 20 Ryan Ranch Road, Monterey, CA 93940-5703. 800-538-9547; fax: 800-282-0266.
California Achievement Tests—5th Edition (CAT-5)
Kuder General Interest Survey (KGIS)
Kuder Occupational Interest Survey (KOIS)
Test of Cognitive Skills
Tests of Adult Basic Education (TABE)

Educational and Industrial Testing Service (EdITS), P.O. Box 7234, San Diego, CA 92167. 800-416-1666; fax: 619-226-1666.
    Career Occupational Preference System (COPS)
    Career Ability Placement Survey (CAPS)
    Career Orientation Placement and Evaluation Survey (COPES)
    Comrey Personality Scales (CPS)
    Eysenck Personality Questionnaire–Revised (EPQ-R)
    Profile of Mood States (POMS)
    Study Attitudes and Methods Survey (SAMS)

Educational and Psychological Consultants, 601 E. Broadway, Suite 301, Columbia, MD 65201. 573-875-6640.
    Personal Styles Inventory (PSI)

Educational Testing Service (ETS), Rosedale Road, Princeton, NJ 08541. 609-921-9000.
    Advanced Placement Program (APP)
    College Level Examination Program (CLEP)
    Graduate Record Examinations (GRE)
    LearningPlus
    Preliminary Scholastic Aptitude Test (PSAT)
    Scholastic Assessment Test I & II (SAT)
    System of Interactive Guidance and Information Plus More (SIGI PLUS)

Institute for Personality and Ability Testing Incorporated (IPAT), P.O. Box 1188, Champaign, IL 61824-1188. 800-225-4728.
    Children's Personality Questionnaire
    Clinical Analysis Questionnaire
    Culture-Fair Intelligence Tests
    Early School Personality Questionnaire
    High School Personality Questionnaire
    16 Personality Factor Questionnaire (16 PF)

Mind Garden, P.O. Box 60669, Palo Alto, CA 94306. 415-424-8493; fax: 415-424-4075.
    State-Trait Anxiety Inventory (STAI)
    State-Trait Anxiety Inventory for Children (STAI-C)
    Test Anxiety Inventory

University Residence Environment Scale (URES)
Ways of Coping Questionnaire

Multi-Health Systems Inc., 908 Niagra Falls Boulevard, North
Tonawanda, NY 14120-2060. 800-456-3003; fax: 416-424-1736.
   Children's Depression Inventory (CDI)
   Conners' Rating Scales (CRS)
   Coping Inventory for Stressful Situation (CISS)

National Computer Systems (NCS), P.O. Box 1416, Minneapolis,
MN 55440. 800-NCS-7271; fax: 612-939-5199.
   Alcohol Use Inventory
   Bender Visual Motor Gestalt Test
   Brief Symptom Inventory (BSI)
   Campbell-Hallam Team Development Survey
   Campbell Interest and Skill Survey (CISS)
   Campbell Leadership Index
   Campbell Organizational Survey
   Career Assessment Inventory (CAI)
   IDEAS: Interest Determination, Exploration and Assessment
      System
   Inventory for Counseling and Development (ICD)
   Millon Adolescent Clinical Inventory (MACI)
   Millon Adolescent Personality Inventory (MAPI)
   Millon Clinical Multiaxial Inventory–III (MCMI-III)
   Minnesota Multiphasic Personality Inventory–2 (MMPI-2)
   Minnesota Multiphasic Personality Inventory–Adolescent (MMPI-A)
   Quickview Social History
   Symptom Checklist–90–Revised (SCL-90-R)
   Temperament and Values Inventory (TVI)

Psychological Assessment Resources (PAR), P.O. Box 998, Odessa,
FL 33556. 800-331-TEST; fax: 800-727-9329.
   Adolescent Drinking Index (ADI)
   Bricklin Perceptual Scales (BPS)
   Career Attitudes and Strategies Inventory (CASI)
   Career Decision Scale (CDS)
   College Adjustment Scales (CAS)
   Eating Disorder Inventory–2 (EDI-2)

Employee Assistance Program Inventory (EAPI)
Interpersonal Adjective Scales (IAS)
Life Stressors and Social Inventory–Adult Form (LISRES-A)
Life Stressors and Social Inventory–Youth Form (LISRES-Y)
My Vocational Situation
NEO Personality Inventory-Revised (NEO PI-R)
Occupational Stress Inventory (OSI)
Personal Style Inventory (PSI)
Personality Assessment Inventory (PAI)
Position Classification Inventory (PCI)
Self-Directed Search (SDS)
State-Trait Anger Expression Inventory (STAXI)
Vocational Exploration and Insight Kit (VEIK)
Vocational Preference Inventory (VPI)

The Psychological Corporation (Psych. Corp.), (Including Harcourt Brace) P.O. Box 839954, San Antonio, TX 78283-3954. 800-228-0752; fax: 800-232-1223.
Adult Basic Learning Examination (ABLE)
Beck Anxiety Inventory
Beck Depression Inventory (BDI)
Career Interest Inventory
Differential Aptitude Tests (DAT)
Edwards Personal Preference Schedule (EPPS)
Metropolitan Achievement Test
Millon Index of Personality Styles (MIPS)
Mooney Problem Checklist
Ohio Vocational Interest Survey–II (OVIS-II)
Otis-Lennon School Ability Test (OLSAT)
Raven's Progressive Matrices
Rorschach Inkblot Test
Rotter Incomplete Sentences Blank
Stanford Achievement Test
Survey of Study Habits and Attitudes (SSHA)
Thematic Apperception Test (TAT)
Weschler Adult Intelligence Scale–Revised (WAIS-R)
Weschler Intelligence Scale for Children–III (WISC-III)
Weschler Preschool and Primary Scale of Intelligence–Revised (WPPSI-R)

Psychological Publications, Inc., 290 Conejo Ridge Avenue, Suite 100, Thousand Oaks, CA 91361-4928. 800-345-TEST.
  Family Relationship Inventory (FRI)
  Taylor-Johnson Temperament Analysis

Riverside Publishing Company, 8420 Bryn Mawr Avenue, Chicago, IL 60631. 800-323-9540; fax: 312-693-0325.
  Allport-Vernon-Lindzey Study of Values (AVL)
  Cognitive Abilities Test (COGAT)
  Henmon-Nelson Test of Mental Ability (Henmon-Nelson Test)
  Iowa Tests of Basic Skills (ITBS)
  Iowa Tests of Educational Development (ITED)
  Scales of Independent Behavior (SIB)
  Stanford-Binet Intelligence Scale (Stanford-Binet)
  Work Values Inventory
  Woodcock-Johnson Psycho-Educational Battery-Revised (WJ-R)

Scholastic Testing Service Incorporated, 480 Meyer Road, Bensenville, IL 60106-1617. 708-766-7150; fax: 708-766-8054.
  Kuhlman Anderson Tests
  Torrance Tests of Creative Thinking

Sigma Assessment Systems Inc., 1110 Military Street, P.O. Box 610984, Port Huron, MI 48061-0984. 800-265-1285; fax: 800-361-9411.
  Basic Personality Inventory (BPI)
  Jackson Personality Inventory–Revised (JPI-R)
  Jackson Vocational Interest Survey (JVIS)
  Multidimensional Aptitude Battery (MAB)
  Personality Research Form (PRF)
  Psychological Screening Inventory (PSI)

Slosson Educational Publications, Inc., P.O. Box 280, East Aurora, NY 14052. 800-828-4800; fax: 716-655-3840.
  Slosson Intelligence Test-Revised (SIT-R)

U.S. Department of Labor, Division of Testing, Employment and Testing Administration, 200 Constitution Avenue, N.W., Washington, D.C. 20213. 202-535-0157.

General Aptitude Test Battery (GATB)
USES Interest Inventory
USES Interest Check List

U.S. Military Entrance Processing Command (USMEPCOM), 2500 Green Bay Road, North Chicago, IL 60064-3094. 800-323-0513.
   Armed Services Vocational Aptitude Battery (ASVAB)

Western Psychological Services, 12031 Wilshire Boulevard, Los Angeles, CA 90025-1251. 800-648-8857; fax: 310-478-7838.
   Assessment of Career Decision Making (ACDM)
   Bender Visual-Motor Gestalt Test
   Marital Satisfaction Inventory (MSI)
   Personality Inventory for Youth (PIY)
   Personal Experience Inventory (PEI)
   Personal Experience Screening Questionnaire (PESQ)
   Shipley Institute of Living Scale
   Tennessee Self-Concept Scale (TSCS)
   The Vocational Interest Inventory—Revised (VII-R)

Wonderlic Personnel Test, Inc., 1509 N. Milwaukee Avenue, Libertyville, IL 60048-1380. 800-323-3742.
   Wonderlic Basic Skills Test
   Wonderlic Personnel Test

PERMISSIONS

We are grateful to the following authors and publishers for permission to reproduce sample items from the assessment instruments named below:

The Values Scale by Donald E. Super and Dorothy D. Nevill. Modified and reproduced by special permission of the publisher, Consulting Psychologists Press, Inc., Palo Alto, CA 94303. © 1985 by Consulting Psychologists Press, Inc. All rights reserved. Further reproduction is prohibited without the publisher's written consent.

SCL-90-R by L. R. Derogatis, professor and director of Division of Clinical Psychology, Hahnemann University Medical Center. Published by Clinical Psychometric Research, Baltimore, MD. © 1983.

Strong Interest Inventory of the Strong Vocational Interest Blanks Form T317. Modified and reproduced by special permission of the publisher, Consulting Psychologists Press, Inc., Palo Alto, CA 94303. © 1994 by Consulting Psychologists Press, Inc. All rights reserved. Further reproduction is prohibited without the publisher's written consent.

Adult Career Concerns Inventory by Donald E. Super, Albert S. Thompson, and Richard H. Lindeman. Modified and reproduced by special permission of the publisher, Consulting Psychologists Press, Inc., Palo Alto, CA 94303. © 1990 by Consulting Psychologists Press, Inc. All rights reserved. Further reproduction is prohibited without the publisher's written consent.

Minnesota Multiphasic Personality Inventory-2 (MMPI-2). © 1942, 1943 by the Regents of the University of Minnesota (renewed 1970, 1989. This booklet 1989).

My Vocational Situation by John L. Holland, Denise C. Daiger, and Paul G. Power. Modified and reproduced by special permission of the publisher, Consulting Psychologists Press, Inc., Palo Alto, CA 94303. © 1980 by Consulting Psychologists Press, Inc. All rights reserved. Further reproduction is prohibited without the publisher's written consent.

Career Attitudes and Strategies Inventory by J. L. Holland and G. D. Gottfredson. Adapted and reproduced by special permission of the publisher, Psychological Assessment Resources, Inc., Odessa, FL 33556. © 1994 by PAR, Inc. Further reproduction is prohibited without permission from PAR, Inc.

Eating Attitudes Test by David M. Garner and Paul E. Garfinkel. Published by Cambridge University Press. © 1979.

REFERENCES

Adams, D. P. (1993). *Stories we live by: Personal myths and the making of the self.* New York: Morrow.

Adler, T. (1990, April). Does the "new" MMPI beat the "classic"? *APA Monitor,* pp. 18–19.

Aiken, L. R. (1996). *Personality assessment methods and practices.* Seattle: Hogrefe & Huber.

Allport, G. W. (1937). *Personality: A psychological interpretation.* New York: Holt.

Allport, G. W., Vernon, P. E., & Lindzey, G. (1960). *Manual for study of values* (3rd ed.). Boston: Houghton-Mifflin.

Alpert, R., & Haber, R. N. (1960). Anxiety in academic achievement situations. *Journal of Abnormal and Social Psychology, 61,* 207–215.

Ambrosini, P. J., Bianchi, M. D., Metz, C., & Rabinovich, H. (1994). Evaluating clinical response of open nortriptyline pharmacotherapy in adolescent major depression. *Journal of Child and Adolescent Psychopharmacology, 4,* 233–244.

American Association for Counseling and Development, & Association for Measurement and Evaluation in Counseling and Development. (1989, May). The responsibilities of users of standardized tests. *Guidepost,* pp. 12–28.

American College Testing Program. (1985). *Proficiency examination program (PEP) technical handbook.* Iowa City, IA: Author.

American College Testing Program. (1988a). *Interim psychometric handbook for the 3rd edition ACT Career Planning Program.* Iowa City, IA: Author.

American College Testing Program. (1988b). *User's handbook for vocational interest, experience and skills assessment (levels 1 & 2)* (2nd ed.). Iowa City, IA: Author.

American College Testing Program. (1989a). The enhanced ACT assessment. Iowa City, IA: Author.

American College Testing Program. (1989b). *P-ACT plus program, technical manual.* Iowa City, IA: Author.

American College Testing Program (1994). *ACT Career Planning Program counselor's manual.* Author: Iowa City, IA.

375

American College Testing Program (1995). *Technical manual: Revised Unisex Edition of the ACT Interest Inventory (UNIACT).* Author: Iowa City, IA.

American Counseling Association. (1995). *Code of ethics and standards of practice.* Alexandria, VA: Author.

American Educational Research Association, American Psychological Association, & National Council on Measurement in Education. (1985). *Standards for educational and psychological testing.* Washington, DC: American Psychological Association.

American Psychiatric Association (1994). *Diagnostic and statistical manual of mental disorders* (4th ed.). Washington, D.C.

American Psychological Association. (1993). *Ethical principles of psychologists and code of conduct.* Washington, DC: Author.

American Rehabilitation Counseling Association, Commission on Rehabilitation Counselor Certification, & National Rehabilitation Counseling Association. (1995). *Code of professional ethics for rehabilitation counselors.* Chicago: Author.

American School Counselor Association. (1992). *Ethical standards for school counselors.* Alexandria, VA: Author.

Anastasi, A. (1988). *Psychological testing* (6th ed.). New York: Macmillan.

Anastasi, A. (1992). What counselors should know about the use and interpretation of psychological tests. *Journal of Counseling and Development, 70,* 610–615.

Anderson, W. (1995). Ethnic and cross-cultural differences on the MMPI-2. In J. C. Duckworth & W. P. Anderson (Eds.), *MMPI and MMPI-2 interpretation manual for clinicians (4th ed.).* Bristol, PA: Accelerated Development.

Arbona, C. (1990). Career counseling research and Hispanics: A review of the literature. *The Counseling Psychologist, 18,* 300–323.

Archer, R. P., Maruish, M., Imhof, E. A., & Piotrowski, C. (1991). Psychological test usage with adolescent clients: 1990 survey findings. *Professional Psychology: Research and Practice, 22,* 247–252.

Association of American Medical Colleges. (1994). *Medical College Admissions Test (MCAT) interpretative manual.* Washington, DC: Author.

Athelstan, G. T. (1966). *An exploratory investigation of response patterns associated with low profiles on the Strong Vocational Interest Blank for men.* Unpublished doctoral dissertation, University of Minnesota, Minneapolis.

Baker, R. W., & Siryk, B. (1984). Measuring adjustment to college. *Journal of Counseling Psychology, 31,* 179–189.

Barker, R. G. (1968). *Ecological psychology: Concepts and methods for studying the environment of human behavior.* Stanford, CA: Stanford University.

Barrios, B. A. (1988). On the changing nature of behavioral assessment. In A. S. Bellack & M. Hersen (Eds.), *Behavioral assessment: A practical handbook* (pp. 3–41). New York: Pergamon.

Barrons Educational Series. (1995). *Profiles of American colleges.* Hauppauge, NY: Author.

Bartling, H. C., & Hood, A. B. (1981). An 11-year follow-up of measured interest and vocational choice. *Journal of Counseling Psychology, 28,* 27–35.

Baxter-Magolda, M. B., & Porterfield, W. (1988). *Assessing intellectual development: A link between theory and practice.* Alexandria, VA: American College Personnel Association.

Beck, A. T., & Steer, R. A. (1993a). *Beck Anxiety Inventory manual.* San Antonio, TX: Psychological Corporation.

Beck, A. T., & Steer, R. A. (1993b). *Beck Depression Inventory manual.* San Antonio, TX: Psychological Corporation.

Benbow, C. P. (1988). Sex differences in mathematical reasoning ability in intellectually talented preadolescents: Their nature, effects and probable causes. *Behavioral and Brain Sciences, 11,* 169–232.

Bennett, G. K., Seashore, H. G., & Wesman, A. G. (1989). *Differential Aptitude Tests for Personnel and Career Assessment.* San Antonio, TX: Psychological Corporation.

Ben-Porath, Y. S., & Butcher, J. N. (1989). The comparability of MMPI and MMPI-2 scales and profiles. *Psychological Assessment, 1,* 345–347.

Benson, P. G. (1988). Review of the Minnesota Importance Questionnaire (MIQ). In J. T. Kapes & M. M. Mastie (Eds.), *A counselor's guide to career assessment instruments* (2nd ed.) (pp. 144–149). Alexandria, VA: National Career Development Association.

Berven, N. L. (1980). Psychometric assessment in rehabilitation. In B. Bolton and D. W. Cook (Eds.), *Rehabilitation client assessment* (pp. 46–64). Baltimore, MD: University Park.

Blocher, D. H. (1989). *Career actualization and life planning.* Denver, CO: Love.

Block, J. (1961). *The Q-Sort method in personality assessment and psychiatric research.* Palo Alto, CA: Consulting Psychologists.

Bogatz, G. A., & Greb, A. (1980). *School and college ability tests (SCAT Series 111) manual and technical report.* Monterey, CA: CTB/McGraw-Hill.

Bolles, R. N. (1990). *The quick job-hunting map for beginners* (Advanced version). Berkeley, CA: Ten Speed.

Bolles, R. N. (1991). *How to create a picture of your ideal job or next career: Advanced version (revised) of the quick job hunting (and career-changing) map.* Berkeley, CA: Ten Speed.

377

Bolles, R. N. (1996). *The 1996 what color is your parachute?: A practical manual for job-hunters and career-changers.* Berkeley, CA: Ten Speed.

Bolton, B. (1980). Second-order dimension of the Work Values Inventory (WVI). *Journal of Vocational Behavior, 17,* 33–40.

Bolton, B. (1994). Review of USES General Aptitude Test Battery (GATB)/ USES Interest Inventory (USES-II). In J. T. Kapes, M. M. Mastie, & E. A. Whitfield (Eds.), *A counselor's guide to career assessment instruments* (pp. 115–123). Alexandria, VA: National Career Development Association.

Borgen, F. H. (1985). Predicting career choices of able college men from occupational and basic interest scales of the Strong Vocational Interest Blank. *Journal of Counseling Psychology, 19,* 202–211.

Bradley, R. W. (1995). Book review: ETS Test Collection Catalog. *Measurement and Evaluation in Counseling and Development, 28,* 114–115.

Brandt, J. E., & Hood, A. B. (1968). Effect of personality adjustment on the predictive validity of the Strong Vocational Interest Blank. *Journal of Counseling Psychology, 15,* 547–551.

Brescio, W., & Fortune, J. C. (1989). Standardized testing of American Indian students. *The College Student Journal, 23,* 98–104.

Brickman, P., Rabinowitz, V. C., Karuza, J., Coates, D., Cohn, E., & Kidder, L. (1982). Models of helping and coping. *American Psychologist, 37,* 368–384.

Brown, D. (1995). A values-based approach to facilitating career transitions. *Career Development Quarterly, 44,* 4–11.

Brown, R. D. (1985). College Student Experiences Questionnaire. In J. V. Mitchell (Ed.), *Ninth mental measurement yearbook* (pp. 365–366). Lincoln, NE: University of Nebraska.

Brown, W. F., & Holtzman, W. H. (1984). *Survey of Study Habits and Attitudes manual.* San Antonio, TX: Psychological Corporation.

Bubenzer, D. L., Zimpfer, D. G., & Mahrle, C. L. (1990). Standardized individual appraisal in agency and private practice: A survey. *Journal of Mental Health Counseling, 12,* 51–66.

Buck, J. N., & Daniels, M. H. (1985). *Assessment of career decision making manual.* Los Angeles: Western Psychological Services.

Burns, D. D. (1989). *The feeling good handbook.* New York: Morrow.

Butcher, J. N. (1989a). *User's guide for the Minnesota report: Adult clinical system.* Minneapolis: National Computer System.

Butcher, J. N. (1989b). *User's guide for the Minnesota report: Personnel selection system.* Minneapolis: National Computer System.

Butcher, J. N. (1990a, August). Education level and MMPI-2 measured psychopathology: A case of negligible influence. *News and profiles: A newsletter of the MMPI-2 workshops and symposia,* p. 3.

Butcher, J. N. (1990b). *MMPI-2 in psychological treatment*. New York: Oxford University.

Butcher, J. N., Dahlstrom, W. G., Graham, J. R., Tellegen, A., & Kaemmer, B. (1989). *Minnesota Multiphasic Personality Inventory–2: Manual for administration and scoring*. Minneapolis: University of Minnesota.

Butcher, J. N., Graham, J. R., Williams, C. L., & Ben-Porath, Y. (1989). *Development and use of the MMPI-2 content scales*. Minneapolis: University of Minnesota.

Butcher, J. N., & Williams, C. L. (1992). *Essentials of MMPI-2 and MMPI-A interpretation*. Minneapolis: University of Minnesota.

Butcher, J. N., Williams, C. L., Graham, J. R., Archer, R. P., Tellegen, A., Ben-Porath, Y. S., & Kaemmer, B. (1992). *Minnesota Multiphasic Personality Inventory–Adolescent (MMPI-A): Manual for administration, scoring, and interpretation*. Minneapolis: University of Minnesota.

Campbell, D. P. (1972). *Handbook for the Strong Vocational Interest Blank*. Stanford, CA: Stanford University.

Campbell, D. P. (1993). A new integrated battery of psychological surveys. *Journal of Counseling & Development, 71,* 575–587.

Campbell, D. P., Hyne, S. A., & Nilsen, D. L. (1992). *Manual for the Campbell Interest and Skill Survey*. Minneapolis: National Computer System.

Canfield, A. A., & Canfield, J. S. (1988). *Canfield Learning Styles Inventory*. Los Angeles, CA: Western Psychological Services.

Carney, C. G., & Wells, C. F. (1995). *Discover the career within you* (4th ed.). Monterey, CA: Brooks/Cole.

Carroll, J. B. (1993). *Human cognitive abilities*. New York: Cambridge University.

Carter, M. M., & Barlow, D. H. (1995). Assessing the severely anxious patient. In J. N. Butcher (Ed.), *Clinical personality assessment: Practical approaches* (pp. 353–366). New York: Oxford.

Cass, J., & Birnbaum, M. (1995). *The comparative guide to American colleges: For students, parents, and counselors*. New York: Harper & Row.

Cattell, R. B. (1973). *Measuring intelligence with the Culture-Fair Test*. Champaign, IL: Institute of Personality and Ability Testing.

Cattell, R. B., Cattell, A. K., & Cattell, H. E. (1993). *The 16-PF test booklet*. Champaign, IL: Institute for Personality and Ability Testing.

Center on Education and Work. (1995). *Career skills workbook*. Madison, WI: University of Wisconsin: Author.

Centers for Disease Control and Prevention. (1994). Prevalence of disabilities and associated health conditions—United States, 1991–1972. *Journal of the American Medical Association, 272,* 1735–1737.

Cesnik, B. I., & Nixon, S. K. (1977). Counseling suicidal persons. In C. Zastrow & D. H. Chang (Eds.), *Personal problem solver* (pp. 275–289). Englewood Cliffs, NJ: Prentice-Hall.

379

Chaplin, W. F. (1985). Review of State-Trait Anxiety Inventory. In D. J. Keyser & R. C. Sweetland (Eds.), *Test critiques: Volume 2* (pp. 626–632). Kansas City, MO: Test Corporation of America.

Chartrand, J. M. (1991). The evolution of trait-and-factor career counseling: A person × environment fit approach. *Journal of Counseling & Development, 69*, 518–524.

Chickering, A. W., & Reisser, L. (1993). *Education and identity, 2nd edition.* San Francisco, CA: Jossey-Bass.

Cicchetti, D. V. (1994). Guidelines, criteria, and rules of thumb for evaluating normed and standardized assessment interests in psychology. *Psychological Assessment, 6*, 284–290.

Clark, K. E. (1961). *The vocational interests of nonprofessional men.* Minneapolis: University of Minnesota.

Clark, L. A., Watson, D., & Reynolds, S. (1995). Diagnosis and classificiation of psychopathology: Challenges to the current system and future directions. *Annual Review of Psychology, 46*, 121–153.

Cochran, L. (1983). Implicit versus explicit importance of career values in making a career decision. *Journal of Counseling Psychology, 30*, 188–193.

Code of Fair Testing Practices in Education. (1988). Washington, DC: Joint Committee on Testing Practices. (Available from Joint Committee on Testing Practices, American Psychological Association, 750 First Street, N.E., Washington, DC 20002).

Cohen, R. J., Swerdlik, M. E., & Smith, D. K. (1992). *Psychological testing and assessment.* Mountain View, CA: Mayfield.

College Board. (1991). *SAT.* New York: Author.

College Board. (1992a). *The new PSAT/NMSQT.* New York: Author.

College Board. (1992b). *The official handbook for the CLEP examinations.* New York: Author.

College Board. (1994a). *A guide to the advanced placement program.* New York: Author.

College Board. (1994b). *Balancing the SAT scales.* New York: Author.

College Entrance Examination Board. (1978). *Implementing the Career Skills Assessment Program: A handbook for effective program use.* New York: Author.

College Entrance Examination Board. (1988). *Working with the PSAT/ NMSQT: Preparation, administration, interpretation.* New York: Author.

College Entrance Examination Board. (1995). *The college handbook.* New York: Author.

Conoley, J. C., & Impara, J. C. (Eds.). (1995). *The Twelfth Mental Measurements Yearbook.* Lincoln, NE: Buros Institute of Mental Measurements.

Consulting Psychologists Press. (1996). *CPP 1996 catalog.* Palo Alto, CA: Author.

Cooper-Patrick, L., Crum, R. M., & Ford, D. E. (1994). Identifying suicidal ideation in general medical patients. *Journal of American Medical Association, 272,* 1757–1762.

Coopersmith, S. (1981). *Self-Esteem Inventories (SEI).* Palo Alto, CA: Consulting Psychologists.

Coopersmith, S., & Gilberts, R. (1982). *Professional manual: Behavioral Academic Self-Esteem (BASE), a rating scale.* Palo Alto, CA: Consulting Psychologists.

Costa, P. T., & McCrae, R. (1992). *NEO-PI-R professional manual.* Odessa, FL: Psychological Assessment Resources.

Costa, P. C., Jr., & Widiger, T. A. (Eds.). (1994). *Personality disorders and the five-factor model of personality.* Washington, DC: American Psychological Association.

Crace, R. K., & Brown, D. (1992). *The Life Values Inventory.* Minneapolis, MN: National Computer Systems.

Craig, J. R., & Craig, P. (1995). *The multidimensional model of the substance abuse disorders: Implications for assessment, intervention, rehabilitation, and research.* Kokomo, IN: Diagnostic Counseling Services.

Craighead, W. E., Curry, J. F., & Ilardi, S. S. (1995). Relationship of Children's Depression Inventory factors to major depression among adolescents. *Psychological Assessment, 7,* 171–176.

Crites, J. O. (1978). *Career Maturity Inventory: Theory and research handbook* (2nd ed.). Monterey, CA: CTB/McGraw-Hill.

Crites, J. O. (1993). *Career Mastery Inventory sourcebook.* Boulder, CO: Crites Career Consultants.

Cronbach, L. J. (1990). *Essentials of psychological testing* (5th ed.). New York: HarperCollins.

Cronbach, L. J., & Gleser, G. C. (1965). *Psychological tests and personnel decisions* (2nd ed.). Urbana: University of Illinois.

CTB/Macmillan/McGraw-Hill. (1992). *California Achievement Tests technical bulletin.* Monterey, CA: Author.

CTB/Macmillan/McGraw-Hill. (1993). *Test of Cognitive Skills test coordinator's handbook and guide to interpretation.* Monterey, CA: Author.

CTB/Macmillan/McGraw-Hill. (1994). *TABE examiner's manual.* Monterey, CA: Author.

Cummings, W. H. (1995). Age group differences and estimated frequencies of the Myers-Briggs Type Indicator preferences. *Measurement and Evaluation in Counseling and Development, 2,* 69–77.

Cyr, J. J., McKenna-Foley, J. M., & Peacock, E. (1985). Factor structure of the SCL90-R: Is there one? *Journal of Personality Assessment, 49,* 571–577.

Dahlstrom, W. G. (1993). Tests: Small samples, large consequences. *American Psychologist, 48,* 393–399.

Dana, R. H. (1993). *Multicultural assessment perspectives in professional psychology.* Boston: Allyn & Bacon.

Dance, K. A., & Neufeld, R. W. (1988). Aptitude-treatment interaction research in the clinical setting: A review of attempts to dispel the "patient uniformity" myth. *Psychological Bulletin, 104,* 192–113.

Dawis, R. V., & Lofquist, L. H. (1984). *A psychological theory of work adjustment: An individual-differences model and its applications.* Minneapolis: University of Minnesota.

Denzine, G. (1995). Psychometric resources for student affairs professionals. *Journal of College Student Development, 36,* 495–496.

Derogatis, L. R. (1979). *Sexual Functioning Inventory manual.* Baltimore, MD: Clinical Psychometric Research.

Derogatis, L. R. (1983). *Administration, scoring, and procedures manual–II for the SCL-90-R.* Baltimore, MD: Clinical Psychometric Research.

Derogatis, L. R. (1992). *The Brief Symptom Inventory (BSI) administration, scoring, and procedures manual–II.* Baltimore, MD: Clinical Psychometric Research.

Derogatis, L. R., & Melisaratos, N. (1983). The Brief Symptom Inventory: An introductory report. *Psychological Medicine, 13,* 595–605.

Diamond, R. J. (1989). *Psychiatric presentations of medical illness: An introduction for non-medical mental health professionals.* Unpublished manuscript, University of Wisconsin–Madison, Department of Psychiatry, Madison, WI.

Division of Educational Measurements, Council on Dental Education. (1994). *Dental Admission Testing Program (DATP) overview.* Chicago, IL: American Dental Association.

Dolliver, R. H. , Irvin, J. A., & Bigley, S. S. (1972). Twelve-year follow-up of the Strong Vocational Interest Blank. *Journal of Counseling Psychology, 19,* 212–217.

Dolliver, R. H., & Will, J. A. (1977). Ten-year follow-up of the Tyler Vocational Card Sort and the Strong Vocational Interest Blank. *Journal of Counseling Psychology, 24,* 48–54.

Dolliver, R. H., & Worthington, E. L., Jr. (1981). Concurrent validity of other-sex and same-sex twin Strong-Campbell Interest Inventory Occupational scales. *Journal of Counseling Psychology, 28,* 126–134.

Dorn, F. J. (1988). Utilizing social influence in career counseling: A case study. *Career Development Quarterly, 36,* 269–280.

Drasgow, J., & Carkhuff, R. R. (1964). Kuder neuropsychiatric keys before and after psychotherapy. *Journal of Counseling Psychology, 11,* 67–69.

Droege, R. C. (1987). The USES testing program. In B. Bolton (Ed.), *Handbook of measurement and evaluation in rehabilitation* (2nd ed.) (pp. 169–182). Baltimore, MD: Brookes.

Droege, R. C., & Hawk, J. (1977). Development of a U. S. Employment Service Interest Inventory. *Journal of Employment Counseling, 14,* 65–71.

Drummond, P. J. (1988). *Appraisal procedures for counselors and helping professionals.* Columbus, OH: Merrill.

Duckworth, J. (1990). The counseling approach to the use of testing. *The Counseling Psychologist, 18,* 198–204.

Duckworth, J. C., & Anderson, W. P. (1995). *MMPI & MMPI-2: Interpretation manual for counselors and clinicians* (4th ed.). Bristol, PA: Accelerated Development.

Dunn, R., Dunn, K., & Price, G. E. (1987). *Manual for the Learning Style Inventory (LSI).* Lawrence, KS: Price Systems.

D'Zurilla, T. J., & Goldfried, M. R. (1971). Problem solving and behavior modification. *Journal of Abnormal Psychology, 78,* 107–126.

Eagly, A. H. (1995). The science and politics of comparing women and men. *American Psychologist, 50,* 145–158.

EdITS. (1995). *COPSystem: A career awareness unit.* San Diego, CA: Author.

Educational Testing Service (1993). *The ETS Test Collection Catalog, Volume 1: Achievement tests and measurement devices* (2nd ed.). Phoenix, AZ: Oryx.

Educational Testing Service. (1994). *Guide to the use of the Graduate Record Examination program.* Princeton, NJ: Author.

Educational Testing Service. (1995). *Graduate Management Admission Test Bulletin.* Princeton, NJ: Author.

Elizur, D., Borg, I., Hunt, R., & Beck, I. M. (1991). The structure of work values: A cross cultural comparison. *Journal of Organizational Behavior, 12,* 21–38.

Elizur, D., & Tziner, A. (1977). Vocational needs, job rewards, and satisfaction: A canonical analysis. *Journal of Vocational Behavior, 10,* 205–211.

Ellis, A. (1988). *How to stubbornly refuse to make yourself miserable about anything—yes, anything!* Secaucus, NJ: Stuart.

Elmore, P. B., & Bradley, R. W. (1994). Review of Armed Services Vocational Aptitude Battery (ASVAB) Career Exploration Program. In J. T. Kapes, M. M. Mastie, & E. A. Whitfield (Eds.), *A counselor's guide to career assessment instruments* (pp. 71–77). Alexandria, VA: National Career Development Association.

Elmore, P. B., Ekstrom, R. B., & Diamond, E. E. (1993). Counselors' test use practices: indicators of the adequacy of measurement training. *Measurement and Evaluation in Counseling and Development, 26,* 116–124.

Elmore, P. B., Ekstrom, R. B., Diamond, E. E., & Whittaker, S. (1993). School counselors' test use patterns and practices. *The School Counselor, 41,* 73–80.

Endler, N. S., & Parker, J. D. A. (1994). Assessment of multidimensional coping task, emotion, and avoidance strategies. *Psychological Assessment, 6,* 50–60.

Engen, H. B., Lamb, R. R., & Prediger, D. J. (1982). Are secondary schools still using standardized tests? *Personnel and Guidance Journal, 60,* 287–290.

Epperson, D. L., Bushway, D. J., & Warman, R. E. (1983). Client self-terminations after one counseling session: Effects of problem recognition, counselor gender, and counselor experience. *Journal of Counseling Psychology, 30,* 307–315.

Epperson, D. L., & Hammond, D. C. (1981). Use of interest inventories with Native Americans: A case for local norms. *Journal of Counseling Psychology, 28,* 213–220.

Erikson, E. H. (1968). *Identity, youth and crisis.* New York: Norton.

Erwin, T. D. (1983). The Scale of Intellectual Development: Measuring Perry's scheme. *Journal of College Student Personnel, 24,* 6–12.

Ewing, J. A. (1984). Detecting alcoholism: The CAGE Questionnaire. *Journal of American Medical Association, 252,* 1905–1907.

Exner, J. E. (1986). *The Rorschach: A comprehensive system: Volume 1. Basic foundations* (2nd ed.) New York: Wiley.

Eyde, L. D., Moreland, K. L., Robertson, G. J., Primoff, E. S., & Most, R. B. (1988). *Executive Summary. Test user qualifications: A data-based approach to promoting good test use. Issues in Scientific Psychology.* Report of the Test User Qualifications Working Group of the Joint Committee on Testing Practices. Washington, DC: American Psychological Association.

Eyde, L. D., Robertson, G. J., Krug, S. E., Moreland, K. L., Robertson, A. G., Shewan, C. M., Harrison, P. L., Porch, B.E., Hammer, A. L., & Primoff, E. S. (1993). *Responsible test use: Case studies for assessing human behavior.* Washington, DC: American Psychological Association.

Eysenck, H. J., & Eysenck, S. B. G. (1993). *Manual: Eysenck Personality Questionnaire (junior & adult).* San Diego, CA: Educational and Industrial Testing Service.

Feldt, L. S., Forsyth, R. A., Ansley, T. N., & Alnot, S. D. (1994). *Teacher, administrator, and counselor manual, Iowa Tests OF Educational Development.* Chicago, IL: Riverside.

Figler, H. E. (1993). *PATH: A career workbook for liberal arts students* (3rd ed.). New York: Sulzburger & Graham.

Finn, S. E., & Tonsager, M. E. (1992). Therapeutic effects of providing

MMPI-2 test feedback to college students awaiting therapy. *Psychological Assessment, 4,* 278-287.

Fischer, J., & Corcoran, K. (1994). *Measures for clinical practice: A sourcebook* (2nd ed., Vols. 1-2). New York: Free Press.

Flowers, J. V., Booream, C. D., & Schwartz, B. (1993). Impact of computerized rapid assessment instruments on counselors and client outcome. *Computers in Human Services, 10,* 9–18.

Folkman, S., & Lazarus, R. S. (1988). *Manual for the Ways of Coping Questionnaire: Research edition.* Palo Alto, CA: Consulting Psychologists.

Fong, M. L. (1995). Assessment and DSM-IV diagnosis of personality disorders: A primer for counselors. *Journal of Counseling & Development, 73,* 635–639.

Fouad, N. A., & Arbona, C. (1994). Careers in a cultural context. *Career Development Quarterly, 43,* 96–104.

Fouad, N. A., Harmon, L. W., & Hansen, J. C. (1994). Cross-cultural use of the Strong. In L. W. Harmon, J. C. Hansen, F. H. Borgen, F. H., & A. L. Hammer (Eds.), *Strong Interest Inventory applications and technical guide.* Stanford, CA: Stanford University.

French, J. W. (1962). Effective anxiety on verbal and mathematical examination scores. *Educational and Psychological Measurement, 22,* 553–564.

Friedenberg, L. (1995). *Psychological testing: Design, analysis, and use.* Needham Heights, MA: Allyn & Bacon.

Fuqua, D. R., & Newman, J. L. (1994). Review of Campbell Interest and Skill Survey. In J. T. Kapes, M. M. Mastie, & E. A. Whitfield (Eds.), *A counselor's guide to career assessment instruments* (pp. 138–143). Alexandria, VA: National Career Development Association.

Garner, D. M. (1991). *Eating Disorder Inventory–2: Professional manual.* Odessa, FL: Psychological Assessment Resources.

Garner, D. M., & Garfinkel, P. E. (1979). The Eating Attitudes Test: An index of the symptoms of anorexia nervosa. *Psychological Medicine, 9,* 273–279.

Gay, G. H. (1990). Standardized tests: Irregularities in administration of tests affect test results. *Journal of Instructional Psychology, 17,* 93–103.

Geisinger, K. F. (1994). Cross-cultural normative assessment: Translation and adaptation issues influencing the normative interpretation of assessment instruments. *Psychological Assessment, 6,* 304–312.

Gellerman, S. W. (1963). Personnel testing: What the critics overlook. *Personnel, 40,* 18–26.

Giannetti, R. A. (1992). *User's guide for Quickview Social History–Clinical Version.* Minneapolis: National Computer Systems.

Goldberg, L. R. (1993). The structure of phenotypic personality traits. *American Psychologist, 48,* 26–34.

Goldenson, R. M. (Ed.). (1984). *Longman dictionary of psychology and psychiatry*. New York: Longman.

Goldfried, M. R. , Stricker, G., & Weiner, I. R. (1971). *Rorschach handbook of clinical and research applications*. Englewood Cliffs, NJ: Prentice-Hall.

Goldman, L. (1972). Tests and counseling: The marriage that failed. *Measurement and Evaluation in Guidance, 4,* 197–205.

Goldman, L. (1990). Qualitative assessment. *The Counseling Psychologist, 18,* 205–213.

Goldman, L. (1994). The marriage is over. . . for most of us. *Measurement and Evaluation in Counseling and Development, 26,* 217–218.

Goldman, R. D., Kaplan, R. M., & Platt, B. B. (1973). Sex differences in the relationship of attitudes toward technology to choice of field of study. *Journal of Counseling Psychology, 20,* 412–418.

Goodyear, R. K. (1990). Research on the effects of test interpretation: A review. *The Counseling Psychologist, 18,* 240–257.

Gottfredson, L. S. (1982). The sex fairness of unnormed interest inventories. *Vocational Guidance Quarterly, 31,* 128–132.

Gottfredson, G. D., & Holland, J. L. (1989). *Dictionary of Holland Occupational Codes* (2nd ed.). Odessa, FL: Psychological Assessment Resources.

Gottfredson, G. D., & Holland, J. L. (1991). *Manual for position classification inventory*. Odessa, FL: Psychological Assessment Resources.

Gough, H. G. (1987). *California Psychological Inventory administrator's guide*. Palo Alto, CA: Consulting Psychologists.

Gough, H. G., & Bradley, P. (1995). *CPI Manual*. Palo Alto, CA: Consulting Psychologists.

Graham, J. R. (1993). *MMPI-2: Assessing personality and psychopathology* (2nd ed.). New York: Oxford.

Graham, J. R., & Strenger, V. E. (1988). MMPI characteristics of alcoholics: A review. *Journal of Consulting & Clinical Psychology, 56,* 197–205.

Greenberg, L. (1994). *Interpretation manual for Test of Variables of Attention*. Circle Pines, MN: American Guidance Service.

Greene, R. L. (1987). Ethnicity and MMPI performance: A review. *Journal of Consulting and Clinical Psychology, 35,* 497–512.

Greene, R. L. (1991). *The MMPI-2/MMPI: An interpretive manual*. Boston: Allyn & Bacon.

Gross, M. L. (1962). *The brain watchers*. New York: New American Library.

Groth-Marnat, G. (1990). *Handbook of psychological assessment* (2nd ed.). New York: Van Nostrand Reinhold.

Guilford, J. P. (1959). *Personality*. New York: McGraw-Hill.

Hammen, C. L. (1980). Depression in college students: Beyond the Beck Depression Inventory. *Journal of Consulting and Clinical Psychology, 45,* 126–128.

Han, L., & Hoover, H. D. (1994). *Gender differences in achievement test scores.* Paper presented at annual meeting of the National Council on Measurement in Education, New Orleans, LA.

Haney, W. (1981). Validity, vaudeville, and values: A short history of social concerns over standardized testing. *American Psychologist, 36,* 1021–1034.

Hansen, J. C. (1994). Review of the Salience Inventory (SI). In J. T. Kapes, M. M. Mastie, & E. A. Whitfield (Eds.), *A counselor's guide to career assessment instruments* (3rd ed.) (pp. 231–235). Alexandria, VA: National Career Development Association.

Hansen, J. C., & Fouad, N. A. (1984). Translation and validation of the Spanish form of the Strong-Campbell Interest Inventory. *Measurement and Evaluation in Guidance, 16,* 192–197.

Hanson, G. R., Noeth, R. J., & Prediger, D. J. (1977). Validity of diverse procedures for reporting interest scores: An analysis of longitudinal data. *Journal of Counseling Psychology, 24,* 487–493.

Harcourt Brace. (1993). *MAT7 technical manual.* San Antonio, TX: Author.

Harcourt Brace. (1996). *Stanford 9 technical data report.* San Antonio, TX: Author.

Harmon, L. W. (1994). Review of the Career Decision Scale. In J. T. Kapes, M. M. Mastie, & E. A. Whitfield (Eds.), *A counselor's guide to career assessment instruments* (pp. 258–262). Alexandria, VA: National Career Development Association.

Harmon, L. W., Hansen, J. C., Borgen, F. H., & Hammer, A. L. (1994). *Strong Interest Inventory applications and technical guide.* Stanford, CA: Stanford University.

Harrell, A. V., & Wirtz, P. W. (1989). *Adolescent Drinking Index: Professional manual.* Odessa, FL: Psychological Assessment Resources.

Harren, V. A. (1979). A model of career decision making for college students. *Journal of Vocational Behavior, 14,* 119–133.

Harrington, T. F., & O'Shea, A. J. (1992). *Career Decision-Making System Revised.* Circle Pines, MN: American Guidance Service.

Harris, R., & Lingoes, J. (1968). *Subscales for the Minnesota Multiphasic Personality Inventory.* Mimeographed materials, The Langley Porter Clinic, 401 Parnassus Ave., San Francisco, CA 94143.

Hasin, D. S. (1991). Diagnostic interviews for assessment: Background, reliability, validity. *Alcohol Health and Research World, 15,* 293–302.

Hay, R. G. (1988). Screening counseling center clients for drinking problems. *Journal of College Student Development, 29,* 79–81.

Healy, C. C. (1990). Reforming career appraisals to meet the needs of clients in the 1990s. *The Counseling Psychologist, 18,* 214–226.

Healy, C. C. (1994). Review of Career Maturity Inventory. In J. T. Kapes, M. M. Mastie, & E. A. Whitfield (Eds.), *A counselor's guide to career assessment instruments* (pp. 268–272). Alexandria, VA: National Career Development Association.

Heck, E. J. (1991). Developing a screening questionnaire for problem drinking in college students. *Journal of American College Health, 39,* 227–234.

Helmes, E., & Reddon, J. R. (1993). A perspective on developments in assessing psychopathology: A critical review of the MMPI and MMPI-2. *Psychological Bulletin, 113,* 453–471.

Hendel, D. D., & Weiss, D. J. (1970). Individual inconsistency and reliability of measurement. *Educational and Psychological Measurement, 30,* 579–593.

Heppner, P. P. (1988). *The Problem-Solving Inventory: Manual.* Palo Alto, CA: Consulting Psychologists.

Heppner, P. P., Cook, S. W., Wright, D. M., & Johnson, W. C., Jr. (1995). Progress in resolving problems: A problem-focused style of coping. *Journal of Counseling Psychology, 42,* 279–293.

Heppner, P. P., & Krauskopf, C. J. (1987). An information-processing approach to personal problem solving. *The Counseling Psychologist, 15,* 371–447.

Herman, D. O. (1985). Review of Career Decision Scale. In J. V. Mitchell, Jr. (Ed.), *The ninth mental measurements yearbook* (pp. 270–271). Lincoln, NE: Buros Institute of Mental Measurements.

Hersh, J. B., Nazario, N. S., & Backus, B. A. (1983). DSM-III and the college mental health setting: The University of Massachusetts experience. *Journal of American College Health, 31,* 247–252.

Hinkle, J. S. (1994). Practitioners and cross-cultural assessment: A practical guide to information and training. *Measurement and Evaluation in Counseling and Development, 27,* 103–115.

Hoffman, J. A., & Weiss, B. (1986). A new system for conceptualizing college students' problems: Types of crises and the Inventory of Common Problems. *Journal of American College Health, 34,* 259–266.

Holland, J. L. (1985). *Making vocational choices: A theory of vocational personalities and work environments* (2nd ed.). Englewood Cliffs, NJ: Prentice-Hall.

Holland, J. L. (1992). *Vocational exploration and insight kit.* Odessa, FL: Psychological Assessment Resources.

Holland, J. L., Daiger, D. C., & Power, P. G. (1980). *My Vocational Situation.* Palo Alto, CA: Consulting Psychologists.

Holland, J. L., & Gottfredson, G. D. (1976). Using a typology of persons and environments to explain careers: Some extensions and clarifications. *The Counseling Psychologist, 6,* 20–29.

Holland, J. L., & Gottfredson, G. D. (1994a). *CASI: Career Attitudes and Strategies Inventory.* Odessa, FL: Psychological Assessment Resources.

Holland, J. L., & Gottfredson, G. D. (1994b, April). *Career Attitudes and Strategies Inventory: A new tool for counseling adults.* Program presented at the annual convention of the American Counseling Association, Minneapolis, MN.

Holland, J. L., Powell, A. B., & Fritzsche, B. A. (1994). *Self-Directed Search professional user's guide.* Odessa, FL: Psychological Assessment Resources.

Holmberg, K., Rosen, D., & Holland, J. L. (1990). *The leisure activities finder.* Odessa, FL: Psychological Assessment Resources.

Hood, A. B. (1968). *What type of college for what type of student?* Minneapolis: University of Minnesota.

Hood, A. B. (1986). *The Iowa Student Development Inventories.* Iowa City, IA: Hitech.

Hoover, H. D., & Han, L. (1995). *The effect of differential selection on gender differences in college admission test scores.* Paper presented at the annual meeting of the American Educational Research Association, San Francisco, CA.

Hoover, H. D., Hieronymus, A. N., Frisbie, D.A., & Dunbar, S. B. (1993). *Iowa Tests of Basic Skills, Manual for school administrators.* Chicago, IL: Riverside.

Horan, J. J. (1979). *Counseling for effective decision-making: A cognitive-behavioral perspective.* North Scituate, MA: Duxbury.

Horn, J. L., Wanberg, K. W., & Foster, F. M. (1986). *Alcohol Use Inventory.* Minneapolis, MN: National Computer System.

Hoyt, D. P. (1960). Measurement and prediction of the permanence of interests. In W. L. Layton (Ed.), *The Strong Vocational Interest Blank: Research and uses* (pp. 93–103). Minneapolis: University of Minnesota.

Jackson, D. N. (1984a). *Multidimensional aptitude battery manual.* Port Huron, MI: Research Psychologists.

Jackson, D. N. (1984b). *Personality research form manual.* Port Huron, MI: Research Psychologists.

Jackson, D. N. (1989). *Basic Personality Inventory manual.* Port Huron, MI: Sigma Assessment Systems.

Jackson, D. N. (1993). *Jackson Vocational Interest Survey manual* (2nd ed.). Port Huron, MI: Sigma Assessment Systems.

Jackson, D. N. (1994). *Jackson Personality Inventory–Revised Manual.* Port Huron, MI: Sigma Assessment Systems.

Jaeger, R. M. (1985). Graduate record examination—General test. In J. D. Mitchell, Jr. (Ed.), *The ninth mental measurements yearbook.* Lincoln, NE: University of Nebraska Press, pp. 624–626.

Jenkins, J. O., & Ramsey, G. A. (1991). Minorities. In M. Herson, A. E. Kazdin, & A. S. Bellack (Eds.), *The clinical psychology handbook*. New York: Pergamon.

Jepsen, D. A. (1994). Review of Jackson Vocational Interest Survey. In J. T. Kapes, M. M. Mastie, & E. A. Whitfield (Eds.), *A counselor's guide to career assessment instruments* (3rd ed.) (pp. 183–188). Alexandria, VA: National Career Development Association.

Jepsen, D. A., & Kapes, J. T. (1994). Sources of information about testing and career assessment. In J. T. Kapes, M. M. Mastie, & E. A. Whitfield (Eds.), *A counselor's guide to career assessment instruments* (3rd ed.) (pp. 423–434). Alexandria, VA: National Career Development Association.

Johansson, C. B. (1984). *Manual for Career Assessment Inventory* (2nd ed.). Minneapolis: National Computer Systems.

Johansson, C. B. (1986). *Manual for career assessment inventory: The enhanced version*. Minneapolis: National Computer Systems.

Johansson, C. B., & Campbell, D. P. (1971). Stability of the Strong Vocational Interest Blank for Men. *Journal of Applied Psychology, 55*, 34–36.

Johnson, R. W. (1977). Relationships between female and male interest scales for the same occupations. *Journal of Vocational Behavior, 11*, 239–252.

Johnson, R. W. (1987). Review of Assessment of Career Decision Making. *Journal of Counseling and Development, 65*, 567–569.

Johnson, R. W., Ellison, R. A., & Heikkinen, C. A. (1989). Psychological symptoms of counseling center clients. *Journal of Counseling Psychology, 36*, 110–114.

Johnson, R. W., Heikkinen, C. A., & Ellison, R. A. (1988). Frequency of symptoms indicating depression among counseling service clients. Unpublished raw data.

Johnson, R. W., & Johansson, C. B. (1972). Moderating effect of basic interests on predictive validity of SVIB Occupational scales. *Proceedings of the 80th Annual Convention of the American Psychological Association, 7,* 589–590.

Juhnke, G. A. (1992). An evaluation of a method of suicide assessment (Doctoral dissertation, Western Michigan University, 1991). *Dissertation Abstracts International, 52*, 3827A.

Kane, S. T. (1989). A review of the COPS Interest Inventory. *Journal of Counseling and Development, 67,* 361–363.

Kapes, J. T., Borman, C. A., & Frazier, N. (1989). An evaluation of the SIGI and DISCOVER microcomputer-based career guidance systems. *Measurement and Evaluation in Counseling and Development, 22*, 126–136.

Kapes, J. T., Mastie, M. M., & Whitfield, E. A. (1994). *A counselor's guide to career assessment instruments* (3rd ed.). Alexandria, VA: National Career Development Association.

Kapes, J. T., & Vansickle, T. R. (1992). Comparing paper-and-pencil and computer-based versions of the Harrington-O'Shea Career Decision-Making System. *Measurement and Evaluation in Counseling and Development, 25, 5–13.*

Kaufman, A. S., & Kaufman, N. L. (1983). *KABC: Kaufman Assessment Battery for Children, administration and scoring manual.* Circle Pines, MN: American Guidance Service.

Kaufman, A. S., & Kaufman, N. L. (1990). *Kaufman Brief Intelligence Test manual.* Circle Pines, MN: American Guidance Service.

Kaufman, A. S., & Kaufman, N. L. (1993). *Manual, Kaufman Adolescent and Adult Intelligence Test.* Circle Pines, MN: American Guidance Service.

Keesling, J. W., & Healy, C. C. (1988). Review of the USES General Aptitude Test Battery. In. J. T. Kapes & M. M. Mastie (Eds.), *A counselor's guide to career assessment instruments* (2nd ed.) (pp. 69–74). Alexandria, VA: National Career Development Association.

Kenrick, D. T., & Funder, D. C. (1988). Profiting from controversy: Lessons from the person-situation debate. *American Psychologist, 43, 23–34.*

Kessler, R. C., McGonagle, K. A., Zhao, S., Nelson, C. B., Hughes, M., Eshleman, S., Wittchen, H., & Kendler, K. S. (1994). Lifetime and 12-month prevalence of DSM-III-R psychiatric disorders in the United States. *Archives of General Psychiatry, 51, 8–19.*

Keyser, D. J., & Sweetland, R. C. (Eds.). (1984–1994). *Test critiques: Volumes I–X.* Kansas City, MO: Test Corp. of America.

Kiesler, D. J. (1987). *Checklist of Psychotherapy Transactions–Revised (CLOPT-R), Checklist of Interpersonal Transactions–Revised (CLOIT-R).* Richmond, VA: Virginia Commonwealth University.

Kinnier, R. T. (1987). Development of a values conflict resolution assessment. *Journal of Counseling Psychology, 34, 31–37.*

Kinnier, R. T. (1995). A reconceptualization of values clarification: Values conflict resolution. *Journal of Counseling & Development, 74, 18–24.*

Kiresuk, T. J., & Sherman, R. (1968). Goal attainment scaling: A general method for evaluating comprehensive mental health programs. *Community Mental Health Journal, 4, 443–453.*

Kishline, A. (1994). *Moderate drinking: The moderate management guide for people who want to reduce their drinking.* New York: Crown Trade.

Kitchener, K. S., & King, C. M. (1981). Reflective judgment: Concepts of justification and their relationship to age and education. *Journal of Applied Developmental Psychology, 2, 89–116.*

Kitchens, J. M. (1994). Does this patient have an alcohol problem? *Journal of American Medical Association, 272, 1782–1787.*

Klerman, G. (1987). Clinical epidemiology of suicide. *Journal of Clinical Psychiatry, 48, 33–38.*

Knapp-Lee, L., Knapp, L., & Knapp, R. (1990). A complete career guidance program: The COPSystem. In C. E. Watkins, Jr., and V. L. Campbell (Eds.), *Testing in counseling practice* (pp. 241–284). Hillsdale, NJ: Erlbaum.

Kohlberg, L. (1969). Stage and sequence: The cognitive developmental approach to socialization. In D. Goslin (Ed.), *Handbook of socialization theory and research* (pp. 347–480). Chicago: Rand McNally.

Kohlberg, L. (1971). Stages of moral development. In C. M. Beck, V. S. Crittenden, & E. B. Sullivan (Eds.), *Moral education* (pp. 23–92). Toronto: University of Toronto.

Kolb, D. A. (1985). *Learning Style Inventory.* Boston: McBer.

Kovacs, M. (1992). *Children's Depression Inventory manual.* North Tonawanda, NY: Multi-Health Systems.

Kramer, J. J., & Conoley, J. C. (Eds.). (1992). *Eleventh Mental Measurements Yearbook.* Lincoln, NE: Buros Institute of Mental Measurements.

Kroeger, O., & Thuesen, S. M. (1988). *Type talk.* New York: Delacorte.

Krug, S. E. (Ed.). (1993). *Psychware sourcebook: A reference guide to computer-based products for behavioral assessment in psychology, education, and business* (4th ed.). Kansas City, MO: Test Corporation of America.

Krumboltz, J. D. (1991). *Manual for the Career Beliefs Inventory.* Palo Alto, CA: Consulting Psychologists.

Krumboltz, J. D. (1994). The Career Beliefs Inventory. *Journal of Counseling and Development, 72,* 424–428.

Krumboltz, J. D., Blando, J. A., Kim, H., & Reikowski, D. J. (1994). Embedding work values in stories. *Journal of Counseling and Development, 73,* 57–62.

Kuder, F. (1988). *General manual for Kuder General Interest Survey, Form E.* Monterey, CA: CTB/McGraw-Hill.

Kuder, F., & Zytowski, D. G. (1991). *Kuder Occupational Interest Survey general manual.* Monterey, CA: CTB/McGraw-Hill.

LaBruzza, A. L., & Mendez-Villarrubia, J. M. (1994). *Using DSM-IV: A clinician's guide to psychiatric diagnosis.* Northvale, NJ: Jason Aronson.

Lachar, B. (1992). Review of Minnesota Importance Questionnaire. In J. J. Kramer & J. C. Conoley, *Eleventh Mental Measurements Yearbook* (pp. 542–544). Lincoln, NE: Buros Institute of Mental Measurements.

Lachar, D., & Wrobel, T. A. (1979). Validating clinicians' hunches: Construction of a new MMPI critical item set. *Journal of Consulting and Clinical Psychology, 47,* 277–284.

Laing, J., & Farmer, M. (1984). *Use qf the ACT assessment by examinees with disabilities.* Research Report #84. Iowa City, IA: American College Testing Program.

Lamb, R. R. (1974). *Concurrent validity of the American College Testing Interest Inventory for minority group members.* Unpublished doctoral dissertation, University of Iowa.

Lambe, T. A., Nelson, M. J., & French, J. L. (1973). *Manual for the Henman-Nelson Test of Mental Ability.* Chicago: Riverside.

Lampe, R. E. (1985). Self-scoring accuracy of the Kuder General Interest Survey. *The School Counselor, 32,* 319–324.

Lanier, C. W. (1994). *ACT composite scores of re-tested students.* Iowa City, IA: American College Testing Program.

Lanyon, R. I. (1978). *Manual for Psychological Screening Inventory.* Port Huron, MI: Research Psychologists.

Law School Admission Council. (1995). *LSAT/LSDAS registration and information book.* Newton, PA: Author.

Lawrence, G. (1992). *People types and tiger stripes* (3rd edition). Gainesville, FL: Center for the Application of Type.

Layton, W. L. (1992). Review of Minnesota Importance Questionnaire. In J. J. Kramer & J. C. Conoley, *Eleventh Mental Measurements Yearbook* (pp. 544–546). Lincoln, NE: Buros Institute of Mental Measurements.

LeBold, W. K., & Shell, K. D. (1986). *Purdue Interest Questionnaire: A brief interpretive guide for the revision.* West Lafayette, IN: Purdue University, Department of Freshman Engineering.

Lewak, R. W., Marks, P. A., & Nelson, G. E. (1990). *Therapist guide to the MMPI & MMPI-2: Providing feedback and treatment.* Muncie, IN: Accerlerated Development.

Lewin, K. (1935). *A dynamic theory of personality: Selected papers.* New York: McGraw-Hill.

Locke, D. C. (1988). Review of the Career Development Inventory. In J. T. Kapes & M. M. Mastie (Eds.), *A counselor's guide to career assessment instruments* (2nd ed.) (pp. 175–179). Alexandria, VA: National Career Development Association.

Lonner, W. J., & Ibrahim, F. A. (1985). Assessment in cross-cultural counseling. *The Counseling Psychologist, 13,* 299–332.

Lonner, W. J., & Sundberg, N. D. (1987). Assessment in cross-cultural counseling and therapy. In P. Pederson, *Handbook of cross-cultural counseling and therapy* (pp. 199–205). New York: Praeger.

LoVerde, M., McMahon, B. T., & Morris, G. W. (1992). Employment testing and evaluation. In N. Hablutzel, & B. T. McMahon (Eds.), *The Americans With Disabilities Act: Access and accommodations* (pp. 79–88). Orlando, FL: Deutsch.

Lustman, P. J., Sowa, C. J., & O'Hara, D. J. (1984). Factors influencing college student health: Development of the Psychological Distress Inventory. *Journal of Counseling Psychology, 31,* 28–35.

Maccoby, E. E., & Jacklin, C. N. (1974). *The psychology of sex differences.* Stanford, CA: United.

Maloney, M. P.,& Ward, M. P. (1976). *Psychological assessment: A conceptual approach*. New York: Oxford University.

Maris, R. W. (1992). The relationship of nonfatal suicide attempts to completed suicides. In R. W. Maris, A. L. Berman, J. T. Maltsberger, & R. I. Yufit (Eds.), *Assessment and prediction of suicide* (pp. 362–380). New York: Guilford.

Marks, I. M., & Mathews, A. M. (1978). Brief standard self-rating for phobic patients. *Behavior Research and Therapy, 17,* 263–267.

Marlatt, G. A., & Miller, W. R. (1984). *Comprehensive drinking profile*. Odessa, FL: Psychological Assessment Resources.

Maze, M. (1991). *The enhanced guide for occupational exploration*. Menomonie, WI: University of Wisconsin–Stout.

McAllister, L. W. (1996). *A practical guide to CPI interpretation* (3rd ed.) Palo Alto, CA: Consulting Psychologists.

McArthur, C. (1954). Long-term validity of the Strong Interest Test in two subcultures. *Journal of Applied Psychology, 38,* 346–354.

McArthur, C., & Stevens, L. B. (1955). The validation of expressed interests as compared with inventoried interests: A fourteen year follow-up. *Journal of Applied Psychology, 39,* 184–189.

McCrae, R. R., & Costa, P. T. (1986). Clinical assessment can benefit from recent advances in personality psychology. *American Psychologist, 41,* 1001–1003.

McDivitt, P. J. (1994). Using portfolios for career assessment. In J. T. Kapes, M. M. Mastie, & E. A. Whitfield (Eds.), *A counselor's guide to career assessment instruments* (pp. 423–434). Alexandria, VA: National Career Development Association.

McGoldrick, M., & Gerson, R. (1985). *Genograms in family assessment*. New York: Norton.

Mehrens, W. A. (1988). Review of Vocational Interest, Experience, and Skill Assessment (VIESA). In J. T. Kapes, & M. M. Mastie (Eds.), *A counselor's guide to career assessment instruments* (pp. 132–136). Alexandria, VA: National Career Development Association.

Mehrens, W. A. (1994). Review of Kuder General Interest Survey, Form E (KGIS). In J. T. Kapes, M. M. Mastie, & E. A. Whitfield (Eds.), *A counselor's guide to career assessment instruments* (pp. 189–193). Alexandria, VA: National Career Development Association.

Mendelsohn, G. A., & Kirk, B. A. (1962). Personality differences not used. *Journal of Counseling Psychology, 9,* 341–346.

Messick, S. (1980). Test validity and the ethics of assessment. *American Psychologist, 35,* 1012–1027.

Messick, S. (1981). The controversy over coaching: Issues of effectiveness and equity. In B. F. Green (Ed.), *Issues in testing: Coaching, disclosure, and ethnic bias* (pp. 21–53). San Francisco: Jossey-Bass.

Michael, W. B., Michael, J. J., & Zimmerman, W. S. (1980). *Study attitudes and methods survey, manual of instructions and interpretations*. San Diego, CA: EdITS.

Miller, W. R. (1976). Alcoholism scales and objective assessment methods: A review. *Psychological Bulletin, 83*, 649–674.

Miller, S. D., & Berg, I. K. (1995). *The miracle method: A radically new approach to problem drinking*. New York: Norton.

Miller, W. R., & Munoz, R. F. (1982). *How to control your drinking: A practical guide to responsible drinking* (Rev. ed.). Albuquerque, NM: University of New Mexico.

Millon, T. (1969). *Modern psychopathology*. Philadelphia: Saunders.

Millon, T. (1981). *Disorders of personality: DSM-IV, axis II*. New York: Wiley.

Millon, T. (1990). *Toward a new personology: An evolutionary model*. New York: Wiley-Interscience.

Millon, T. (1995). *Millon Index of Personality Styles Manual*. San Antonio, TX: Psychological Corporation.

Millon, T., & Davis, R. D. (1993). The Millon Adolescent Personality Inventory and the Millon Adolescent Clinical Inventory. *Journal of Counseling & Development, 71*, 570–574.

Millon, T., Millon, C., & Davis, R. (1994). *Millon Clinical Multiaxial Inventory-III: Manual for MCMI-III*. Minneapolis: National Computer Systems.

Mintz, L. B., & Betz, N. E. (1988). Prevalence and correlates of eating disordered behaviors among undergraduate women. *Journal of Counseling Psychology, 35*, 463–471.

Mitchell, L. K., & Krumboltz, J. D. (1987). The effects of cognitive restructuring and decision-making training on career indecision. *Journal of Counseling and Development, 66*, 171–174.

Moore, W. S. (1988). *The Measure of Intellectual Development: An instrument manual*. Farmville, VA: Center for the Study of Intellectual Development.

Moos, R. H. (1974). *The social climate scales: An overview*. Palo Alto, CA: Consulting Psychologists.

Moos, R. H. (1976). *The human context: Environmental determinants of behavior*. New York: Wiley.

Moos, R. H., & Moos, B. S. (1986). *Family Environment Scale manual*. Palo Alto, CA: Consulting Psychologists.

Moos, R. H., & Moos, B.S. (1994a). *Life Stressors and Social Resources Inventory–Adult Form*. Odessa, FL: Psychological Assessment Resources.

Moos, R. H., & Moos, B.S. (1994b). *Life Stressors and Social Resources Inventory–Youth Form*. Odessa, FL: Psychological Assessment Resources.

Moreland, K. L. (1985). Validation of computer-based test interpretations: Problems and prospects. *Journal of Consulting and Clinical Psychology, 53*, 816–825.

Moreland, K. L., Eyde, L. D., Robertson, G. J., Primoff, E. S., & Most, R. B. (1995). Assessment of test user qualifications: A research-based measurement procedure. *American Psychologist, 50,* 14–23.

Morey, L. (1991). *Personality Assessment Inventory: Professional manual.* Odessa, FL: Psychological Assessment Resources.

Morrison, J. (1995a). *DSM-IV made easy: The clinician's guide to diagnosis.* New York: Guilford.

Morrison, J. (1995b). *The first interview: Revised for DSM-IV.* New York: Guilford.

Muhs, W. F., Popp, G. E., & Patterson, H. F. (1979). The Mexican-American in higher education: Implications for educators. *Personnel and Guidance Journal, 58,* 20–24.

Murphy, G. (1985). Suicide and attempted suicide. In R. Michels (Ed.), *Psychiatry* (pp. 1–17). Philadelphia: Lippincott.

Murphy, L. L., Conoley, J. C., & Impara, J. C. (Eds.). (1994). *Tests in Print IV* (Vols. 1–2). Lincoln, NE: Buros Institute of Mental Measurements.

Murray, H. A. (1938). *Explorations in personality.* New York: Oxford University.

Murray, H. A. (1943). *Thematic Apperception Test manual.* Cambridge, MA: Harvard University.

Myers, I. B. (1980). *Introduction to type.* Palo Alto, CA: Consulting Psychologists.

Myers, I. B., & McCaulley, M. H. (1985). *Manual: A guide to the development and use of the Myers-Briggs Type Indicator.* Palo Alto, CA: Consulting Psychologists.

Myers, I. B., & Myers, P. B. (1993). *Gifts differing.* Palo Alto, CA: Consulting Psychologist.

Myers, R. A., Thompson, A. S., Lindeman, R. H., Super, D. E., Patrick, T. A., & Friel, T. W. (1972). *The Educational and Career Exploration System: A two-year field trial.* New York: Teachers College, Columbia University.

Naugle, R. I., Chelune, G. J., & Tucker, G. D. (1993). Validity of the Kaufman Brief Intelligence Test. *Psychological Assessment, 5,* 182–186.

Naylor, F. D., & Krumboltz, J. D. (1994). The independence of aptitudes, interests, and beliefs. *Career Development Quarterly, 43,* 152–160.

Neimeyer, G. J. (1989). Applications of repertory grid technique to vocational assessment. *Journal of Counseling and Development, 67,* 585–589.

Neisser, U., Boodoo, G., Bouchardt, T. J., Boykin, A. W., Brody, N., Ceci, S. J., Halpern, D. F., Loehlin, J. C., Perloff, R., Sternberg, R. J., & Urbina, S. (1996). Intelligence: Knowns and unknowns. *American Psychologist, 51,* 77–101.

Nevill, D. D., & Super, D. E. (1986a). *Manual for the Salience Inventory.* Palo Alto, CA: Consulting Psychologists.

396

Nevill, D. D., & Super, D. E. (1986b). *Manual for the Values Scale.* Palo Alto, CA: Consulting Psychologists.

Nguyen, T. D., Attkisson, C. C., & Stegner, B. L. (1983). Assessment of patient satisfaction: Development and refinement of a service evaluation questionnaire. *Evaluation and Program Planning, 6,* 299–314.

Norris, L., & Cochran, D. J. (1977). The SIGI prediction system: Predicting college grades with and without tests. *Measurement and Evaluation in Guidance, 10,* 134–140.

Novy, D. M., Nelson, D. V., Goodwin, J., & Rowzec, R. D. (1993). Psychometric comparability of the State-Trait Anxiety Inventory for different ethnic populations. *Psychological Assessment, 5,* 343–349.

Osgood, C. E., Suci, G. J., & Tannenbaum, P. H. (1957). *The measurement of meaning.* Urbana, IL: University of Illinois.

Osipow, S. H. (1987). *Manual for the Career Decision Scale* (rev. ed.). Odessa, FL: Psychological Assessment Resources.

Otis, A. S., & Lennon, R. T. (1989). *Otis-Lennon School Ability Test, sixth edition, preliminary technical manual.* San Antonio, TX: Psychological Corporation.

Owens, W. A. (1983). Background data. In M. D. Dunnette (Ed.), *Handbook of industrial and organizational psychology* (pp. 609–644). New York: Wiley.

Pace, C. R. (1987). *CSEQ: Test manual and norms.* University of California, Los Angeles: Center for the Study of Evaluations.

Paniagua, F. A. (1994). *Assessing and treating culturally diverse clients.* Thousand Oaks, CA: Sage.

Paritzky, R. S., & Magoon, T. M. (1982). Goal attainment scaling models for assessing group counseling. *Personnel and Guidance Journal, 60,* 381–384.

Parker, J., & Hood, A. B. (1986). The Parker Cognitive Development Inventory. In A. B. Hood, (Ed.), *The Iowa Student Development Inventories* (pp. 1–26). Iowa City, IA: Hitech.

Parks, C. W., Jr., & Hollon, S. D. (1988). Cognitive assessment. In A. S. Bellack & M. Hersen (Eds.), *Behavioral assessment: A practical handbook* (pp. 161–212). New York: Pergamon.

Parsons, F. (1909). *Choosing a vacation.* Boston: Houghton-Mifflin.

Patterson, W. M. , Dohn, H. H. , Bird, J., & Patterson, G. A. (1983). Evaluation of suicidal patients: The SAD PERSONS Scale. *Psychosomatics, 24,* 343–349.

Pekarik, G. (1988). Relation of counselor identification of client problem description to continuance in a behavioral weight loss program. *Journal of Counseling Psychology, 35,* 66–70.

Perry, W. (1970). *Forms of intellectual and ethical development in college years: A scheme.* New York: Holt, Rinehart & Winston.

Peterson, C., & Austin, J. T. (1985). Review of Coopersmith Self-Esteem Inventories. In J. V. Mitchell, Jr. (Ed.), *The ninth mental measurements yearbook* (pp. 396–397). Lincoln, NE: Buros Institute of Mental Measurements.

Piaget, J. (1965). *The moral judgment of the child.* New York: Free Press.

Piers, E. B. (1984). *Piers-Harris Children's Self-Concept Scale, Revised manual.* Los Angeles, CA: Western Psychological Services.

Pittenger, D. J. (1993). The utility of the Myers-Briggs Type Indicator. *Review of Educational Research, 63,* 467–488.

Plake, B. S., Conoley, J. C., Kramer, J. J., & Murphy, L. U. (1991). The Buros Institute of Mental Measurements: Commitment to the tradition of excellence. *Journal of Counseling and Development, 69,* 449–455.

Plake, B. S., & Parker, C. S. (1982). The development and validation of a revised version of the Mathematics Anxiety Rating Scale. *Educational and Psychological Measurement, 42,* 551–557.

Ponterotto, J. G. , Pace, T. M., & Kavan, M. G. (1989). A counselor's guide to the assessment of depression. *Journal of Counseling and Development, 67,* 301–309.

Porteus, M. A. (1985). *Porteus Problem Checklist.* Windsor, England: NFER-Nelson.

Prediger, D. (Ed.). (1972). Symposium: Tests and counseling—The marriage that failed? *Measurement and Evaluation in Guidance, 5,* 395–429.

Prediger, D. J. (1988). Review of Assessment of Career Decision Making. In J. T. Kapes & M. M. Mastie (Eds.), *A counselor's guide to career assessment instruments* (2nd ed.) (pp. 165–169). Alexandria, VA: National Career Development Association.

Prediger, D. J. (Ed.). (1993). *Multicultural assessment standards: A compilation for counselors.* Alexandria, VA: American Counseling Association.

Prediger, D. J. (1994a). Multicultural assessment standards: A compilation for counselors. *Measurement and Evaluation in Counseling and Development, 27,* 68–73.

Prediger, D. J. (1994b). Tests and counseling: The marriage that prevailed. *Measurement and Evaluation in Counseling and Development, 26,* 227–234.

Prediger, D. J., & Swaney, K. B. (1985). *Role of counselee experiences in the interpretation of vocational interest scores.* (ACT Research Report No. 86). Iowa City, IA: American College Testing Program.

Prediger, D. J., & Swaney, K. B. (1992). *Career counseling validity of DISCOVER's job cluster scales for the revised ASVAB score report (Report No. 92-2).* Iowa City, IA: American College Testing Program.

Prochaska, J. O., DiClemente, C. C., & Norcross, J. C. (1992). In search of how people change: Applications to addictive behaviors. *American Psychologist, 47,* 1102–1114.

Provost, J. A., & Anchors, S. (1987). *Applications of the Myers-Briggs Type Indicator in higher education.* Palo Alto, CA: Consulting Psychologists.

Pryor, R. G. L., & Taylor, N. B. (1986). On combining scores from interest and value measures for counseling. *Vocational Guidance Quarterly, 34,* 178–187.

Psychological Corporation. (1987). *Miller Analogies Test manual.* San Antonio, TX: Author.

Psychological Corporation (1992). *Differential Aptitude Tests manual* (5th ed.). San Antonio, TX: Author.

Psychological Corporation. (1994). *Miller Analogies Test candidate information booklet.* San Antonio: TX: Author.

Pyle, K. R. (1984). Career counseling and computers: Where is the creativity? *Journal of Counseling & Development, 63,* 141–144.

Randahl, G. J., Hansen, J. C., & Haverkamp, B. E. (1993). Instrumental behaviors following test administration and interpretation: Exploration validity of the Strong Interest Inventory. *Journal of Counseling & Development, 71,* 435–439.

Raths, L., Harmin, M., & Simon, S. (1978). *Values and teaching: Working with values in the classroom* (2nd ed.). Columbus, OH: Merrill.

Raven, J. C. , Court, J. H., & Raven, J. (1993). *Manual for Raven's Progressive Matrices and Vocabulary Scales.* San Antonio, TX: Psychological Corporation.

Rayman, J. R. (1976). Sex and the Single Interest Inventory: The empirical validation of sex-balanced interest inventory items. *Journal of Counseling Psychology, 23,* 239–246.

Regier, D. A., Boyd, J. H., Burke, J. D., Rae, D. S., Myers, J. K., Kramer, M., Robins, L. N., George, L. K., Karno, M., & Locke, B. Z. (1988). One-month prevalence of mental disorders in the United States. *Archives of General Psychiatry, 45,* 977–986.

Renzulli, J. S., & Smith, L. H. (1978). *Learning Styles Inventory: A measure of student preference for instructional techniques.* Mansfield Center, CT: Creative Learning.

Rest, J. R. (1974). *Manual for the Defining Issues Test.* (Available from J. R. Rest, 330 Burton Hall, University of Minnesota, Minneapolis, MN 55455).

Rest, J. (1979). *Development in judging moral issues.* Minneapolis: University of Minnesota.

Reynolds, W. M., & Kobak, K. A. (1995). *Professional manual for Hamilton Depression Inventory: A self-report version of the Hamilton Depression Rating Scale.* Odessa, FL: Psychological Assessment Resources.

Riverside Publishing Co. (1994). *Technical Summary I Riverside 2000 Cognitive Abilities Test.* Chicago: Author.

Robins, L. N., Heizer, J. E., Weissman, M. M., Orvaschel, H., Gruenberg, E., Burke, J. D., & Regier, D. A. (1984). Lifetime prevalence of specific psychiatric disorders in three sites. *Archives of General Psychiatry, 41,* 949–958.

Robinson, J. P., Shaver, P. R., & Wrightsman, L. S. (1991). (Eds.). *Measures of personality and social psychological attitudes: Volume 1 in measures of social psychological attitudes series.* San Diego, CA: Academic.

Roid, G. H., & Fitts, W. H. (1988). *Tennessee Self-Concept Scale, Revised manual.* Los Angeles, CA: Western Psychological Services.

Roselle, B. E., & Hummel, T. J. (1988). Intellectual development and interaction effectiveness with DISCOVER. *Career Development Quarterly, 36,* 241–250.

Rosen, D., Holmberg, K., & Holland, J. L. (1994). *The Educational Opportunities Finder.* Odessa, FL: Psychological Assessment Resources.

Rosen, J. C. , Silberg, N. T., & Gross, J. (1988). Eating Attitudes Test and Eating Disorders Inventory: Norms for adolescent girls and boys. *Journal of Consulting & Clinical Psychology, 56,* 305–308.

Rosenthal, R. (1990). How are we doing in soft psychology? *American Psychologist, 45,* 775–776.

Rosnow, R. L., & Rosenthal, R. (1988). Focused tests of significance and effect size estimation in counseling psychology. *Journal of Counseling Psychology, 35,* 203–208.

Rotter, J. B., & Rafferty, J. E. (1950). *Manual for the Rotter Incomplete Sentence Blank, College Form.* San Antonio, TX: Psychological Corporation.

Rounds, J. B. (1989). Review of the Career Assessment Inventory. In J. C. Conoley & J. J. Kramer (Eds.), *Tenth mental measurements yearbook* (pp. 139–141). Lincoln, NE: Buros Institute of Mental Measurements.

Rounds, J. B. (1990). The comparative and combined utility of work value and interest data in career counseling with adults. *Journal of Vocational Behavior, 37,* 32–45.

Rounds, J. B., Jr., Henly, G. A., Dawis, R. V., Lofquist, L. H., & Weiss, D. J. (1981). *Manual for the Minnesota Importance Questionnaire: A measure of vocational needs and values.* Minneapolis: University of Minnesota, Department of Psychology.

Russell, M., & Karol, D. (1993). *16-PF, fifth edition, administrator's manual.* Champaign, IL: Institute for Personality and Ability Testing.

Sabourin, S., Laferriere, N., Sicuro, F., Coallier, J., Cournoyer, L., & Gendreau, P. (1989). Social desirability, psychological distress, and consumer satisfaction with mental health treatment. *Journal of Counseling Psychology, 36,* 352–356.

Sampson, J. P. (1990). Computer-assisted testing and the goals of counseling psychology. *The Counseling Psychologist, 18,* 227–239.

Sampson, J. P., Jr., Peterson, G. W., Lenz, J. G., & Reardon, R. C. (1992). A cognitive approach to career services: Translating concepts into practice. *Career Development Quarterly, 41,* 67–74.

Sampson, J. P., Jr., Peterson, G. W., Lenz, J. G., Reardon, R. C., & Saunders, D. E. (1994). *My Career Thoughts Inventory: Professional manual.*

Samuda, R. J. (1975). Compendium of tests for minority adolescents and adults. In R. J. Samuda (Ed.), *Psychological testing of American minorities* (pp. 177–204). New York: Dodd, Mead.

Sarason, I. G. (Ed.). (1980). *Test anxiety: Theory, research, and applications.* Hillsdale, NJ: Erlbaum.

Sarason, I. G., Johnson, J. H., & Siegel, J. M. (1978). Assessing the impact of life changes: Development of the Life Experiences Survey. *Journal of Consulting and Clinical Psychology, 46,* 932–946.

Sattler, J. M. (1989). Vineland Adaptive Behavior Scales. In J. C. Conoley & J. J. Kramer (Eds.), *Tenth mental measurements yearbook* (pp. 878–881). Lincoln, NE: University of Nebraska.

Saunders, J. B., Aasland, O. G., Amundsen, A., & Grant, M. (1993). Alcohol consumption and related problems among primary health care patients: WHO collaborative project on early detection of persons with harmful alcohol consumption, I. *Addiction, 88,* 349–362.

Savickas, M. L. (1990). The use of career choice process scales in counseling practice. In C. E. Watkins, Jr., & V. L. Campbell (Eds.), *Testing in counseling practice* (pp. 373–418). Hillsdale, NJ: Erlbaum.

Savickas, M. L., Brizzi, J. S., Brisbin, L. A., & Pethtel, L. L. (1988). Predictive validity of two medical specialty preference inventories. *Measurement and Evaluation in Counseling and Development, 21,* 106–112.

Schinka, J. A. (1984). *Personal Problems Checklist—Adult.* Odessa, FL: Psychological Assessment Resources.

Schinka, J. A. (1985). *Personal Problems Checklist—Adolescent.* Odessa, FL: Psychological Assessment Resources.

Scholastic Testing Service. (1982). *Kuhlmann-Anderson tests manual of directions.* Bensenville, IL: Author.

Schuerger, J. M. (1992). The sixteen personality factor questionnaire and its junior versions. *Journal of Counseling & Development, 71,* 231–244.

Schutte, N. S., & Malouff, J. M. (1995). *Sourcebook of adult assessment strategies.* New York: Plenum.

Selzer, M. L. (1971). The Michigan Alcoholism Screening Test: The quest for a new diagnostic instrument. *American Journal of Psychiatry, 127,* 1653–1658.

Sewell, T. E. (1985). Review of Coopersmith Self-Esteem Inventories. In J. V. Mitchell, Jr. (Ed.), *The ninth mental measurements yearbook* (pp. 397–398). Lincoln, NE: Buros Institute of Mental Measurements.

Shimizu, K., Vondracek, F. W., Schulenberg, J. E., & Hostetler, M. (1988). The factor structure of the Career Decision Scale: Similarities across selected studies. *Journal of Vocational Behavior, 32,* 213–225.

Shrauger, J. S., & Osberg, R. M. (1981). The relative accuracy of self-predictions and judgments by others in psychological assessment. *Psychological Bulletin, 90,* 322–351.

Simon, S. B., Howe, L. W., & Kirschenbaum, H. (1978). *Values clarification: A handbook of practical strategies for teachers and students.* New York: Dodd, Mead.

Skidmore, J. E., & Berg, I. K. (1994, April). *A follow-up study of therapists trained in the use of the solution-focused brief therapy model.* Paper presented at the meeting of the American Counseling Association, Minneapolis, MN.

Slaney, R. B., Moran, W. J., & Wade, J. C. (1994). Vocational card sorts. In J. T. Kapes, M. M. Mastie, & E. A. Whitfield (Eds.), *A counselor's guide to career assessment instruments* (pp. 347–360). Alexandria, VA: National Career Development Association.

Slaney, R. B., & Suddarth, B. H. (1994). Review of the Values Scale (VS). In J. T. Kapes, M. M. Mastie, & E. A. Whitfield (Eds.), *A counselor's guide to career assessment instruments* (3rd ed.) (pp. 236–240). Alexandria, VA: National Career Development Association.

Smart, R. M., & Peterson, C. C. (1994). Super's stages and the four-factor structure of the Adult Career Concerns Inventory in an Australian sample. *Measurement and Evaluation in Counseling and Development, 26,* 243–257.

Smith, D. L. (1976). Goal attainment scaling as an adjunct to counseling. *Journal of Counseling Psychology, 23,* 22–27.

Snyder, D. K. (1981). *Marriage Satisfaction Inventory manual.* Los Angeles, CA: Western Psychological Services.

Sobell, M. B., Maisto, S. A., Sobell, L. C., Cooper, A. M., Cooper, T. C., & Sanders, B. (1980). Developing a prototype for evaluating alcohol treatment effectiveness. In L. C. Sobell, M. B. Sobell, & E. Ward (Eds.), *Evaluating alcohol and drug abuse treatment effectiveness: Recent advances* (pp. 129–150). New York: Pergamon.

Sparrow, S. S., Balla, D. A., & Cicchetti, D. V. (1985). *Vineland adaptive behavior scales. Classroom edition manual.* Circle Pines, MN: American Guidance Service.

Spengler, P. M., Strohmer, D. C., Dixon, D. N., & Shivy, V. A. (1995). A scientist-practitioner model of psychological assessment: Implications for training, practice, and research. *The Counseling Psychologist, 23,* 506–534.

Spielberger, C. D. (1988). *Manual for the State-Trait Anger Expression Inventory (STAXI)*. Odessa, FL: Psychological Assessment Resources.

Spielberger, C. D., Gorsuch, R. L., Lushene, R., Vagg, P. R., & Jacobs, G. A. (1983). *Manual for State-Trait Anxiety Inventory*. Palo Alto, CA: Consulting Psychologists.

Spielberger, C.D., Sydeman, S. J., Ritterband, L. M., Reheiser, E. C., & Unger, K. K. (1995). Assessment of emotional states and personality traits: Measuring psychological vital signs. In J. N. Butcher (Ed.), *Clinical personality assessment: Practical approaches* (pp. 42–58). New York: Oxford.

Spitzer, R. L., Gibbon, M., Skodol, A. E., Williams, J. B. W., & First, M. B. (Eds.). (1994). *DSM-IV casebook: A learning companion to the Diagnostic and Statistical Manual of Mental Disorders, Fourth edition*. Washington, DC: American Psychiatric.

Spitzer, R. L., Williams, J. B. W., Kroenke, K., Linzer, M., de Gruy, F. V., III, Hahn, S. R., Brody, D., & Johnson, J. G. (1994). Utility of a new procedure for diagnosing mental disorders in primary care: the PRIME-MD 1000 study. *Journal of the American Medical Association, 272*, 1749–1756.

Stelmachers, Z. T. (1995). Assessing suicidal clients. In J. N. Butcher (Ed.), *Clinical personality assessment: Practical approaches* (pp. 367–379). New York: Oxford.

Sternberg, R. J. (1985). *Beyond IQ*. Cambridge: Cambridge University.

Sternberg, R. J. (1987). *The triangle of love: Intimacy, passion, commitment*. New York: Basic Books.

Sternberg, R. J. (1988). *The triarchic mind*. New York: Viking Penguin.

Sternberg, R. J., Wagner, R. K., Williams, W. M., & Horvath, J. A. (1995). Testing common sense. *American Psychologist, 50*, 912–927.

Stewart, E. S., Greenstein, S. M., Holt, N. C., Henly, G. A., Engdahl, B. E., Dawis, R. V., Lofquist, L. H., & Weiss, D. J. (1986). *Occupational reinforcer patterns* (Rev. ed.). Minneapolis: University of Minnesota, Department of Psychology, Vocational Psychology Research.

Strong, E. K., Jr. (1955). *Vocational interests 18 years after college*. Minneapolis: University of Minnesota.

Stuart, R. B., & Stuart, F. (1975). *Premarital Counseling Inventory manual*. Ann Arbor, MI: Compuscore.

Sturgis, E. T., & Gramling, S. (1988). Psychophysiological assessment. In A. S. Bellack & M. Hersen (Eds.), *Behavioral assessment: A practical handbook* (pp. 213–251). New York: Pergamon.

Sue, D. W. (1978). Work views and counseling. *Personnel and Guidance Journal, 56*, 458–462.

Sue, D. W. (1990). Barriers to effective cross-cultural counseling. In D. W. Sue & D. Sue (Eds.), *Counseling the culturally different: Theory and practice* (pp. 27–48). New York: Wiley.

Sue, S., & Sue, D. W. (1974). MMPI comparisons between Asian-American and non-Asian students utilizing a student health psychiatric clinic. *Journal of Counseling Psychology, 21,* 423–427.

Super, D. E. (1957). *The psychology of careers: An introduction to vocational development.* New York: Harper.

Super, D. E. (1970). *Manual for the Work Values Inventory.* Boston: Houghton-Mifflin.

Super, D. E. (1980). A life-span, life-space approach to career development. *Journal of Vocational Behavior, 16,* 282–298.

Super, D. E. (1984): Career and life development. In D. Brown & L. Brooks (Eds.), *Career choice and development* (pp. 192–234). San Francisco: Jossey-Bass.

Super, D. E., & Thompson, A. S. (1979). A six-scale, two-factor measure of adolescent career or vocational maturity. *Vocational Guidance Quarterly, 28,* 6–15.

Super, D. E., Thompson, A. S., & Lindeman, R. H. (1988). *Adult Career Concerns Inventory: Manual for research and exploratory use in counseling.* Palo Alto, CA: Consulting Psychologists.

Sweetland, R. C., & Keyser, D. J. (Eds.). (1991). *Tests: A comprehensive reference for assessments in psychology, education, and business* (3rd ed.). Kansas City, MO: Test Corp. of America.

Taylor, R. M., Morrison, W. L., & Nash, L. (1985). *Taylor-Johnson Temperament Analysis handbook.* Los Angeles, CA: Western Psychological Services.

Taylor, S. E. (1989). *Positive illusions: Creative self-deception and the healthy mind.* New York: Basic.

Technical Education Research Centers. (1977). *Guidance, counseling, and support services for high school students with physical disabilities.* Cambridge, MA: Author.

Tennen, H., Affleck, G., & Herzberger, S. (1985). SCL-90-R. In D. J. Keyser & R. C. Sweetland (Eds.), *Test critiques* (vol. III) (pp. 583–594). Kansas City, MO: Test Corporation of America.

Thompson, A. S., Lindeman, R. H., Super, D. E., Jordaan, J. P., & Myers, R. A. (1981). *Career Development Inventory* (Vol. 1). Palo Alto, CA: Consulting Psychologists.

Thompson, A. S., Lindeman, R. H., Super, D. E., Jordaan, J. P., & Myers, R. A. (1982). *Career Development Inventory: College and University Form. Supplement to user's manual.* Palo Alto, CA: Consulting Psychologists.

Thorndike, R. L., Hagen, E. P., & Sattler, J. M. (1986a). *The Stanford-Binet Intelligence Scale: Fourth edition, guide for administering and scoring.* Chicago: Riverside.

Thorndike, R. L., Hagen, E. P., & Sattler, J. M. (1986b). *The Stanford-Binet Intelligence Scale: Fourth edition, technical manual.* Chicago: Riverside.

Thorne, A., & Gough, H. (1991). *Portraits of type: An MBTI research compendium*. Palo Alto, CA: Consulting Psychologists.

Tieger, P. D., & Barron-Tieger, B. (1992). *Do what you are: Discover the perfect career through the secrets of personality type*. Boston: Little-Brown.

Timbrook, R. E, & Graham, J. R. (1994). Ethnic differences on the MMPI-2? *Psychological Assessment, 6*, 212–217.

Tracey, T. J. G., & Schneider, P. L. (1995). An evaluation of the circular structure of the checklist of interpersonal transactions and the checklist of psychotherapy transactions. *Journal of Counseling Psychology, 42*, 496–507.

Trimble, J. T. (1966). A ten-year longitudinal follow-up of inventoried interests of selected high school students (Doctoral dissertation, University of Missouri). *Dissertation Abstracts International, 24*, 5252–5253.

Tyler, L. E. (1961). Research explorations in the realm of choice. *Journal of Counseling Psychology, 8*, 195–210.

Urbina, S. (1995). Review of Basic Personality Inventory. In J. C. Conoley & J. C. Impara (Eds.), *Twelfth mental measurements yearbook* (pp. 105–106). Lincoln, NE: Buros Institute of Mental Measurements.

U.S. Department of Defense, Defense Manpower Data Center (1992). *Armed Services Vocational Aptitude Battery 18/19 counselor manual*. Monterey, CA: Author.

U.S. Department of Labor. (1979). *USES Interest Check List*. Washington, DC: U.S. Government Printing Office.

U.S. Department of Labor. (1981). *USES Interest Inventory*. Washington, DC: U.S. Government Printing Office.

U.S. Department of Labor. (1982). *Manual for General Aptitude Test Battery, section 1: Administration and scoring, Forms A and B*. Washington, DC: U.S. Government Printing Office.

U.S. Department of Labor. (1992). *Validity generalization manual, section C: Counseling and test interpretation*. Washington, DC: Author.

U.S. Department of Labor. (1993). *Dictionary of occupational titles* (4th ed.). Washington, DC: U.S. Government Printing Office.

Vacc, N. A., & Hinkle, J. S. (1994). Review of Career Assessment Inventory—Enhanced Version and Vocational Version (CAI-EV/CAI-VV). In J. T. Kapes, M. M. Mastie, & E. A. Whitfield (Eds.), *A counselor's guide to career assessment instruments* (pp. 145–150). Alexandria, VA: National Career Development Association.

VanDenberg, T. F., Schmidt, J. A., & Kiesler, D. J. (1992). Interpersonal assessment in counseling and psychotherapy. *Journal of Counseling and Development, 71*, 84–90.

Vansickle, T. R. (1994). Review of Harrington-O'Shea Career Decision-Making System—Revised (CDM-R). In J. T. Kapes, M. M. Mastie, & E. A.

Whitfield (Eds.), *A counselor's guide to career assessment instruments* (3rd ed.) (pp. 172–177). Alexandria, VA: National Career Development Association.

Vilas, R. C. (1988). *Counseling outcome as related to MBTI client type, counselor type and counselor-client type similarity.* Unpublished doctoral dissertation, The University of Iowa, Iowa City.

Vondracek, F. W. (1991). Osipow of the Career Decision Scale: Some comments. *Journal of Counseling and Development, 70,* 327.

Vuchinich, R. E., Tucker, J. A., & Harllee, L. N. (1988). Behavioral assessment. In D. M. Dononvan & G. A. Marlart (Eds.), *Assessment of addictive behaviors* (pp. 51–83). New York: Guilford.

Wagner, E. E. (1987). A review of the 1985 Standards for Educational and Psychological Testing: User responsibility and social justice. *Journal of Counseling and Development, 66,* 202–203.

Waldinger, R. J. (1986). *Fundamentals of psychiatry.* Washington: American Psychiatric Press.

Walker, C. E., & Kaufman, K. (1984). Review of State-Trait Anxiety Inventory for Children. In D. J. Keyser & R. C. Sweetland (Eds.), *Test critiques: Volume 2* (pp. 633–640). Kansas City, MO: Test Corporation of America.

Walsh, W. B., & Betz, N. E. (1994). *Tests and assessment* (3rd ed.). Englewood Cliffs, NJ: Prentice-Hall.

Wang, L. (1995). Review of Differential Aptitude Tests (DAT). *Measurement and Evaluation in Counseling and Development, 28,* 168–170.

Watkins, C. E., Jr., Campbell, V. L., & Nieberding, R. (1994). The practice of vocational assessment by counseling psychologists. *The Counseling Psychologist, 22,* 115–128.

Watkins, C. E., Jr., Campbell, V. L., Nieberding, R., & Hallmark, R. (1995). Contemporary practice of psychological assessment by clinical psychologists. *Professional Psychology: Research and Practice, 26,* 54–60.

Wechsler, D. (1974). *Manual for the Wechsler Intelligence Scale for Children— revised manual,* San Antonio, TX: Psychological Corporation.

Wechsler, D. (1981). *WAIS-R Manual: Wechsler Adult Intelligence Scale–Revised.* San Antonio, TX: Psychological Corporation.

Wechsler, D. (1989). *Manual: Wechsler Preschool and Primary Scale of Intelligence.* San Antonio, TX: Psychological Corporation.

Wechsler, D. (1991). *Manual for the Wechsler Intelligence Scale for Children.* San Antonio, TX: Psychological Corporation.

Wechsler, H., Davenport, A., Dowdall, G., Moeykens, B., & Castillo, S. (1994). Health and behavioral consequences of binge drinking in college: A national survey of students at 140 campuses. *Journal of the American Medical Association, 272,* 1672–1677.

Weinstein, C. E. (1987). *LASSI User's Manual.* Clearwater, FL: H & H.

Weinstein, C. E., Palmer, D. R., & Schulte, A. C. (1987). *Learning and Study Strategies Inventory.* Clearwater, FL: H & H.

Werts, C. E., & Watley, D. J. (1969). A student's dilemma: Big fish–little pond or little fish–big pond. *Journal of Counseling Psychology, 16,* 14–19.

Wickwire, P. N., & Faldet, B. (1994). Review of Career Occupational Preference System Interest Inventory (COPS). In J. T. Kapes, M. M. Mastie, & E. A. Whitfield (Eds.). *A counselor's guide to career assessment instruments* (pp. 156–161). Alexandria, VA: National Career Development Association.

Widiger, T. A., Mangine, S., Corbitt, E. M., Ellis, C. G., & Thomas, G. V. (1995). *Personality Disorder Interview–IV.* Odessa, FL: Psychological Assessment Resources.

Wiggins, J. D. (1985). Review of Career Skills Assessment Program. In J. V. Mitchell, Jr., (Ed.), *The ninth mental measurements yearbook* (pp. 202–203). Lincoln, NE: Buros Institute of Mental Measurements.

Wiggins, J. S. (1993). *Interpersonal adjective scales professional manual.* Odessa, FL: Psychological Assessment Resources.

Williams, C. L., Butcher, J. N., Ben-Porath, Y. S., & Graham, J. R. (1992). *MMPI-A content scales: Assessing psychopathology in adolescents.* Minneapolis: University of Minnesota.

Williams, R. L. (1972). *Black Intelligence Test of Cultural Homogeneity manual.* St. Louis, MO: Williams.

Williamson, E. G. (1939). *How to counsel students.* New York: McGraw-Hill.

Winston, R. B., & Miller, T. K. (1987). *Student developmental task and lifestyle inventory.* Athens, GA: Student Development Associates.

Winters, K. C. (1991). *Personal Experience Screening Questionnaire (PESQ) manual.* Los Angeles: Western Psychological Services.

Winters, K. C., & Henley, G. A. (1989). *The Personal Experience Inventory.* Los Angeles: Western Psychological Services.

Wisconsin Clearinghouse. (1996). *Alcohol and other drugs Self test: A guide to help you examine how and why you use chemicals.* Madison, WI: Author.

Wise, S. L., & Plake, B. S. (1990). Computer-based testing in higher education. *Measurement and Evaluation in Counseling and Development, 23,* 3–10.

Wonderlic, E. F. (1983). *Wonderlic Personnel Test manual.* Northfield, IL: E. F. Wonderlic Personnel Test.

Worthington, E. L., McCullough, M. E., Shortz, J. L., Mindes, E. J., Sandage, S. J., & Chartrand, J. M. (1995). Can couples assessment and feedback improve relationships? Assessment as a brief relationship enrichment procedure. *Journal of Counseling Psychology, 42,* 466–475.

Yelland, T. (1995). Review of Basic Pesonality Inventory. In J. C. Conoley & J. C. Impara (Eds.), *Twelfth mental measurements yearbook* (pp. 106–107). Lincoln, NE: Buros Institute of Mental Measurements.

Yu, J., & Williford, W. R. (1992). Perception, style, and consumption: Specifying and testing a structural model on problem drinking. *The Journal of Drug Issues, 22,* 75–90.

Zachery, R. A. (1986). *Shipley Institute of Living Scale: Revised manual.* Los Angeles: Western Psychological Services.

Ziemelis, A. (1988). *Report of University of Wisconsin–La Crosse Alcohol and Drug Issues Survey.* La Crosse, WI: Counseling and Testing Center, University of Wisconsin.

Zimet, G. D., Dahlem, N. W., Zimet, S. G., & Farley, G. K. (1988). The Multidimensional Scale of Perceived Social Support. *Journal of Personality Assessment, 52,* 30–41.

Zimny, G. H., & Senturia, A. G. (1976). *Medical Specialty Preference Inventory.* St. Louis, MO: St. Louis University Medical Center, Department of Psychiatry.

Zytowski, D. G. (1974). Predictive validity of the Kuder Preference Record, Form B, over a 25-year span. *Measurement and Evaluation in Guidance, 7,* 122–129.

Zytowski, D. G. (1976a). Predictive validity of the Kuder Occupational Interest Survey: A 12- to 19-year follow-up. *Journal of Counseling Psychology, 23,* 221–233.

Zytowski, D. G. (1976b). Long-term profile stability of the Kuder Occupational Interest Survey. *Educational and Psychological Measurement, 36,* 689–692.

Zytowski, D. G. (1977). The effects of being interest-inventoried. *Journal of Vocational Behavior, 11,* 153–157.

Zytowski, D. G. (1992). Three generations: The continuing evolution of Frederic Kuder's interest inventories. *Journal of Counseling & Development, 71,* 245–248.

Zytowski, D. G. (1994a). A super contribution to vocational theory: Work values. *The Career Development Quarterly, 43,* 25–31.

Zytowski, D. G. (1994b). Test and counseling: We are still married and living in discriminant analysis. *Measurement and Evaluation in Counseling and Development, 26,* 219–223.

Zytowski, D. G., & England, R. J. L. (1994). Indices of interest maturity in the Kuder Occupational Interest Survey. *Measurement and Evaluation in Counseling and Development, 28,* 148–151.

Zytowski, D. G., & Laing, J. (1978). Validity of other-gender-normed scales on the Kuder Occupational Interest Survey. *Journal of Counseling Psychology, 25,* 205–209.

Zytowski, D., & Warman, R. E. (1982). The changing use of tests in counseling. *Measurement and Evaluation in Guidance, 15,* 147–152.

INDEX

academic aptitude and achievement, 95–96

academic achievement tests, 110–15

administering and interpreting academic aptitude tests, 108–10

American College Testing (ACT), 96, 98–99, *See also* American College Testing Program (ACT)

California Achievement Tests, 111, 113, 115

coaching, 108–10

cognitive developmental theories, 116–17

college-level achievement tests, 114

criticisms of using diagnostic testing in, 337

Defining Issues Test (DIT), 117

graduate and professional school admissions tests, 104–7

Graduate Record Examination (GRE), 40, 44, 76, 104–6, 317

Iowa Tests of Basic Skills/Iowa Tests of Educational Development, 41, 44, 51, 90, 111, 112

Metropolitan Achievement Tests, 91, 111, 112, 115, 312

Miller Analogies Test (MAT), 106–7, 317

Parker Cognitive Development Inventory (PCDI), 117

Preliminary Scholastic Aptitude Test/National Merit Scholarship Qualifying Test (PSAT/NMSQT), 97–98, 334

professional school tests, 107

reliability and validity, 113–15

Scale of Intellectual Development (SID), 117

Scholastic Assessment Test (SAT), 41, 49, 96–97, 110, 334

Stanford Achievement Test, 91, 111, 112, 312

study habit inventories, 115–16

test anxiety, 108

test selection, 72

tests of adult basic education, 114–15

tests for higher education, 96–104

validity of scholastic aptitude tests, 99–104

acculturation, 299

achievement tests, difference between aptitude and, 18–19

Adler, Alfred, 232

adolescents and children

achievement tests, 111–13

Adolescent Drinking Index, 290

Children's Depression Inventory (CDI), 283–84

Diagnostic Interview for Children and Adolescents (DICA), 72

informing minors of test results, 332

Kaufman Adolescent and Adult Intelligence Test (KAIT), 87–88

Kaufman Assessment Battery for Children (K-ABC), 87–88

Life Stressors and Social Resources Inventory-Youth Form, 259

Millon Adolescent Clinical Inventory (MACI), 278

Millon Adolescent Personality Inventory (MAPI), 226

Minnesota Multiphasic Personalty Inventory-Adolescent (MMPI-A), 276–77

Personal Experience Inventory for Adolescents (PEI), 291

Personal Problems Checklists—Adolescent, 63

psychosocial theories, 235–36

Raven's Progressive Matrices for Children, 305

State-Trait Anxiety Inventory for Children (STAIC), 286

test administration for small children, 74
Wechsler Intelligence Scale for Children (WISC-III), 85, 87
Wechsler Preschool and Primary Scale of Intelligence (WPPSI-R), 87
See also school counseling
Adult Basic Education, tests of, 114–15
Advanced Placement Program (APP), 114
African Americans. *See* Black Americans
alcohol use
   alcohol abuse, 263, 288–91
   assessment of, 261–67
   suicide and, 258
American Association for Counseling and Development. *See* American Counseling Association
American College Testing Program (ACT), 96, 98–99, 109, 111, 365
   ACT Career Planning Program (CPP), 189–90, 193, 194–95
   CLEP, 114
   DISCOVER program, 192
   options for examinees with disabilities, 311
   Preliminary ACT Battery (P-ACT), 99
   professional school tests, 107
   reliability factors, 45, 49
   standard scores, 41
   UNIACT, 336
American Counseling Association
   AAC and, 28
   Code of Ethics and Standards of Practice, 25, 298, 328, 343–47
   JCTP member, 26
American Educational Research Association (AERA), 25–26, 328, 359
American Psychological Association (APA)
   ethical codes, 25, 298
   Ethical Principles of Psychologists and Code of Conduct, 328
   JCTP member, 26
   Standards for Educational and Psychological Testing, 25–26, 328, 359
American Rehabilitation Counseling Association, ethical codes, 25

American School Counselor Association, ethical codes, 25
American Sign Language (ASL), 312
American Speech-Language-Hearing Association, 26
Americans With Disabilities Act of 1990, 311
Anchors, S., 212
anger, 287–88
anorexia nervosa, 291–94
anxiety and fear, 285–87
Applications of the MBTI in Higher Education (Provost and Anchors), 212
aptitude tests, 41
   difference between achievement and, 18–19
   gender bias in aptitude testing, 333–34
   test administration, 74
   See also academic aptitude and achievement
Armed Services Vocational Aptitude Battery (ASVAB), 194, 200–201
Asian Americans, assessment of, 303–4, 306–7, 309
assessment of interests
   Career Assessment Inventory (CAI), 178–80
   interest inventories, 6, 7, 9, 74
   interpretation of interest inventories in counseling, 182–83
   Jackson Vocational Interest Survey (JVIS), 180–82
   Kuder General Interest Survey (KGIS), Form E, 76, 171–74, 312
   Kuder Occupational Interest Survey (KOIS), Form DD, 76–77, 171, 174–78, 335
   Medical Specialty Preference Inventory, 154
   Missouri Occupational Card Sort, 155
   Missouri Occupational Preference Inventory, 155
   Nonsexist Vocational Card Set, 155
   Occ-U-Sort, 155
   popular interest inventories, 155–82
   Purdue Interest Questionnaire, 154
   selection of interest inventories for counseling, 153–55
   Slaney Vocational Card Sort, 155

Strong Interest Inventory, 11, 13, 49, 50, 55, 73, 76, 155–71, 208, 303, 312, 332, 335
types of interest inventories, 151–53
See also interest inventories
assessment of interpersonal relationships, 239–40
Checklist of Interpersonal Transactions (CLOIT), 244
Checklist of Psychotherapy Transactions (CLOPT), 244
Derogatis Sexual Functioning Inventory (DSFI), 240–41
Family Environment Scale (FES), 242
genograms, 246–47, 248
Interpersonal Adjective Scales (IAS), 244–45
interpersonal assessment inventories, 244–46
inventories for marriage, couples, and family counseling, 240–44
Marital Precounseling Inventory, 241
Marital Satisfaction Inventory (MSI), 240
Myers-Briggs Type Indicator (MBTI), 243–44
Stuart Couples' Precounseling Inventory (SCPI), 241–42
Taylor-Johnson Temperament Analysis (TJTA), 241
Triangular Love Scale (TLS), 242–43
assessment of minority and special populations
aptitude and cognitive assessment, 300–306
Asian Americans, 303–4
assessment of clients with disabilities, 310–14
Black Americans, 300–302
career assessment, 306–7
Cattell's Culture-Fair Intelligence Test, 303, 304
cultural bias in testing, 297–300
cultural differences, 305–6
culture-fair tests, 304–5
DSM-IV diagnoses of culture-bound syndromes, 254
Hispanics, 302–3
Multicultural Assessment Standards, 28
Native Americans, 303

Peabody Picture Vocabulary Test, 312
personality assessment, 308–10
psychological and educational diagnoses of culturally diverse clients, 316–17
Raven's Progressive Matrices, 305, 312
Vineland Adaptive Behavior Scales, 313–14
assessment procedure, defined, 7
assessment process. See use of assessment procedures in counseling
Association for Assessment in Counseling (AAC)
Multicultural Assessment Standards, 28, 298
RUST statement, 25
Association for Measurement and Evaluation in Counseling and Development. See Association for Assessment in Counseling
Athelstan, G. T., 167

Barker, R. G., 233
base rates, 51–52
Beck, Aaron T., 281, 282–84
Ben-Porath, Y., 273
Binet, Alfred, 82
biofeedback devices, 19, 24
biographical data, 23–24
bipolar scales, 22
Birnbaum, M., 103
Black Americans
assessment of, 300–302, 306, 308–9
use of the ASVAB with, 201
Blocher, D. H., 193
Block, J., 18
Bolles, Richard N., 193
Borgen, F. H., 153
brain fag, 254
Brickman, P., 59, 60
Briggs, Katherine, 209
Brown, D., 148
bulimarexia, 291
bulimia, 291–94
Buros Institute of Mental Measurements, University of Nebraska—Lincoln, 29
Buros, Oscar K., 29
Butcher, J. N., 272, 273

California Achievement Tests, 111, 113, 115

California Test of Mental—Maturity Short Form, 91

Campbell, David, 155, 170, 191

Campbell Development Surveys, 191

Campbell Interest and Skill Survey (CISS), 186, 191–92

card sorts, 154–55

Career Actualization and Life Planning (Blocher), 193

career counseling. *See* measures of career choice and development

career and life planning. *See* comprehensive assessment programs for career and life planning

Career Skills Assessment Program (CSAP), 129

Carney, C. G., 193

Cass, J., 103

Cattell, Raymond B., 209, 221

Center for Applications of Psychological Type (CAPT), 243

Chaplin, W. F., 286

checklists, 6
  interpersonal interactions, 244
  problem, 63–69

Chickering, Arthur, 236

children. *See* adolescents and children

Chinese Americans, assessment of, 303

Choosing A Vocation (Parsons), 151

coaching programs, commercial, 109

Code of Fair Testing Practices in Education, 27

Cognitive Abilities Test, 90, 112

College Adjustment Scale, 63

College Entrance Examination Board (CEEB)
  Career Skills Assessment Program (CSAP), 129–30
  coaching methods study, 109, 110
  options for examinees with disabilities, 311–12
  Preliminary Scholastic Aptitude Test/ National Merit Scholarship Qualifying Test (PSAT/NMSQT), 97–98, 334
  SAT scores, 41, 49
  Scholastic Aptitude Test (SAT), 96–97, 334
  standard scores, 40

College Handbook, The, 103

College Student Experiences Questionnaire: Test Manual and Norms (Pace), 235

College-Level Examination Program (CLEP), 114

Commission on Rehabilitation Counselor Certification, ethical codes, 25

communication of test results, 315–17
  general guidelines for communicating test results, 317–19
  guidelines for the test interpretation interview, 319–21
  report writing, 321–25

community mental health counseling, 12–13

Comparative Guide to American Colleges: For Students, Parents, and Counselors, The (Cass and Birnbaum), 103

Composite International Diagnostic Interview (CIDI), 72

comprehensive assessment programs for career and life planning
  ACT Career Planning Program (CPP), 193, 194–95
  Armed Services Vocational Aptitude Battery (ASVAB), 193, 200–201
  Campbell Interest and Skill Survey (CISS), 186, 191–92
  Career Decision-Making System Revised (CDM-R), 186, 188–89
  Career Interest Inventory (CII), 195, 196
  career and life planning workbooks, 193
  Career Occupational Preference System (COPSystem), 193, 201–2
  Career Planning Questionnaire (CPQ), 195
  computer-based programs, 192
  Counselee Assessment/Occupational Exploration System, 193, 197–200
  Differential Aptitude Tests (DAT), 76, 193, 195–97
  Self-Directed Search (SDS), 11, 186–88, 303, 336
  self-rating career and life planning, 185–93
  self-report inventories, 186–90

standardized career and life planning programs, 193–202
use of comprehensive assessment programs in counseling, 202–3
Vocational Exploration Insight Kit (VEIK), 155, 188
Vocational Interest, Experience, and Skill Assessment (VIESA), 186, 189–90
computer scoring, 76–77, 140, 196, 272–73
computer-based assessment packages, sourcebook of, 30
computer-based career and life planning programs, 192, 196–97
computer-based test administration, 75–76
computer-based test interpretations (CBTIs), 77, 332
confidentiality
  public and private data and, 20
  test results and, 331
confirmatory bias, 71
Conoley, J. C., 29
Consulting Psychologists Press, 29, 156, 212, 366
Coping Inventory for Stressful Situations, 62
Coopersmith, Stanley, 226–27
Corcoran, K., 281
Counseling and Testing centers, 3
Counselor's Guide to Career Assessment Instruments, A (Jepsen), 30
Crace, R. K., 148
criterion-referenced interpretation, 34
Crites, John, 133, 134, 135
Cronbach's alpha reliability coefficient, 46
culture. See assessment of minority and special populations

Dawis, R. V., 140
Defining Issues Test (DIT), 117
Dental Admission Test (DAT), 107
depression, 281–85
Derogatis, L. R., 67, 240–41
Diagnostic & Statistical Manual of Mental Disorders, 4th Edition (DSM-IV), 250–54, 262, 291

Diagnostic Interview for Children and Adolescents (DICA), 72
Diagnostic Interview Schedule (DIS), 71
DiClemente, C. C., 58
Dictionary of Occupational Titles, 187, 197, 198, 199
Differential Aptitude Tests (DAT), 76, 193, 195–97
disabilities, assessment of clients with, 310–14
Discover the Career Within You (Carney and Wells), 193
DISCOVER (computer program), 192
Doll, Edgar, 313
D'Zurilla, T. J., 4

eating disorders, 291–94
Educational Occupational Finder, 187
Educational Testing Service (ETS), 367
  ETS Test Collection, 30
  GRE administration, 104–7
  professional school tests, 107
  SAT administration, 96
  SIGI+ program, 192
Enhanced ACT Assessment, 98
Enhanced Guide for Occupational Exploration, The (Maze), 197, 198
Erikson, Erik, 235, 236
error of central tendency, 21
ethical and social issues in testing
  client welfare issues, 330–33
  counseling process issues, 337–39
  counselor competence in testing, 328–29
  ethical standards, 327–29
  ethical standards for test quality, 328
  gender bias in aptitude testing, 333–34
  gender bias in interest measurement, 335–36
  gender bias in personality measurement, 334–35
  issues of gender bias in testing, 333–36
ETS Test Collection Catalog, Volume I: Achievement Tests and Measurement Devices, The), 30
Exner, J. E., 230
Exploring Careers: The ASVAB Workbook, 201

"faking bad" profile, 216, 222, 224
"faking good" profile, 216
false negative and false positive cases, validity and, 53
family counseling. *See* assessment of interpersonal relationships
Family Education Rights and Privacy Act of 1974, 330
fear, anxiety and, 285–87
Fischer, J., 280
Fong, M. L., 252–53
free association tests, 6
Funder, D. C., 22
Fuqua, D. R., 192

gender bias in testing, 333–36
General Aptitude Test Battery (GATB), 41, 51, 197, 198–200
General Education Tests (GED), 115
ghost sickness, 254
Gifts Differing (Myers and Myers), 212
Gilberts, R., 227
Goldfried, M. R., 4
Goldman, L., 10, 11
Gottfredson, G. D., 187
Gough, Harrison, 212, 214, 216
grade point averages (GPAs), 99, 100, 103–4, 106
Graduate Management Admission Test (GMAT), 107
Graduate Record Examination (GRE), 104–6, 317
  computer-based test version, 76
  scores, 40, 44
Graham, J. R., 273, 274, 309
group tests, 75
Guide for Occupational Exploration, The (Maze), 197, 198
Guilford, J. P., 18

halo effect, 21
Halstead-Reitan Neuropsychological Test Battery, 21
Hammen, C. L., 283
Hammer, A. L., 153
Hansen, J. C., 55, 153
Hansen, Jo-Ida, 155
Harmon, L. W., 125, 153

Harren, Vincent, 126
Harrington, T. F., 188
Hathaway, Starke, 270
Haverkamp, B. E., 55
Healy, C. C., 134, 200
Heck, E. J., 263
Helmes, E., 274
Henmon-Nelson Tests of Mental Ability, 90
Hispanics
  assessment of, 302
  use of the ASVAB with, 201
hit rates, 52
Hoffman, Jeffrey, 63
Holland, J. L.
  Classification of Personality Types, 157, 164, 179, 188, 194
  Self-Directed Search, 336
  theory of vocational choice, 186, 187, 234
Howe, L. W., 148

Impara, J. C., 29
in-basket technique (work assignment basket), 22
individual tests, 75
initial assessment in counseling, 57
  Brief Symptom Inventory (BSI), 67
  client orientation toward problem solving, 58–62
  compensatory model, 59, 60
  defining the problem, 62–72
  enlightenment model, 59–60
  intake form, 62–63
  intake interview, 69–72
  Inventory of Common Problems (ICP), 63–66
  medical model, 60
  models of helping and coping, 59–60
  moral model, 59, 60
  problem checklists, 63–69
  problem-solving style, 61–62
  readiness for counseling, 58–59
  Symptom Check List–90-Revised (SCL–90-R), 66–67, 257
  test selection, administration, and scoring, 72–77
intake form, 62–63
intelligence assessment, 41, 81–83

advantages of individual intelligence tests, 88–89
Cognitive Abilities Test, 90
crystallized intelligence, 82–83, 88
fluid intelligence, 83, 88
group intelligence tests, 89–94
group intelligence tests for school use, 90–91
Henmon-Nelson Tests, 90
interpreting intelligence results, 92–93
Kuhlmann-Anderson test, 90–91
Multidimensional Aptitude Battery, 92
other group intelligence tests, 91–92
Otis-Lennon School Ability Test, 91
popular individual intelligence tests, 83–89
Shipley Institute of Living Scale, 91
Stanford-Binet Intelligence Scale, 41, 82, 83–84, 91, 312, 329
Test of Cognitive Skills, 91
Wechsler Scales, 84–88
Wonderlic Personnel Test, 91–92
Intelligence Quotient (IQ), 41, 82
interest inventories
alternative solutions and, 6
gender bias in interest measurement, 335–36
nomothetic approach, 9
questionnaires and, 7
test administration, 74
See also assessment of interests
internal consistency, measures of, 54–55, 84
interpersonal relationships. See assessment of interpersonal relationships
interviews
during problem-solving process, 60
intake interview, 69–72
interview schedules, 71–72, 263–64
mental health interview procedures, 249–67
Introduction to Type (I. B. Myers), 212
Inventory of Common Problems (ICP), 63–66
Iowa Student Development Inventories, 236
Iowa Tests of Basic Skills, 90, 111, 112
Iowa Tests of Educational Development (ITED), 41, 44, 51, 111, 112

ipsative interpretation measure, 34
item response theory (IRT), 196

Jackson, Douglas N., 92, 224–25
Jackson Vocational Interest Survey (JVIS), 180–81
Japanese Americans, assessment of, 303–4
Jepsen, D. A., 30, 181
Job and College Majors Charts, 173
Johansson, Charles, 178
Joint Committee on Testing Practices (JCTP), 26–28
Journal of Counseling and Development, 30
Journal of Counseling Psychology, 30
Jung, Carl, 209
Jungian concepts, 54, 210, 211

Kaufman Batteries, 87–88
Kavan, M. G., 281
Keesling, J. W., 200
Kenrick, D. T., 22
Kessler, R. C., 249, 281
Keyser, D. J., 29–30
Kinnier, R. T., 149
Kirschenbaum, H., 148
Kohlberg, L., 116–17, 236
Kroeger, O., 212
Krumboltz, J. D., 122
Kuder General Interest Survey (KGIS), Form E, 76, 171–74, 312
Kuder Occupational Interest Survey (KOIS), Form DD, 76–77, 171, 174–77, 335
Kuder-Richardson Formula 20, 46
Kuhlmann-Anderson Test, 90–91

laboratory settings, test results in, 19
Lachar, D., 272
Laing, J., 177
Law School Admission Test (LSAT), 107
Lawrence, G., 212
Learning and Study Strategies Inventory (LASSI), 116
leniency error, 21
level a, b, and c tests, 28

Lewin, Kurt, 233
life planning, career and. *See*
  comprehensive assessment programs
  for career and life planning
Likert scale, 122
Locke, D. C., 132
locus of control, internal and external,
  60
Lofquist, L. H., 140
Logically Consistent Triad (LCT) score,
  141–42
Lorge-Thorndike Intelligence Tests, 90
LoVerde, M., 311

McArthur, C., 169
McKinley, J. Charnley, 270
McMahon, B. T., 311
marriage counseling. *See* assessment of
  interpersonal relationships
Maze, M., 197
measurement concepts and test
    interpretation, 33–34
  alternate-form reliability, 45–46
  concurrent validity, 50–51
  considerations in reliability, 47–48
  construct validity, 54–55
  content validity, 50
  convergent validity, 54
  correlation, 42–43
  criterion-related validity, 50–54, 55
  discriminant validity, 54
  grade equivalents, 38–39
  incremental validity, 52
  interitem consistency, 46–47
  norms, 34–42
  parallel-form reliability, 45
  percentile rank, 35–38
  predictive validity, 51
  profile reliability, 45
  rank, 35
  reliability, 43–49
  split-half reliability, 46, 87
  standard deviation, 39–40
  standard error of measurement (SEM),
    48–49
  standard scores, 40–42
  test development, 55–56
  test-retest reliability, 44–45, 87
  treatment validity, 55
  validity, 49–55

*Measurement and Evaluation in
  Counseling and Development*
  (journal), 30
measures of career choice and
    development, 121–22
  Adult Career Concerns Inventory
    (ACCI), 127–28
  Assessment of Career Decision Making
    (ACDM), 126–27
  attitudes toward career planning, 122–
    29
  Career Assessment Inventory (CAI),
    178–80
  career assessment portfolios, 24
  Career Attitudes and Strategies
    Inventory (CASI), 127, 128–29
  Career Beliefs Inventory (CBI), 122–23
  career counseling, 13, 14, 72
  Career Decision Scale (CDS), 124–25
  Career Development Inventory (CDI),
    130–32, 133
  career exploration process, 155
  Career Mastery Inventory (CMAS),
    134–35
  Career Maturity Inventory (CMI),
    133–34
  career planning competencies, 129–30
  Jackson Vocational Interest Survey
    (JVIS), 180–81
  measures of career concerns for adults,
    127–29
  measures of career concerns for
    students, 124–27
  measures of career maturity, 130–35
  My Career Thoughts Inventory
    (MCTI), 123–24
  My Vocational Situation, 68, 125–26
  use of career development in
    counseling, 135–36
measures of work and personal values,
    139
  Life Values Inventory, 148–49
  Minnesota Importance Questionnaire
    (MIQ), 140–44
  Minnesota Job Description
    Questionnaire (MJDQ), 142
  Minnesota Satisfaction Questionnaire,
    143
  personal values inventories, 144–46
  Salience Inventory (SI), 145–46
  Study of Values inventory, 144–45

use of value inventories in counseling, 146–47
values clarification exercises, 147–49
Values Conflict Resolution Assessment (VCRA), 149
values inventories, 140–47
Values Scale (VS), 145
work values inventories, 140–44
Work Values Inventory (WVI), 144
Medical College Admission Test (MCAT), 45, 52, 107, 331
Medical Economics Data, 70
mental health assessment, interview procedures, 249–50
assessment of alcohol use, 261–66
Brief Drinker Profile, 264
CAGE Questionnaire, 263–64
Comprehensive Drinking Profile (CDP), 264
Diagnostic & Statistical Manual of Mental Disorders, 4th Edition (DSM-IV), 250–54, 262, 291
Follow-up Drinker Profile, 264
Life Events Scale, 258
Life Stressors and Social Resources Inventory, 258–59
Multidimensional Scale of Perceived Social Support, 259
Personality Disorder Interview-IV, 253
Primary Care Evaluation of Mental Disorders (PRIME-MD), 253–54
SAD PERSONS Scale, 260–61
suicide risk assessment, 254–61
Time-Line Follow-Back (TLFB), 264
mental health assessment, standardized inventories
Achievement Anxiety Inventory, 287
Achievement Anxiety Scale, 287
Adolescent Drinking Index, 290
alcohol abuse, 288–91
Alcohol Use Inventory (AUI), 290–91
anger, 287–88
anxiety and fear, 285–87
AUDIT—Alcohol Use Disorders Identification Test, 290
Basic Personality Inventory (BPI), 274, 279–80
Beck Anxiety Inventory (BAI), 286–87
Beck Depression Inventory (BDI), 274, 277, 281–83

Children's Depression Inventory (CDI), 283–84
depression, 281–85
Eating Attitudes Test (EAT), 68, 292–93
eating disorders, 291–94
Eating Disorders Inventory–2 (EDI–2), 292, 293–94
Fear Questionnaire, 287
general-purpose measures, 269–80
Hamilton Depression Inventory (HDI), 284–85
Inventory of Common Problems, 277
Mathematics Anxiety Rating Scale-Revised, 287
Michigan Alcoholism Screening Test (MAST), 68, 288–90
Millon Clinical Multiaxial Inventory-III (MCMI-III), 274, 277–78
Minnesota Multiphasic Personality Inventory–2 (MMPI–2), 11, 208, 270–75
Minnesota Multiphasic Personality Inventory-Adolescent (MMPI-A), 276–77
Multidimensional Additions and Personality Profile, 290
Personal Experience Inventory (PEI), 291
Personal Experience Screening Questionnaire, 290
Personality Assessment Inventory (PAI), 274, 278–79
specific-purpose measures, 280–94
State-Trait Anger Expression Inventory (STAXI), 287
State-Trait Anxiety Inventory (STAI), 285–86, 287
Test Anxiety scale, 287
mental health counseling, community, 12–13
Mental Measurement Yearbook series, 29, 77
Metropolitan Achievement Tests, 91, 111, 112, 115, 312
Miller Analogies Test (MAT), 106–7, 317
Millon Index of Personality Styles (MIPS), 61, 225–26
Millon, T., 226, 278

Minnesota Multiphasic Personalty
Inventory (MMPI)
computer-based test interpretation, 77,
332
decision-making process and, 6–7
factor analytic method, 209
suicide ideation, 53
test reliability, 44
treatment validity, 55
use in marriage counseling, 239
use in mental health counseling, 12–
13, 269–70, 271
use in minority assessment, 308–9
Minnesota Multiphasic Personalty
Inventory–2 (MMPI–2), 11, 208,
270–75
Minnesota Multiphasic Personalty
Inventory-Adolescent (MMPI-A),
276–77
"Minnesota normals", 270
minority and special populations. *See*
assessment of minority and special
populations
Mitchell, L. K., 122
Moos, Rudolph, 234
Morgan, Christina, 231
Morris, G. W., 311
Multicultural Assessment Standards, 28
Multidimensional Aptitude Battery, 92
Murphy, L. L., 29
Murray, Henry, 231
My Vocational Situation, 68, 125–26
Myers, Isabel B., 210, 212
Myers, P. B., 212
Myers-Briggs Type Indicator (MBTI),
209–13
construct validity of the, 54
problem-solving style of the, 61
self-scorable answer sheets, 76
Spanish language edition, 303
theoretical method approach, 208
use in marriage counseling, 239, 243–
44

National Association of School
Psychologists, 26
National Comorbidity Study, 281
National Computer Systems (NCS), 178,
368
National Council on Measurement in

Education (NCME), 25–26, 328,
359
National Merit Scholarships, 97–98, 334
National Rehabilitation Counseling
Association, ethical codes, 25
Native Americans, assessment of, 300,
303, 309
natural settings
behavior observations in, 23
test results in, 19
nature of psychological assessment in
counseling, 17
*ACA Code of Ethics and Standards of
Practice*, 25
behavioral observations, 23
biographical measures, 23–24
*Code of Fair Testing Practices in
Education*, 27
distinctions among psychological
assessment procedures, 18–20
how is the assessment conducted, 20
Multicultural Assessment Standards,
28
physiological measures, 24
projective techniques, 22–23
rating scales, 21–22
Responsibilities of Users of
Standardized Tests (RUST
Statement-Revised), 25
sources of information about
assessment procedures, 28–31
standardized tests, 21
*Standards for Educational and
Psychological Testing*, 25–26
standards for evaluating tests and test
usage, 24–28
test publisher requirements, 28
test user qualifications, 26–27
types of psychological assessment
methods, 20–24
what is being assessed, 18–19
when is the assessment occurring, 19
where is the assessment taking place,
19
who is making the assessment, 18
why is the assessment being
undertaken, 20
Nevill, D. D., 139
Newman, J. L., 192
Norcross, J. C., 58
norm-referenced interpretation, 34

O-data, 18
obesity, 291
OCCU-FIND, 201
occupational ability patterns (OAPs), 199
Occupational Outlook Handbook, 171
Occupational Reinforcer Patterns Notebook (Stewart et al.), 142
Occupational Reinforcer Patterns (ORPs), 142–43
occupational scales, 152
Occupations Finder, 187
Osgood, C. E., 22
O'Shea, A. J., 188
Osipow, Samuel, 124
Otis-Lennon School Ability Test, 91

Pace, C. R., 235
Pace, T. M., 281
Parker Cognitive Development Inventory (PCDI), 117
Parsons, Frank, 151
People Types and Tiger Stripes (Lawrence), 212
Perry, W., 117, 236
Personal Problems Checklists—Adolescent, 63
Personal Problems Checklists—Adult, 63
personal values. *See* measures of work and personal values
personality disorders, 252–53
personality inventories, 207
   Behavioral Academic Self-Esteem (BASE) rating scale, 227
   California Psychological Inventory (CPI), 209, 213–21
   Coopersmith Self-Esteem Inventories (SEI), 226–27
   criterion group method, 208–9
   criticisms of, 337
   Eysenck Personality Questionnaire-Revised (EPQ-R), 222–23
   factor analytic method, 209
   inventory development, 208–9
   Jackson Personality Inventory-Revised (JPI-R), 224–25
   Jackson's Personality Research Form (PRF), 208

logical content method, 208
Millon Index of Personality Styles (MIPS), 61, 225–26
Myers-Briggs Type Indicator (MBTI), 54, 61, 76, 208, 209–13, 239, 243–44, 302
NEO Personality Inventory-Revised (NEO PI-R), 209, 223–24
nomothetic approach, 9
Personality Research Form (PRF), 224
problem identification and, 5
questionnaires and, 7
self-report personality inventories, 209–27
Sixteen Personality Factor Questionnaire (16 PF), 209, 221–22, 302
Tennessee Self-Concept Scale (TSCS), 227
test administration, 74
theoretical method, 208
personality measures
   Early Recollections, 232
   gender bias in personality measurement, 334–35
   person-environment interaction, 232–35
   projective techniques, 229–32
   psychosocial theories, 235–36
   Rorschach Ink Blot test, 23, 230, 329
   Rotter Incomplete Sentence Blank, 23, 232
   Thematic Apperception Test (TAT), 23, 231, 329
Physicians' Desk Reference, 70
Piaget, J., 116, 117
Ponterotto, J. G., 281
Porteus Problem Checklist, 63
Portraits of Type: An MBTI Research Compendium (Thorne and Gough), 212
Position Classification Inventory (PCI), 234
power tests, 75
Prediger, D. J., 11
Preliminary Scholastic Aptitude Test/National Merit Scholarship Qualifying Test (PSAT/NMSQT), 97–98, 334
Present State Examination (PSE), 72
problem checklists, 63–69

Problem-Focused Style of Coping (PF-SOC) instrument, 61
problem-solving instruments, 61–62
Problem-Solving Inventory, 62
Prochaska, J. O., 58
Proficiency Examination Program (PEP), 114
Profiles of American Colleges, 103
projective tests, 22–23
Provost, J. A., 212
psychoactive drugs, 262
Psychological Assessment Resources (PAR), 29, 368
Psychological Corporation, 29, 106, 369
Psychological Distress Inventory, 63
Psychological Screening Inventory, 63
psychosocial inventories, 24
public and private data, confidentiality and, 20

questionnaires, inventories and, 7
Quick Job-Hunting Map for Beginners (Bolles), 24, 193
Quickview Social History, 24, 63

Randahl, G. J., 55
rating scales, 20, 21–22
Reddon, J. R., 274
Rehabilitation Act of 1973, 311
reliability. *See* measurement concepts and test interpretation
research, ethical use of tests in, 332
Responsibilities of Users of Standardized Tests (RUST Statement—Revised), 25, 328, 349–58
Responsible Test Use: Case Studies for Assessing Human Behavior (Eyde et al.), 27
Rest, J. R., 117
Rorschach, Hermann, 230
Rorschach Ink Blot Test, 23, 230, 329
Rosen, J. C., 292
Rosenthal, R., 53
Rosnow, R. L., 53
Rotter Incomplete Sentence Blank, 23, 232
Rutgers University, 29

S-data, 18
Scale of Intellectual Development (SID), 117
Schedule for Affective Disorders and Schizophrenia (SADS), 70–71
Scholastic Aptitude Test (SAT), 41, 49, 96–97, 110, 334
school counseling, 13, 15
  achievement tests, 111–13
  Behavioral Academic Self-Esteem (BASE) rating scale, 227
  group intelligence tests for, 89–91
  measures of career concerns for students, 124–27
  See also adolescents and children
scoring stencils, 20
Self-Directed Search (SDS), 11, 186–88, 303, 336
self-referenced measure, 34
self-report inventories, 186–90
semantic differential technique, 22
sensitivity and specificity, validity and instrument, 53
Shipley Institute of Living Scale (SILS), 91
SIGI+ (System of Interactive Guidance and Information), computer program, 192
Simon, S. B., 148
situational tests, 22
Spearman-Brown Prophecy Formula, 46
special populations. *See* assessment of minority and special populations
speed tests, 75
Spielberger, Charles, 285
standard error of measurement (SEM), 48–49
standardized tests
  in counseling with other cultures, 299–300
  defined, 21
  test administration of, 73–74
  See also measurement concepts and test interpretation
Standards for Educational and Psychological Testing, 7, 25–26, 328, 359–63
Stanford Achievement Tests, 91, 111, 112, 312
Stanford University, 82

Stanford-Binet Intelligence Scale, 41, 82, 83–84, 91, 312, 329
stanines, 41–42
Steer, R. A., 282–83
Sternberg, Robert J., 93, 242
Stevens, L. B., 169
Stewart, E. S., 142
stress, environmental, 258–59
Strong Interest Inventory, 11, 73, 155–71
  computer interpretation of, 332
  computer scoring, 76
  gender bias in, 335
  logical content method, 208
  occupational and basic interest scales, 152, 157, 164–71, 208
  Spanish language edition, 303
  test validity, 49, 50
  treatment validity, 55
  use in mental health and career counseling, 13
  use with visually impaired persons, 312
Strong-Campbell Interest Inventory, 13, 155, 191
Structured Clinical Interview for DSM-IV (SCID), 71
Student Developmental Task and Lifestyle Inventory, 236
Study Attitudes and Methods Survey (SAMS), 115
Suci, G. J., 22
suicide
  SAD PERSONS Scale, 260
  suicide risk assessment, 67, 254–60
  validity and, 52–53
Super, Donald E.
  Career Development Inventory (CDI), 130–31, 132
  work values, 139, 144, 145
Survey of Study Habits and Attitudes, 15
Susto, 254
Sweetland, R. C., 29–30
Symptom Check List–10 (SCL–10), 67
Symptom Check List–90-Revised (SCL–90-R), 66–67, 257

T-scores, 40, 216
Tannenbaum, P. H., 22

Technical Education Research Centers, 311
Terman, Lewis, 82
test bias
  cultural bias in testing, 297–300
  gender bias in testing, 333–34
Test of Cognitive Skills, 91
Test Corporation of America, 29–30
Test Critiques (Keyser and Sweetland), 29–30
test publishers, 29–31, 365–71
  requirements for test usage, 28
Test User Qualification Working Group, 329
Test of Variables of Attention (TOVA), 76
testing, defined, 7
Tests: A Comprehensive Reference for Assessments in Psychology, Education, and Business (Sweetland and Keyser), 29
Tests of General Education (GED), 115
Tests in Print IV (Murphy, Conoley and Impara), 29
Thematic Apperception Test (TAT), 23, 231, 329
Thorne, A., 212
Thuesen, S. M., 212
Timbrook, R. E., 274, 308
Twelfth Mental Measurements Yearbook (Conoley and Impara), 29
Tyler, L. E., 154
Type Talk (Kroeger and Thuesen), 212

UNIACT, 336
U.S. Census Bureau, 272
U.S. Department of Labor, 198, 370
U.S. Employment Service (USES)
  Counselee Assessment/Occupational Exploration System of the, 197–200
  General Aptitude Test Battery of the, 41, 51, 197, 198–200
  USES Interest Inventory (USES-II), 197–98
use of assessment procedures in counseling
  attitudes toward psychological tests, 10–11

career counseling, 13, 14
community mental health counseling,
    12–13
decision making, 6–7
definition of psychological assessment,
    7–10
generation of alternatives, 5–6
individual vs. environmental
    assessment, 10
nomothetic vs. idiographic assessment,
    8–9
problem identification, 5
problem orientation, 4–5
purpose of psychological assessment,
    4–7
quantitative vs. qualitative assessment,
    9–10
role of counseling, 3–4
school counseling, 13, 15
standardized vs. unstandardized
    assessment, 8
surveys of test usage, 12–14
verification, 7

validity. *See* measurement concepts and
    test interpretation
values. *See* measures of work and
    personal values
vector scales, 216–18
voluntary and involuntary responses, 19

Ways of Coping Questionnaire, 62
Wechsler, David, 84
Wechsler Scales, 84–88
    counselor competence in using, 329
    Kaufman Adolescent and Adult
        Intelligence Test (KAIT), 87–88
    Kaufman Assessment Battery for
        Children (K-ABC), 87–88

Kaufman Brief Intelligence Test
    (K-BIT), 88
options for examinees with disabilities,
    311, 312
reliability factor, 49
Spanish language edition, 303
standard scores, 41
Wechsler Adult Intelligence Scale
    (WAIS-R), 13, 84–85, 86, 88
Wechsler Bellevue Intelligence Scale,
    84, 85
Wechsler Intelligence Scale for
    Children (WISC-III), 85, 87
Wechsler Preschool and Primary Scale
    of Intelligence (WPPSI-R), 87
Weiss, Bahr, 63
Wells, C. F., 193
*What Color is Your Parachute?: A
    Practical Manual for Job-Hunters
    and Career-Changers* (Bolles), 193
Williams, C. L., 273
Williamson, E. G., 233
Wonderlic Personnel Test, 92, 371
Woodcock-Johnson Psycho-Educational
    Battery, 21
work and personal values. *See* measures
    of work and personal values
World War I
    group tests for U.S. Army recruits
        during, 89
    popularity of psychological testing
        during, 10
World War II, popularity of
    psychological testing during, 10
World of Work Map, 189, 190, 194
Wrobel, T. A., 272

z-scores, 40
Ziemelis, A., 265
Zytowski, D. G., 11, 173, 174, 177